BALI

TIME, RITES, ART AND MAGIC

Jean Couteau & Georges Breguet
Illustrations by I Gusti Nyoman Darta

TUTTLE Publishing
Tokyo | Rutland, Vermont | Singapore

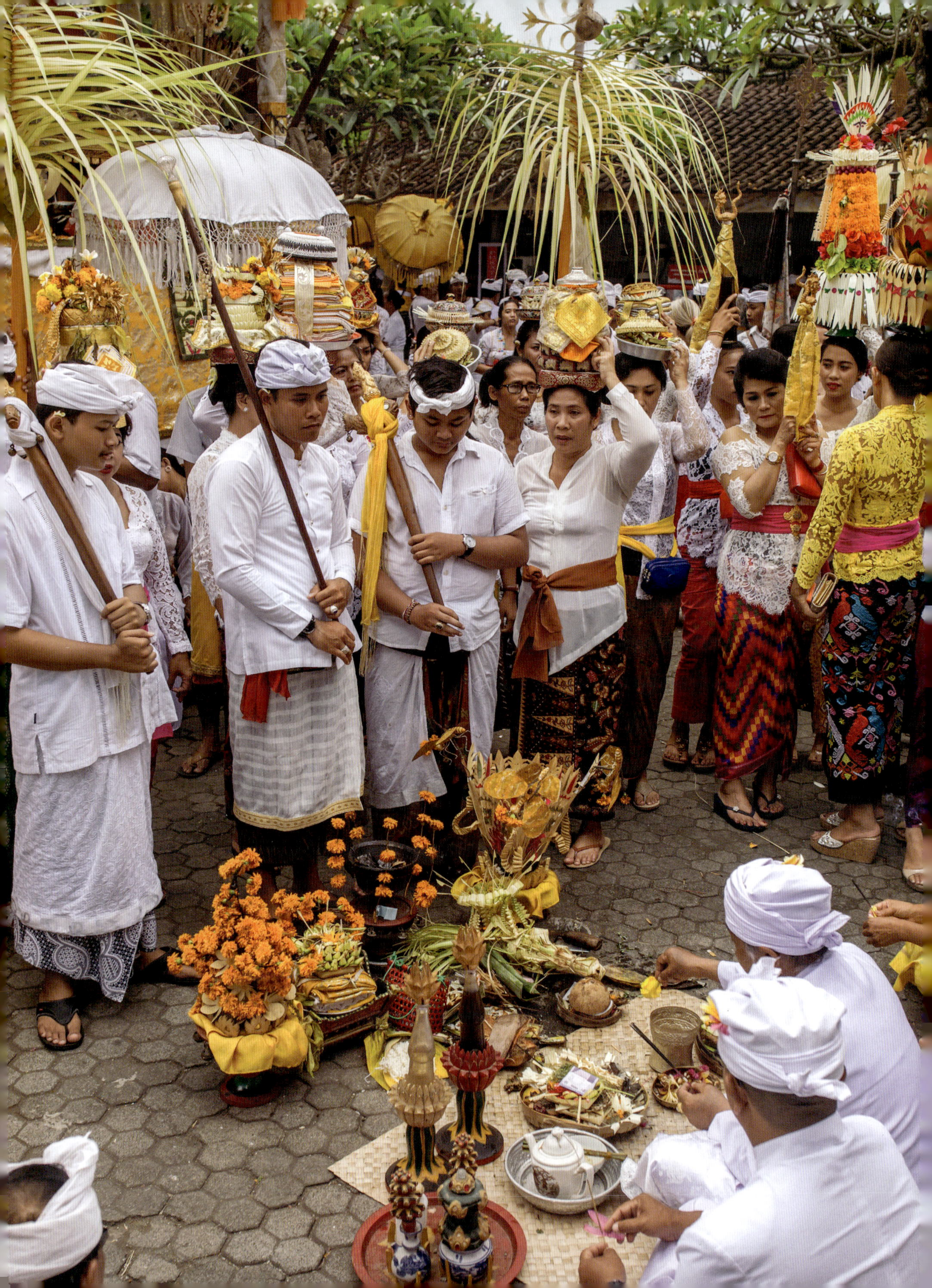

CONTENTS

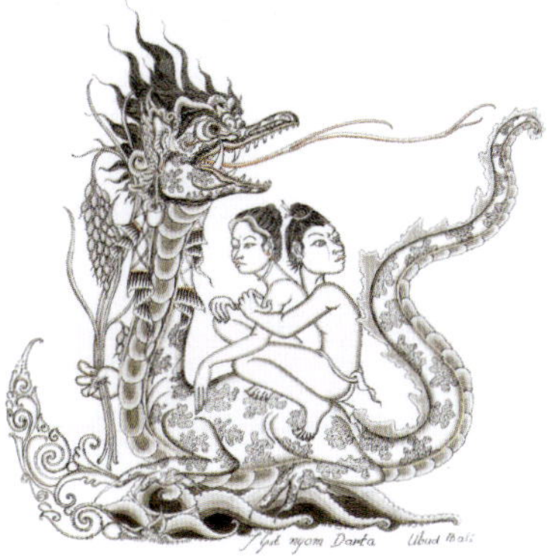

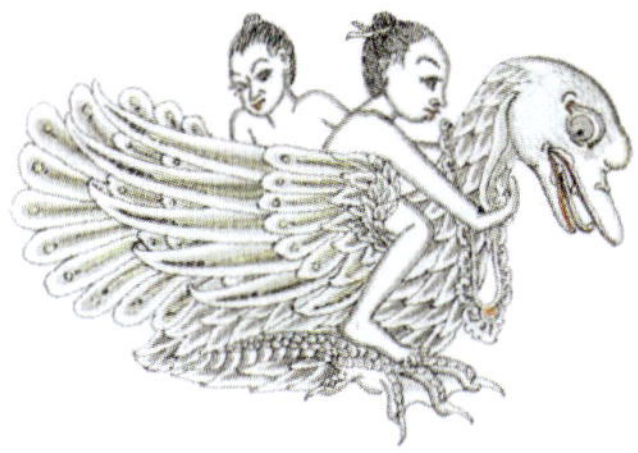

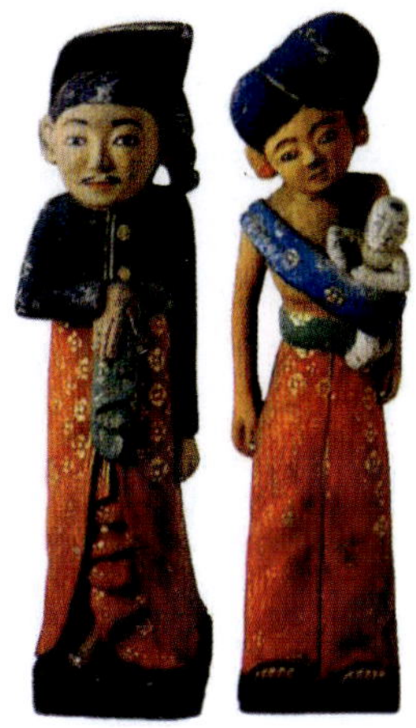

A Note on the Spelling of Balinese

The spelling of Balinese names and words in this book follows conventions now used in Bali for the transcription of Balinese script into Roman characters. These conventions are, however, not strictly followed, and thus one can read in modern Bali the word Kliwon spelt as Klion, Soma spelt as Çoma, and Redite spelt as Radite. Variations in writing are also common, in particular the 'a' becoming 'e', as it is pronounced, such as in *api takep/api tekep*, *wraspati/wrespati*, and *palelintangan/pelelintangan*. Except when quoted, words of Sanskrit origin are presented in their modern orthography, for example, Saka rather than Śaka. Balinese nouns are not pluralized by the addition of 's', as in English, but the plural may be inferred from the context. Balinese terms are italicized and explained the first time they occur in the text of each chapter, and subsequently in main chapter sections and in captions.

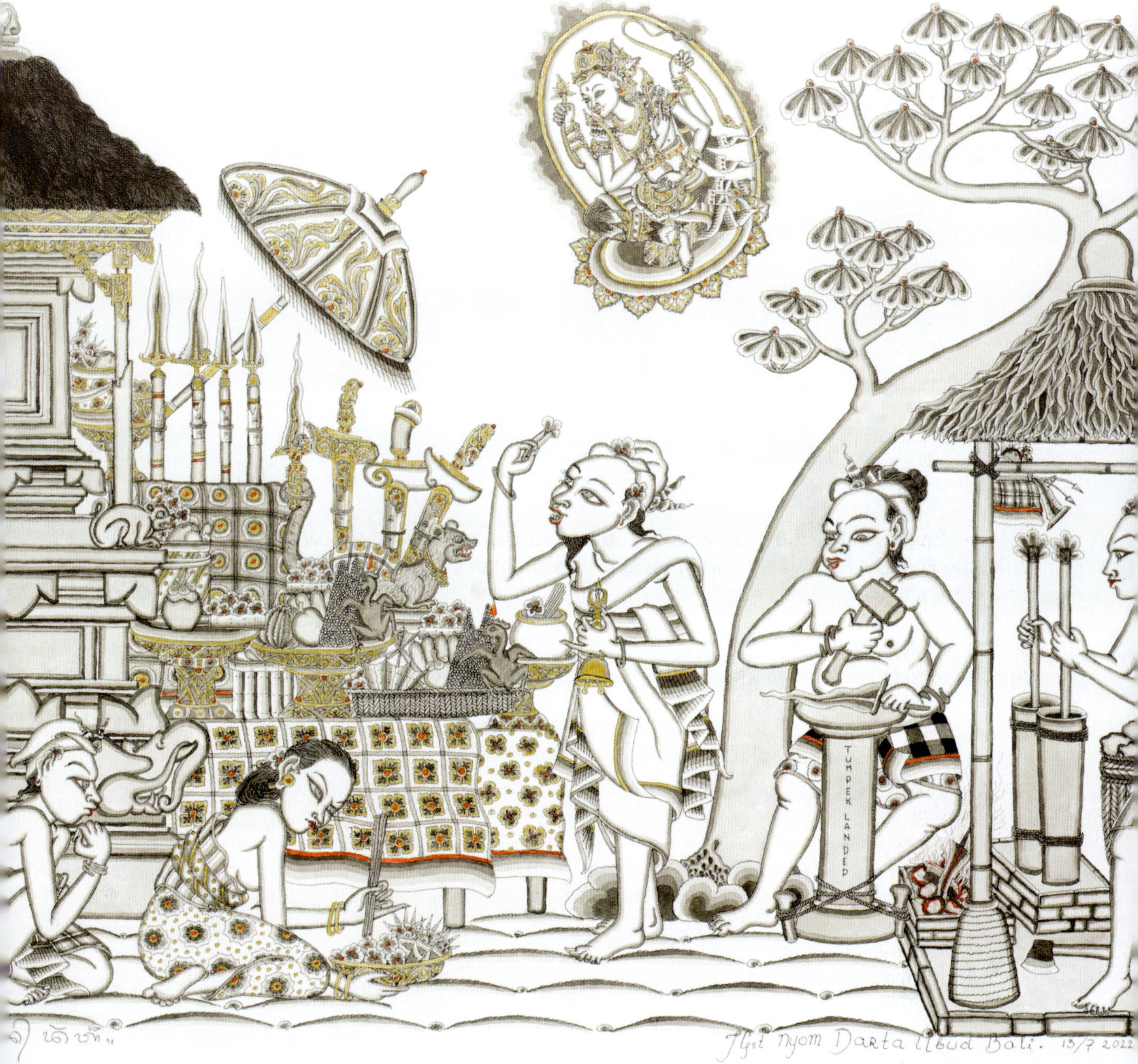
TUMPEK LANDEP
I Gst Nyom Darta Ubud Bali. 13/7 2022

How This Book Came About

Bali: Time, Rites, Art and Magic is the outcome of a long-term collaboration between three friends: French writer Jean Couteau, Swiss scientist and museum consultant Georges Breguet, and Balinese artist-cum healer I Gusti Nyoman Darta. The seed for this book was planted when the Musée d'Horlogerie Le Locle in Switzerland acquired, upon Georges's suggestion, a collection of Balinese *tika* (wooden and painted calendars) owned by Dominique Gardan. When the museum first exhibited the works in 2002, it decided to produce, under Georges's direction, a hardcover catalog titled *Un Autre Temps, les Calendriers tika de Bali* (Somogy Éditions) with illustrations by Darta and an analysis of the Balinese calendar system by Jean. During this work, it became clear that while almost everyone had heard about Balinese rites and festivals, hardly anyone knew much about its calendar system. We then decided to work on an English publication that would build upon the French-language exhibition catalog to give the general public a thorough, yet accessible presentation of the Balinese calendar system and related festivals and rites. New illustrations were commissioned to Darta for the purpose, all accompanied by explanations given by Jean. The whole illustration corpus is now the property of the new Branly Museum in Paris. Most of the texts were written by Jean, then reviewed by all three of us. Published by BAB Books in 2013, the book met with immediate success. It would have been republished sooner were it not for the death from Covid-19 of the previous publisher. Thus, it is to a new publisher, Tuttle Publishing, that we owe the present edition, significantly revised, reorganized, and, in parts, pruned. It was decided, for example, to remove the section about Tenganan. The title was slightly modified. New diagrams were designed and different illustrations were selected.

The present book is structured into two parts, each with four chapters. Part One discusses Balinese calendars and the concepts of time. Part Two then explores how the calendar system applies in practice. Chapter 1 begins with a discussion of the dual character of Balinese religion, with its indigenous core but Indian mantle. What follows is a genealogy of the notion of time, depicting its shift from myths to history. Then comes a presentation of agricultural time and its connection to natural and stellar cycles. It continues with a discussion about the transmigration of ancestral souls, and concludes with reflections on the cosmic aspect of time. Chapter 2 presents the myth of Watugunung, Bali's Oedipus, at the origin of the calendar. Chapter 3 explains the workings of the two traditional calendar systems, the first the 210-day Pawukon, composed of overlapping cycles of one-day to ten-day 'weeks', and the second the Balinese variant of the Indian Saka calendar, which has numbered years and consists of 12 lunar months, presented one by one, followed by a depiction of the Pengerupukan that closes the year. Chapter 4 deals with everyday time. Part Two deals with Rites and Festivals. Chapter 5 pinpoints the role of date intersections or moon positions to define holy days, followed by a description of festivals. Chapter 6 offers an account of Balinese rites of passage from conception to birth, birth to death, and beyond. Chapter 7 provides readers with a glimpse of Balinese divination and the 'horoscope'—the schemes and charts used to determine auspicious days—followed by a depiction of two visits, one to a priest to obtain a date for a ceremony, the other to a *balian* (medium) to read someone's character. The book ends with a brief reflection on the modern evolution of the Balinese notion of time.

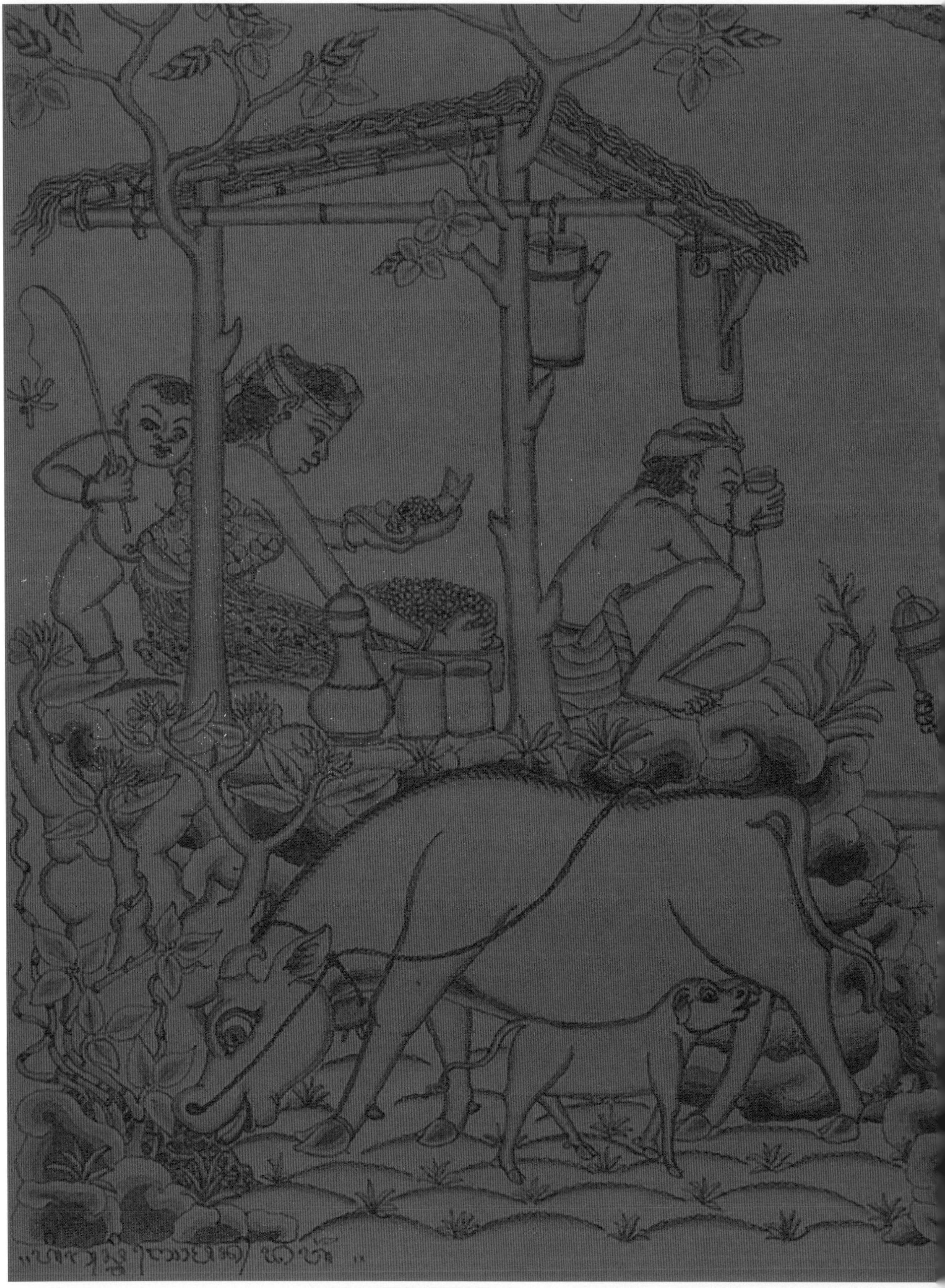

PART ONE

TIME

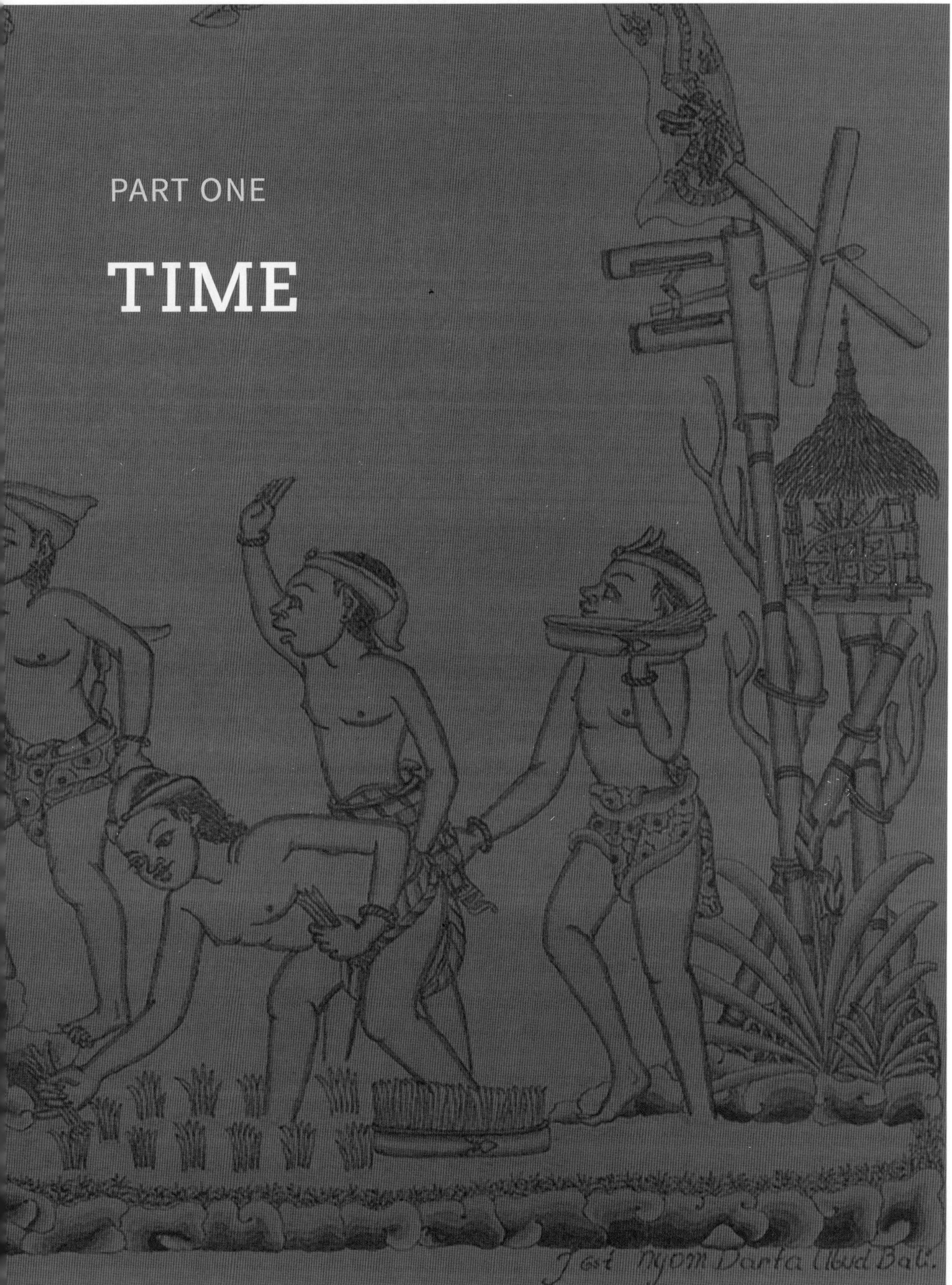

CHAPTER 1

TIME AND THE BALINESE

The Complexities of the Balinese Belief System

As we shall find as we explore this book, the Balinese time system consists of two distinct yet intermingling calendars: the 210-day Pawukon, indigenous to Indonesia (Java and Bali), and the 354-day Saka calendar of Indian origin. To these two calendars correspond to two poles of religious belief: the indigenous core, focused on ancestor-cum-mountain worship, and the Hindu-Buddhist court tradition, resting on cosmological concepts of Indian origin. This needs explaining.

Despite centuries of Javanese-inflected Indianization, the fundamental reality for the majority of Balinese remains the cult of the ancestors combined with the worship of natural forces, most notably the mountainous ancestral abode of Gunung Agung. In this traditional world view, the individual is born from an ancestral realm 'above the mountains' and returns to it following death rites to become water (*yeh/tirta*). The soul spends its life navigating a dense, rite-laden path to maintain balance. Following death, the soul is cleansed in purgatory before reincarnating back in Bali, reborn among its own kin as a *titisan* water drop.

This water path is reflected in the stark, intimate language of *balian* (medium) seances, in which ancestors addressing their descendants may use the startling term of endearment—"Oh, *warih* of mine"—referring to their sacred effluence or bodily outflow—"What can I do for you?" Within this logic, the incarnated descendant is viewed as the 'spent outflow' of a divine ancestor.

If cleansed of Indianized terminology, the practiced cult can be described as entirely hydraulic, with the mountain and its waters at its center. In such a context, defining 'godly' entities around a final pantheon is less vital than maintaining the cohesive ritual system surrounding them. Thus, while deities carry fluid, indigenous names (Sesuhunan, Ratu) and the worship of ancestors remains paramount. When these ancestors descend during temple anniversaries, they are welcomed by possession rites, dance, and music. Worshippers are then blessed by holy waters beseeched from water temples, some local, others obtained from sacred sites at lakes and mountain peaks. This facet of Balinese belief is most aptly named Agama Tirta: The Religion of Holy Water.

While the Agama Tirta described above retains its inherent resilience, it was subjected to successive layers of 'lettered' influence from Java—primarily through the 1343 Majapahit invasion, and later following the 16th-century arrival of Buda and Siwa Brahmins fleeing an Islamized Java. These Brahmins refined and further Indianized the existing court culture.

Through this process, the courts and their priests, with their Kawi-language theater and literature, served as the primary vehicles of 'Indianization', giving the belief system a 'Vedic look'. While Indian tradition appeared to sit at the heart of the system, the Brahmins and their mantras never replaced the ancestor-cum-mountain cult. They simply 'Indianized' it with a lettered tradition, leading to the sacrality of *weda*-based mantras and *tirta* holy water. In reality, however, this knowledge provided a prestigious mantle for an ancient, hydraulic-based soul-map.

The result is a complex layering of indigenous inputs and Indianized cosmology. While Brahmins and the high-caste elite, conscious of retaining their sociological distinction, occupy the top of the lowland hierarchy, the mountain Bali Aga villages remain largely outside court influence. This has given rise to deep paradoxes. Today, while the Bali Aga and many lowland Balinese hope to return after death to *nunas baas*—to look for rice in the good land of Bali—many Brahmins, influenced by the Vedaic mantle, insist on the real possibility of *moksha* (liberation) and *samsara* (the cycle of suffering).

This Indianization has accelerated following the shock of colonization and modernity. In 1958, for national recognition the Balinese were required to adopt the concept of the 'Oneness of God' (Ketuhanan Yang Maha Esa) and refer to a corpus of holy books. In response, scholars 'unearthed' the deity Sang Hyang Widhi Wasa from ancient Kawi manuscripts, re-envisioning it as a singular, supreme God.

Yet, this ongoing evolution, accelerated by the institutionalization of 'Balinese religion', raises a crucial question: Is Hinduism still being 'Balinized' or is it that Bali is now being fully 'Hinduized'? Despite intense questioning and the growing presence of Indian sects, the traditional calendar system remains to this day the ultimate anchor of Balinese relevance.

From Myth to History: The Genealogy of Balinese Time

If, in the West, time is viewed as a relentless linear progression, in Bali it is a complex tapestry of overlapping cycles where myth, ethics, and history are woven together to define the present. This temporal architecture moves from the destructive power of mythic origin to the social legitimacy of ancestral descent, and finally to the 'stable world' of pre-colonial memory.

When referring to its mythical origin, Balinese time is inherently destructive. Personified as Kala, the god of time, was born from Siwa's 'fallen sperm' (*kama salah*) after the supreme god was overcome by desire for his consort-cum-sakti, the goddess Uma. Born outside the boundaries of cosmic order, Kala emerged as a monstrous, insatiable being—a man-eater. In the Balinese imagination, Time does not merely 'pass', it devours. Kala must therefore be continuously placated by offerings (*caru*), while those born on inauspicious dates must be redeemed through a special Sapuh Leger *wayang* performance.

Kala and his feminine counterpart, Kali, also refer to Balinese demons. While Kala represents the masculine, devouring the maw of time, Kali (often manifest as the demoness Kalika) represents the feminine era of discord and decay. Equally significant, the very notion of 'disaster' is expressed by the term *sengkala*, suggesting that a catastrophe is, at its root, a demonic encounter. In terms of mythic time, the Balinese also refer to the Hindu cycles of the world (*yuga*), but apart from men of letters, the four yuga cycles are generally reduced to two: Kali Yuga (the era of destruction and chaos) and Kerta Yuga (the era of prosperity and order).

If the myth of Kala explains the nature of time, the stories of Maya Danawa and Watugunung explain how humans must behave within it; they define the passage from cosmology to human ethics. The legend of Maya Danawa, the demon-king of Bedulu, is the founding myth of the Galungan festival. By forbidding the worship of the Hindu gods, Maya Danawa represented Adharma, the inversion of cosmic law. His defeat by the god Indra marks the triumph of Dharma. Thus, the survival of the world depends on the 'victory' over primal impulses. The symbolic recurrence of Indra's victory during the Galungan and Kuningan cycle is a perpetual reminder of the primacy of ethics.

Similarly, the story of the culture hero Watugunung is at the foundation of the 210-day Pawukon calendar. Watugunung's tragic fate—marrying his mother only to be defeated after challenging the gods—serves as a warning about the need to transcend primal life and structure taboos, obligations, and rituals through a ritually organized time. Every moment carries a 'character' (*dewasa*). To ignore its *ala/ayu* (negative or positive) qualities is to invite sengkala. To act in harmony with this dewasa is to head toward *kerta raharja*, or prosperity.

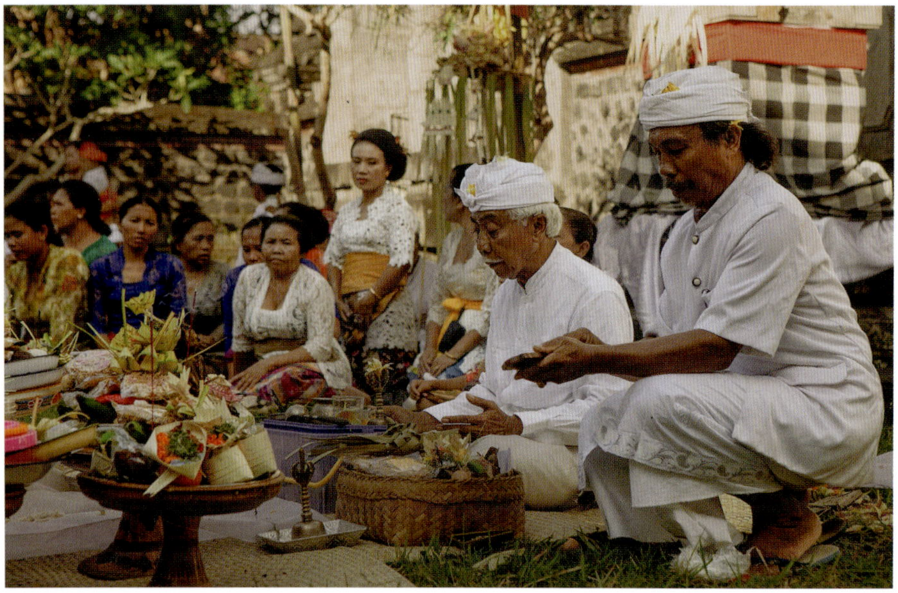

Temple priest with offerings during the Galungan-Kuningan cycle of ceremonies, at the heart of the indigenous Pawukon 210-day calendar, when all the ancestors are said to come down for a 10-day visit among their descendants.

As we move from myth toward history, time takes on a more social dimension. The arrival of the Majapahit empire in 1343 CE serves as the foundation of the social structure. For the majority of Balinese clans, history begins here. Balinese clans refer to chronicles, or Babad, to define their origin and status. However, no dates are attributed to the events related. Instead, the narrative focuses on the Kawitan—the point of origin. A clan's legitimacy is established not by *when* an ancestor lived, but by *whom* they served and from *where* they migrated. The history of a family is a living map of ritual responsibilities linking the modern household to the warriors and nobility of the Majapahit invasion.

The only date usually found in a Babad is at the end of the palm-leaf manuscript (*lontar*). This colophon provides the Saka year and Pawukon references for the completion of the physical manuscript, not the events within it. Thus, these chronicles exist in a space that is as much mythical as historical. Their key episodes are not meant for academic knowledge but for symbolic identification with the past. For example, when a dancer dons the mask of a Majapahit king, the past is not merely 'remembered,' it is made present.

When dates are recorded, they are rarely presented as simple numbers. Instead, they are hidden within an esoteric system known as Candra Sengkala. This system uses words or images with numerical values to create a short, poetic sentence. For example, the phrase "Sirna hilang kertaning bhumi" (Vanish, disappear, the prosperity of the earth) codes for the fall of Majapahit in 1400 Saka (1478 CE). This method of dating reveals that the 'quality' of a year is more important than its 'quantity.' By turning a date into an image, the Balinese ensure that even the recording of history remains an act of art and divination.

When it comes to more recent historical events, the Balinese have adopted the Gregorian calendar. Yet, among the elderly, it is not the numerical years that are meaningful but the quality of the situation. They generally refer to the period before the full Dutch takeover in the early 20th century as "dugas gumi nu enteg" (the time when the world was quiet or stable). Subsequent 'times' are marked by similar cosmic ruptures: the Japanese occupation (*jaman Jepang*), the 1963 eruption of Mount Agung, or the political upheavals of 1965.

Balinese time is a sophisticated layering of meanings. It begins with the devouring hunger of Kala, is shaped by the ethical triumphs of Maya Danawa, is classified by the ancestral lines of Majapahit, and is remembered through the 'stability' of the world before the modern era. To this day, the past remains conceptualized as a means to ensure that the present remains in balance with the gods, the ancestors, and the devouring maw of Time itself.

Agricultural and Celestial Cycles

Long before the rice-farming people of Bali (and the neighboring island of Java) adopted or developed any calendar, their time was regulated by agricultural cycles based on close observation of the seasons in relation to the movements and positions of stars in the sky.

It was not the Plough (or Big Dipper) of the Ursa Major constellation that formed the Plough of Balinese farmers, but a group of stars of the constellation of Orion. Since Java and Bali are close to the equator, the constellation appears on its side, and Orion's belt (Alnitak, Alnilam, and Mintaka), together with three of the four outer stars (Saiph, Rigel, and Bellatrix, excluding Betelgeuse), make up a constellation that looks like a traditional plough (*tenggala* or *wuluku*) and is known locally as *bintang wuluku*, or other variations of its spelling, such as *walaku* or *huluku*.

The changing appearance of this constellation over the year, together with that of the Pleiades (Kartika), an open-star cluster, was traditionally used to regulate the seasonal activities associated with agriculture and, more specifically, the cycles of rice cultivation on both dry and wet land.

For dry-land rice, in pre-modern days, the beginning of the new agricultural year corresponded to the first appearance of Kartika and Wuluku in the pre-dawn sky (heliacal rise). This happens around the time of the June solstice (during the Saka months Kasa or Karo). At this time, the celestial plough is upright, like regular ploughs when in use. The observation of the dawn apparition of the first star of Kartika, followed by the apparition of Wuluku, was still common practice by a couple of *pemangku* (temple priests) from Besakih (the mother temple of Bali) in the 1980s. They interpreted their observations with the help of a calendrical text called *Wariga Surya Sewana*, and decided the date for the opening of the local agricultural cycle accordingly.

Three months later, with Kartika and Wuluku rising progressively earlier each night, came the onset of the rainy season and the time to prepare tools and maintain and repair water channels ahead of the first wet-land rice cycle (*kerta masa*). When Wuluku eventually rose at sunset (achronical rise), generally in November or December (or during the Saka month Kanem), and thus looked once again upright, this meant the time had come to sow the rice in the nursery and start ploughing the fields. It was thus the opening of the first wet-land rice season.

A month or so later, around the time of the December solstice (during the Saka months Kapitu or Kawulu), came the time for the fields to be harrowed and the seedlings to be transplanted into the fields. At that time of year, Kartika and Wuluku could be seen rising increasingly higher in the sky after sunset, with their highest point in the sky occurring at dusk.

Around four months later, when the rain had stopped and the rice had ripened, the harvesting of the first rice crop could begin. This season was marked by the celestial plough appearing progressively lower in the western sky after sunset. It looked as if it were upside down, 'like a farmer's plough when the work is done'. Soon afterwards, Kartika and Wuluku disappeared completely (heliacal set) until they appeared again later, thus opening a new annual cultivation cycle.

Of Rice and Men

Natural elements are, in Balinese thought, perceived as analogous in structure and life process to Man. Both are considered as *bhwana* (cosmic) seen in a dynamic, cyclic perspective. Nature belongs to the macrocosm, or *bhwana agung*, and Man, to the microcosm, or *bhwana alit*. In a 2000 study of the agricultural rites of Bali, Arlette Ottino commented that "Since life can only arise from a living being, the apprehension of the land as a living being is deduced daily from the fact that plants grow and crops mature, and that human beings regularly return to the earth after death." About rice, she further added, "Both human beings and rice share the same destiny. They are similarly born from the earth, bear fruit, mature, and eventually die, returning to the timeless and undifferentiated domain of the sky before coming back to this world and begin another cycle anew. Conversely, events such as the emergence of new seedlings from the grains at the beginning of the cycle, and the sublimation of the whole plant into the panicle at the end, inform people's appreciation of the cyclical dynamism of life itself. Like the grain of rice, which, to germinate, must first be severed from the plant, so human being[s] must die in order for the first generation to be born. The perceived analogies between the two cycles create [a] web of meaning according to which the distinction between people and rice is blurred...."

This cyclical analogy between Man and Rice is one of the founding elements of the Javanese-Balinese Pawukon calendar. The traditional slow-growing variety of rice (*padi taun*), now rarely planted, takes 210 days to mature. This corresponds to the 210-day cycle of the Pawukon calendar, which, as we shall see, is the basis for the distribution of almost all Balinese rites.

The History of Rice Cultivation

Paddy cultivation was introduced to Bali in the first millennium BCE. As noted in the description of the stellar cycle above, it is traditionally linked to the astronomical year and to the succession of dry and wet seasons. The dry season usually begins in May and lasts until October, while the wet season runs from October to April. However, important discrepancies may occur from year to year due to various factors, in particular to recurrent changes in sea currents across the Pacific (La Niña and El Niño).

Initially cultivated on dry fields (*ladang*), paddy has long been cultivated on irrigated rice fields (*sawah*). This led to the constitution of irrigation communities (*subak*) which organize the distribution of water through a complex system of rites and collective work.

The first species of paddy (padi taun) introduced to Bali were of slow growth with a cycle of 210 days. New species were later introduced, which made two crops a year possible. The species used for the first crop (*kerta masa*) had a growth cycle that was two weeks slower than those used for the second crop (*gagadon*).

Since the 1970s, these traditional species have for the most part been replaced by hybrid species that can give up to three high-yield crops per year. In the present discussion, we are not talking about these hybrid species, many of which no longer correspond to the traditional time cycles, and are also criticized for ecological reasons.

The Traditional Wet-rice Cycle

In the traditional wet-rice cycle, rice fields are prepared and cleansed followed by the flooding of the fields and the replanting of young seedlings. This process differs significantly from place to place according to the location and the ecological conditions of the rice fields.

For example, the replanting takes place in December and January in mountainous areas, in February on the middle slopes, in March and April on the lower plains, and in May by the beaches. However, in a 1987 paper on "Balinese 'Water Temples' and the Management of Irrigation," J. S. Lansing, demonstrated it is of paramount importance that the rice cycles be coordinated among rice fields on a large scale, and hence across a broad territory in order to optimize the use of water at the end of the rainy season, as well as to achieve the best possible pest control.

From one rice-growing season to the next, there is a fallow period of roughly one month between plantings, and if this period occurs at the same time on a large scale it prevents pests from easily spreading from one rice field area to the other. This is only possible if the surface cultivated is large enough and includes one or several subak working in coordination with one another.

The management of water for the rice cycle has to be decided at the highest level of the irrigation system, that is, for most of South Bali at the Ulun Danau temple on Mount Batur. This temple, dedicated to Danu, goddess of the lake, holds sway over no fewer than 204 downstream subak, thus functioning as the 'mother temple' of those units.

In the past, the priests of Ulun Danau used to send handwritten invitation letters to the respective subak leaders (*pekaseh*) to attend the full-moon ceremony at the temple at the end of the

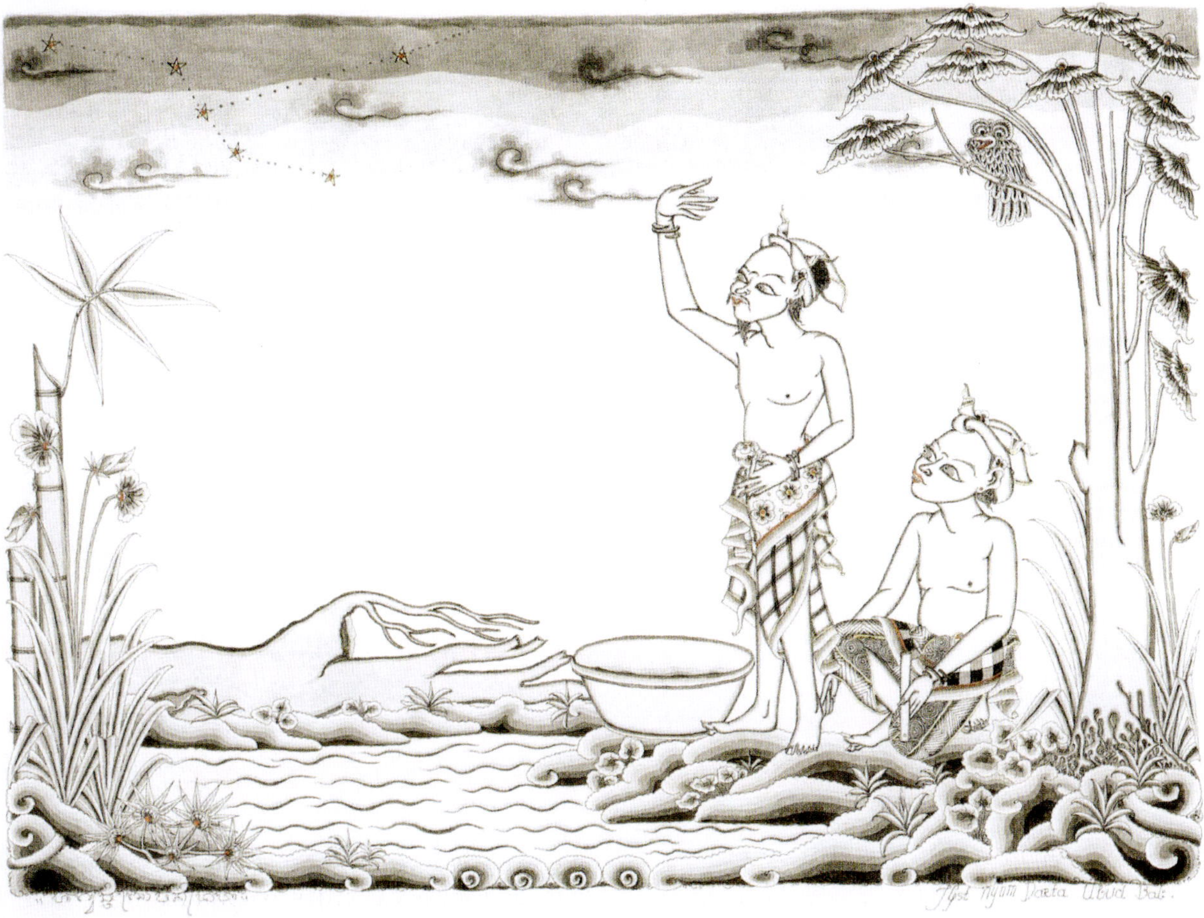

WATCHING THE SKY: This drawing shows two priests observing the positions of the stars of the Wuluku and Kartika constellations. The plough-shaped *bintang wuluku* is visible in the sky in the upper left of the picture. The Kartika constellation, which would be located further to the left, is outside the illustration. Other stars considered unimportant to the Balinese are not shown. Waluku is reflected in the basin water, and the squatting man will note its position on the *lontar* leaf in his hand. Is it vertical (*jejeg*), tilting slightly (*sendeh*), or inclining to the east (*ngorokang kangin*)? It remains for a traditional astronomy specialist to interpret the data so that relevant agricultural decisions can be made. Notice the owl, symbol of the night, at upper right.

rainy season (in the tenth month of the Saka calendar year), during which the chronological distribution of water among the subak units would be set. Owing to discrepancies in the readings and adjustments made to the lunar calendar by the priests of different kingdoms in pre-colonial times, the invitations also made mention of the Pawukon day corresponding to the full-moon ceremony date. From that point onward, all decisions taken, such as those pertaining to the second rice planting, also followed the Pawukon cycle.

Steps in the Wet-rice Production Cycle

Land preparation is the first step of rice growing. The farmer must plough the soil, turn it over, and level it before bringing in irrigation water (*betengin*). Many tools are used for this purpose—hoe (*pacul*), spade (*sorok*), leveler (*tulud*), weeding knife (*penampad*), harrow (*lampid*), and a plough (*tenggala* or *waluku*), the shape of which inspired the naming of the Wuluku star constellation that guides the timing of the steps in the production cycle.

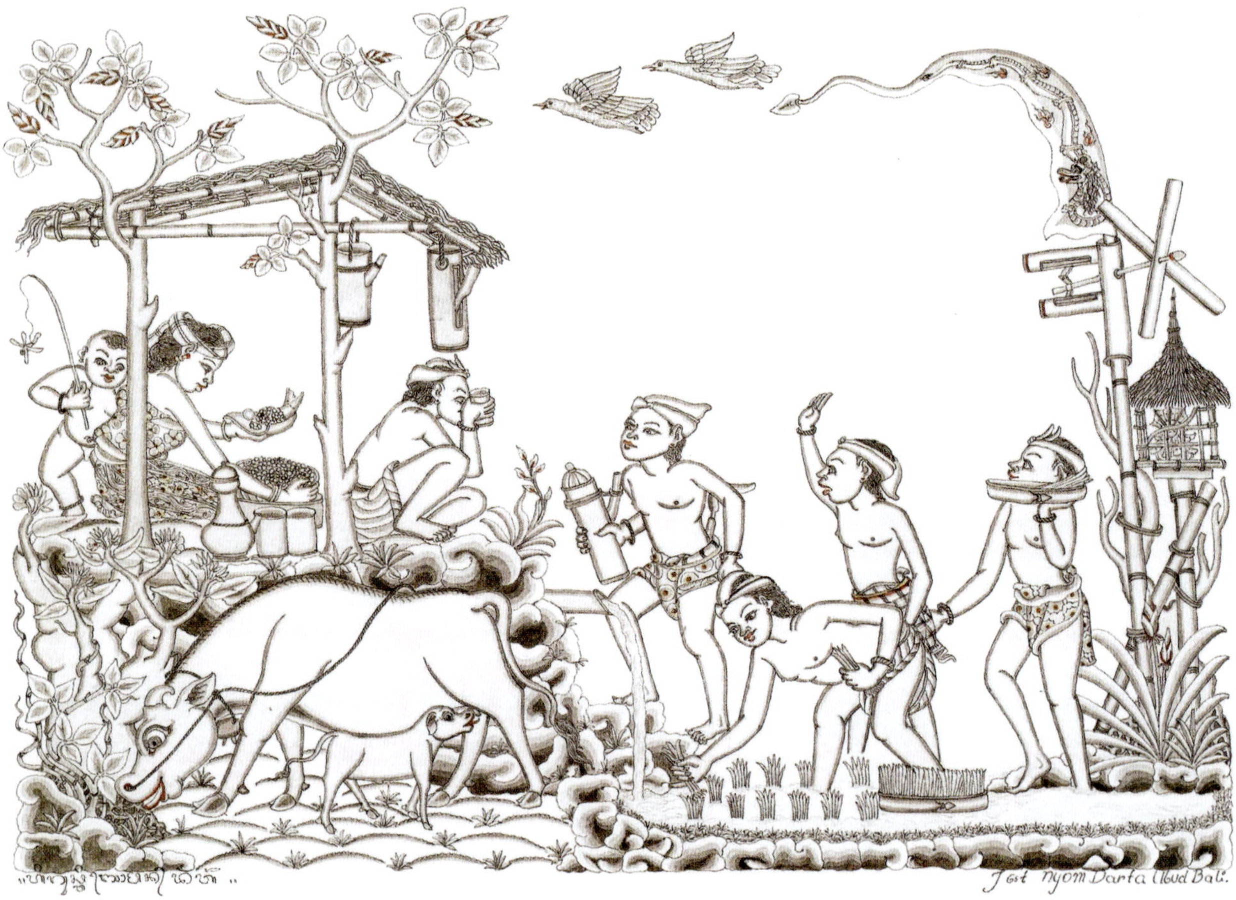

PLANTING RICE: The main scene is the planting of the first crop of rice, which usually occurs toward the end of the raining season. The woman to the left is bringing food to the workers. One of the men squats, eating. A buffalo is resting after ploughing. Notice the bamboo receptacles in the middle used to carry water, and the wooden drum (*kulkul*) hanging under the roof. To the right is the 'head' of the rice field shrine (*ulun carik*) holding a bamboo rod (*andung*) that is used to separate water into two flows, and a crackling wind-wheel (*pindekan*) that is used to scare birds.

While the soil is being prepared, a nursery is set up on a small plot of land. The seedlings emerge after six weeks. At this point, the fields have already been irrigated, so the transplanting (*tandurin*) can take place.

All sorts of weeds grow in the rice fields. They must be regularly removed. Natural fertilization is done through various means, such as using duck herds and the burning of left-over stems. Growing rice is related to water and associated with the female world. But it is men who are in charge of this part of the rice cycle. While waiting for the rice to ripen, farmers make scarecrows (*lelakut*) to protect crops from sparrows and other birds. They also set up crackling bamboo noise-makers for the same purpose.

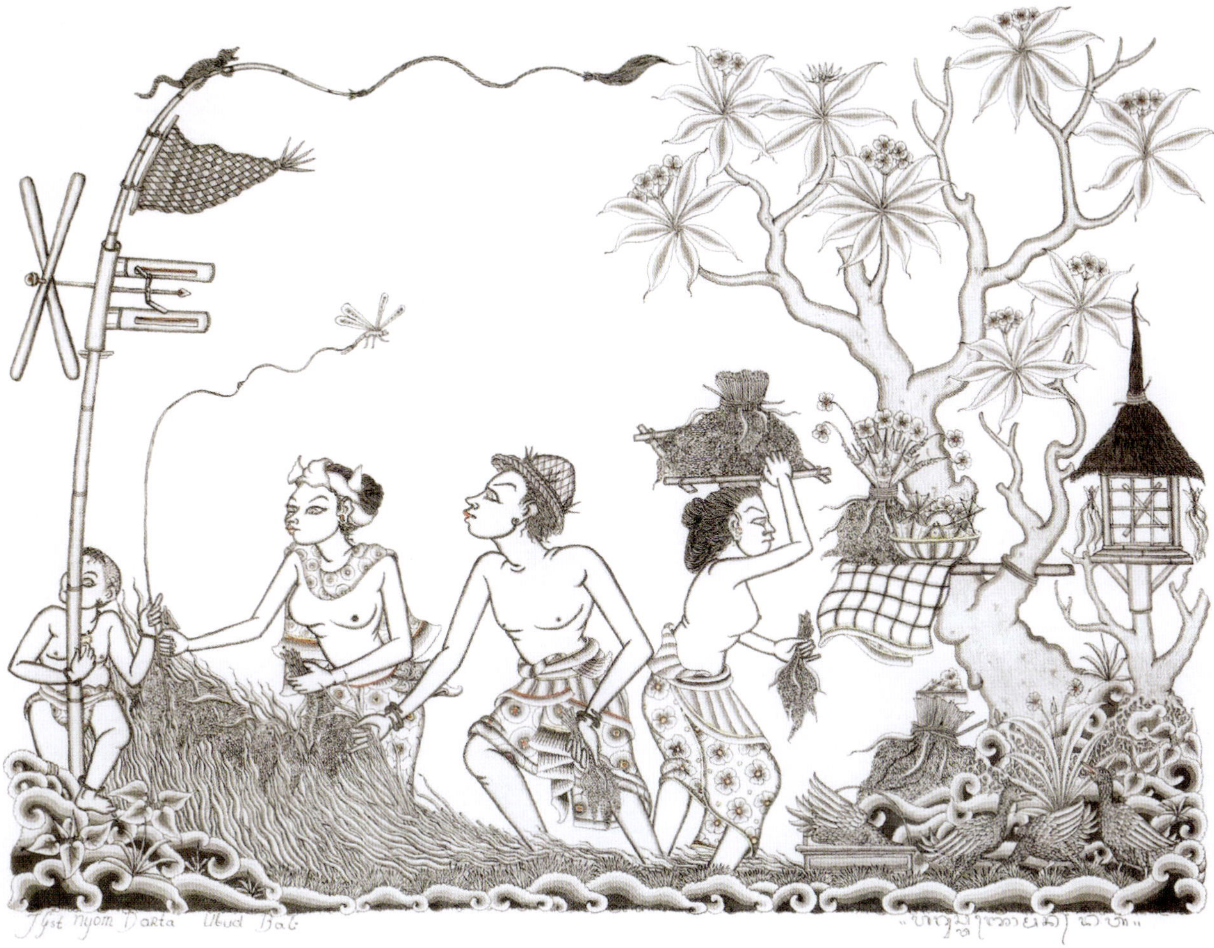

OFFERINGS TO DEWI SRI: On the right is the spirit house (Sanggah Dewa) of the female spirit of rice, Dewa Nini. Offerings are being made to the goddess of rice, Dewi Sri, just before starting to harvest. The effigy of the goddess is here attached to a big tree trunk next to the head shrine of the rice field with the offering (Nini Pantun). This effigy is made using a handful of paddy straws, which must be androgynous (*kedi*), that is, composed of male and female panicles. The harvest may not start before proper respect has been paid to Dewi Sri. Here, the woman to the left is shown gathering paddy straws, whereas the one on the right has collected enough to carry back to her home granary (*lumbung*). Notice the crackling wind-wheel to the left.

Once the panicles are ripe, harvesting can begin. This is always a moment of joy, but also hard work. Farmers harvest the rice using a special panicle cutter (*anggapan*) and a sickle (*arit*). They also use a special tool (*penatapan*) to level the paddy bundles and string (*pangeran tali*) to tie them tightly together.

After the harvest, the bundles are taken to the granary (*lumbung*), usually located in the farmers' private compounds. Women carry the bundles on their heads whereas men carry them on their shoulders with a palanque (*sanan*). The last phases of the rice-cycle work, to dry and process the grain, are usually done by women in the family compound. After being stored in the lumbung the paddy is processed into rice

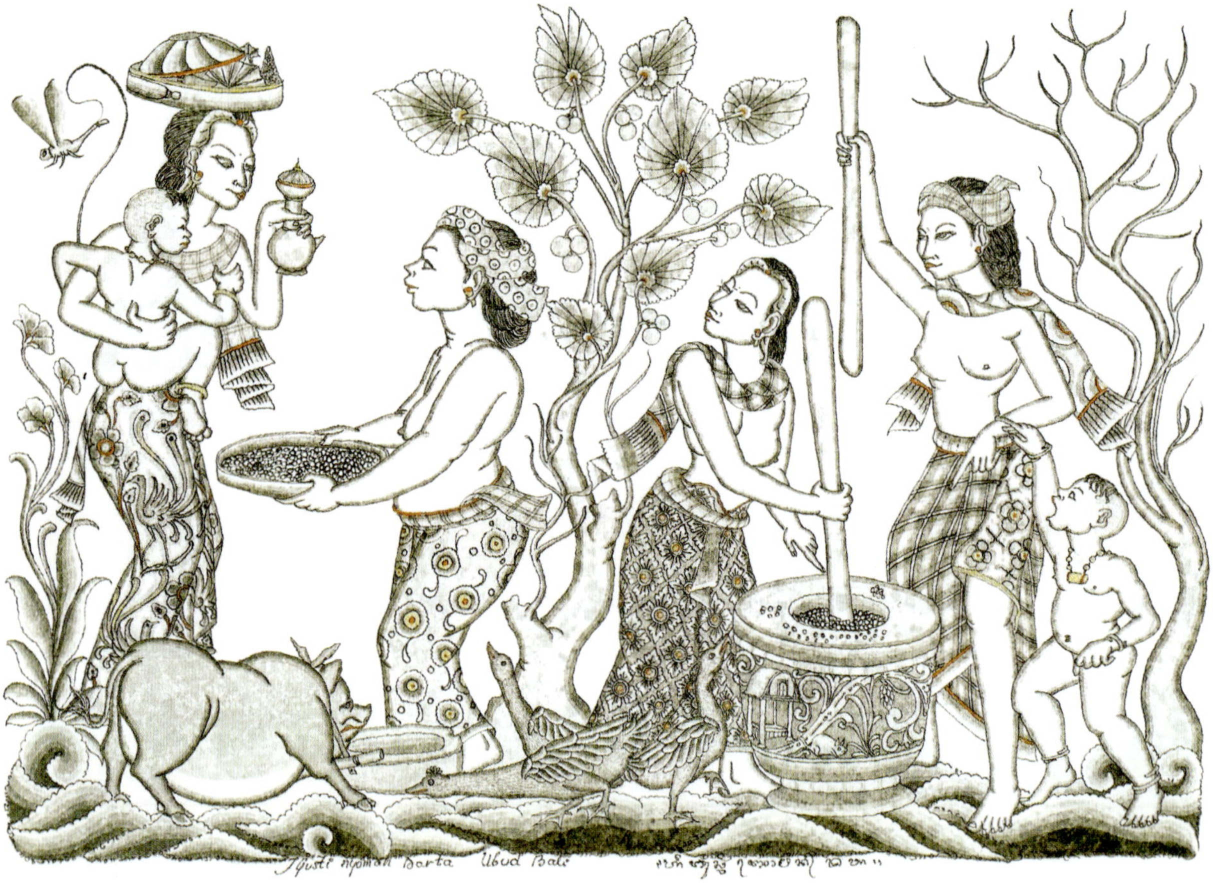

POUNDING THE RICE: The mechanical treatment of paddy is something relatively new, even though it is now commonplace. Up until 20 years ago, most rice was pounded by hand, as shown in this picture. Notice the *lumbung* granary carved on the pounding stone (*lesung*). The woman at center left is winnowing the rice grains.

through successive phases of winnowing, sieving, and pounding. The storing of rice is linked to the sky and thus associated with the male world, although it is women who are in charge of this part of the cycle.

The Circulation of the Soul

Throughout most of Bali, the circulation of the soul is enshrined in people's minds not as a 'belief' but as a fact of life. Everything begins in the mountainous heights of the 'Old Country' (*tanah ane wayah*). There reside the ancestral gods and other deities. Yet, these ancestral souls remain 'subject to desire and hunger', longing to return to the island of Bali (Bali Kulino).

Birth is a process in which an ancestor 'casts their shadow to earth and comes down asking for rice' (*mepewayangan nunas baas*). The ancestor is also symbolized as water that flows down as *warih*—the ancestor's sacred effluence—to dwell temporarily among humans. They are born not as a stranger, but as a manifestation of an ancestral divinity, often called for this reason 'dewa' after birth.

However, once incarnated, the individual must navigate a rite-laden path, maintaining a strict balance between *ayu* (virtue) and *ala* (vice) through offerings and exorcism. Yet, all along they bear an unbroken obligation to the ancestors and the local deities who guard the land and the waters. Death, in the end, is not a point of cessation but a gateway to purification. Through layered funerary rites, the soul is cleansed of worldly remnants to be sent back to the ancestral abode atop the mountain. This cycle is part of a cosmic movement orchestrated by the gods, ensuring that humans live in accord with the universal order.

Indian influences interfere in this tradition through mantras and literature. Yet, the ultimate goal, rarely formulated, is not endless incarnation. The soul hopes one day to transcend the illusory limits of time. It seeks to merge with Sang Hyang Embang—the Sublime Void—where all lineage, desire, and duality finally dissolve into eternal silence.

Is the quest for Embang an influence of the notion of *samsara*? Probably, as there have always been, in the Brahmins' mansions, men of letters talking of the samsara transmigration of the souls, and of the possibility, for saints like Dang Hyang Nirartha, of achieving *moksha*. The 'mantle' of Hinduism is thus sometimes, and increasingly so, penetrating the skin.

Cosmic Time

In keeping with the precepts of Balinese cosmology, the purpose of the traditional Balinese calendar system (*pedewasan*) is not to keep chronological track of human events, but to organize time so as to delineate the ritual behavior deemed necessary to preserve cosmic order both at the levels of the *bhwana alit* and the *bhwana agung*.

In this context, it is the quality, not the quantity, of time that matters, and determines the propitious moment for any rite. As anthropologist Clifford Geertz in a 1966 Cultural Report, puts it, the Balinese calendars "don't tell us which day we are in, but what sort of day we are in."

Geertz also says that Balinese time is divided into 'full' and 'empty' time. Yet, the Balinese have no real 'empty' time. Their calendar system consists of overlapping units, all charged with divine and demonic influences of varied power. Their perceived time accordingly pulsates in a way that is partially regular, partially irregular, as it hovers between the many forces that inhabit it.

It pertains to everyone to try to understand this system and to adapt their behavior as closely as possible to the pulsating temporal rhythms to which they are subject, in order to properly harmonize their microcosmic selves to the macrocosmic forces that surround them.

This means that no important event or action should be undertaken without considering the quality of the day(s) or moment(s) on which it should be scheduled, based on a complex body of knowledge related to calendar divination (*wariga*). There are auspicious and inauspicious days and moments, not only to hold rites but also to start a business, plant rice, leave on a journey, choose a good rooster, start a new carving, put a roof on a house, and many more.

Meanwhile, the social scope of the rites prescribed by the calendar system is astounding. Some ritual events, on holy days called *rerainan gumi*, apply to the whole Balinese community. The whole ritual time takes between one-fourth and one-fifth of social time. Others apply to specific groups or communities, variously involving the family, clan, village, kingdom, and rice irrigation society, all of which are living microcosmic units complete with their respective temples and congregations. These events principally include *odalan* or temple 'anniversaries' that may last from one to ten days or even more.

Considering that every Balinese is an active member of six to ten different congregations, the time they spend on ritual events increases accordingly. To this should be added the days consecrated to rituals of the life and death cycle, also regulated by the calendar: pre- and post-birth rituals, *otonan* ('birthdays' in the 210-day cycle), weddings, tooth filings, and death rituals.

Pedewasan-related concerns indeed literally saturate the flow of Balinese time, making it in a mirror reversal of the philosopher Hölderlin's image of "God, who is nothing but Time"—into a "Time which is only God"—a time pervaded by sacred rituals. In short, humans do not so much manage time as they are managed by it.

CHAPTER 2

THE MYTH OF WATUGUNUNG AND THE BIRTH OF CIVILIZATION

There are different versions of the Watugunung myth, but the arc of the story remains the same, even if the names of some characters or places change. Precise times and distances are irrelevant. Again and again, the storyteller keeps his audience enchanted with the tale, even if they already know it by heart, for this is the story of the gods and heroes whose names are given to the weeks of the Balinese Pawukon calendar.

Once upon a time, there was a king named Dang Hyang Kulagiri who ruled over the kingdom of Jalasanggara. He had two wives—Dewi Sinta Kasih, the daughter of the high priest Gadiswara—and Dewi Landep, the daughter of Dang Hyang Pasupati, lord of Kundawipa.

Sinta became pregnant, and everyone in the kingdom prayed for a son to be born to succeed Kulagiri. Great rejoicing took place in Jalasanggara, whereupon Kulagiri went to the sacred mountain Mahameru to meditate, as was the custom under such circumstances. The king's duty was to thank the gods for granting him an heir and to implore them to bestow the child with supernatural powers.

The meditation lasted longer than usual and the date of the birth was approaching. Sinta and Landep were distressed at the thought that the king would not be present when his heir was born, which was considered an inauspicious omen.

The women decided to leave for the sacred mountain in search of Kulagiri. They rode on a cart specially suited to Sinta's condition and drawn by two mules familiar with the narrow paths leading to Mahameru.

Before long, Sinta felt the first pains of childbirth. The party interrupted their journey and stopped near a large rock where Sinta rested, while Landep prepared to help deliver the baby. Soon Landep became unable to assist Sinta any longer. The baby kicked his mother's womb with such force that a violent storm erupted, with thunder and lightning and gale-force winds.

The frightened women implored the gods for help. Brahma, the god of fire, appeared and helped with the delivery. A child was born, a huge baby boy with a remarkably red complexion.

The god comforted the women: "Women! The storm has subsided. You must take care of the child now, for he will grow in strength and power. I predict that he will become invulnerable. You must name him Jabang Bayi, as he is a newborn child, but later he will be known as Watugunung, which means 'stone' and 'mountain', in remembrance of his birth on this large rock on the slope of the sacred mountain."

The god of fire continued predicting: "Watugunung will be the almighty overlord of the lands around the sacred mountain. The twenty-seven princes who now rule over these lands will challenge him but they will eventually become his vassals. Neither giants nor men nor beasts, neither fire nor the wind of the cyclones will ever overpower Watugunung. Only one with the power to stalk the whole earth in three giant steps, one who has a tortoise head and is armed with five nails, namely, Wisnu, the god of water, will do so."

Thus spoke the god of fire, then he vanished into the air.

Sinta and Landep found solace in the words of the god. They rode back home with the newborn

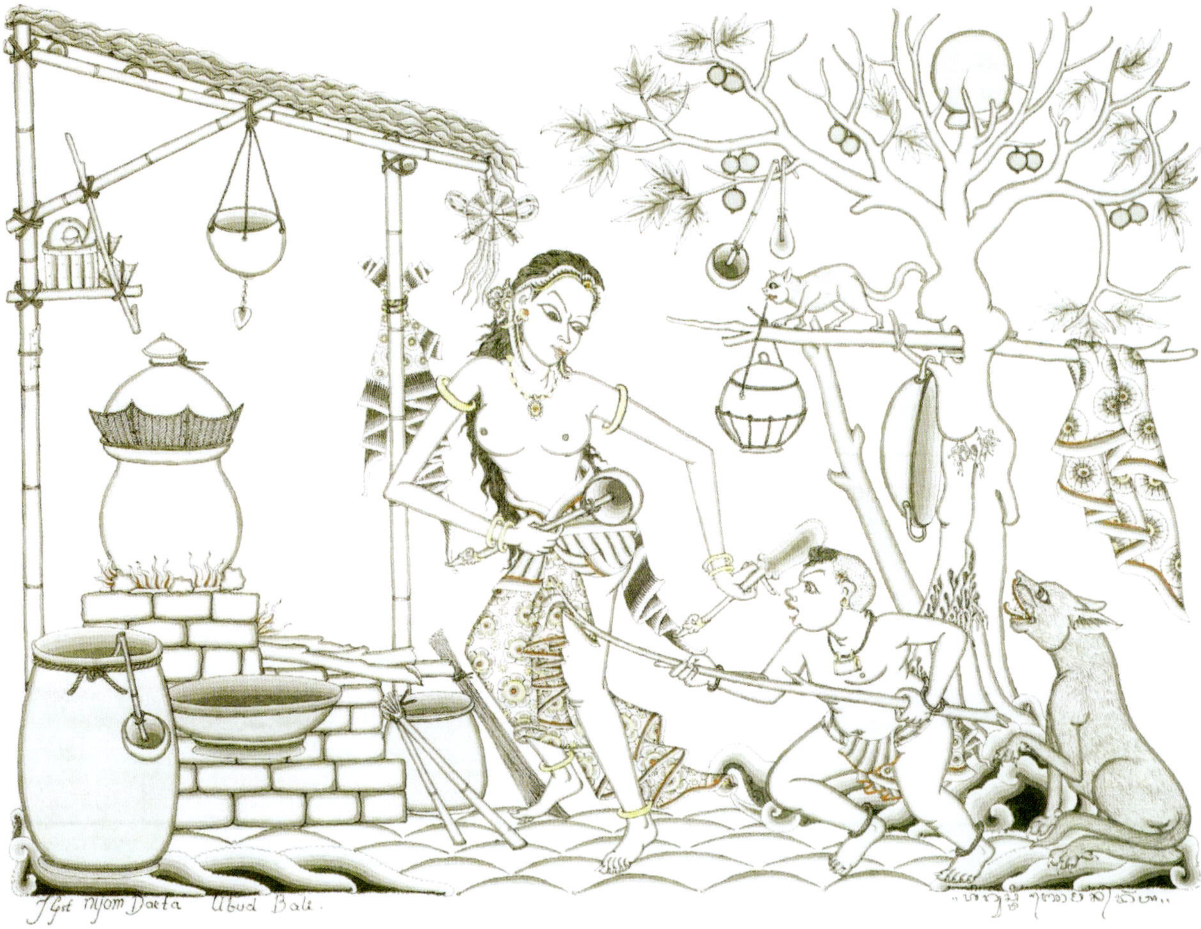

SINTA HITTING YOUNG WATUGUNUNG: This illustration shows Sinta hitting her son with a long bamboo ladle. The scene takes place in the kitchen. People say this is why mothers *may* not beat their children with kitchen instruments. Notice the offering shrine (*plangkiran*) attached to the left post.

Jabang Bayi and gave him tender loving care. However, they were amazed at the speed at which he grew. At only seven days of age, Jabang Bayi could talk. And he was always hungry, always asking for more food.

"Please, mother," the child would cry, addressing Sinta, "I want more rice."

"More rice? I have just given you plenty," his mother replied.

Jabang Bayi then turned to Landep and implored, "I'm so hungry. Will you give me more rice?"

Landep spoilt the child with more food. And Jabang Bayi grew bigger and bigger. At ten days of age he could walk! He was ill-tempered and threw tantrums on every possible occasion. The women were exhausted.

One day, Jabang Bayi, clinging to his mother's sarong, again asked for food. Sinta lost her patience.

"More rice? You want more rice?" she cried. "Well, take this!" And she smacked the child on the head with the ladle she was using.

Jabang Bayi ran out of the kitchen and left the palace screaming and cursing his mother. He produced a noise louder than the sound of the gong in a temple. Sinta and Landep tried to catch him, but he was already out of reach.

"He'll be back soon and we'll nurse the wound," said Landep.

But the child never came back.

Jabang Bayi had fled to the sacred mountain, hoping to find his father, the lord of the mountain Giriswara. He soon reached the slopes of

Mahameru. Once there, he meditated and became a man.

As Jabang Bayi prayed, sitting cross-legged on a large rock, the supreme god Siwa,who had witnessed his devotion, came down from his celestial abode and spoke to him: "Jabang Bayi, from now on I shall call you Watugunung, in remembrance of the place on the sacred mountain where you were born. I praise your devoutness, but I have the feeling that there is something you want to ask me."

"Oh Batara Siwa, my master, I want you to give me the power to rule over these lands," said Watugunung, stretching his arms over the horizon.

Siwa made a sign and said, "I will grant you your wish, Watugunung, so that the prediction made to your mother when you were born is fulfilled. Indeed, you will rule over the kingdoms all around the sacred mountain, and indeed, you will overpower all of the twenty-seven lords who now rule these lands. You will fear neither the giants, nor the men, nor the beasts, nor the fire, nor the winds of the cyclones."

"Oh Batara Siwa," Watugunung asked, "Can you tell me how and when I shall meet my destiny?"

"You will face death when you confront a monster with the head of a giant turtle and with *panca naka* (five nails). On this very day, my child, remember what I have predicted: your time has come."

With that pronouncement, Siwa disappeared. His vanished figure was replaced by Mount Siwagunungphala, the cosmic phallic lingam.

Watugunung went on his way so that the predictions would come true. He reached the kingdom of Himalaya, which was ruled by Ukir, lord of the mountain. Covered with dust from the road and tired of walking under the scorching sun, he came to a river and decided to rest and bathe.

Once in the water, Watugunung heard the voice of a woman singing a beautiful song. Intrigued, he approached to see where the singing was coming from. When the woman saw Watugunung gazing at her with great lust, she cried for help, and her husband, who was working in a rice field nearby, came to help.

Outraged at Watugunung's behavior, the man threatened him with his scythe. Others, who were working not far away, were attracted by the commotion. They realized what had happened and rushed to tell the king that a man in the river was trying to seduce a married woman. King Ukir and his men came and challenged Watugunung, but he overpowered them all. As it had been written, Watugunung would conquer the world.

Ukir surrendered, as did all of the other princes (*wuku*) who dared challenge Watugunung. Together with Ukir, they numbered 27: Kulantir, Taulu, Gumbreg, Wariga, Warigadian, Julungwangi, Sungsang, Dungulan, Kuningan, Langkir, Medangsiya, Pujut, Pahang, Krulut, Merakih, Tambir, Medangkungan, Matal, Uye, Menail, Perangbakat, Bala, Ugu, Wayang, Kulawu, and Dukut.

Watugunung now ruled all the lands around the sacred mountain. When he was not hunting or inspecting work in the rice fields, he spent his time in his palace with his entourage.

One evening, as they gathered in the main hall of the palace, Watugunung said, "My lords! Would you tell me, whom should I choose to be my wedded companion? For the future of my kingdom, I must father a child to succeed me."

"Oh Watugunung! In the kingdom of Jalasanggara are not one but two princesses who would be worthy of becoming our queen." Thus spoke Dungulan, one of the princes in the room.

"I thought those princesses were already married," said Watugunung.

Dungulan replied that, indeed, the princesses had been married, but both their husband and their only son had mysteriously vanished.

That night, Watugunung dreamt of the two princesses. The next morning, his decision was made. He would send one of his princes to the kingdom of Jalasanggara and ask the princesses to become his wives. If necessary, he would fight for them!

The two princesses, Sinta and Landep, resisted Watugunung's overtures. He therefore went to war. The princesses lost the battle, surrendered, and became his wives and queens.

Some time afterwards, Watugunung, upon returning from the hunt, rested under the awning of the palace. He asked Sinta to comb his hair, as was the custom. As she ran the comb through her husband's hair, Sinta made a discovery. On the

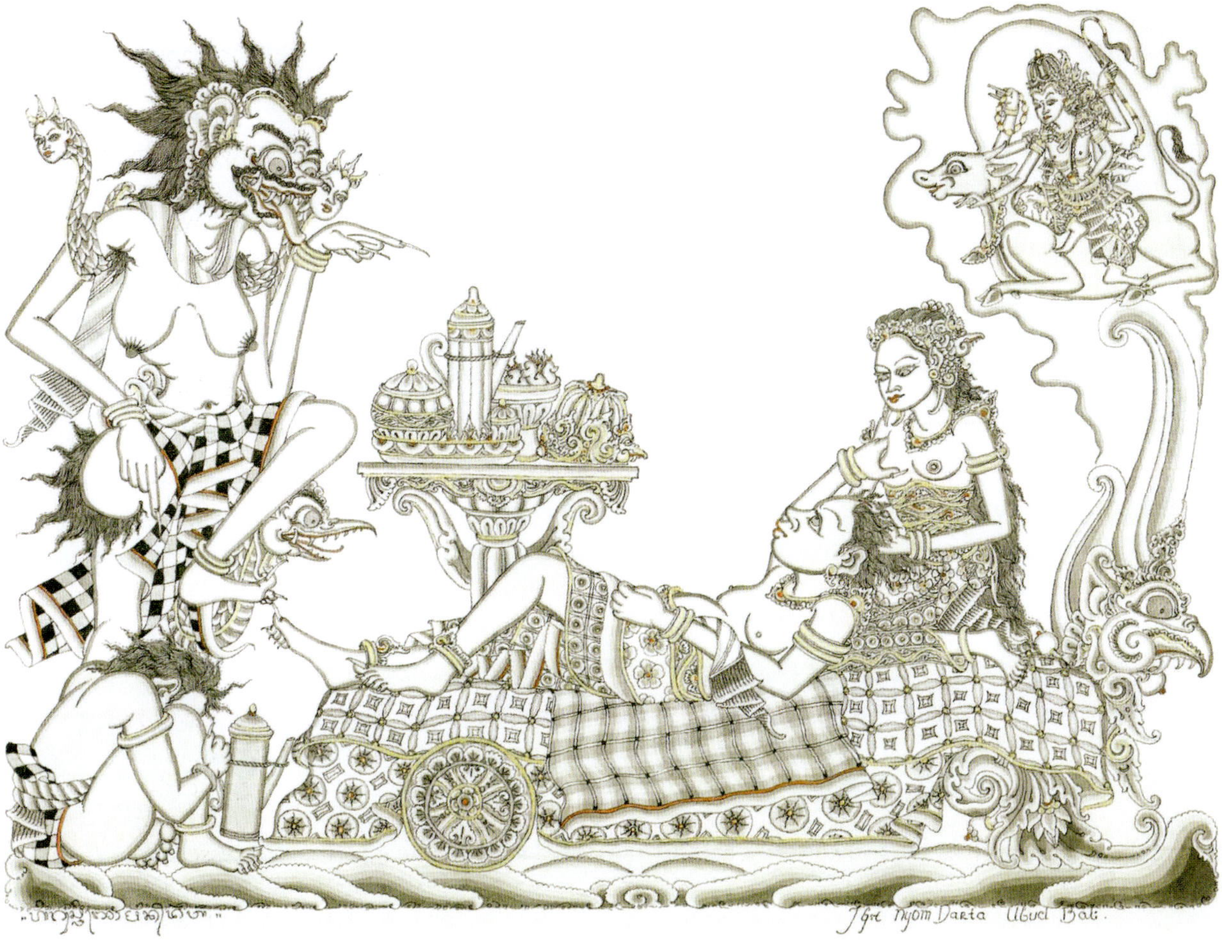

SINTA DISCOVERS THE SCAR: Watugunung is shown here lying on his couch while his wife, who happens to be his mother, combs his hair, and upon discovering the scar made by the ladle awakens to her fate as an incestuous mother. Witnessing the scene are Durga, the goddess of destruction, to the left, accompanied by her demon companions (*rencang*), and Siwa, to the right, riding his vehicle, the bull Nandini. Durga is, in fact, Siwa's wife Uma, who was turned into a demonic goddess after betraying Siwa with the herdsman Rare Angon, who happened to be Siwa in disguise.

top of his head, there was a scar. So strange was its shape that she concluded it could only have come from the ladle she had struck her son with so many years before.

Too confused to proceed any further, Sinta pretended to be tired, and asked Landep to finish the job. She also instructed her to carefully examine the scar. Landep went further. She asked Watugunung what had caused the scar.

"When I was a child," Watugunung replied, "my mother struck me because I was hungry and I wanted more rice."

As soon as she had finished her task, Landep went to Sinta's room and reported the conversation. Both women now realized with horror that their husband was, in fact, their son and stepson!

Watugunung noticed a dramatic change in the behavior of his wives. He asked them, "My sweet ladies ... what has happened to you so suddenly? You look sad and dejected. Tell me, what is the matter?"

Sinta spoke first. "Oh our lord! We have both had a strange dream in which we saw ourselves getting older while you retained the strength of youth. We think that you should take another wife to satisfy your desires and bear the son you expect." Watugunung protested. Yet, he was curious to know who this other wife was in his queens' dreams?

"We dreamt that you should marry Nawang Ratih," Landep replied. "What?" cried Watugunung, "Do you mean Wisnu's wife, the spouse of the god of water?"

"You have named her!"

Watugunung was shocked. It was inconceivable to think he could covet the wife of a god! He was unaware that Sinta and Landep knew the true origin of the scar on his head and were ashamed of the incest. Sinta and Landep had also learned that if Watugunung were to marry a god's wife, this would make him a god himself, and thus the stain of incest would be cleansed.

Watugunung, after reviewing the situation, summoned one of his counselors, Warigadian. He instructed him to go to the kingdom of the gods and ask Wisnu to part from his wife Nawang Ratih.

Wisnu was furious. How could a mere mortal dare to covet a god's wife? He told Watugunung's ambassador to return to his master and tell him that if the king was so impudent as to ask for his wife, he should come himself and fight for her. Should he, Wisnu, lose the battle, then Watugunung could marry Nawang Ratih.

When Watugunung was told of Wisnu's words, he marshaled his troops and *wuku* allies. Nothing was spared in the preparation of his army for a battle that would be the mother of all battles.

Wisnu, being a god, was aware of Watugunung's reaction, and he also prepared his own troops for the mighty clash. Indeed, his troops were a formidable lot, comprised of all the principal inhabitants of the abode of the gods, including the *sapta rsi* (seven seers), the *panca rsi* (five seers), and the *caturlokaphala* (four lords of the directions of the compass).

When the two armies met, the confrontation was terrifying. The soldiers fought fiercely for a whole day, from sunrise to sunset. The dead were counted by the thousands. All the wuku princes had been killed and, as nothing had been settled that day, the armies repaired to their quarters to rest for the night. The fight was to resume the next day.

Meanwhile, Wisnu was despondent. Many gods had been killed and, until then, no one had ever resisted him. He confided in his father-in-law Wrespati, who suggested that Wisnu should dispatch his brother-in-law Lumanglang to the land of the mortals. Lumanglang, whose name means 'he who sees', could take the form of a spider, so it would be easy for him to spy on Watugunung. Based on what Lumanglang learned, they would decide on what tactics to adopt when the struggle resumed.

Lumanglang entered the tent where Watugunung and his wives rested. Sinta and Landep had just asked their husband to tell the story of the battle and the origin of his supernatural powers.

"My sweet ladies," Watugunung said, "if I tell you the secret of my supernatural powers, which was revealed to me when I meditated on the slope of the sacred mountain, you must keep this secret to yourselves, or I shall die."

The women promised not to tell. Watugunung told them that only the god of water could overpower him when he took the shape of a monster with the head of a giant turtle and armed with the five nails. Lumanglang, who was hiding behind a pillar in the tent, remembered every word of the conversation. He returned to the realm of the gods and reported to Wisnu what he had heard.

The next day, the two armies resumed the fight. To his dismay, Watugunung found himself facing a monster with the head of a turtle and five lethal nails. He realized that his time was nearly up. The armies soon ceased fighting to watch the single challenge between Watugunung and Wisnu.

The struggle raged on for a long while. Try as he might, Watugunung could not overcome the formidable nails. No sooner had he severed one or two of the nails, they grew anew to lash at him again. He was losing too much blood. Finally, he was defeated. Wisnu threw him to the ground, where he lay, mortally wounded.

The following day, Watugunung's corpse was defiled. The next day, Watugunung's body was dragged on the ground. And the next day, Batara Buda brought him back to life. But barely an hour later, Wisnu killed him again. The next day, Siwa revived him once more.

Realizing that Wisnu was planning to kill Watugunung yet again, and intended to continue this infernal cycle indefinitely, Siwa said, "Wisnu, forget the idea of killing Watugunung. Each time one of us will resuscitate him. For with him dead, the lessons we must teach mankind will never be conveyed to the generations to come."

Wisnu argued, "Oh Batara Siwa, I must kill Watugunung, for great were his sins. He has lusted after a married woman, he has married his mother and his stepmother, and he has coveted the wife of a god. This is too much to be tolerated in the world of the mortals!"

Siwa replied, "It is true that Watugunung has committed all these abominable sins. It shall not be permitted, henceforth, to covet anyone else's spouse or to marry one's own mother. But let us punish Watugunung in another way."

Wisnu then addressed Watugunung: "Every six months—counting thirty-five days each, that is, 210 days—you shall be impure."

Watugunung repented and asked for forgiveness. "So be it, according to thy will, Oh Wisnu," he said. Yet, he implored, "Please, when I fall into the depths of the seas, might I warm the world so mankind does not shiver with cold any more? When I fall on the land before the harvest, might I bring the rains with me so that crops do not wither? And might it be that, henceforth, mankind knows what happened to me so the gods' teachings will be heeded?"

After Watugunung was sentenced, Siwa resuscitated the 27 *wuku* and the *panca rsi*. All the gods descended from the sacred mountain to earth to purify Watugunung. Ganesha, the elephant god, gave mankind the *wariga* (knowledge of the calendar and calendar-based divination) so that they would know what is good and what is evil.

Then the gods wrote down this story, and thus established the *dewasa* or *pedewasan*—the god-given calendar system—with Watugunung as the lord of the calendar. They distributed the 27 wuku, in addition to Sinta, Landep, and Watugunung, to form the 30 seven-day weeks of the 210-day Pawukon cycle, which begins with the incestuous mother, Sinta, and ends with the incestuous son, Watugunung.

Watungunung: Bali's Culture Hero

If we analyze the myth of Watugunung from a psychoanalysis-slanted, anthropological perspective, a few things clearly stand out.

At first sight, the myth is a classically Freudian, sex-laden incest story. Signs are found throughout the plot. The incestuous hero is separated from his father and mother at a young age. Like Oedipus, the tragic figure of ancient Greek mythology who kills his father and eventually marries his mother, Watugunung also defeats his father (Kulagiri/Giriswara/Ukir) and marries his mother (Sinta). In both myths, the hero's transgressions throw the abode of the gods into chaos.

Symbolically, all of the alternate names for Watugunung's father refer to mountains: Kulagiri, which means 'mountain range', Giriswara, which means 'lord of the mountain', and Ukir or Wukir, which means 'mountain' in Old Javanese. The mountain is a clear phallic symbol (lingam), which also associates Watugunung's father with the god Siwa. Balinese commonly recognize both Giriswara and Ukir as symbols of Siwa.

Sinta hits her infant son on the head with a long bamboo ladle, another phallic symbol. As for the long wound Sinta catches sight of on her adult son's head, it is a classic vaginal symbol (yoni), as is the river in which the women whom Watugunung tries to rape are bathing. The name Watugunung itself, which means 'stone mountain', can also be seen as a phallic symbol. Finally, there is the presence of the god Siwa, who is the cosmic phallic symbol par excellence. In short, many elements of the myth allude to sexual symbolism in the Freudian sense.

One notices, too, that the sexual transgressions of the hero do not go unnoticed. One of the principal characters of the myth is the 'witness god' Sang Hyang Lumanglang ('he who sees'), who is said to be a form of the sun god Surya. Thus, apart from its sexual symbolism, the story symbolically depicts the origin of Balinese society as it emerges into the light from the dark pit of the world before time.

Before the victory of the gods over Watugunung, the world is in chaos. The family as an institution is not yet structured: Watugunung's mother Sinta is violent toward her infant son and badly wounds him on the head; Watugunung then leaves his mother; and previously, the father abandons his family. Sexual life is in total disorder, even wild. Powerful men like Watugunung can rape women at will. Political life is also in turmoil. War is ubiquitous, and a violent man like Watugunung can become conqueror of the world, including the kingdom of his own parents.

The peak of these cumulative disorders is Watugunung's act of incest with his mother, immediately followed by his mother's awareness of the enormity of this act as a transgression of divine order; that is, only the gods are allowed to commit this kind of act. And Watugunung is not a god, but a human. What results from his transgression is nothing less than total cosmic chaos, which translates into Watugunung's subsequent actions. He feels that he has become the equal of the gods and can wreak havoc on the world, rape women, and even provoke Wisnu, the ultimate guardian of the world's stability.

Wisnu's intervention re-establishes cosmic order and returns Watugunung to his original status. Yet, instead of being killed by the god, Watugunung is enlightened through an epiphany, and then made the master of the calendar and guarantor of the prohibition against incest. Thus, he turns from destroyer, rapist, and threat into a tool through which the gods obtain stability in the world of men.

Stability is achieved through a set of transformations that are concomitant with the appearance of the calendar. The creation of the calendar by the gods after Watugunung's defeat also corresponds to the onset of the prohibition of incest. This is the first enlightenment. The incestuous mother and son now occupy opposite ends of the Pawukon cycle. Sinta is at the beginning of the cycle, while Watugunung is at its end. They are formally separated, and at the same time cleansed by the epiphany at the apex of the cycle, which falls on the day of Saraswati, goddess of knowledge.

Saraswati does not symbolize knowledge in the narrow sense of the word, as mere 'learning'. Rather, she symbolizes human 'consciousness'. The most deeply entrenched and universal manifestation of consciousness among human beings since the origin of humanity is the awareness that sexual life in the family and social environment have to follow rules, to be regulated. Sexual intercourse must not be forced upon any woman and must not take place within the nuclear family, especially between mother and son, like Sinta and Watugunung before their enlightenment.

Thus, the origin of the incest prohibition, as it appears in the story of Watugunung's epiphany and development of a human 'consciousness,' can be understood as the first fully human step of prehistoric humans, the step through which the *homo* became fully *sapiens*. In Freudian lingo, it is the eruption of the 'super-ego' in human life.

Further down the line, the prohibition of incest was the first step in the setting up of a legal system, and therefore marked the onset of the organization of social life. Saraswati day, the day of the goddess of knowledge, thus also celebrates the mythical foundation of social organization.

Implicitly related to the above is the appearance of the 'consciousness of time' as a divine gift, when Siwa appoints the enlightened Watugunung as lord of the Pawukon calendar.

An important point must be emphasized here, which will be underlined again later on. This is that Watugunung's revolt, far from ending in a victory over the gods, ends in his surrender to the gods. Watugunung, the symbol of Man revolting against the gods, *ipso facto*, turns against religion, but at the end of the day, defeated, he 'understands', receives faith and consciousness, and returns to the fold of religion to eventually become the definer, as lord of the calendar, of all its ritual activities. The majority of Balinese rites are indeed defined by the rules of this calendar.

The myth, through its story of incest and revolt, tells us something about the inception of self-consciousness in Man. In his revolt, Watugunung begins to feel he is autonomous from the larger cosmic world, but when he is defeated it is not 'liberty' that he finds but an epiphany that leads him to throw away his autonomy or individual consciousness, to rejoin the very system against which he had revolted.

The ultimate teachings of the myth are unambiguous: Cosmic order must be preserved at all cost! Man as microcosm (*bhwana alit*) must obey the ritual requirements necessary to

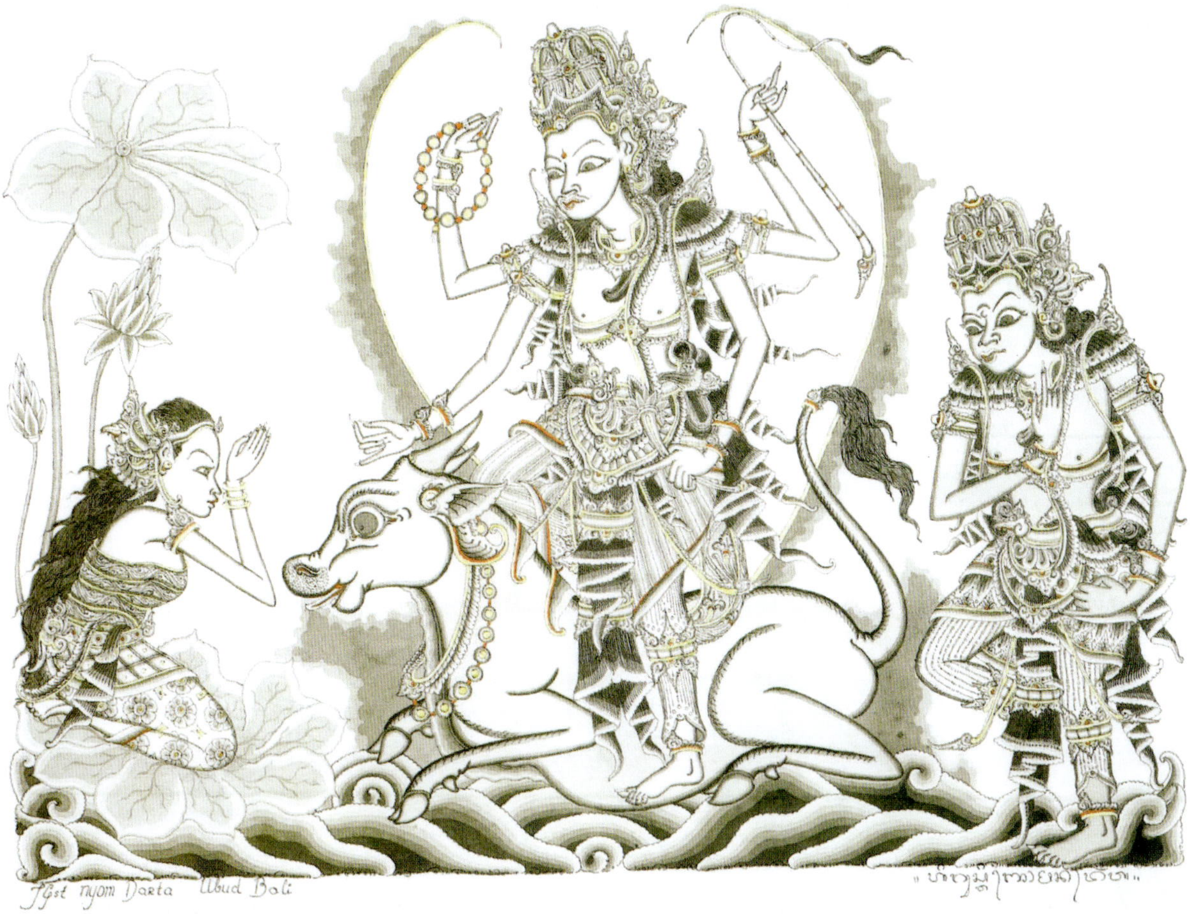

THE SEPARATION: Siwa is shown here separating the incestuous mother, to the left, from the incestuous son, to the right, the action which institutes the notion of time in Bali. Siwa rides his godly vehicle, the bull Nandini, and holds the *ganitri* rosary, symbol of time, as well as the *pecut* whip, symbol of punishment. His hands are held in the position that denotes speech in Balinese dance.

preserve this order. He must therefore organize his action by holding the correct rites at the right times, as determined by the Pawukon calendar and the Wariga divination system. He has to surrender his autonomy.

In conclusion, it can be said that the myth of Watugunung marks the inception of a whole range of human characteristics. Man appears as a primitive *homo* who gives up his animal-hood and fully becomes a *sapiens* with the prohibition of incest; the dawning of a consciousness of time; the establishment of social norms and legal rules, and a religious ideological system.

These features, however, are not presented as universal characteristics of the human anthropos. They are rather those of Man in Java/Bali, as the Balinese view him, at the dawn of civilization. In that sense, Watugunung is the 'culture hero' of Bali—the character who civilized Bali.

Oedipus and Watugunung

From the Balinese point of view, the only type of Man is that symbolized by Watugunung, whose story tells the origin of the awareness of time and rituals. Having challenged the gods, the hero, defeated, becomes the protector of religion, a far cry from Oedipus who, blinded, ends up erring across the land while cursing the gods and fate itself. The two heroes have quite different roles, leading to two roads of life: one of hope and faith, the other of despair and disbelief.

CHAPTER 3

THE BALINESE CALENDARS

Balinese time is framed by the interplay of two distinct systems that anchor the island in both the cosmos and the community. While they overlap, their roles are clearly demarcated: the Saka calendar serves as the link to the macrocosm and the celestial order, while the Pawukon functions as the primary engine of social and ritual life.

Derived from Indian Hindu tradition, the Saka calendar is a luni-solar system that aligns Balinese life with the great rhythms of the universe. By tracking the lunar phases, it connects the human experience to the Bhuana Agung (the macrocosm). This calendar is the guardian of historical memory and ecological time, regulating agricultural seasons and tides. Its most critical points are the Purnama (Full Moon) and Tilem (New Moon), moments when the veil between the divine and the earthly thins. The Saka is essentially a cosmic dialogue, whose purification rites, culminating in the 'total reset' of Nyepi, are designed to harmonize the island with the celestial cycles and cleanse the environment of universal decay.

In contrast, the Pawukon is a strictly indigenous, 210-day cyclical system that ignores celestial bodies entirely, focusing instead on the Bhuana Alit (the microcosm) and the social fabric. It is the master organizer of 'human time'. Because it dictates the schedules of most *odalan* (temple anniversaries) and life cycle rites, from tooth-filing to weddings, it ensures the constant socialization of the individual within the community and the spirit world. The Pawukon is a qualitative system where time is seen as a recurring pattern of positive and negative energies that have to be kept in balance. Combined, in a more minor way with

Opposite above **CLASSIC WOODEN TIKA: Light wood with pigments and lime. An engraved and painted tika crowned by a simple pediment. The result obtained by the use of alternate black and white colors is very decorative, albeit not very informative. No decoration on the back.**

40 x 16 x 1 cm; Gianyar, Central Bali; Second quarter of the 20th century; MHL collection (inv. 2428).

Opposite center **CLASSIC WOODEN TIKA: Hardwood with horn and brass fragments. A stylized engraved tika crowned by a geometrical pediment. On the back, an engraved *nawa sanga* (not illustrated).**

29 x 12 x 1 cm; Karangasem, East Bali; First quarter of the 20th century; MHL collection (inv. 2430).

Opposite below **CLASSIC WOODEN TIKA: Brownish-red hardwood, with an iron hook (4 cm) and bone fragments. A geometric pediment crowns a classic engraved tika enhanced by bone fragments. No decoration on the back.**

44 x 19 x 1 cm; Tabanan, Central Bali; Second quarter of the 20th century; MHL collection (inv. 2456).

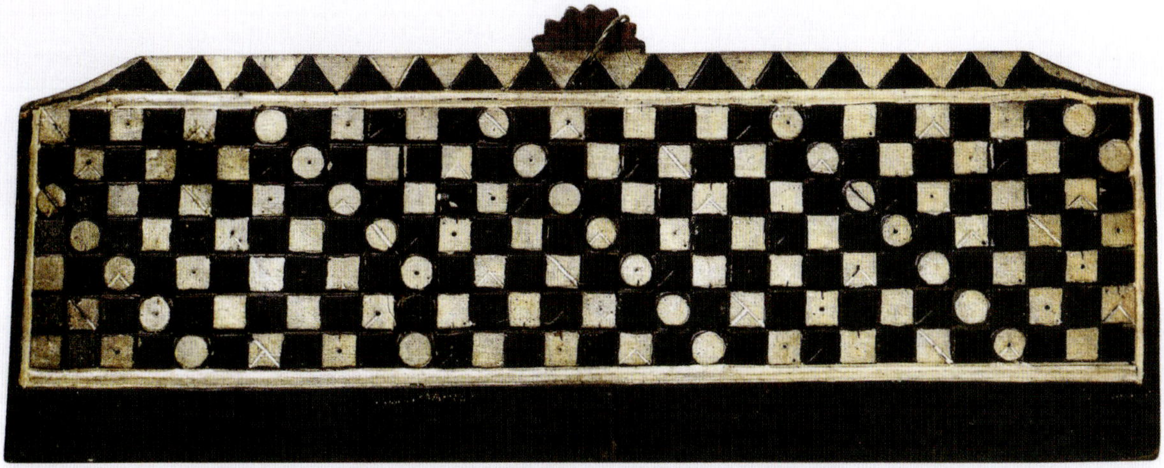

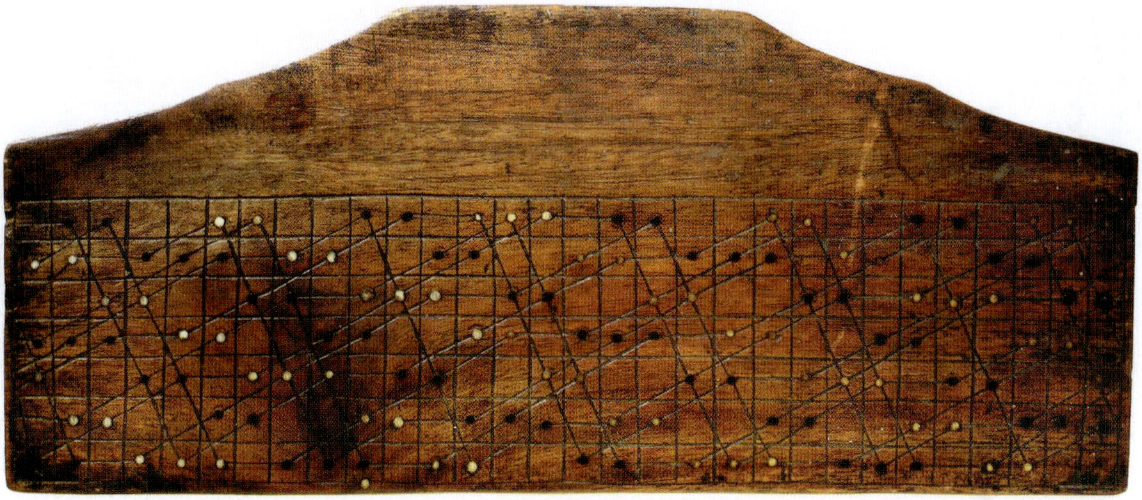

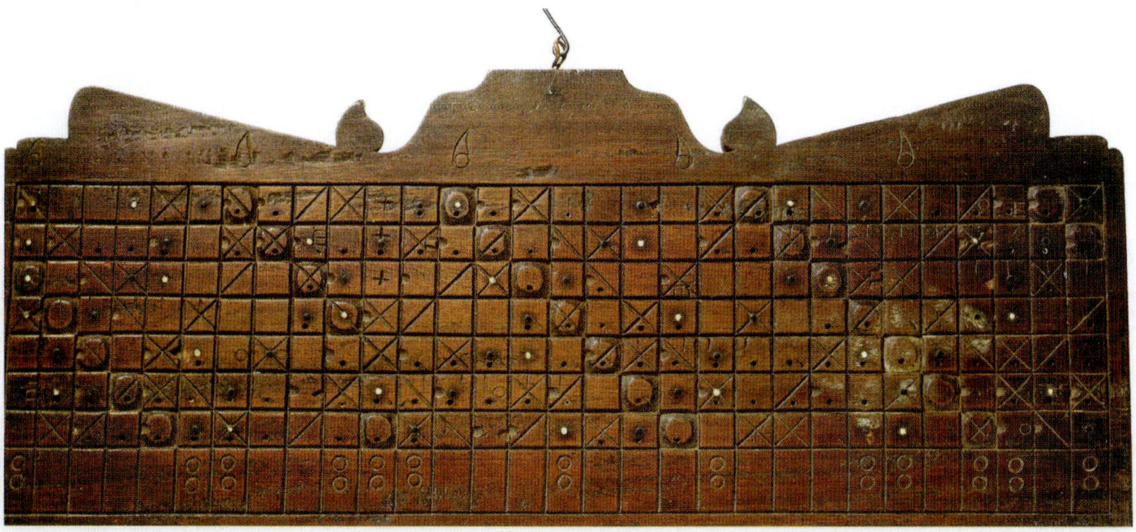

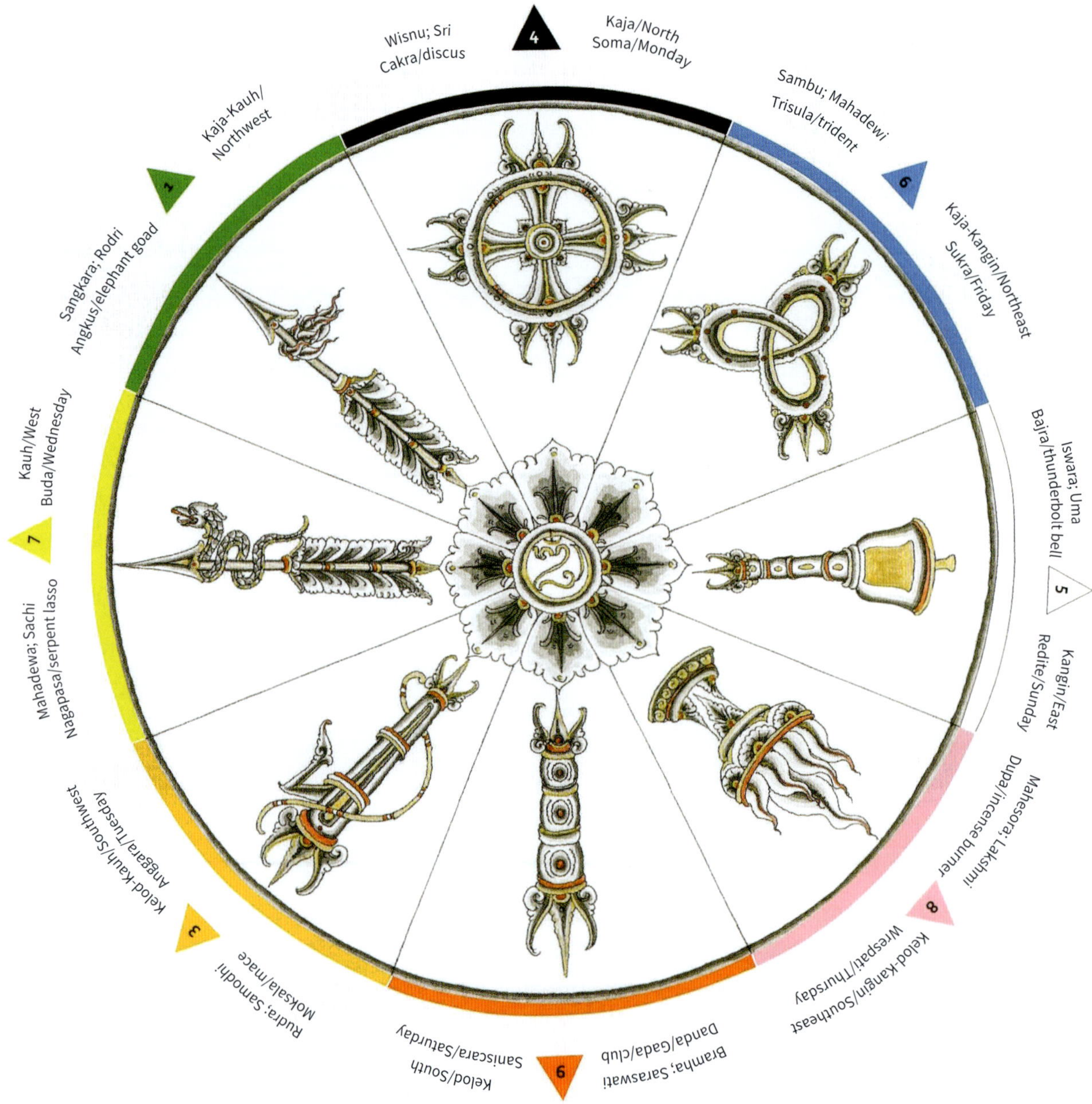

NAWA SANGA MANDALA: The *nawa sanga* is a sacred 'compass rose' or mandala of the world. This circular nawa sanga features the deities and their weapons (shown as drawings here as well as named in English and Balinese), colors, magic numbers (*urip*, in the small triangles), and days of the seven-day week corresponding to each of the eight cardinal directions. At the center is Siwa, who is multi-colored, his weapon is the lotus (*padma*), and his number is 8.

All aspects of reality can, in fact, potentially be mapped onto this compass, including time units, body parts, sounds, letters, animals, plants, demons, mythical heroes, and so on. For a more complete inventory of correspondences, including time units, see the table on the right.

Nawa Sanga correspondences, including elements of the calendar system

Direction	Kaja North/Upstream	Kaja-Kangin Northeast	Kangin East/Downstream	Kelod-Kangin Southeast	Kelod South	Kelod-Kauh Southwest	Kauh West	Kaja-Kauh Northwest	Tengah Center
God	Wisnu	Sambu	Iswara	Mahesora	Brahma	Rudra	Mahadewa	Sangkara	Siwa
Goddess	Sri	Mahadewi	Uma	Lakshmi	Saraswati	Samodhi	Sachi	Rodri	Durga
Weapon	Cakra (discus)	Trisula (trident)	Bajra (thunderbolt bell)	Dupa (incense burner)	Danda/Gada (club)	Moksala (mace)	Nagapasa (serpent lasso)	Angkus (elephant goad)	Padma (lotus)
Vehicle	Garuda (king of birds)	Wilmana (demonic bird)	Gajah (elephant)	Macan (tiger)	Angsa (goose)	Kerbau (buffalo)	Naga (dragon)	Singa (lion)	Lembu (bull)
Color	Black	Blue-Gray	White	Pink	Red	Orange	Yellow	Green	Multi-colored
Temple	Ulundanu	Besakih	Lempuyang	Goa Lawah	Andakasa	Uluwatu	Batukaru	Puncak Mangu	Besakih
Demon	Taruna	Pelung	Jangkitan	Dadu	Langkir	Jingga	Lembu Kanya	Gadang	Tiga Sakti
Letter	A	Wa	Sa	Na	Ba	Ma	Ta	Si	I/Ya
Urip (number)	4	6	5	8	9	3	7	1	8
Ekawara day	-	-	-	-	-	-	-	Luang	-
Dwiwara day	-	-	Menga	-	-	-	Pepet	-	-
Triwara day	Beteng	-	-	-	Pasah	-	Kajeng	-	-
Caturwara day	-	Sri	Laba	Jaya	Menala	-	-	-	-
Pancawara day	Wage	-	Umanis	-	Paing	-	Pon	-	Kliwon
Sadwara day	-	Aryang	Urukung	Paniron	Was	Maulu	Tungleh	-	-
Saptawara day	Soma (Monday)	Sukra (Friday)	Redite (Sunday)	Wrespati (Thursday)	Saniscara (Saturday)	Anggara (Tuesday)	Buda (Wednesday)	-	-
Astawara day	Uma	Sri	Indra	Guru	Yama	Ludra	Brahma	Kala	-
Sangawara day	Urungan	Tulus	Dangu	Jangur	Gigis	Nohan	Ogan	Erangan	Dadi
Dasawara day	Duka	Sri	Pandita	Raja	Dewa	Manusa	Pita	Raksasa	Suka, Manuh
Wuku week	Ukir, Dungulan, Tambir, Wayang	Kulantir, Kuningan, Medangkungan Kulawu	Tolu, Langkir, Matal, Dukut	Gumbreg, Medangsia, Uye, Watugunung	Wariga, Pujut, Menail	Warigadian, Pahang, Prangbakat	Sinta, Julungwangi, Krulut, Bala	Landep, Sungsang, Merakih, Ugu	-
Sasih (Saka lunar month)	Kasa	Karo, Katiga	Kapat	Kalima, Kanem	Kapitu	Kawulu, Kasanga	Kadasa	Desta, Sadha	- -
Tithi (Saka days) **Pananggal (waxing moon)** **Panglong (waning moon)**	3 11	4 12	5 13	6 14	7 15	8	1 9	2 10	

This table shows the same elements as the circular *nawa sanga* 'compass rose' (left), plus others, including elements of the Balinese calendar system related to each of the nine sacred directions: the *wuku* weeks, the *wewaran* weeks and their corresponding days, the Saka lunar months (*sasih*), and the Saka lunar days (*tithi*) of the waxing/waning moon (*pananggal/panglong*).

a reading of moon auspiciousness, it provides the main framework for *wariga* (interpretation-cum-divination), thus allowing practitioners to determine the auspiciousness (*ala/ayu*) of any private or public social or architectural undertaking based on the intersection of various multi-day weeks.

Both systems are integrated through the *pangider-ider*, a sacred mandala that maps every unit of time onto a compass rose. This system links specific days to cardinal directions, deities, colors, and sacred numbers (*urip*). By situating a day within this cosmic map, specialists like the *pedanda* or *balian* can interpret its unique character. Whether through a *tika* (wooden calendar chart) or a *pelelintangan* (astrological painting), these calendars transform the abstract concept of 'time' into a tangible guide for living.

While examples of the tika are discussed in this chapter, whereas the pelelintangan and pelelindon (earthquake divination charts) are explored in Chapter 7, the most common modern reference is the printed Balinese calendar. This contemporary tool synthesizes these ancient complexities into a single grid, embedding Gregorian dates alongside the intricate names of Pawukon and Saka units. It serves as a daily visual guide, ensuring that even in a globalized world a Balinese person remains precisely positioned at the intersection of the stars above and the community around them.

The Pawukon Calendar

The 30 Wuku Weeks

The 210-day Pawukon calendar consists of 30 seven-day weeks. Each of these weeks is named after a *wuku*, one of the noble indigenous characters from the Watugunung saga (as opposed to the *wewaran* characters of Indian and Javanese origin), and has a corresponding deity and geographical direction on the *pengider-ider*, along with an *urip*.

The names of the 30 wuku weeks and corresponding deities, in order of appearance on the calendar, are given in the table at right.

	Wuku name		Corresponding deity
1.	Sinta	-	Yamadipati
2.	Landep	-	Mahadewa
3.	Ukir (Wukir)	-	Mahayekti
4.	Kulantir	-	Langsur
5.	Taulu (Tolu)	-	Bayu
6.	Gumbreg	-	Cakra
7.	Wariga	-	Asmara
8.	Warigadian	-	Maharesi
9.	Julungwangi	-	Sambu
10	Sungsang	-	Gana
11.	Dungulan	-	Kamajaya
12.	Kuningan	-	Indra
13.	Langkir	-	Kala
14.	Medangsia	-	Brahma
15.	Pujut	-	Guritha
16.	Pahang	-	Tantra
17.	Krulut	-	Wisnu
18.	Merakih	-	Surenggana
19.	Tambir	-	Siwa
20.	Medangkungan	-	Basuki
21.	Matal	-	Sakri
22.	Uye	-	Kuwera
23.	Menail	-	Citragotra
24.	Prangbakat	-	Bisma
25.	Bala	-	Durga
26.	Ugu	-	Singajalma
27.	Wayang	-	Sri
28.	Klawu	-	Sadana
29.	Dukut	-	Baruna
30.	Watugunung	-	Antaboga

The Wewaran Cycles

What makes the Pawukon a one-of-a-kind calendar is that it has not only one but ten different types of 'weeks' or cycles, known as *wara.* Each wara is composed of a different number of days, ranging from one day to ten. All ten wara run simultaneously through each Pawukon cycle, and together they make up the wewaran system.

Thus, the seven-day wuku week discussed above is only one of the 'weeks' of the wewaran system. It corresponds to the seven-day week (Saptawara), which is similar to the standard week of the Gregorian calendar. It is also the only one in which the individual weeks are named.

The names of the ten kinds of wara making up the wewaran system:

Ekawara	-	one day
Dwiwara	-	two days
Triwara	-	three days
Caturwara	-	four days
Pancawara	-	five days
Sadwara	-	six days
Saptawara	-	seven days
Astawara	-	eight days
Sangawara	-	nine days
Dasawara	-	ten days

Together, the days of the ten different wara add up to 55 days, each with a name and meaning of its own as well as a position on the pangider-ider.

The Days of the Wara and Their Meanings

The names of the days in each wara of the wewaran system are as follows:

Ekawara, the one-day week: The day is called Luang, which means 'empty'.

Dwiwara, the two-day week: The days are called Menga and Pepet, meaning 'open' and 'closed', respectively.

Triwara, the three-day week: The days are called Pasah, Beteng, and Kajeng. Kajeng, dedicated to demons, is inauspicious. Pasah means 'market day'. Bedeng means 'plenty of water' and refers to irrigation. The Triwara may refer to a traditional market-day cycle among neighboring villages.

Caturwara, the four-day week: The days are called Sri, Laba, Jaya, and Mendala (Menala), respectively, meaning 'prosperity, 'profit', 'victory', and 'territory'. The auspicious day Jaya is repeated on three days before Galungan day, offsetting the influences of inauspicious Kala, also repeated three times, from the Astawara on the same days.

Pancawara, the five-day week: The days are called Manis (Umanis), Paing (Pahing), Pon, Wage, and Kliwon (Klion). These words are very likely of Javanese origin and are associated with an old market-day cycle. The qualities of these days are those of the gods corresponding to them on the pangider-ider: lswara, Brahma, Mahadewa, Wisnu, and Siwa. Kliwon, associated with the center of the compass rose, is the most propitious. Following is Manis, which occupies the east and therefore the position of the rising sun. Most festivals fall on one of these two days. Paing and Pon, corresponding to the south and west, respectively, are associated with human life and ancestors and are suitable for events such as *subak* (irrigation community) meetings. The least propitious day is Wage, associated with death.

Sadwara, the six-day week: The days are called Tungleh, Aryang, Urukung, Paniron, Was, and Maulu. In a 1992 publication, Wayan Gina gives the following meanings and values for these days: Tungleh, 'not lasting' and Urukung, 'exterminated' are considered dangerous days, and Aryang, 'lean', is deemed unlucky. On the other hand, Paniron, 'imitation', Was, 'healed', and Maulu, 'in height' or 'increasing', are lucky days. Arlette Ottino, referring to village rituals in *The Universe Within* (2000), gives a more precise presentation of the Sadwara: "The Sadwara is associated with good fortune in a way that relates human destiny to the ebb and flow of natural forces in the environment. The first day, Aryang, carries a value of dryness and suffering, Urukung, mould and decay, Paniron is associated with burgeoning and breaking out (of buds), Was has a value of healthy, growing and whole, Mahulu is associated with flowering and fruition, and Tungleh, aged—if a tree: losing its leaves."

Saptawara, the seven-day week: This makes up every wuku-named week. The names of the days are the same as those in the ancient Sumerian hebdomad, which became romanized in the West. Each day of the week is named in its Indian version after a planet in the solar system: Redite is Sunday, the day of the Sun; Soma is Monday, the day of the Moon; Anggara is Tuesday, the day of Mars; Boda or Buda is Wednesday, the day of Mercury; Wrespati is Thursday, the day of Jupiter; Sukra is Friday, the day of Venus, and Saniscara is Saturday, the day of Saturn.

The days of the Saptawara are at the core of the visual representations of the Pawukon in illustrated

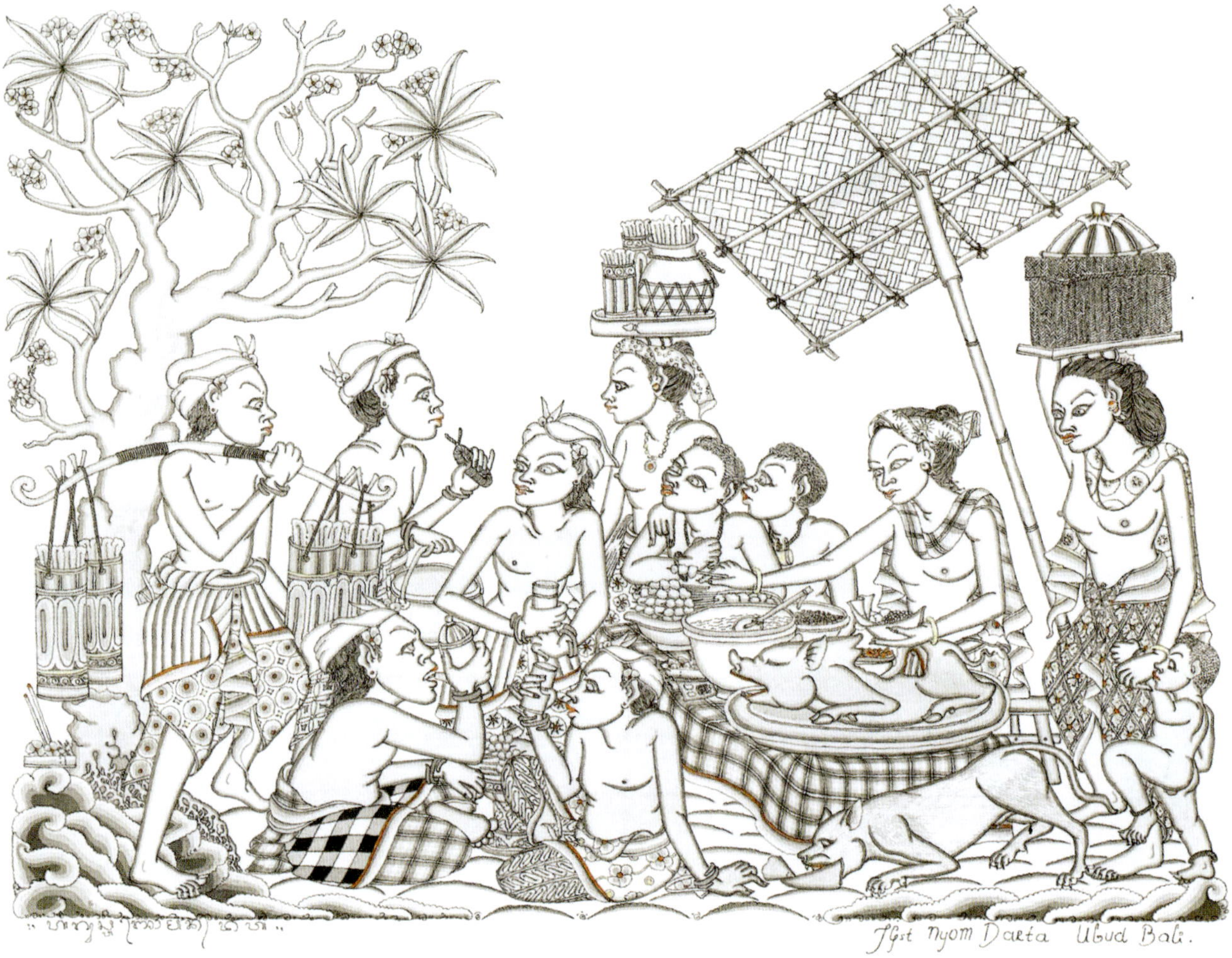

MARKET DAY: In many Balinese villages, life is punctuated by the market (*pasah*) day, which falls traditionally on Pasah, the first day in the Triwara three-day week. The illustration shows several scenes. A man is arriving at the market carrying large bamboo containers of palm-wine (*tuak*) over his shoulder, while a woman is shown selling roast suckling pork. In the middle, three seated men are chatting and drinking palm wine. Notice also the plaited rectangular bamboo parasol.

tika and pelelintangan charts. Tuesdays, Wednesdays, and Saturdays are favorite days for temple festivals, but interestingly, from the point of view of agriculture, things are different. According to Ottino, Friday, associated with Sri and the northeast, is the most propitious day. Sunday and Monday are also auspicious, while Tuesday and Wednesday are associated with death and the ancestors. This is a good example of how a single unit of time may have dual value, according to the context or type of event involved.

Astawara, the eight-day week: The days are called Sri, Indra, Guru, Yama, Ludra (or Rudra), Brahma, Kala, and Uma. These are all names of gods from the Hindu-Balinese pantheon. Ludra (Rudra) and Kala, named after two destructive gods, are particularly inauspicious. The days named after Sri, the goddess of rice, Guru and his spouse Uma, and Brahma, are very auspicious. Those named after Yama, the keeper of hell and warrantor of justice, and Indra, the king of the gods, are more ambiguous. The day Kala is repeated three times ahead of Galungan.

Sangawara, the nine-day week: The days are called Dangu, Jangur, Gigis, Nohan, Ogan, Erangan, Urungan, Tu/us, and Dadi. They refer to the following traits, respectively: 'origin' (a long time ago), 'neither good nor bad', 'small quantity', 'joyful', 'hesitation', 'vengeance', 'cancellation', 'continuation', and 'success.' Dangu is repeated four times at the beginning of the Pawukon cycle.

Dasawara, the ten-day week: The days are called Pandita, Pati, Suka, Duka, Sri, Manuh, Manusa, Raja, Dewa, and Raksasa. These days refer, respectively, to 'wisdom' (priest), 'leadership', 'joy', 'contrariety', 'femininity', 'obedience', 'humaneness', 'charismatic' (like a king), 'virtuous/god-inspired', 'harsh', and 'wicked/demon-inspired.'

Auspicious and Inauspicious Days

Each of the 55 days of the various wara is assigned a sacred urip number, and also has an auspicious or inauspicious quality according to its conjunction of wara and its position on the pangider-ider.

On any given day in 'real time', up to ten different days from each of the ten wara, may coincide. The conjunctions of their various qualities will determine the general quality and relative 'strength' or 'weakness' of the actual 24-hour period concerned.

The main Balinese rituals are designed to fall on the 'strong' days in the Pawukon cycle. The conjunctions of certain highly auspicious and inauspicious days of the three-, five-, six-, and seven-day weeks are the ones considered to be particularly important.

For example, Kajeng in the three-day week coincides with Kliwon from the five-day week every 15 days, and this conjunction day, known as Kajeng-Kliwon, is a day of ritual exorcism. Kliwon from the five-day week also coincides with Saniscara from the seven-day week every 35 days (one Pawukon 'month'), or six times during the complete 210-day Pawukon cycle. Saniscara-Kliwon conjunction days, also known as Tumpek, are special days for honoring various kinds of things of value, including weapons or metal objects, musical instruments, livestock, and others.

Chapter 5 provides a detailed exploration of the holy days and holidays that fall on the various important conjunction days throughout the Pawukon cycle.

The Wewaran System: Tika Charts

Clearly, the wewaran system makes the Pawukon calendar complicated. Fortunately, as mentioned in the introduction to this chapter, various types of charts have been devised to visualize it. The first is the *tika,* carved of wood or painted on cloth, which is usually made to facilitate the reading of the whole 210-day Pawukon.

The usual tika shows the 30 weeks of the Pawukon cycle horizontally, and the days of the seven-day week vertically. It is designed to be read from left to right and top to bottom. The boxes of the tika are coded to focus attention on important conjunctions. The most remarkable patterns of recurrence are immediately visible thanks to this coding, as shown on the diagrams accompanying the tika illustrated in this book.

Several different types of tika charts exist, which may vary in their codes and in the particular wara they illustrate, although several important conjunctions are almost always included. Two examples are shown on pages 34 and 35.

Tika chart I
Source: Covarrubias (1937)

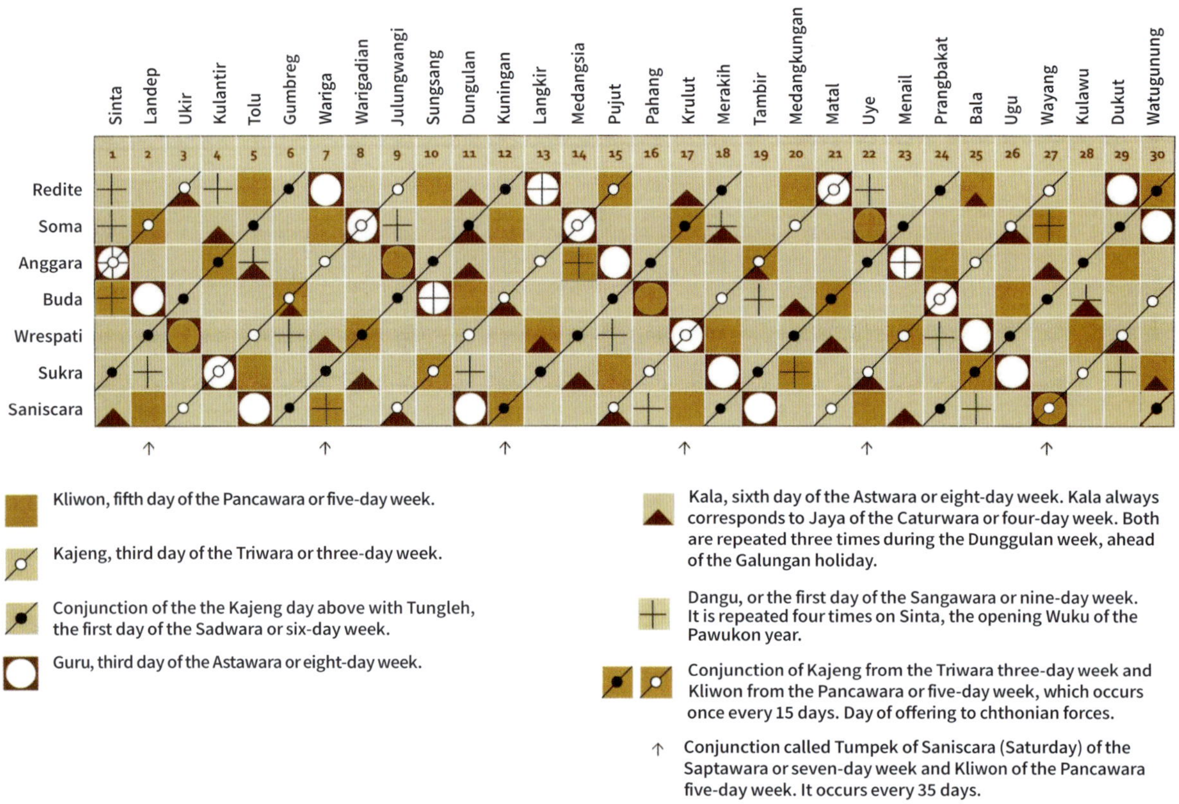

Tika chart I, the most 'classical', presents codes for the reading of days from all except the one-, two-, four-, and ten-day wara. Tika chart II presents different codes for the same, as well as different days of the system, plus codes for reading the four-day wara. It also highlights conjunctions that are important for 'horoscope' interpretations of personal character and the forecasting of auspicious/inauspicious dates.

Irregular Patterns in the Wewaran System

The reading of the Pawukon is more complicated than it appears at first sight from the tika charts, due to irregularities in the distribution of days from some of the wara. The one-day, two-day, and ten-day weeks present oddities, as their days do not appear regularly distributed in a row. As for the four-day, eight-day, and nine-day weeks, their computation within the 210-day calendar produces a remainder. Several adjustments have to be made to compensate for this, which translate into the repetition of the same day of the same wara several days in a row.

Let us take a closer look at the distribution of days of each wara across the 210-day cycle:

The day Luang (meaning 'empty') of the one-day week (Ekawara), seems at first like a paradox. In fact, not all the days in the calendar are Luang.

To find a Luang day, the urip of the day in the seven-day week is added to the urip of the same day in the five-day week. If the sum of the two magic numbers is an even number, then the day is a day without Luang. However, if the sum is an

Tika chart II

Source: Wayan Gina (1992)

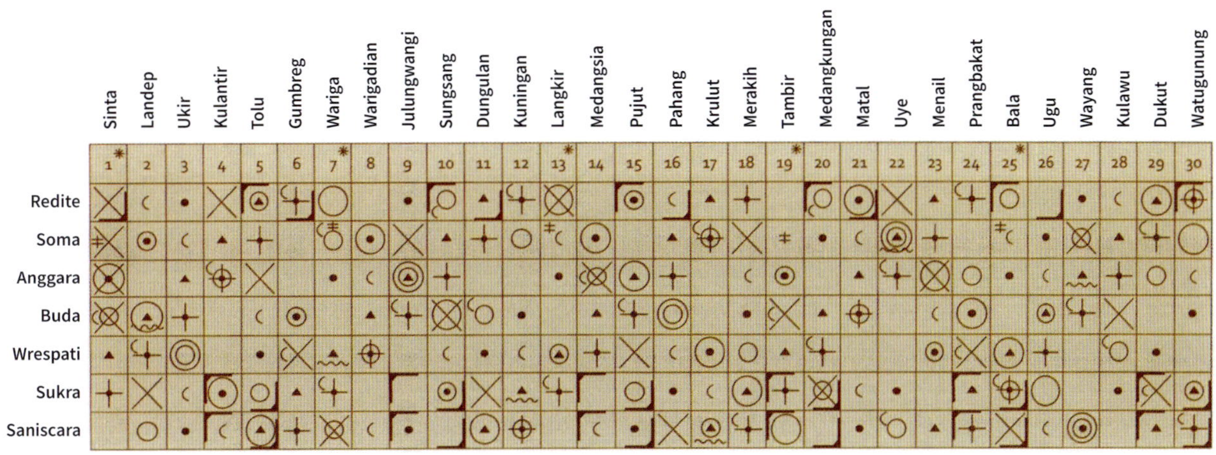

Ingkel, applies to the whole *wuku* (week).

Kajeng from the three-day week (Triwara).

Mendala from the four-day week (Caturwara), followed by Sri, Laba, and Jaya.

Kliwon from the five-day week (Pancawara).

Maulu from the six-day week (Sadwara).

Guru from the eight-day week (Astawara).

Dangu from the nine-day week (Sangawara).

Ingkel: applies to a single day.

Dates with special divinatory meaning:

Semutsadulur: inauspicious for cremations, good for meetings.

Kala Gotongan: inauspicious for cremations, good for beginning an activity.

Taliwangke: inauspicious for important ceremonies, good for agriculture.

Soma Arijang: unfavorable for sexual relations.

odd number, that day is a Luang day. For example, take Redite-Paing: 5 + 9 = 14. The sum is an even number, thus 'empty' of Luang. But Soma-Pon: 4 + 7 = 11, gives an odd number, and therefore it is a Luang day.

The two-day week (Dwiwara) also presents an oddity. The computation of these days is the same as for the one-day week, by adding the urip of the day according to the seven-day week and five-day week. If the sum is an even number, it is a Menga day; if the sum is an odd number, it is a Pepet day. Thus, the Luang day of the one-day week always coincides with the Pepet day of the two-day week.

Practically, the sequence of Menga (M) and Pepet (P) days gives the following result in the first 35 days of the Pawukon cycle, starting from Redite in the first wuku, namely, Wuku Sinta: MPPPPPM, PMMMPMP, MPMPMPM, MMPMPPP, PPMMMMM. Since the computation is based on the seven-day and five-day weeks, this same pattern occurs every subsequent 35 days.

No problem is presented by the three-day cycle (Triwara) since 210 is a multiple of three.

A difficulty arises with the four-day week (Caturwara) and the eight-day week (Astawara), as both have a residual number of two days when fitted into the 210-day cycle. A repetition occurs to compensate for the residual at the beginning of Wuku Dungulan. In the four-day cycle, Laba is followed by three successive Jaya days, two of which are the extra days. Likewise, in the eight-day cycle, Kala is repeated three times before the cycle resumes its normal course.

1 Sinta	2 Landep	3 Ukir	4 Kulantir	5 Tolu	6 Gumbreg	7 Wariga	8 Warigadian	9 Julungwangi	10 Sungsang	11 Dungulan	12 Kuningan	13 Langkir	14 Medangsia	15 Pujut	16 Pahang	17 Krulut	18 Merakih	19 Tambir	20 Medangkungan	21 Matal	22 Uye	23 Menail	24 Prangbakat	25 Bala	26 Ugu	27 Wayang	28 Kulawu	29 Dukut	30 Watugunung
1	4	3	2	1	4	3	2	1	4	3	4	3	2	1	4	3	2	1	4	3	2	1	4	3	2	1	4	3	2
2	1	4	3	2	1	4	3	2	1	3	1	4	3	2	1	4	3	2	1	4	3	2	1	4	3	2	1	4	3
3	2	1	4	3	2	1	4	3	2	3	2	1	4	3	2	1	4	3	2	1	4	3	2	1	4	3	2	1	4
4	3	2	1	4	3	2	1	4	3	4	3	2	1	4	3	2	1	4	3	2	1	4	3	2	1	4	3	2	1
1	4	3	2	1	4	3	2	1	4	1	4	3	2	1	4	3	2	1	4	3	2	1	4	3	2	1	4	3	2
2	1	4	3	2	1	4	3	2	1	2	1	4	3	2	1	4	3	2	1	4	3	2	1	4	3	2	1	4	3
3	2	1	4	3	2	1	4	3	1	3	2	1	4	3	2	1	4	3	2	1	4	3	2	1	4	3	2	1	4

CATURWARA (four-day week) 1st day 1 *Sri* 2nd day 2 *Laba* 3rd day 3 *Jaya* 4th day 4 *Mandala*

1 Sinta	2 Landep	3 Ukir	4 Kulantir	5 Tolu	6 Gumbreg	7 Wariga	8 Warigadian	9 Julungwangi	10 Sungsang	11 Dungulan	12 Kuningan	13 Langkir	14 Medangsia	15 Pujut	16 Pahang	17 Krulut	18 Merakih	19 Tambir	20 Medangkungan	21 Matal	22 Uye	23 Menail	24 Prangbakat	25 Bala	26 Ugu	27 Wayang	28 Kulawu	29 Dukut	30 Watugunung
1	8	7	6	5	4	3	2	1	8	7	4	3	2	1	8	7	6	5	4	3	2	1	8	7	6	5	4	3	2
2	1	8	7	6	5	4	3	2	1	7	5	4	3	2	1	8	7	6	5	4	3	2	1	8	7	6	5	4	3
3	2	1	8	7	6	5	4	3	2	7	6	5	4	3	2	1	8	7	6	5	4	3	2	1	8	7	6	5	4
4	3	2	1	8	7	6	5	4	3	8	7	6	5	4	3	2	1	8	7	6	5	4	3	2	1	8	7	6	5
5	4	3	2	1	8	7	6	5	4	1	8	7	6	5	4	3	2	1	8	7	6	5	4	3	2	1	8	7	6
6	5	4	3	2	1	8	7	6	5	2	1	8	7	6	5	4	3	2	1	8	7	6	5	4	3	2	1	8	7
7	6	5	4	3	2	1	8	7	6	3	2	1	8	7	6	5	4	3	2	1	8	7	6	5	4	3	2	1	8

ASTAWARA (eight-day week) 1st day 1 *Sri* 2nd day 2 *Indra* 3rd day 3 *Guru* 4th day 4 *Tama* 5th day 5 *Ludra* 6th day 6 *Brahma* 7th day 7 *Kala* 8th day 8 *Uma*

1 Sinta	2 Landep	3 Ukir	4 Kulantir	5 Tolu	6 Gumbreg	7 Wariga	8 Warigadian	9 Julungwangi	10 Sungsang	11 Dungulan	12 Kuningan	13 Langkir	14 Medangsia	15 Pujut	16 Pahang	17 Krulut	18 Merakih	19 Tambir	20 Medangkungan	21 Matal	22 Uye	23 Menail	24 Prangbakat	25 Bala	26 Ugu	27 Wayang	28 Kulawu	29 Dukut	30 Watugunung
1	5	3	1	8	6	4	2	9	7	5	3	1	8	6	4	2	9	7	5	3	1	8	6	4	2	9	7	5	3
1	6	4	2	9	7	5	3	1	8	6	4	2	9	7	5	3	1	8	6	4	2	9	7	5	3	1	8	6	4
1	7	5	3	1	8	6	4	2	9	7	5	3	1	8	6	4	2	9	7	5	3	1	8	6	4	2	9	7	5
1	8	6	4	2	9	7	5	3	1	8	6	4	2	9	7	5	3	1	8	6	4	2	9	7	5	3	1	8	6
2	9	7	5	3	1	8	6	4	2	9	7	5	3	1	8	6	4	2	9	7	5	3	1	8	6	4	2	9	7
3	1	8	6	4	2	9	7	5	3	1	8	6	4	2	9	7	5	3	1	8	6	4	2	9	7	5	3	1	8
4	2	9	7	5	3	1	8	6	4	2	9	7	5	3	1	8	6	4	2	9	7	5	3	1	8	6	4	2	9

SANGAWARA (nine-day week)

1st day 1 *Dangu* 2nd day 2 *Jangur* 3rd day 3 *Gigis* 4th day 4 *Nohan* 5th day 5 *Ogan* 6th day 6 *Erangan* 7th day 7 *Urungan* 8th day 8 *Tulus* 9th day 9 *Dadi (this purple stands for multi-colored)*

Three charts showing the irregular distributions of the *caturwara*, *astawara*, and *sangawara* (four-day, eight-day, and nine-day weeks). Colors correspond to the *nawa sanga*.

FRONT

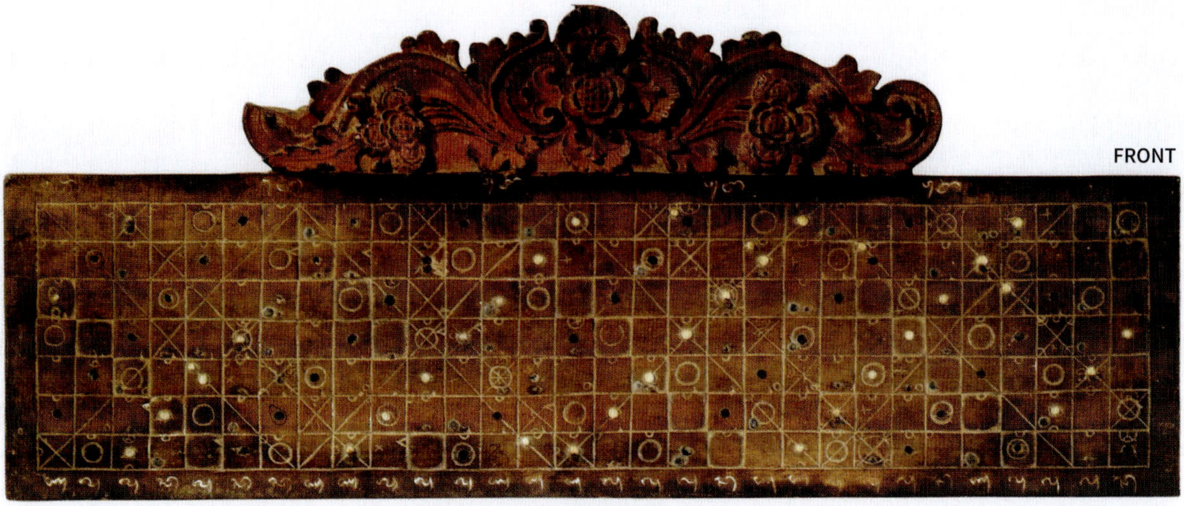

BACK

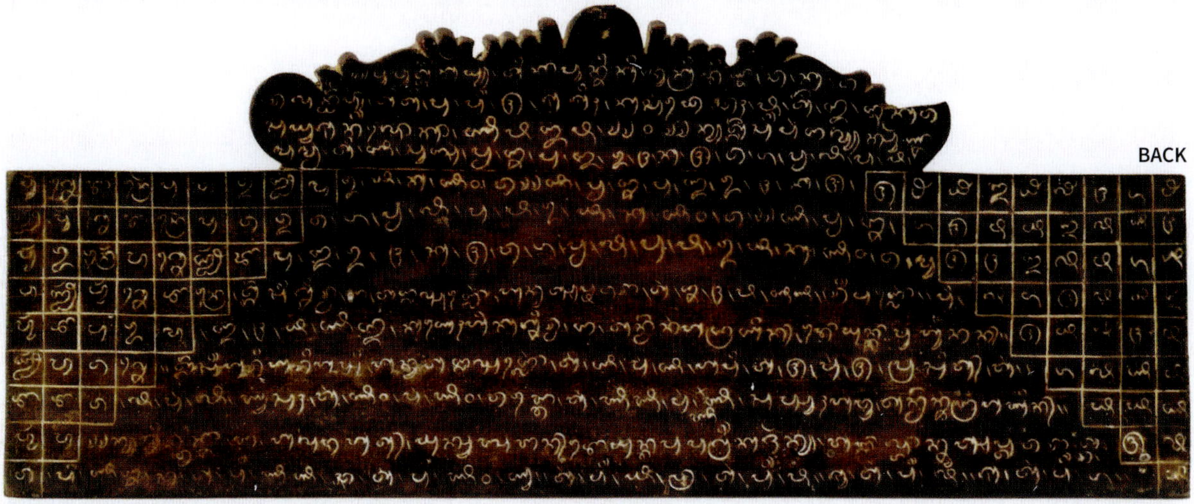

CLASSIC WOODEN TIKA: **Brown wood with iron hook (3 cm), bone fragments, red pigment (*kincu*), and lime. On the pediment, a carved floral decoration (*patera*) heightened with kincu. The pediment crowns a classic engraved tika calendar enhanced by nails, bone fragments, and lime. On the back, an etched text in Balinese and two triangular charts enhanced by lime.**

17 x 41 x 1 cm.
Buleleng, North Bali.
Second quarter of the 20th century.
Private collection.

FRONT

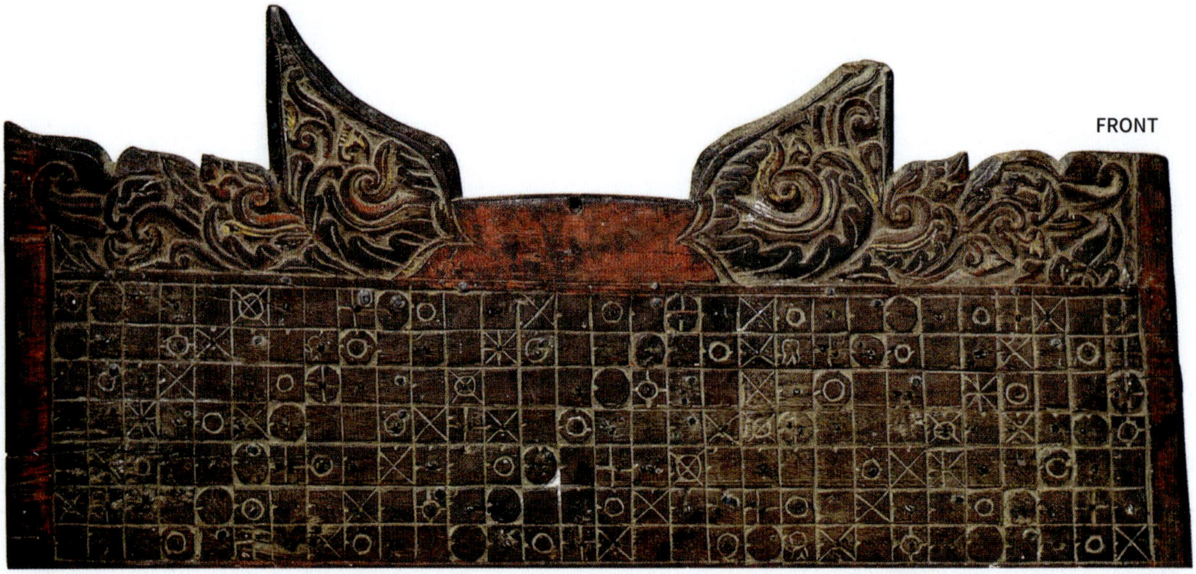

BACK

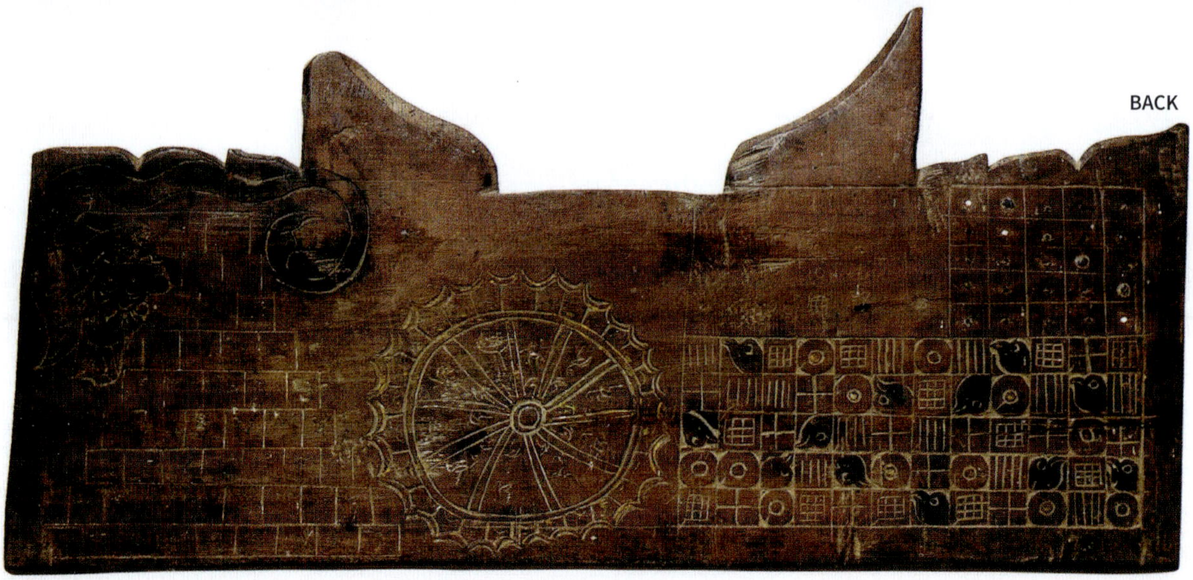

CLASSIC WOODEN TIKA: Hardwood with horn and metallic fragments, red pigment (*kincu*), and lime. The carved pediment, in the form of a pair of wings, crowns an engraved tika, which is unusual in that it is designed to be read from right to left. On the back are a variety of recognizable engraved patterns: a pangider-ider, a naga, and several diagrams, one of which features a symbol resembling a bird's head.

36 x 17 x 1 cm.
Gianyar, Central Bali.
Fourth quarter of the 19th century.
MHL collection (inv. 2324)

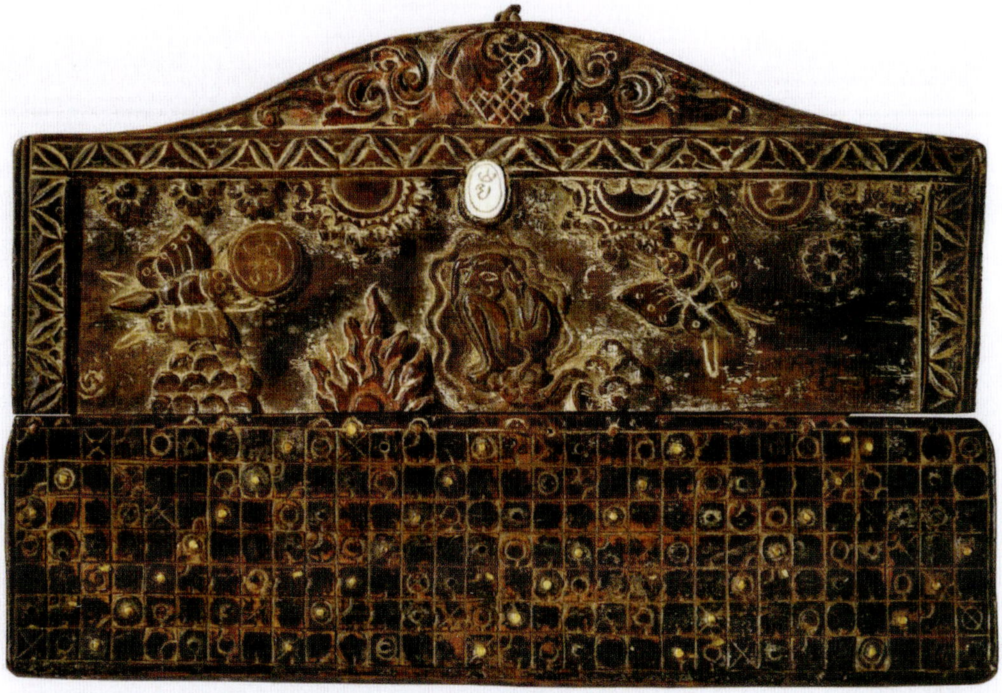

CLASSIC WOODEN TIKA: Hardwood (jackfruit) with iron chain terminated by a hook (16 cm), bone fragments, red pigment (*kincu*), and lime. Composed of two rectangular plates. The upper one is filled with carved decorations—butterflies, flowers, and a monkey—enhanced by kincu and lime, along with a bone fragment etched with Balinese letters. The lower one bears a classic engraved tika enhanced by bone fragments and kincu. No decoration on the back.

19 x 30 x 1 cm.
Central Bali.
Fourth quarter of the 19th century.
Private collection.

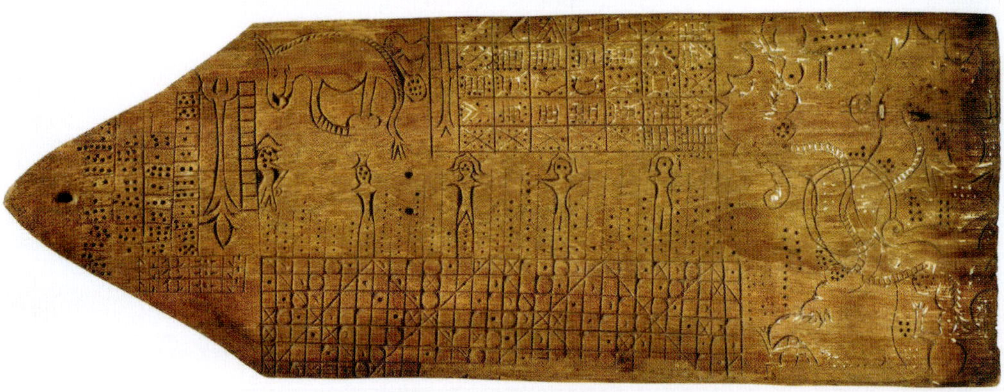

JAVANESE WOODEN TIKA: Hardwood and lime. The board is pierced with three holes. The one at the far left could be used to hang the calendar on a wall. When it was so hung, a string could be passed through the pair of holes closer to the center to suspend a *keris* from the board. The board is covered with etchings, some of them enhanced by lime. The etchings on the front, illustrated here, include a 35-day (5 x 7) diagram (top center) and a classic tika (bottom). Six anthropomorphic figures indicate *ingkel* (weeks with prohibited activities). On the back (not illustrated here) are numerous etchings of animals and more diagrams. This object is evidence that the Pawukon calendar was still in common use in East Java a hundred years ago.

70 x 26 x 1 cm.
Jember, East Java.
Fourth quarter of the 19th century.
MHL collection (inv. 2576).

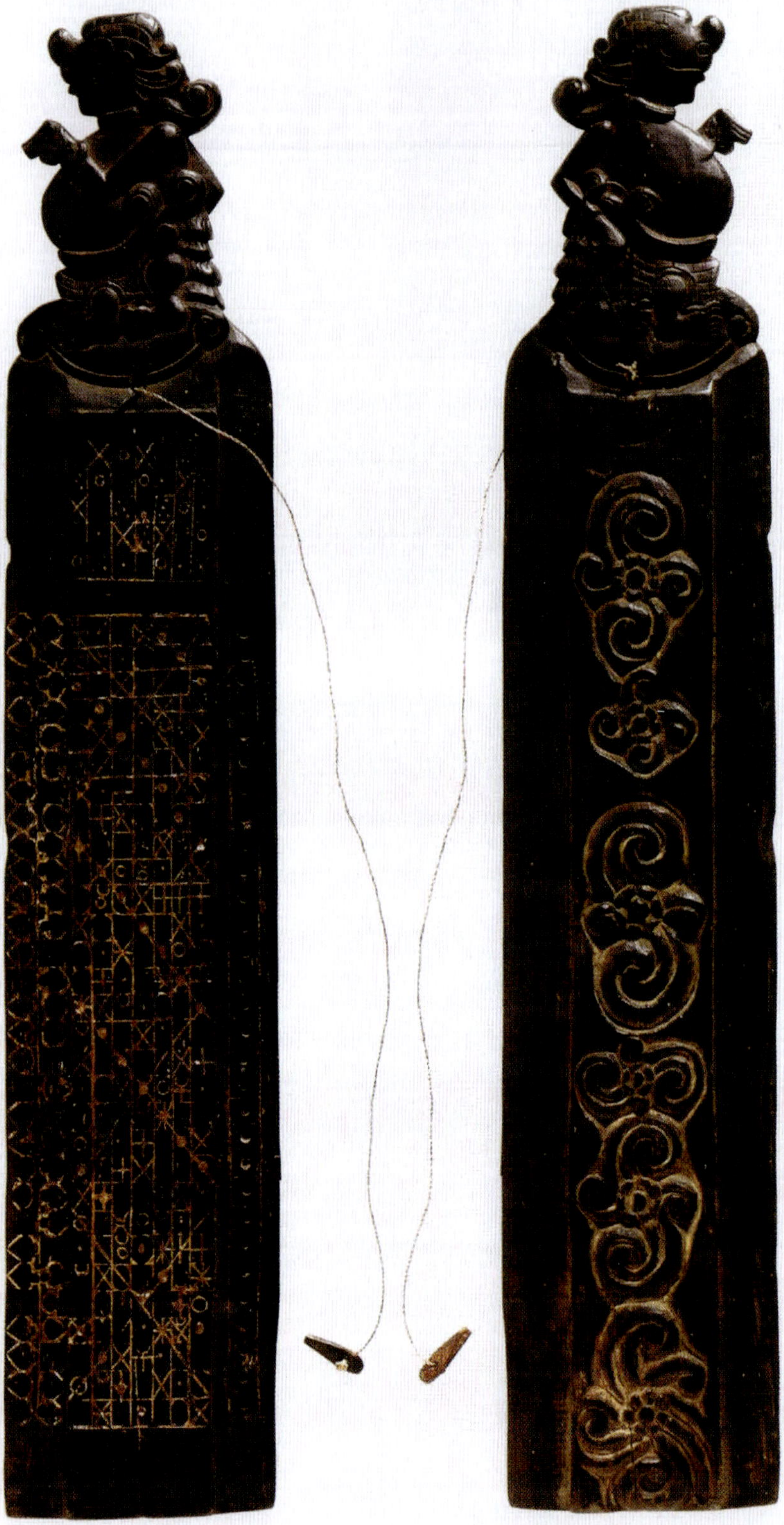

CLASSIC VERTICAL WOODEN TIKA: Hardwood with string and lime. On the top is a carved figure of Merdah, one of the two servants on the good side in the wayang kulit shadow puppet theater, then a 35-day (5 x 7) diagram, followed by a classic tika chart. Most of the etchings are enhanced by lime. On the right is a series of 30 holes representing the 30 weeks of the Pawukon calendar. The little piece of wood attached to the string can be placed in one of these holes as a reminder. On the back is the other side of the carved figure of Merdah and carved floral decorations. Vertical calendars are only encountered in the eastern part of Bali and in Lombok where they are popular.

56 x 11 x 2 cm.
Karangasem, East Bali.
First quarter of the 20th century.
MHL collection (inv. 2531).

Since 210 is a multiple of 5, 6, and 7, the five-day week (Pancawara), six-day week (Sadwara), and seven-day week (Saptawara) are in perfect accord with the 210-day cycle. They are at the heart of Balinese divination by numbers, and their reading is straightforward.

However, the nine-day week (Sangawara) is three days short at the completion of the full cycle. This difference is compensated by adding three extra Dangu days from the nine-day week to Wuku Sinta, the first wuku of the new cycle. This means the day Dangu in the normal sequence is followed by three extra Dangu days before the normal next day of the nine-day week, Jangur.

The ten-day week (Dasawara) is the most irregular of all the weeks. As in the one-day and two-day weeks, no regular pattern is apparent. The ten days seem to be haphazardly distributed over the calendar without any logic. The only recurrent pattern is the repetition of the same combination of Dasawara days every 35 days.

The key lies, again, in the urip. You can find the Dasawara name of a given day by adding its urip in the five-day week (Pancawara) and its urip in the seven-day week (Saptawara). If the total is 10, it is Pandita; if 11, Pati; if 12, Suka; if 13, Duka; if 14, Sri; if 15, Manuh; if 16, Manusa; if 17, Raja; if 18, Dewa, and if 19, Raksasa.

The irregular patterns or anomalies of the repeated days of the four-day and eight-day weeks, as well as the nine-day weeks, are not random and not without meaning. They symbolically underline the special significance of the Galungan-Kuningan series of festivities in the middle of the Pawukon cycle, and of the 'New Year' of the cycle that begins with Wuku Sinta.

The Galungan-Kuningan festivities are all about achieving a balance of positive and negative forces. Jaya, of the four-day week, means 'victory'. It is associated on the pangider-ider with the god Iswara (Siwa). Meanwhile, Kala, of the eight-day week, is the negative form of Siwa. Thus, Jaya is a 'positive' day and Kala is a 'negative' day. The balance of positive and negative is achieved exactly on the day of Galungan, immediately following the sequence of triple Jaya and triple Kala days.

Similarly, the repetition of the four Dangu days (sometimes called Dangupat) to mark the start of the new cycle in Wuku Sinta is rich in symbolic significance. Dangu, in Old Javanese, means 'the time of origin'. The fact that the Dangu days appear where they do confirms the separation between the incestuous son and mother as the origin of cosmic order and consciousness of time in human society. The first Dangu day coincides with Banyu Pinaruh, the day of purification following immediately after the day of knowledge; the last Dangu day coincides with the festival of Pagerwesi, which means 'iron gate'.

The first day of Wuku Sinta also corresponds to the first day of the two-day, three-day, four-day, six-day, seven-day, eight-day, and nine-day weeks. Only the one-day, two-day, five-day, and ten-day weeks do not begin on this same day.

The Saka Calendar

The Saka calendar was introduced during the Indianization of the Indonesian archipelago. Named after a Scythian dynasty that once ruled over Northern India, the Saka era starts in the year 7 BCE. Thus, the Gregorian calendar year 2000 CE corresponds to the Saka year 1922. With the exception of a Sancaya era in the eighth century, the Saka year was in force in the Indonesian archipelago until the introduction of Islam, when it was replaced by the lunar year of the Islamic calendar, which is counted from 622 CE, the year of the *hegira* (the Prophet's migration from Mecca to Medina). Bali is the only location outside of India where the Saka year is still observed.

The Balinese and the Javanese only have a vague memory of the Indian origin of the Saka year. The word Saka, for them, is associated with a legendary guru, the wise man Aji Saka:

"The legend of Aji Saka," says Denys Lombard in *Warisan Kerajaan-Kerajaan Konsentris* (1996), "is the story of a Brahmin's son—using a name later to become that of the Saka era—who came from India to Java and took residence in Medang Kamulan (near Purwodadi). He first fought away all the giants who were holding sway over Java and then underwent to organize and civilize the country: he married a local woman and created the Javanese writing."

The Balinese luni-solar Saka calendar defines the official occurrences of the New Moon (Tilem) and the Full Moon (Purnama) each month, as well as their adjustment to match the natural lunar cycle. It also defines the quality of the lunar days (*tithi*) associated with the waning or waxing of the moon. It adjusts the lunar year to match the length of the solar year, which is based on the revolution of the earth around the sun. Thus, the days and months follow the lunar system, while the year follows, or adapts to, the solar system.

The Saka Months and Days

The Balinese Saka calendar has twelve lunar months, called *sasih*, with 29 or 30 lunar days each. The names of the months refer to their numerical order, except the last two months, which have retained names of Sanskrit origin. Thus we have: 1. Kasa; 2. Karo; 3. Katiga; 4. Kapat; 5. Kalima; 6. Kanem; 7. Kapitu; 8. Kawulu; 9. Kasanga; 10. Kadasa: 11. Jyaistha (or Jhista or Desta), and 12. Asadha (or Sadha).

The sasih and tithi, like all elements of the Balinese calendar system, are located on the pangider-ider, with their corresponding urip sacred numbers (as shown in the last two rows of the Nawa Sanga chart on page 29).

Each month goes from one New Moon (Tilem) to another and is divided into two parts, 'clear' (*sukla*) and 'dark' (*kresna*). First, there are 15 days corresponding to the period of the waxing moon (*tanggal*, or *penanggal*, or *suklapaksa*), computed from the day following the new moon until the day following the Full Moon (Purnama). Then come the 15 days corresponding to the period of the waning moon (*panglong* or *kresnapaksa*) until the next new moon/tilem.

However, this 30-day cycle does not match the real lunar cycle (*candra*), which, from one new moon to another only comprises a little more than 29 lunar days (tithi), precisely 29.531 days. To balance this discrepancy, the Balinese have devised an original system. One lunar day is 'suppressed' every nine wuku, that is, every 63 days. When this occurs, the length of the sasih month is shortened to 29 days.

In Balinese calendar terms, this means that on the 'suppressed' day, two tithi are compounded on the same day. For example, panglong (or tanggal) 6 and 7 are combined on a single day. The sequence becomes panglong (or tanggal) 1-2-3-4-5-6/7-8-9-10-11-12-13-14-15. This 'suppression' of days is called *(pa)ngunalatri* or *pangalihan*, and it normally falls on a Wednesday.

According to Balinese calendar expert Made Suatjana, the *ngunalatri* cycle (also known as *nemu gelang*), based on the movement of the moon, occurs every 1,890 days, and computed on this basis the median length of the Balinese sasih month becomes 29.5313 days, a difference of only 0.002 percent from the actual astronomical lunar cycle. This system is not perfect, and from time to time needs further adjustment. One then 'suppresses' yet another day by accumulating three tithi on the same day. The Balinese month concerned is then reduced to 28 days.

Balinese calendar specialists, however, disagree as to when such further adjustments should take place. Some say every 128 lunar years, others, every 119 solar years. Some *lontar* even say that it should occur whenever a calamity hits Bali. According to Made Suatjana, whose calculations are based on astronomical computations, it should rightly be every 122.47 years. This should have last occurred on November 4, 1998. But following a decision by the Balinese authorities, it was shifted to the end of the year 1999.

The Saka Year

The Balinese Saka year is based on the natural 365-day cycle of the sun (or 366 days during bi-sextile years, commonly known as 'leap years'). Meanwhile, the annual cycle of the 12 Balinese lunar months is 12 x 29.53125 = 354.375 days. Thus, there is a difference of 11 to 12 days between the two systems, which amounts to more than one sasih month over a three-year period.

To compensate for this discrepancy, an additional (intercalary) month (*nampih sasih*) is inserted between the regular sasih every three years or so. For instance, on the Balinese calendar for the year 1999, an extra month called Nampih Desta was inserted after Sasih Desta, following the new

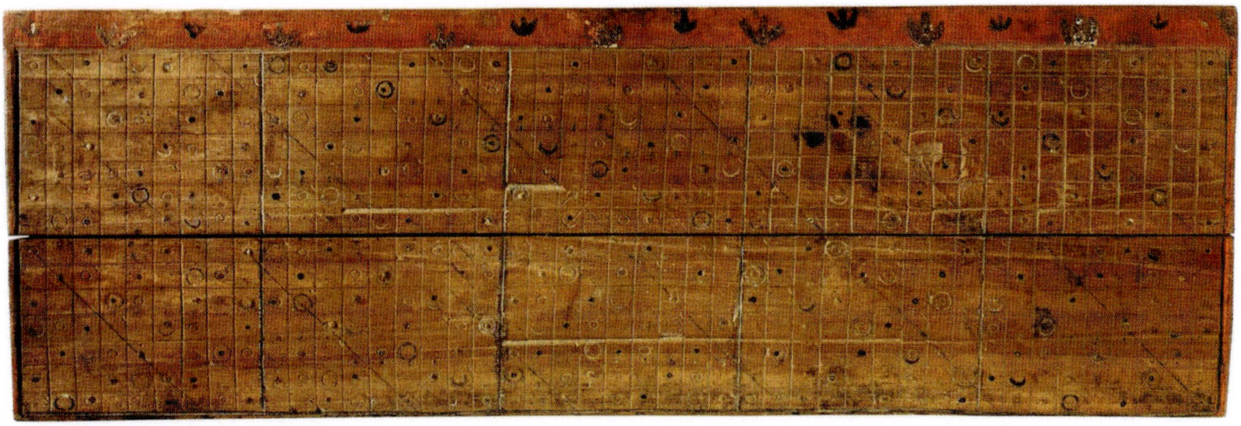

WOODEN NEMU GELANG CALENDAR: Hardwood (jackfruit) with horn fragments and pigments. Consisting of two wooden boards joined together by pegs, this wooden calendar was used to calculate the 1890-day *nemu gelang* or *ngunalatri* cycle, which links the Pawukon and Saka calendars and informs calendar experts when to 'suppress' days by merging two or more days in the lunar Saka calendar so as to adjust it to match the actual astronomical lunar cycle. The chart is divided into two rows of five rectangles, each representing the seven days of the week vertically, and nine *wuku* weeks horizontally. Altogether, they comprise a 630-day cycle (*apa/angtaka*), which repeats three times to form a complete nemu gelang or ngunalatri cycle.

69 x 23 x 1. 5 cm.
Central Bali.
First quarter of the 20th century.
MHL collection (inv. 2577).

moon in May. In 2001, a Nampih Katiga was similarly added after Sasih Katiga, following the new moon in September.

The Balinese Saka year is computed to start around the spring equinox, on the day after the new moon nearest to this equinox. This is the first day of the tenth month, Sasih Kadasa, immediately after the new moon of the ninth month, Sasih Kasanga. This Balinese Saka New Year, called Nyepi, is a day of complete silence.

How can we explain the oddity that Nyepi falls on the tenth month and not the first, in accordance with the numerical order of the sasih months, which would make the cycle start with the month Kasa, around July–August? The most plausible explanation is that in pre-Indianized times, the month Kasa indicated the onset of a solar cycle of agrarian origin. According to researcher Louis-Charles Damais in his article "Le calendrier de l'ancienne Java" (1967), it might have been established based on observations of a group of stars of the Orion constellation known as Wuluku in Balinese. The first ten months of the agricultural cycle would have been followed by a period of rest, called *hapit* (squeezed), waiting for the resumption of the next cycle of months one to ten.

A Journey through the Saka Year

The Balinese luni-solar Saka year runs in parallel with the cycle of seasons, even though there might be small variations from one year to the next, or variations in the seasons from one area to another.

In the following 12 pages, I Gusti Nyoman Darta gives his visual interpretation of the activities that characterize each month, as he knows them to be practiced in the Ubud-Gianyar area of Central Bali.

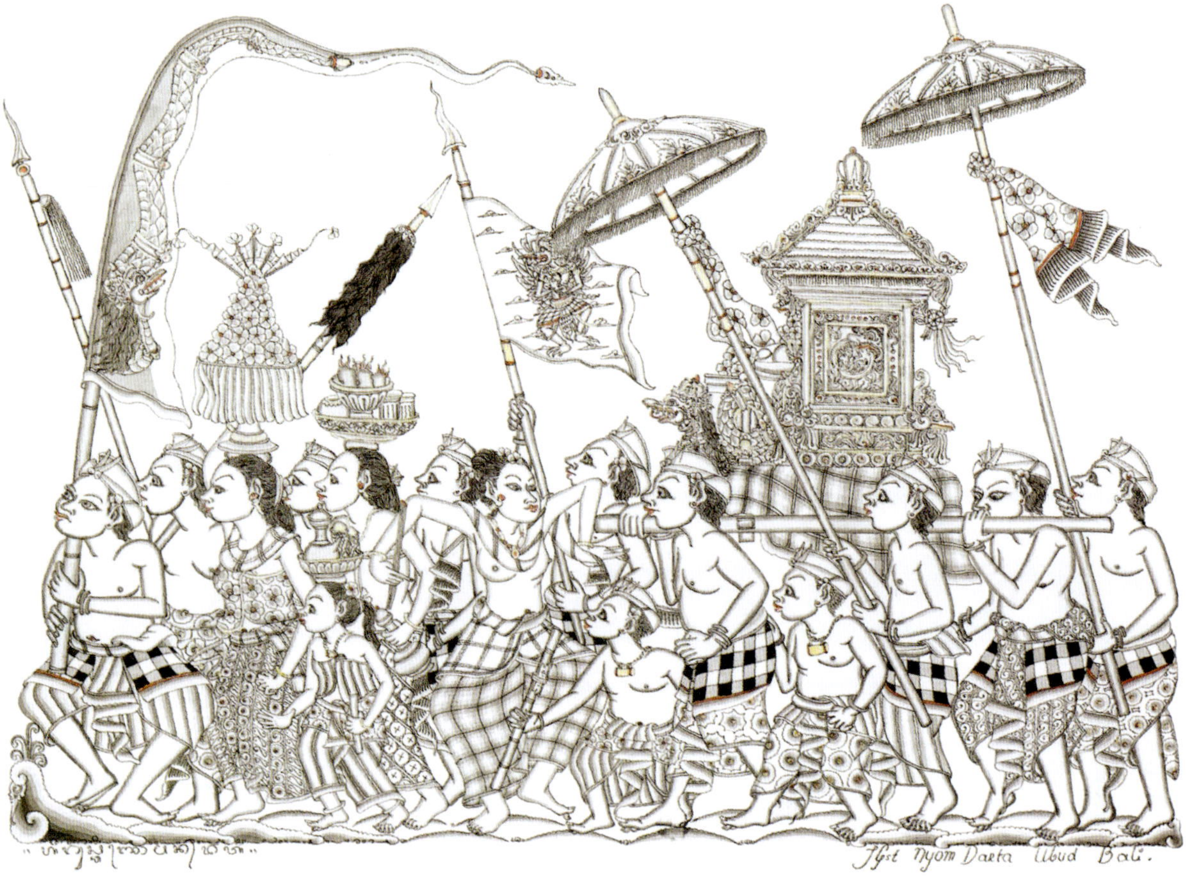

Sasih Kadasa (The Tenth Month) (New Saka Year)
Usually falls in March/April

Among the numerous oddities of time in Bali is the fact that the Balinese Saka New Year does not open with the first month of the year, but with the tenth. Furthermore, it is not celebrated with revelry, but with Nyepi, the day of total silence. Falling on the day following the New Moon (Tilem) closest to the vernal equinox, Nyepi marks the first day of Kadasa.

As seen in the analysis of Sasih Kesanga and the Ngerupuk, all negative energies have been symbolically destroyed by fire at the cemetery, returning them to the chthonian forces of the earth, and creating the spiritual vacuum needed for Nyepi. This month otherwise signals the coming of the dry season. However, while the rains lessen in the lowlands, it may still rain heavily in mountainous areas, causing the 'Kadasa floods' (*blabur Kadasa*). In the lowland plains, people replant rice for the first crop of the year, flowers bloom, tuber plants are harvested, and optimism prevails. It is the month most praised by poets.

On the full moon of Kadasa (Purnama Kadasa), 15 days after the silence of Nyepi, falls Batara Turun Kabeh (The Descent of All the Gods) at the Mother Temple of Besakih, located on the lower slopes of Mount Agung, the abode of the gods. Divine energy is at its absolute zenith: all the island gods come to reside next, and pay their respects to the Tri Purusa: Siwa, Sada Siwa, and Parama Siwa.

On this occasion, beginning a few days prior, the gods are brought from all over Bali on their golden palanquins (*jempana*). They rejoin the temple's sacred effigies in the main assembly pavilion (Balai Pesamuan), where they will stay in state (*nyejer*) in the temple courtyards. Symbolized by their *amerta* (water of immortality), they remain for 21 days, receiving the devotion of the people before returning in similarly colorful and golden processions to their shrines and temples of origin throughout the island.

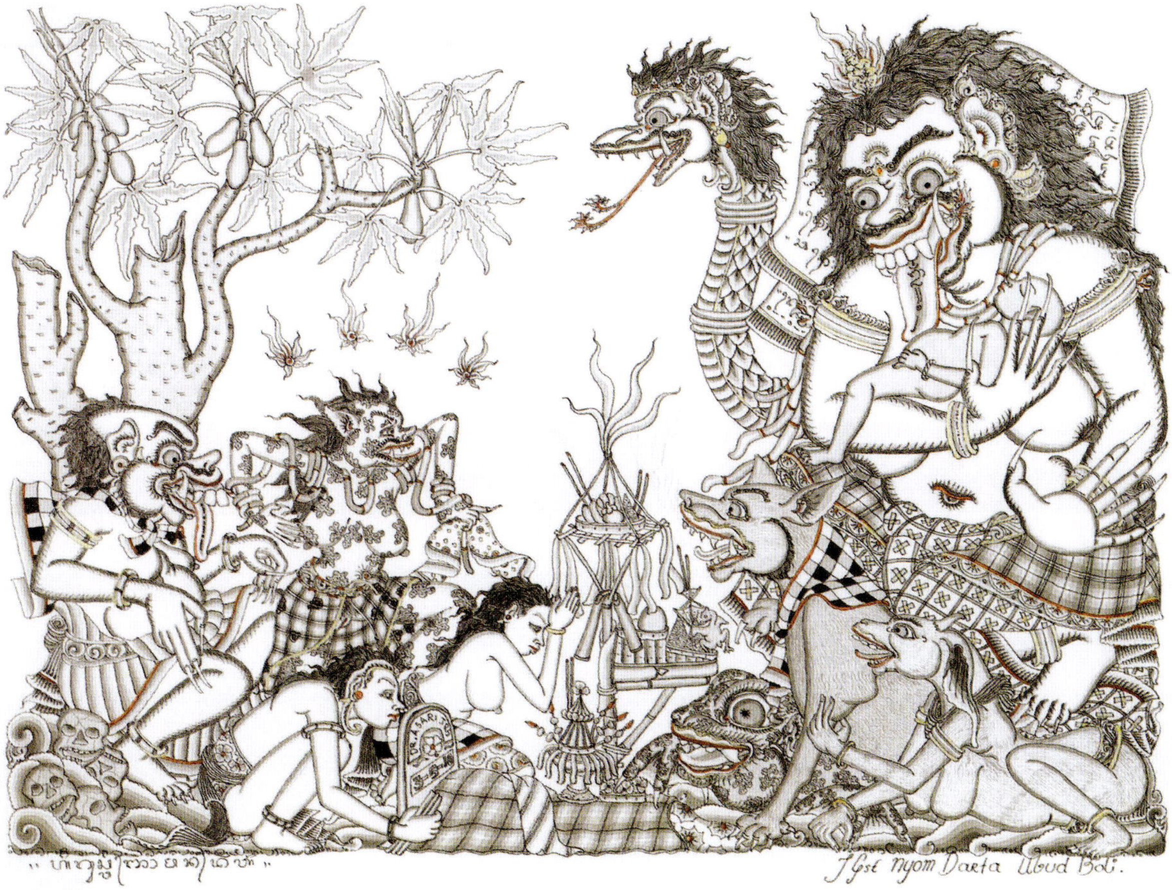

Sasih Desta (The Eleventh Month)

Usually falls in April

On this month, the dry season comes, and with it the harvesting of plants island-wide. It is the best time to plant tubers (*pala bungkah*) and 'hanging vegetables' (*pala gantung*). Rice is still growing in the paddies.

Desta, also called Jyestha, is considered the best period of the year for meditation and the study of magic. It is sometimes, by a play on words, called the month of *desti*, or black magic. Black magic, and endeavors to placate it, are linked in Balinese lore with the temple of death (*pura dalem*) and adjacent cemetery, as well as the nearby *rajapati* shrine, the places where Siwa's demonic consort, the goddess Durga and her disciples rule. She is most famously invoked during the Caton Arang dance, during which performers go to the cemetery to (symbolically) exhume a rotting corpse and endow themselves with magical powers.

As is common in Balinese art, the illustration presents both the visible and invisible worlds in a scene that obviously takes place in a cemetery. On the visible side, in the lower middle part of the work, one sees the figure of a woman addressing prayers and offerings, in particular a standing cane to Durga. She is asking the demonic goddess for the magical powers needed to become a *leyak* (witch). Durga accepts, but she makes her own demands: the sacrifice of the child who is shown cuddled in the arms of the goddess. All the other characters are Durga's demonic companions. Notice the young boy next to the praying woman. He has a tail, which means he is in the process of turning into a monkey *leyak*.

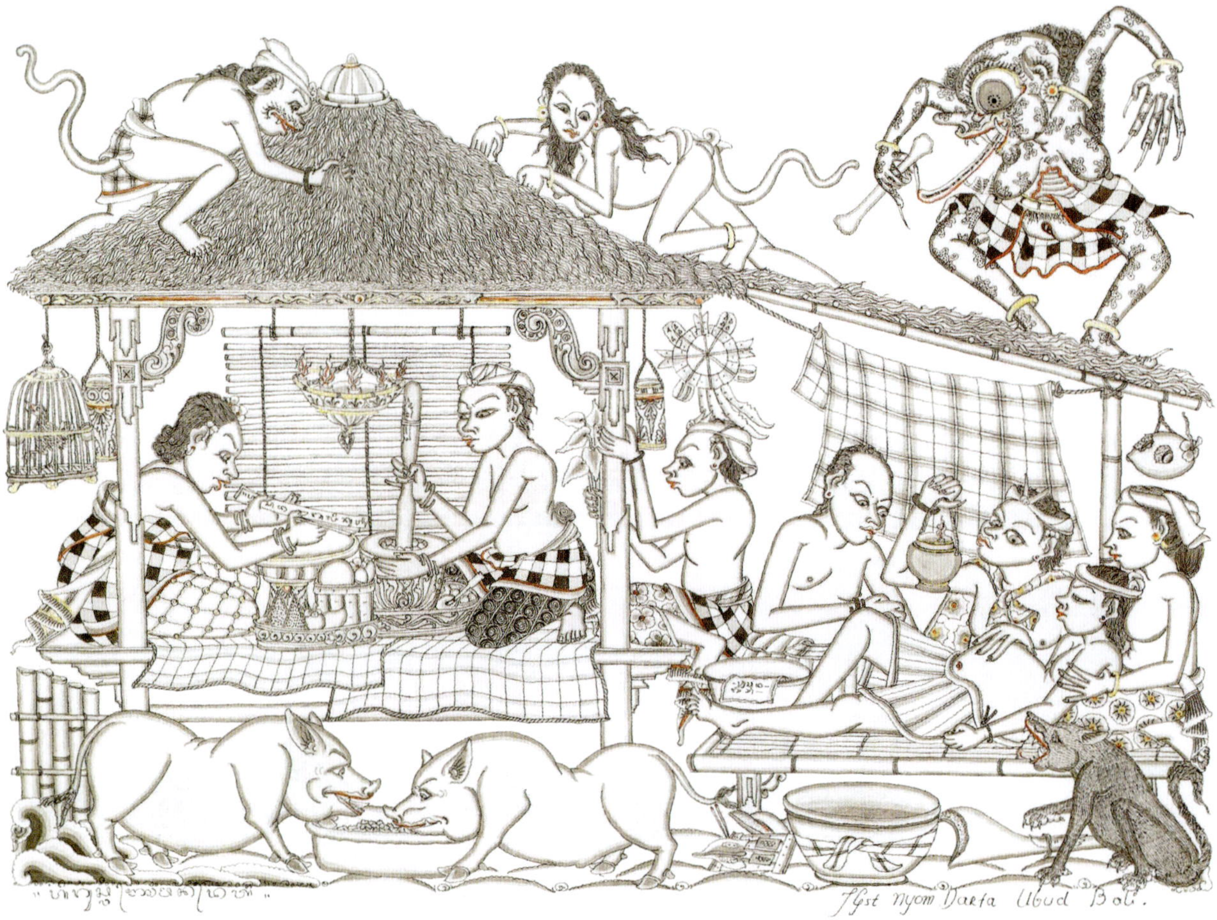

Sasih Sadha (The Twelfth Month)

Usually falls in May

The sun is relatively far to the north. The dry season is setting in, along with the heat. Toward the end of Sadha, though, the nights become fresher. On an auspicious day (*mantanin*), the rice is stored in the granaries (*lumbung*) and new seeds are selected.

In Bali, witchcraft and illnesses, the latter often caused by the former, have both tangible and intangible remedies. This is the specialty of the healers (*balian*). Some of them, *balian-tetakson*, are known as intermediaries of the gods, spirits, and erring souls. Officiating in trance, as shamans they advise on ceremonies to be done to ward off misfortune, to send a lost soul back to its proper abode, or to prepare charms and counter-charms (*jampi*, *rajah*). Others, *balian usadha*, or medicine men, are reputed for their ability to identify plants with curative powers and for their expertise in preparing medicinal concoctions, a task best undertaken during the month of Sadha.

The healing efficacy of the balian is believed to depend on the power (*taksu*) of their shrines, usually the ones set up in their own private family temples. On Saraswati day, the last day of the Pawukon cycle, villagers who have benefited from the help of balian, visit them and their shrines with offerings to express gratitude for their services.

The illustration shows, to the left, a balian reading a medicinal lontar manuscript, while an assistant pounds the plants needed to prepare a remedy. To the right is a patient who is taking the medicine, surrounded by his family. The demonic characters who stand and crawl on the roof, as well as the dog at lower right, are spirits and leyak from the invisible world, probably sent on an evil errand by a malevolent balian competitor.

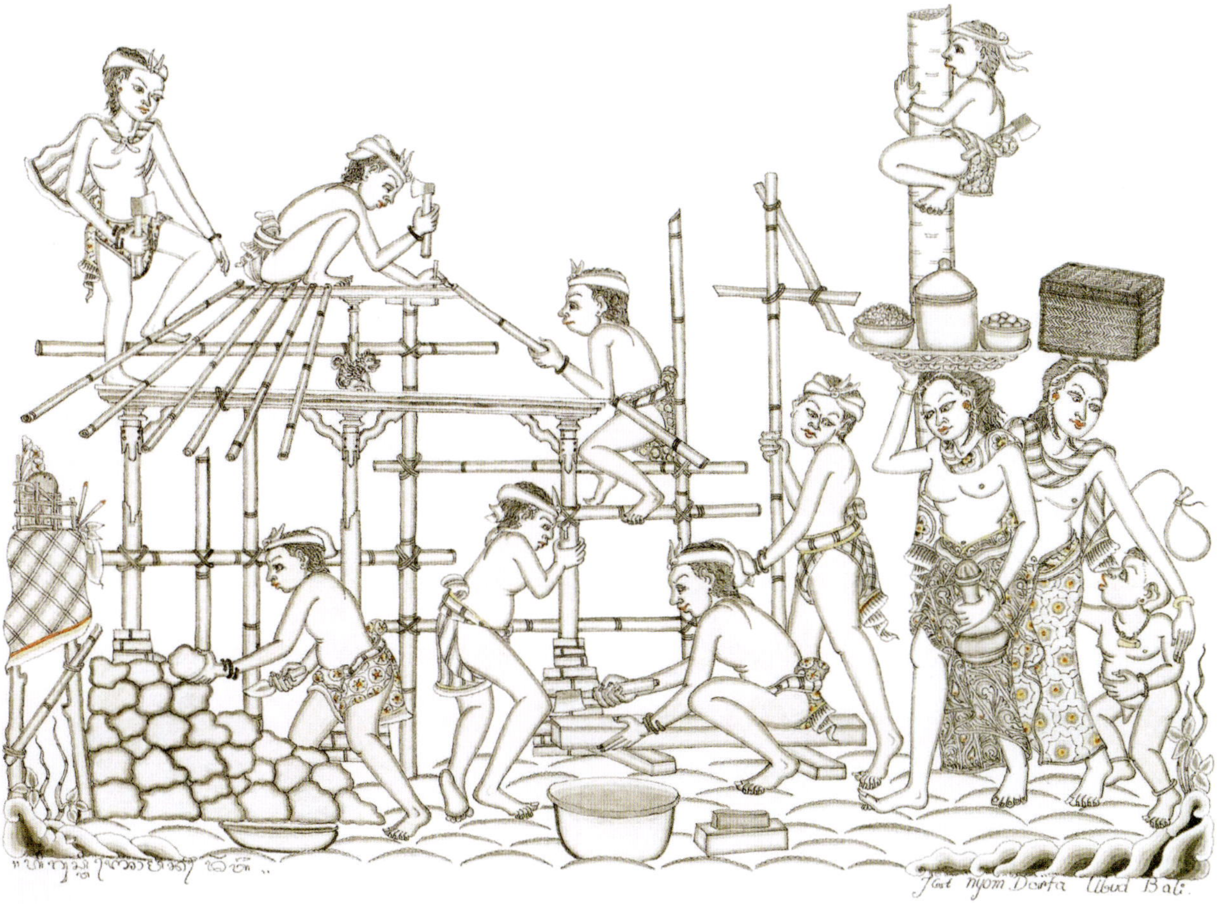

Sasih Kasa (The First Month)

Usually falls in June

In this month, the island approaches the peak of the dry season. Winds from the Austral winter bring bouts of freshness and even cold in the morning. Kites fly all over the sky. This is a suitable period to plant peas and nuts.

This is also the favorite month to start constructing buildings. This illustration shows the way the Balinese traditionally help one another to build a house. The women bring food for their working husbands.

Balinese architecture is based on the understanding that Man is a microcosm and should strive for harmony with the universe. A Balinese house compound is laid out according to the physical proportions of the owner's body, using his foot, forearm, fingers, and outstretched arms as units of measurement. Thus, the house and compound themselves form a symbolic microcosm.

Construction is done under the guidance of a local traditional architect (*undagi*). As shown in the illustration, only local materials, such as bamboo, bricks, and sandstone, were traditionally used. Ropes were made from coconut fiber. Before building, people had to follow a number of ritual requirements, such as sending the rice goddess back to the rice fields (*ngingsirang Batari Sri*); opening the field (*ngeruak*); exorcism (*mecaru*); 'cleaning' the plot with an offering to the earth mother Pertiwi (*mersihang*); and taking the measurements explained above (*nyikut*). Proper days must also be found to initiate these activities, as well as to begin the actual work of cutting trees and erecting the roof. A big house-warming ceremony (*melaspas*) takes place upon completion of the construction.

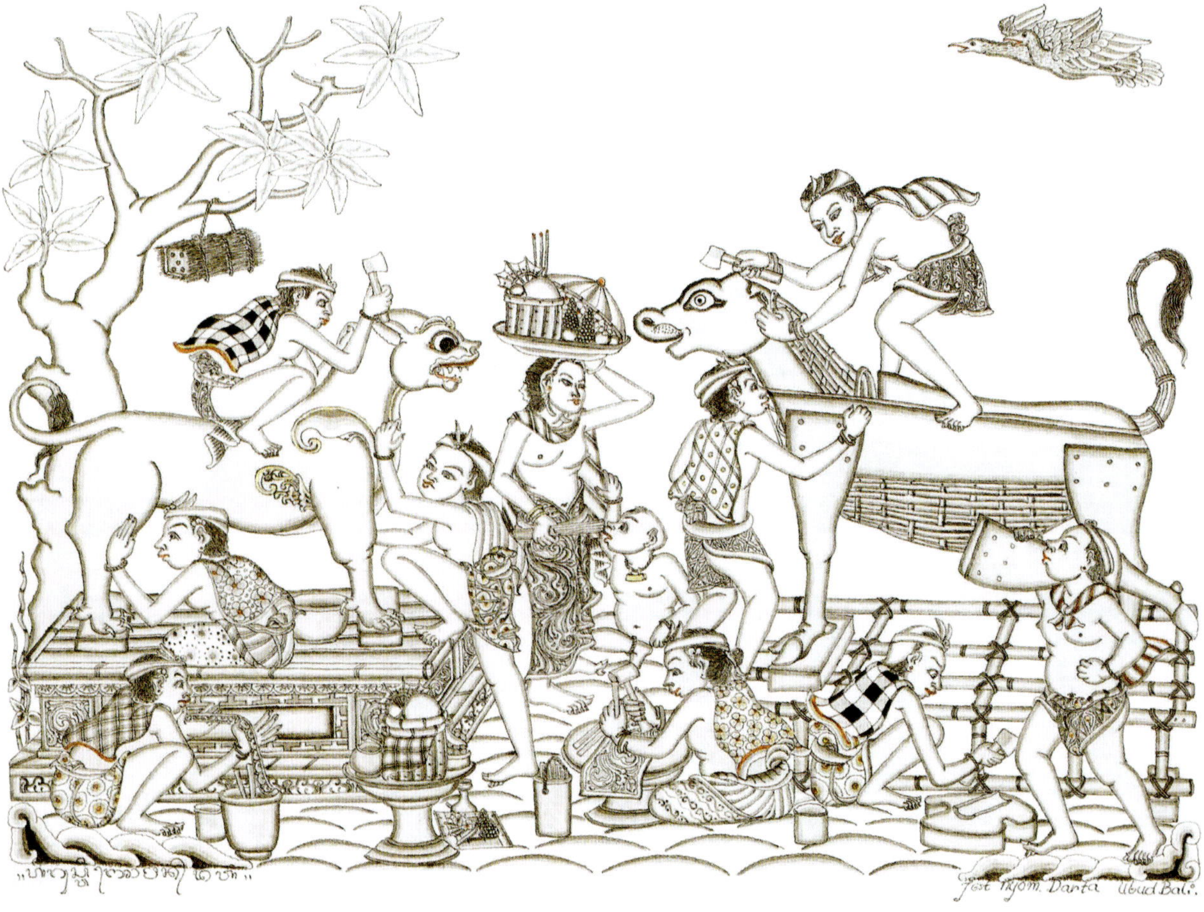

Sasih Karo (The Second Month)

Usually falls in July

The month of Karo is the harshest on men's bones. The dry season fully sets in. In the morning, dew glistens under the reddish rays of the rising sun. Nights are fresh and there might be short rains. Mango is harvested.

This is the month during which, owing to usually fair weather, the preparation of collective cremations takes place. Such cremations are for corpses already buried, sometimes years earlier. The rotting corpses are exhumed and their bones cleansed before the cremation, unless they are replaced by an effigy.

The illustration shows the preparation of the sarcophagi. Bulls are reserved for the nobility, whereas lower castes and kinship groups use lions and other animals, as required by tradition. The making of sarcophagi is supervised by an architect-artist (*undagl*) who personally handles the cutting and carving of the main decorative elements. The illustration also shows, to the right, a man carrying a wooden element to be attached to the bull. Another man, squatting in the middle, is chiseling guilded cardboard ornaments. Yet another, squatting on the lower left, is probably drawing a scene depicting the tortures of Balinese hell. A woman is bringing offerings. Noticeable is a bee's nest hanging from the tree.

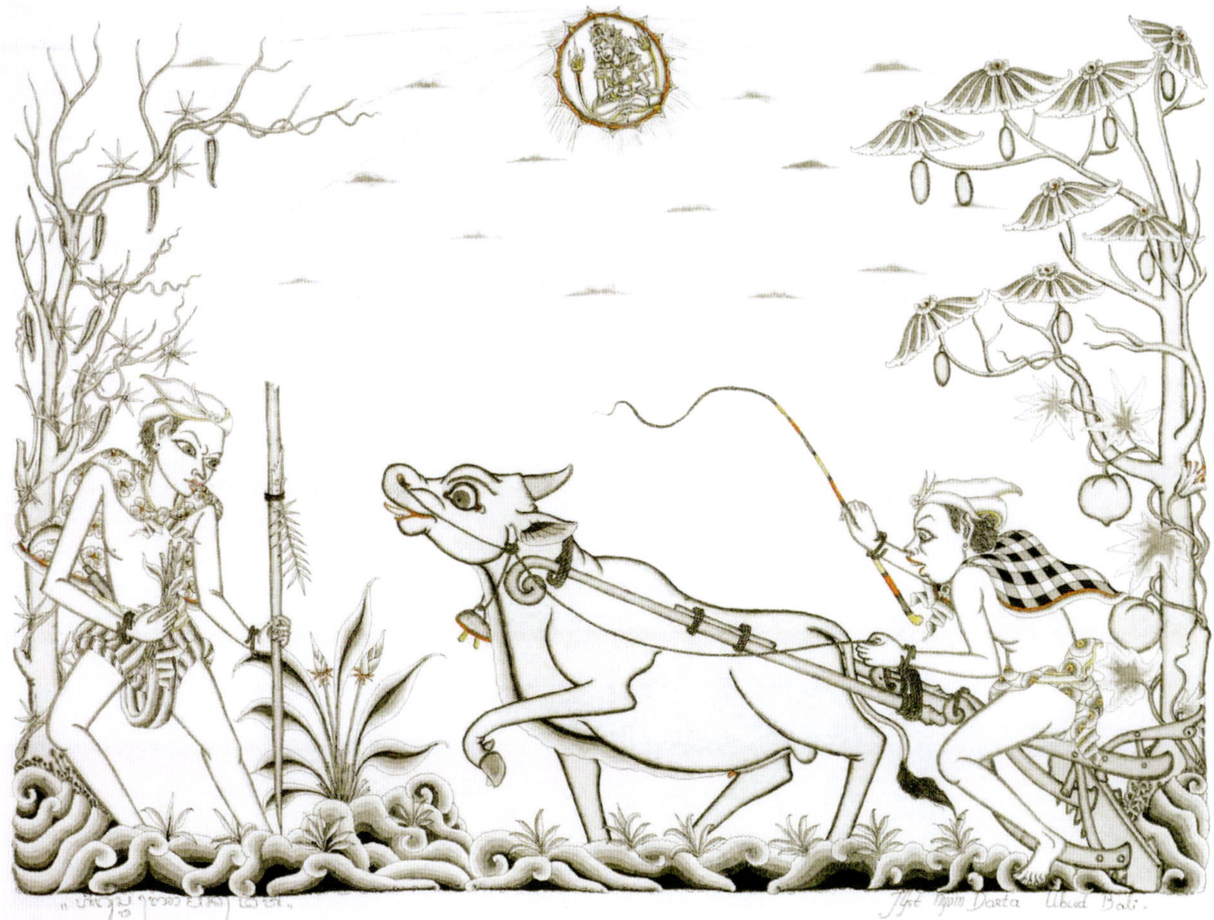

Sasih Katiga (The Third Month)
Usually falls in August

During Sasih Katiga, the third month, heat sets in. Water becomes scarce and grass and leaves tend to yellow. For this reason, this month is considered the most propitious for planting dry crops instead of rice. These crops are categorized into two main groups: *pala gantung*, literally 'hanging crops', which comprise fruits such as oranges and bananas, as well as cucumbers, and *pala bungkah*, literally 'crops to break open', which comprise all sorts of beans and tubers, such as sweet potato or cassava. This month is also the time for preparations to plant the traditional rice crop of the second agricultural season (*gagadon*) by getting the seed beds ready for replanting.

The illustration represents a scene of ploughing in preparation for planting pala bungkah to the left and pala gantung to the right. In the middle, the ploughman has to press heavily on his plough, which is too light to easily penetrate the dry earth. To the left, a man is planting seeds using a sharp bamboo stick. The sun god, supreme witness and source of life, is also there. Planting must be preceded by a small ceremony since the plough is going to open the earth, to the goddess Pertiwi. As for the bull, it symbolizes Siwa's vehicle.

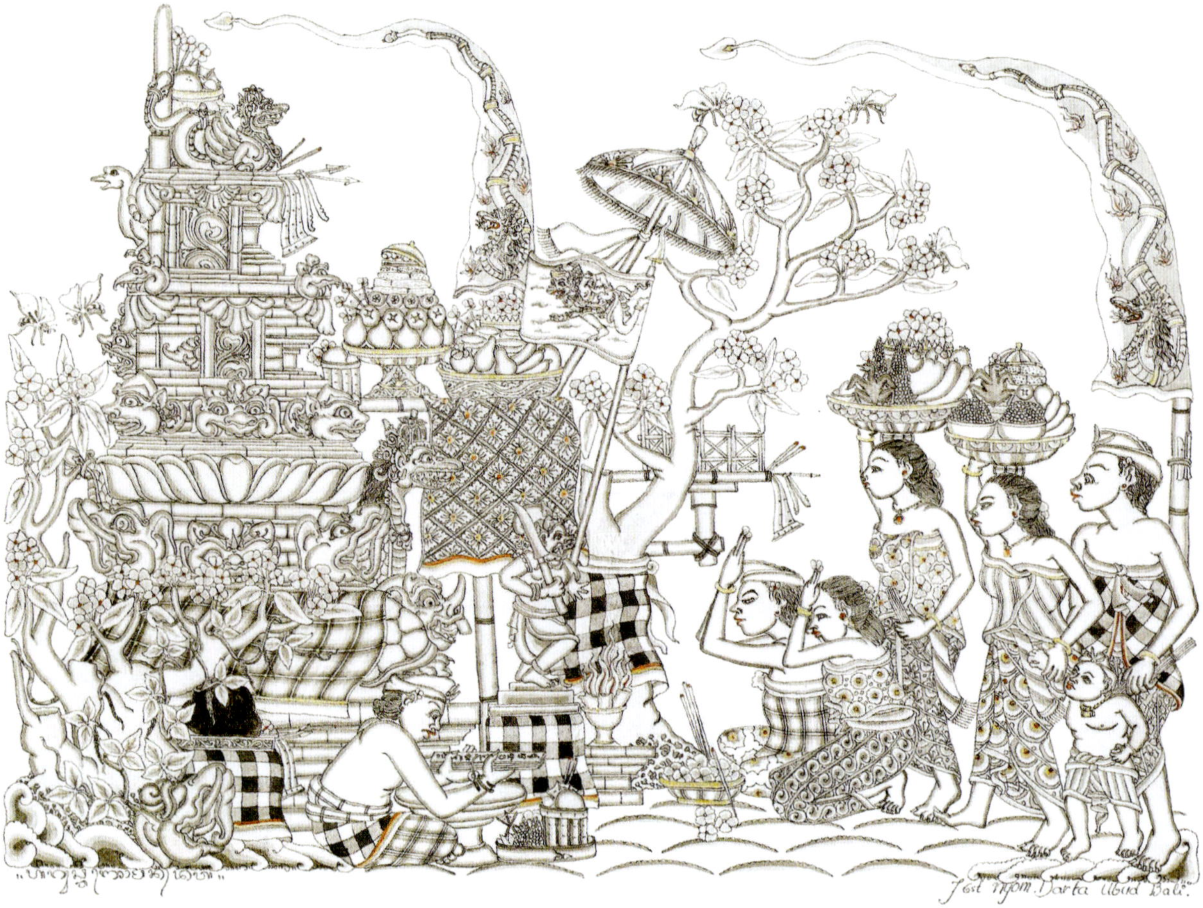

Sasih Kapat (The Fourth Month)

Usually falls in September

This month marks the end of the dry season and the coming of the first rains. Yet, the rainy season is often late and water becomes scarce.

The Kapat full moon is a time when many temple festivals (*odalan*) are held, including the biggest ones at the Besakih and Pura Penataran Agung temples. It is also celebrated at each family's private temple.

The illustration shows a family at prayer at the main altar of their private temple, the *padmasana*, or seat of the lotus, viewed from its side. The padmasana symbolizes the world as it stands, like the cosmic Mount Meru in the milky sea. From the churning of this sea spurts the water of immortality (*amerta*). At the bottom of the padmasana lies Badawang Nala, the cosmic turtle, bearer of the world and symbol of the earth's magma. One can see its protruding mouth just above the man reading a holy manuscript. Above the turtle is one of the two cosmic dragons, Anantaboga and Basuki, symbolizing water and earth. Just above them is the profile of Bhoma, symbolizing the vegetal world. On top of the altar is the open seat of Siwa. Here, one also sees the third dragon, Taksaka, symbolizing air. At the back, seen from the side, one can glimpse the Garuda-Wisnu and the holy goose. The elephant heads are merely decorations.

The padmasana and the trees are literally 'dressed', signaling the presence of the gods in the temple. Two women carry offerings, which they will take home to eat after presenting them to the attending gods. A man and woman are praying with flowers. Their hands are raised level with their heads, the part of the body associated with the divine. On the ground are a fire and offerings presented to the earthly-demonic forces.

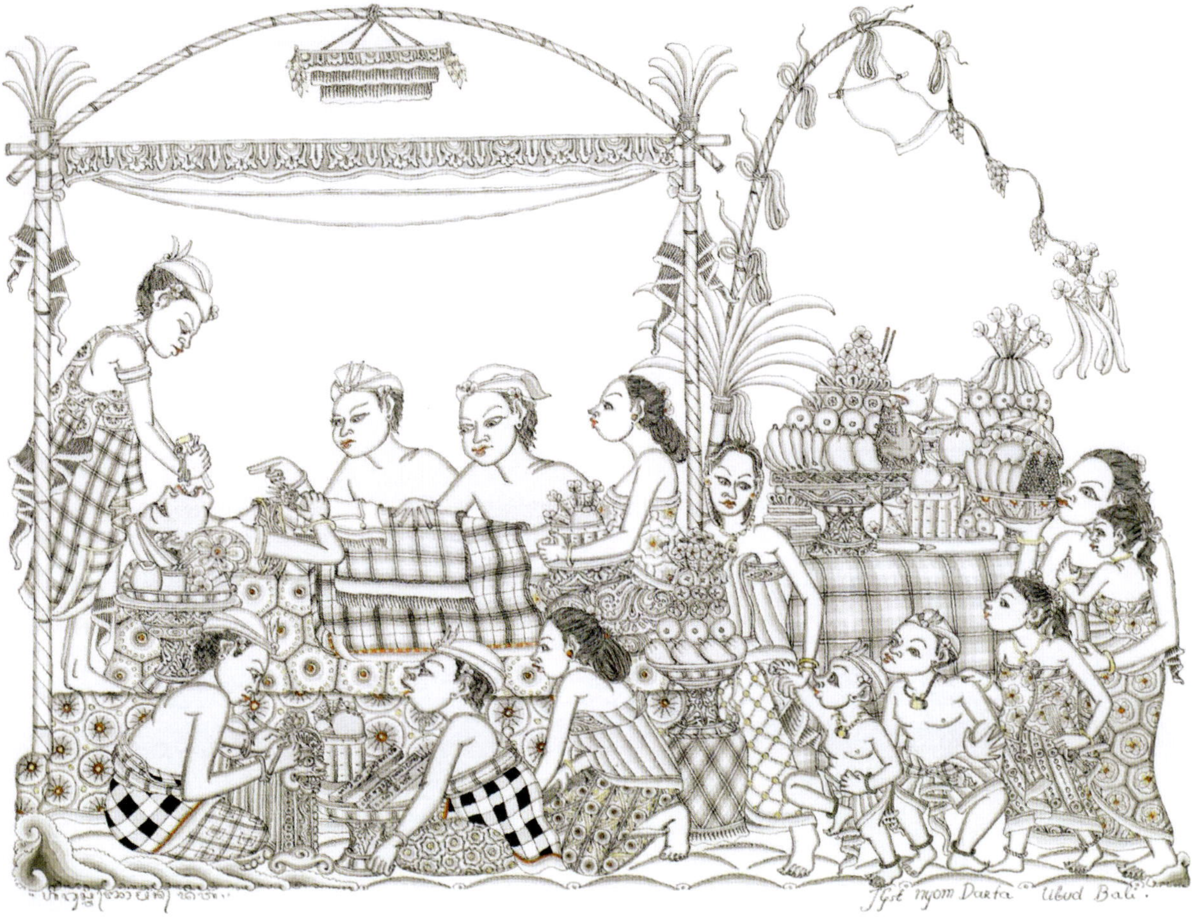

Sasih Kalima (The Fifth Month)

Usually falls in October

The rainy season has started, but it does not rain too much, nor is it too hot. Tomato, eggplant, and chili can already be harvested.

The fifth month is well suited for any rites of the life cycle (*manusa yadnya*). Here, a tooth-filing ceremony is depicted. Upon entering adulthood, the Balinese have to undergo this painful filing of their upper teeth and canines to signify that they will assert proper control over the pleasures that they will now be allowed to enjoy. For this purpose, they must subdue six enemies within the self (*sad ripu*): desire, greed, anger, intoxication, confusion, and jealousy. (See Chapter 6 for more information on the tooth-filing ceremony.)

The illustration shows a *sangging*, usually a non-ordained priest, filing a young man's teeth. At the foot of the ceremonial *bale*, a woman holds a coconut that will be used to collect the saliva. Just below the patient one man is playing the gamelan while another man and a woman next to him are singing while reading from a lontar manuscript. The song and the music must be sweet and harmonious to subdue the demonic forces at work during the ceremony.

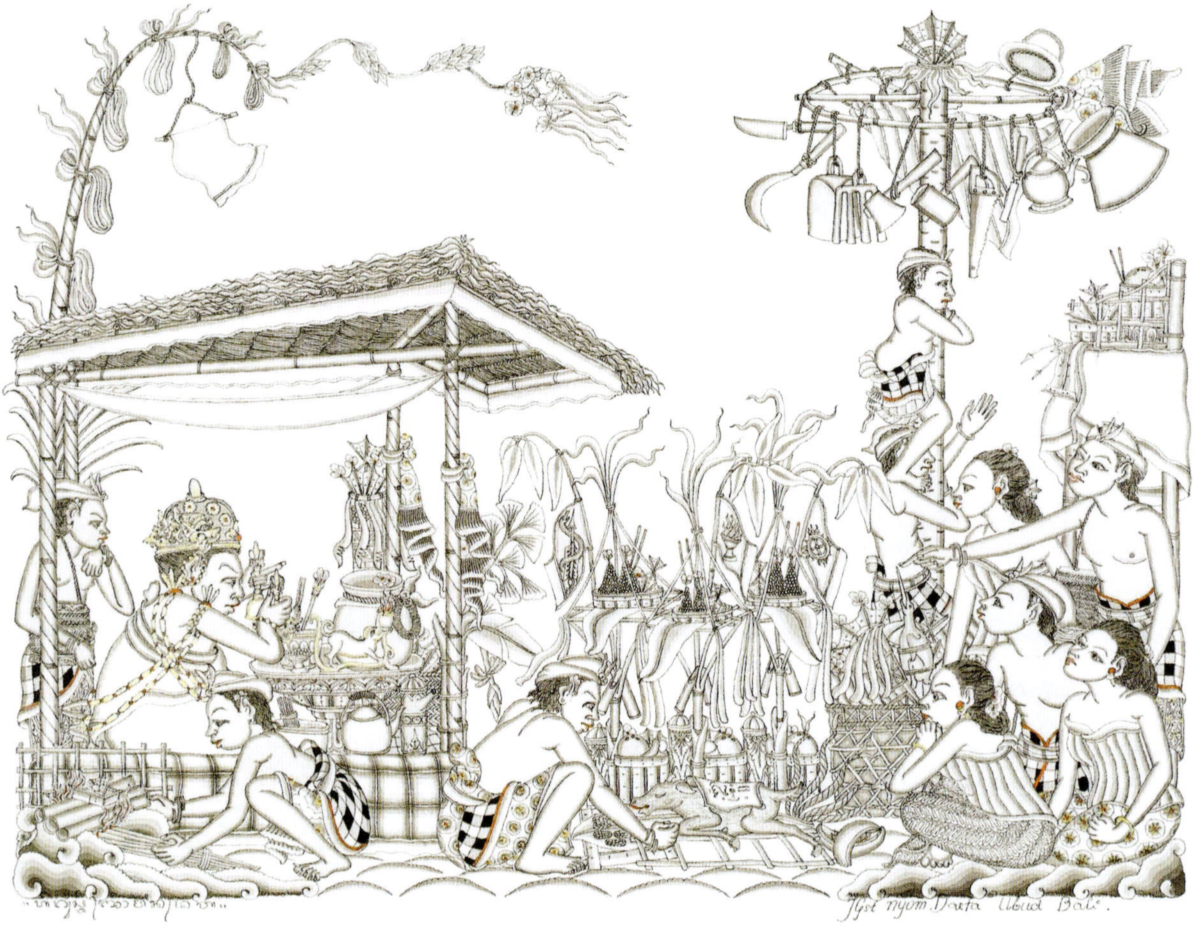

Sasih Kanem (The Sixth Month)

Usually falls in November

In Sasih Kanem, the sixth month, it rains, and with bad, humid weather, accompanied by thunderstorms and lightning, all sorts of woes may befall the island. The weather is good, however, for the growth of leafy vegetables such as spinach and betel.

Even though life-cycle ceremonies are often performed during Sasih Kanem, it is best suited for *buta yadnya*, rites addressed to the demonic beings (*buta*) that the Balinese call 'companions of the gods' (*rencangan ida Batara*). The buta must be heeded and provided with the right offerings.

People believe that during this month the destructive companions who reside in the depths of the sea will come ashore and spread illness to humans and various scourges to crops and the environment: drought, rats, and destruction of crops. When such calamities seem out of control, villagers undertake a cleansing (*nyangkluk merana*), under a priest's guidance, which aims to send the demons back to the sea. They may also put thorny pandanus leaves at the entrances of their houses to prevent demonic forces from entering.

Most exorcist rituals (*caru*) take place in the family compound. The illustration shows a dual ceremony, a big caru, to the left, addressed to the buta, and a *mapedanan*, a ritual presentation of household instruments. The purpose of the caru is to neutralize buta influences in the self and in the world and transform (*nyomia*) them into positive, godly ones. This caru is performed by a Siwa high priest, recognizable by his tiara. On the right are family tools and implements hanging from what looks like a maypole. Men shoulder one another and scramble up the high wishing tree pole (*kalpataru*) to claim gifts at the top.

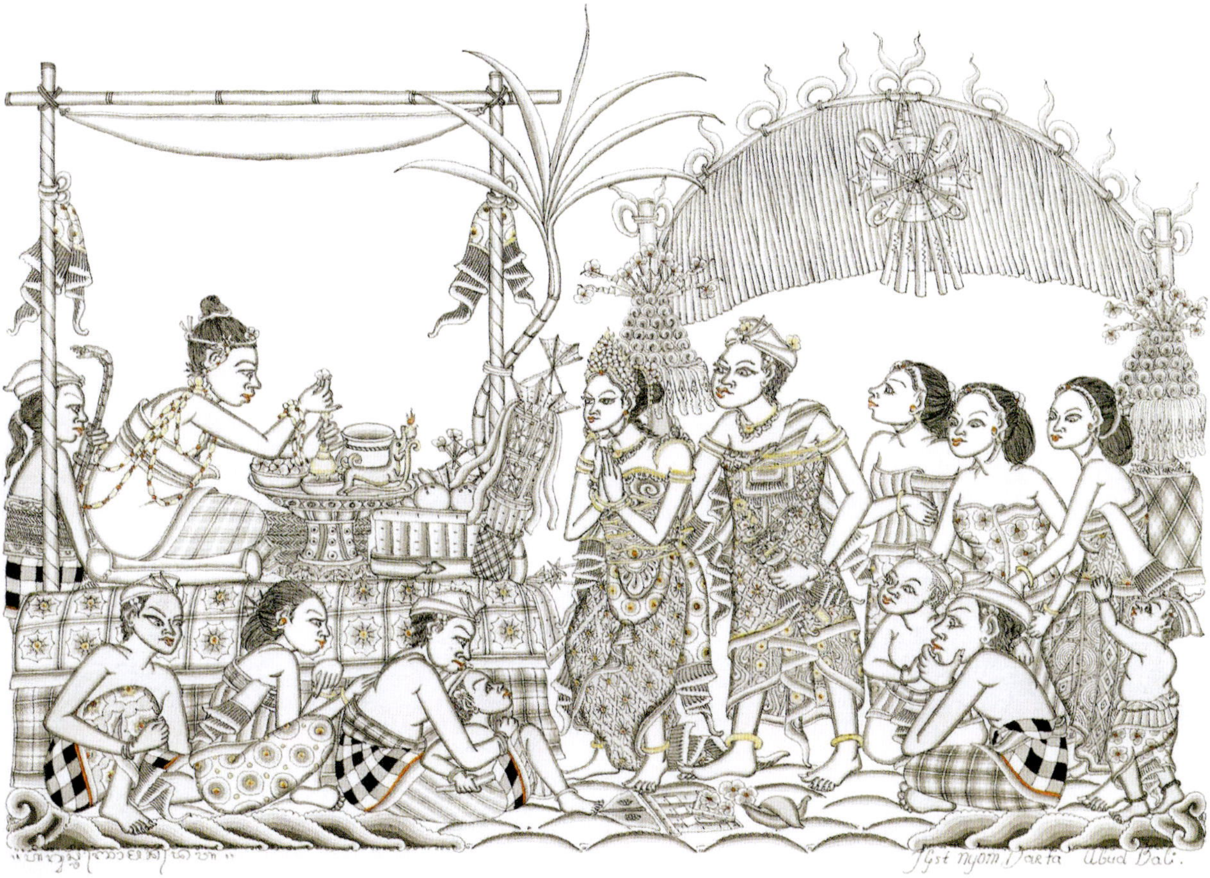

Sasih Kapitu (The Seventh Month)

Usually falls in December

Kapitu, the seventh month, is the peak of the rainy season, with storms and floods. Together with Kawulu, the eighth month, this period is the least pleasant of the year.

This month is often chosen to undertake life-cycle ceremonies (*manusa yadnya*), such as weddings. As usual, the day is chosen by the priest involved, either a high priest (*pedanda/sulinggih*) or a village/temple priest (*pemangku*).

This is also the month with the shortest new moon night of the year, Tilem Kapitu, during which Siwa Ratri takes place at an all-night wake accompanied by prayers and readings of the holy "Siwaratri", a classical Old Javanese poem. This ceremony originates from India, where it is held on the longest new moon of the year, but because Bali is located in the southern hemisphere where the seasons are reversed, it is the shortest new moon.

This illustration, however, does not depict Siwa Ratri, but a wedding. The ceremony is described in more detail in Chapter 6. The crossed coconut (*tekepan*) and nearby *mabiakala* offerings at the feet of the young couple indicate that the wedding has already taken place. The bride and groom are now standing in front of the priest, who is blessing them by sprinkling them with holy water (*majaya-jaya*).

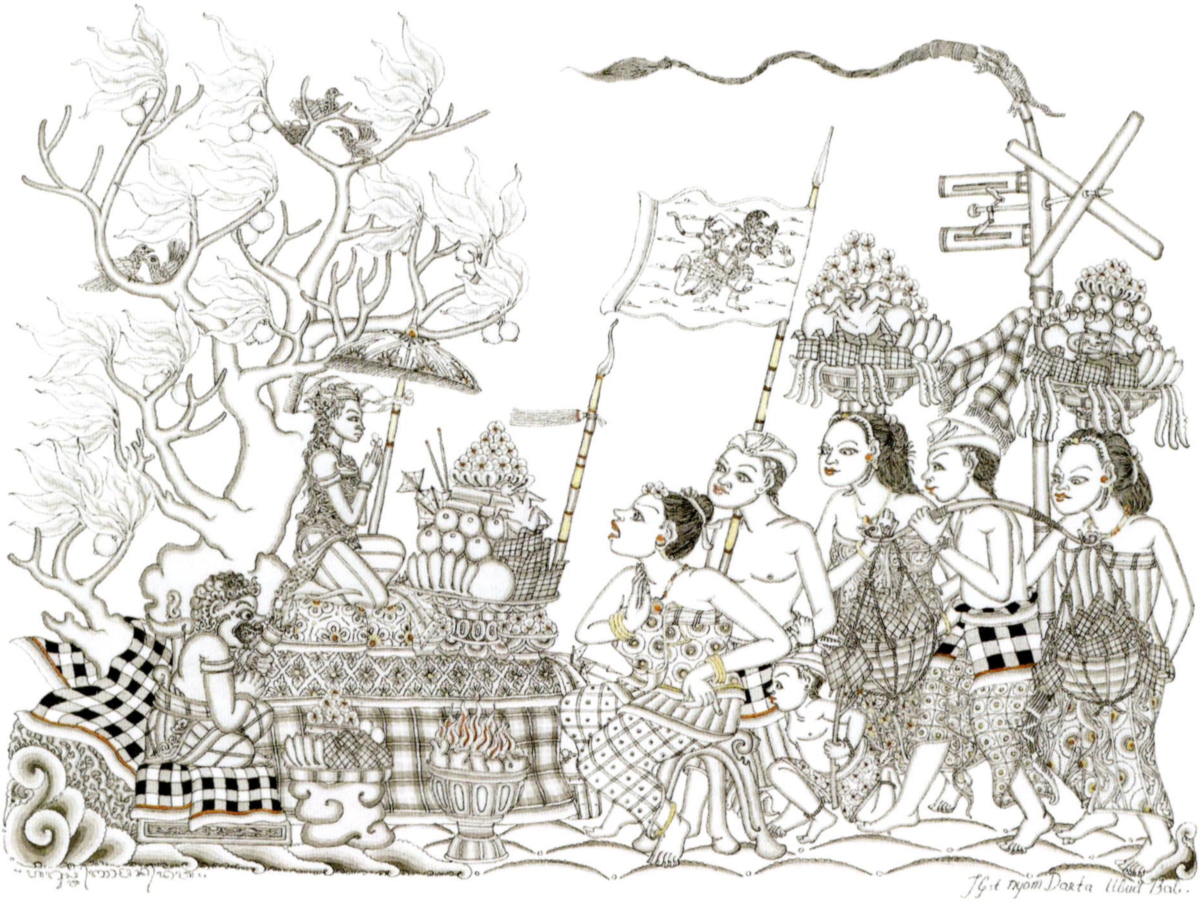

Sasih Kawulu (The Eighth Month)

Usually falls in January

Sasih Kawulu, the eighth month, is known for its strong and sometimes stormy winds and rains. Flooding may occur. Notice the way the artist has depicted the leaves of the tree to show how stormy the weather is.

The main interest of the picture lies in the fact that the ceremony illustrates the animistic substratum of Balinese Hinduism. Small shrines, here a provisional residence (*penyawangan*) for the goddess of rice Dewi Sri and her guardian statue, are frequent features of Balinese natural spaces, such as forests and gorges. One cannot miss seeing Balinese trees wrapped in black-and-white checkered cloth (*poleng*), a sign that the trees are inhabited by spirits. The villagers often present such shrines (*duwe*) with small offerings to placate the residing 'owner' of the shrine.

The purpose of the ceremony shown here is to calm the winds, and thus there is a bigger set of offerings, together with a dance performance. Note the bamboo wind vane and the banner featuring the hero Hanoman from the *Ramayana* epic.

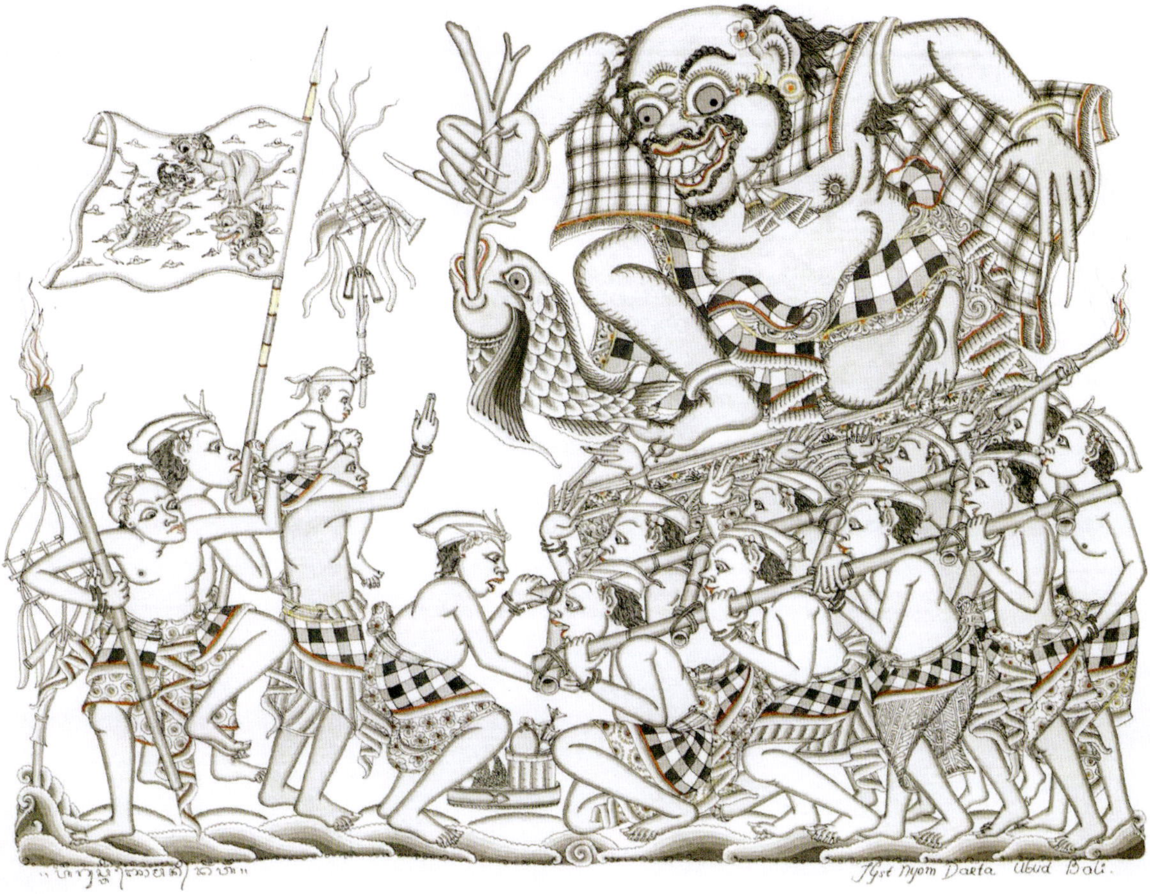

Sasih Kasanga (The Ninth Month)
Usually falls in late February to March

The Great Somya Purifications of the Saka New Year

As the ninth month of the Saka year, Sasih Kesanga, nears its end, Bali emerges from long days of rain. Clouds become rare and the sky begins to clear. It is a time when the dogs are said to be in heat (*cicing kesanga*) and the first rice season (*kerta masa*) begins. Yet, throughout the year, spiritual and physical impurities have accumulated, both within humanity (*manusa*) and in the world at large. It is time for a general 'cleansing', a ritual process of Somya, transmuting the forces of decay into forces of life. It is the realization of "Dewa ya, Buta ya!", the divine becomes the demonic and the demonic becomes the divine.

This purification cycle begins with a ritual bath of the village gods, as their impurities are washed away into the rivers or the sea. It continues with territory-level exorcisms held at all the main crossroads across the island. Then, in a final outburst, the demons are symbolically unleashed, given temporary dominion to roam wild only to be neutralized during the night of the last dark moon of the passing year. It is when the giant *ogoh-ogoh* effigies come out. When the world wakes the next morning on a new Saka year, it is greeted by the absolute silence of Nyepi.

Melasti Procession

The run-up to Nyepi begins with a Melasti pilgrimage just a few days before the new Saka year, when the gods of Bali journey to the water's edge with a singular purpose: to wash away the weight of the passing year. The ritual opens at the village temple (*pura desa*) with the Maspada ritual. Here, the *pemangku* (village priest) performs the sacred invitation, invoking the divine ancestors and summoning them to descend and inhabit their *pratima* (sacred effigies) for a few days. Only once these icons are vitalized by the spirits of the gods can the pilgrimage commence.

As the morning sun rises, the villagers dress the pratima in fine silks and golden cloth, which they then bathe in fragrant flowers. Placed upon ornate palanquins and accompanied by the resonance of the gamelan, the shaggy Barong and a forest of towering *umbul-umbul* flags, a long procession of people and pratima spill onto the roads, winding toward the coast or the nearest sacred riverbank.

There, a *pedanda* high priest is usually waiting atop a bamboo platform. When the procession reaches the water's edge, offerings to the *buta kala*—preferably ducks because they are creatures of both land and water—are cast into the waiting waves (*nganyud*). It is at this moment that Batara Baruna, the god of the sea, intervenes as the 'Divine Transformer'. The ocean is the only force vast enough to 'digest' the collective spiritual weight of the community. Thus, Baruna does not merely receive these impurities, he neutralizes them within his infinite depths.

Then comes the peak of the ceremony. To the steady chime of his bell, the priest invokes and retrieves the *amerta*, the water of immortality, from the now-purified waters. This holy water is then sprinkled toward the pratima and the gathered attendants, often inducing trances as the divine energy takes hold of the crowd.

The holy water and the re-energized effigies are escorted back to the village in yet another grand joyous procession. But rather than returning immediately to their individual shrines, the ancestral deities are enshrined together within their respective vessels upon the long platform of the Bale Agung, the great meeting pavilion in the village territorial temple (*pura desa*). This allows them to sit 'in state' as a council of ancestors. From this central vantage point, they witness the upcoming exorcisms and the chaotic night of the ogoh-ogoh, their presence anchoring the village both in its past and future as the last moments of the year pass away and a new year is born. Now that the effigies have been cleansed and the ancestors honored, the amerta is distributed among the villagers, revitalizing the community and rekindling its unity. The gods will remain at the Bale Agung in their golden vessels through the profound silence of Nyepi, only ascending back to the heavens once the first fires of the New Year are rekindled.

Tawur Agung Exorcism

From the vicinity of the sea during Melasti, the ritual cleansing process will then move, on the Saka calendar's last day, to a more central stage. By that time, it is not simply the local village deities that have to be cleansed, it is the whole world (Gumi Bali), which will undergo a major exorcism through what is called Tawur Agung. This Tawur Agung will involve the symbolic heart of Bali, the residing gods of the Besakih temple, but also all the administrative layers of Bali, from the regency level down, stage by stage, to the districts, the villages, and ultimately, all the important crossroads of the island.

The Tawur Agung is also meant to address not only the horizontal 'human' geography of the island, called *bhwah*, but also the vertical space, including the celestial world (*swah*) and the chthonian one (*bhur*). This island-sized purification begins long before the first prayer is whispered at the village crossroads. Interestingly, it does not start with exorcism but with the preparation of a dedicated Besakih temple holy water. Pura Besakih is indeed the 'Mother Temple' of the island, and the holy water (*tirta*) blessed there by its officiating priests serves as the purification source for the entire island. During the Tawur Agung, this Besakih Tirta emerges as the divine counterbalance to the chthonic forces of the ceremony's cosmic exorcism.

Considering the island-wide scale of the event, the process begins ahead of the Saka New Year. The Tirta Tawur Agung is 'created' in a grand ritual five or six days before the Tawur Agung. It is then mixed with holy water from other key temples, such as Pura Batur and Pura Uluwatu, creating a symbol of the island's divine oneness. Days before Nyepi, this tirta is collected in sacred vessels by representatives from each *kabupaten* (regency), from which it is distributed on the morning of Tawur Kesanga, just before the ceremony begins, to all the districts and then all the villages, reaching the main crossroads at noon precisely when the local purification rites are set to begin.

Meanwhile, at the village level, a high bamboo platform (*bale pawedan*) has been set up at the main crossroads for the *tengai tepet* (midday) event. The people wait, their deities spiritually recharged by the Melasti. They prepare for the night with *wong-wongan* decoys and *ogoh-ogoh* effigies, torches held in readiness to accompany them. As the sun attains its zenith, and once the tirta from Besakih has been poured into large vessels upon the bale pawedan, comes the theological apex: the three Sadhaka priests, fully clothed in their ceremonial regalia and crowned with their respective tiaras, ascend the platform and begin their collective exorcism. At the village level, the reading of mantras addressed to the three layers of the world is often delegated to *mangku* priests.

Through a synthesis of sacred mudras and Vedic mantras, the priests perform the Arga Patra, a complex internal alchemy. They do not merely recite; with every respiration, the priests attract the accumulated impurities of the community and 'cook' them into purity within the furnace of their own anatomy, projecting that transformed energy back into the world through the resonance of their bells.

In their ritual injunctions, they address the three layers of the world. The Pedanda Siwa invokes the celestial world (Swah Loka), calling upon Siwa to purify the soul. The Pedanda Buda focuses on the Bhuwah Loka, the middle world of humans, harmonizing the realm through meditation. The Sengguhu deals with the Bhur Loka, the underworld energies of the *buta kala*. By performing this ritual at the 'navel' of the village, the priests create a vortex of purification. They perform Somya, transforming destructive energy (*buta*) from all levels of the world into a calm, helpful energy (*dewa*), neutralizing the darkness of the year.

As the high priests' bells resonate, village officials, or representatives of the Hindu council, undertake the physical side of the caru exorcism, the Banten Caru. These are sacrificial offerings where the life-force of ducks, pigs, or cattle is surrendered to the earthly forces. These animals are chosen to mirror the *panca warna*, the five cosmic colors of the Balinese mandala: the white of the East, the red of the South, the yellow of the West, the black of the North, and the multicolored *brumbun* of the Center. By spilling blood at the village navel, the community 'feeds' and honors the totality of the underworld. These forces are not merely appeased but 'tamed' and reordered into the cosmic hierarchy, ensuring they remain neutralized and unable to breach the absolute sanctity of the upcoming silence of Nyepi.

Once the three Sadhaka finish their grand ritual performance (around 1:00 p.m. or 2:00 p.m.), they have each 'produced' their own specific brand of holy water, related to their respective layers of the world (Bhur, Bhuwah, Swah). These holy waters, combined with the Besakih 'Mother' tirta, are then distributed to each family, protecting the compound and its inhabitants against the upcoming chaos. This combined tirta is sprinkled upon the family temple (*sanggah*) and the family members, connecting the home to the Mother Temple and the Bhuwana at large. Only once the home is under the gods' tirta protection does it become possible for the family head to perform his own domestic Somya, and thus neutralize the buta kala spirits of the earth.

This is achieved through punctual *caru* exorcism at the intersection of the kitchen and the courtyard, the 'stomach' of the home, and at the front gate, accompanied by rice-paste *wong-wongan*. These wong-wongan are crude, human-looking decoys crafted from rice in five colors (panca warna), representing the cardinal directions and the totality of the physical world. By offering these figures, the family performs a ritual substitution: "Take this representation of our physical form, satisfy your hunger, and leave our actual bodies in peace." By offering the wong-wongan at this exact seam between day and night, the family effectively 'buys' its safety, transforming potentially destructive energy into harmony for the coming year.

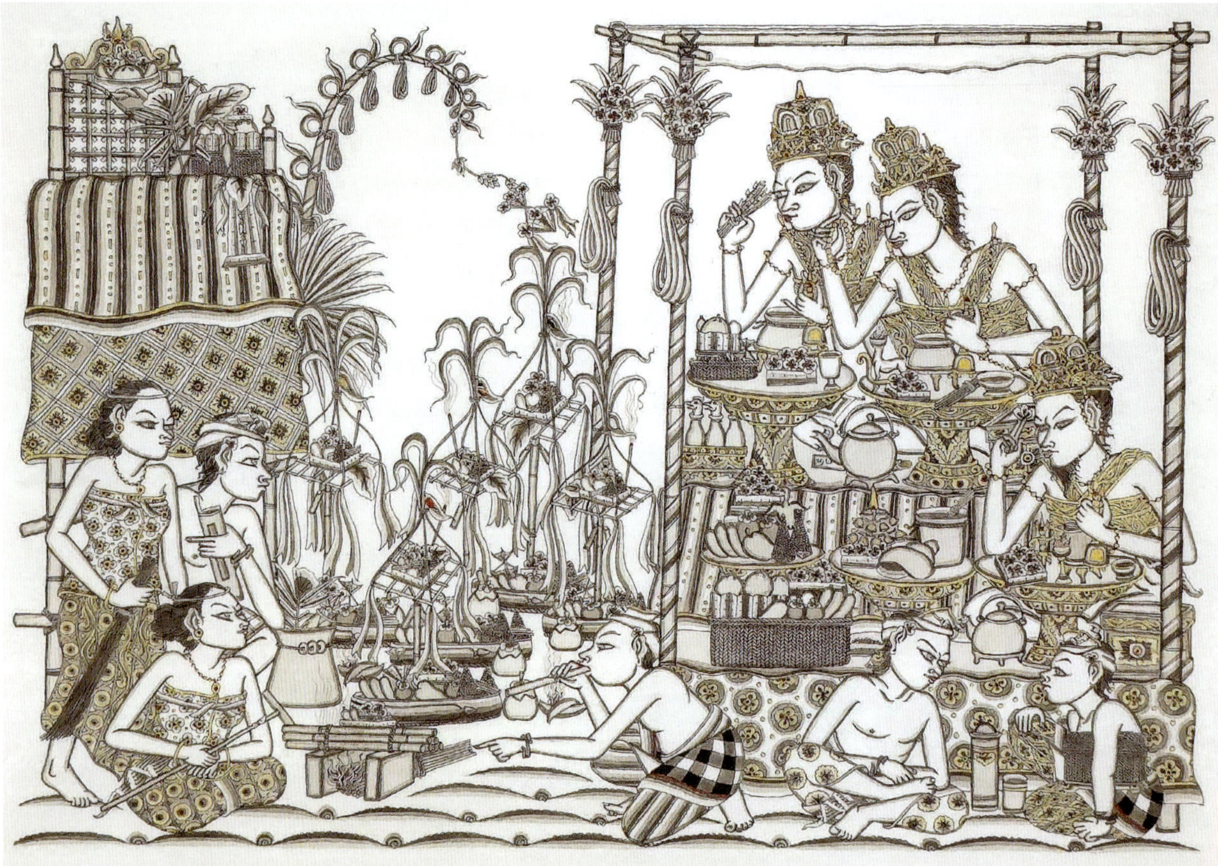

INTERPRETING THE DRAWING OF TAWUR KESANGA: The primary purpose of this ceremony is to expel *mala*, the sum of all negative influences. This process is depicted through two distinct approaches.

The Ritual Conjuration (right): To the right, elevated on a *pewedan* platform, sit three high priests. They harness the metaphysical power of sacred texts to conjure and neutralize negative influences throughout the universe. They operate across the three cosmic levels recognized in scripture, reciting corresponding mantras and performing specialized mudras (sacred hand gestures) to create the purifying *tirta* (holy water).

- The Pedanda Siwa, seated at the highest level, cleanses Swah, the celestial realm of the gods.
- The Pedanda Buda addresses Bhwah, the intermediate realm of humans, a space for which the Buddhist 'Middle Way' is ideally suited.
- The Sengguhu (or Vaishnavite priest) addresses Bhur, the chthonic lower realm.

The Physical Expulsion (lower left): To the lower left, three figures are shown 'physically' driving out the impurities. The man standing strikes a *kulkul* (a wooden slit-drum) to startle and frighten the *buta kala* (demonic forces). Beside him, a woman wields a broom to sweep these energies away, while another woman, seated on the ground, uses a *tulud* (a pushing stick) to shove them out of the sacred space. In the center, a man blows through a pipe to stoke a fire, which will cause bamboo tubes to overheat and explode. Above them stands a *penyawangan*, a temporary altar designed to communicate with ancestral deities from a distance.

The Cosmic Synthesis (center): In the center, five *sanggah cucuk* (bamboo shrines-cum-offerings) symbolize the five cardinal directions that must be purified. Once the three priests have manifested the holy water and restored cosmic balance, the man in the middle stokes the fire. When the third bamboo pops, it signals the start of Ngrupuk, the final, exuberant sweeping and clamor that prepares the island for the silence of the new year.

Ngerupuk and the Birth of Silence

Once the sun has fully set, the ritual transitions from the quiet offerings of the Tawur Kesanga into a period of cacophonous purification. While the Tawur Kesanga at midday was a static, meditative ritual, the Ngerupuk at sunset (Engseb Matanai) is dynamic and visceral. It represents the physical purge of the island. As the shadow energy of the new moon peaks during the gloaming, the community must physically 'sweep' the village, carrying *prakpak* (flaming coconut-leaf torches) and beating *kulkul* (wooden slit drums) to push demonic energies out of human-inhabited spaces.

The peak is reached with the ogoh-ogoh, sent to expel the buta kala from the village. This is the Ngerupuk cavalcade, held all over Bali, though the most fantastic is undoubtedly that of Denpasar. Heading for Gajah Mada Street, the monsters appear by the hundreds—monstrous guitarists, bikers, or even microbes—all with fangs and bulging eyes. Each is carried on the shoulders of dozens of youth who jerk and lunge to give the impression of a dance.

It is a staggering procession, as if Bali possessed an inexhaustible reservoir of demons. The Ngerupuk always culminates at the crossroads, where the ogoh-ogoh are spun three times to disorient the spirits within, before being led to the *setra* (cemetery) to be burned. This ending—the symbolic Pralina of Hindu cosmology—returns the gathered energy to the earth, completing the cycle of Somya.

By the time these three levels of ritual are complete, the world has been 'scrubbed' clean. The wong-wongan has satisfied the home spirits, the Ngerupuk has cleared the streets, and the Tawur Kesanga has realigned the world at the cosmic level. This creates the perfect spiritual vacuum required for the silence to come. If even one level were left undone, the silence of the next day would be 'impure'. But with the demons burned, the world is finally ready for the Nyepi Day of Silence, a day without demons.

Toward Nyepi Silence and a New Saka Year

The hours that immediately follow the Ngerupuk still, however, belong to the final, chaotic end of Tilem Kesanga. As the ogoh-ogoh are burned, turbulence continues, albeit waning, until the horizon meets the first light of the new year. At that first light, Tilem Kesanga is over, and the first day of the tenth month (Sasih Kadasa) begins. With the rising of the sun, the chaos instantly vanishes, replaced by the twenty-four hours of absolute Nyepi silence: Amati Geni (no fire); Amati Karya (no work); Amati Lelunganan (no travel), and Amati Lelanguan (no revelry). Silence is thus total. It is a day when the Balinese practice 'Mulat Sarira', a profound turning inward toward the self as a reflection of the Cosmic Oneness. It also remains a powerful annual assertion of ancestral sovereignty over the Gumi Bali, a day when the island belongs entirely to its own silence.

Nyepi, Ogoh-Ogoh, and the Times of Modernity

While Nyepi is now a cornerstone of Balinese identity, its current rigor is a relatively modern invention. Until the 1980s, the 'Day of Silence' was a loosely observed concept with rules that were vaguely followed and carried out with varying dates across different villages.

The turning point arrived in 1983, when the Balinese successfully lobbied the Indonesian government to recognize Nyepi as a national holiday. This official status placed Balinese Hinduism on an equal footing with other major religions and served as a catalyst for cultural revival. Around this same time, the traditional wong-wongan figures evolved into the monstrous giant ogoh-ogoh to both deepen religious meaning and attract global tourism.

As intellectuals unearthed strict scriptural injunctions banning fire, work, travel and pleasure, the day transformed from a quiet tradition into a powerful assertion of Balinese identity. This new-found religious pride led to the total closure of roads and airspace, with village guards ensuring that even non-Hindu minorities complied. Today, Nyepi is more than a ritual, it is a definitive annual statement of Bali's power to keep control over its own space.

CHAPTER 4
THE BALINESE DAY: EVERYDAY TIME

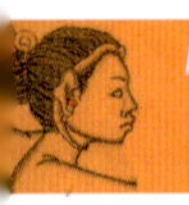

The Balinese day does not start at midnight. It goes instead from one sunrise to the next. The course of the sun is the journey of the god Surya riding his chariot from one side of the horizon to the other. The day cycle's main division is between daytime (*lemah*) and night-time (*peteng*).

Daytime is defined by three 'joints' or turning points (*sandi kala*) of the sun: at sunrise (*galang lemah*), at its zenith (*kali tepet*); and at sunset (*lingsiran*). These are moments of cosmic mutation, moments of danger, when it is inadvisable to move around or to bathe, for instance. Yet, they are also moments when one may gain magical power. Some villages warn their citizens of these moments by striking a wooden signal drum (*kulkul*) in the village commons.

There are corresponding sandi kala of the night. Distinctions between relative degrees of light and darkness affect not only the day but also the night. At each point, the situation of the moon gives a particular quality to the night. When the moon is at its zenith (*nyerepetan bulan*) is a moment of maximum danger. It is also the ideal moment for meditation if one wants to be endowed with magical powers.

The goddess Candra (pronounced 'Chandra') or Ratih, represents the moon. She is often depicted sitting in front of her loom, waiting patiently for the arrival of Semara, the god of love, or expecting to be swallowed by the giant Kala Rau, when there is an eclipse of the moon.

The complementarity between the sun and the moon is symbolized by the mythological couple Candra-Aditya (the luni-solar emanation of Siwa), who are the masters of light, and Durga (the demonic manifestation of Uma, Siwa's consort, or *sakti*), who rules the forces of darkness. These pairs of opposites, day–night and light–darkness, are a manifestation of the Balinese principle of Rwabhinneda, or the ultimate unity of contraries. The symbol of this unity is Acintya, the androgynous God of Gods, the Sublime One.

This cosmic duality blossoms during the night. At dusk, 'when the time to feed the pigs has arrived', witches (*leyak*) gather, hover, and prepare to spread ill-fortune. The darker the night grows, the greater the powers of evil become. Time for black magic is at its height when there is a New Moon (Tilem) or Full Moon (Purnama). Then, the leyak gather around ponds and look at their own hideous reflections in the water.

Night, however, is also the time for meditation, and, most importantly, love. The goddess Ratih finds herself under the spell of the god Semara. The mortals who worship these gods are blessed. Lovers are recommended to wait for the moon to rise before cavorting. Beware of the new moon, though! Before heading home, the visiting lover should wait for the second crowing of the cock (*kruyuk pang pindo*), or the moment when the hens leave their roosts, for this is when Durga rounds up her disciples and returns to the realm of the invisible.

The 'Hours' of the Day: Dauh

In Bali, the unit of time most similar to Western hours is the *dauh*, which literally means 'a call'. The nearest equivalent to dauh in English would be 'a stroke of time', or the 'striking' of a clock.

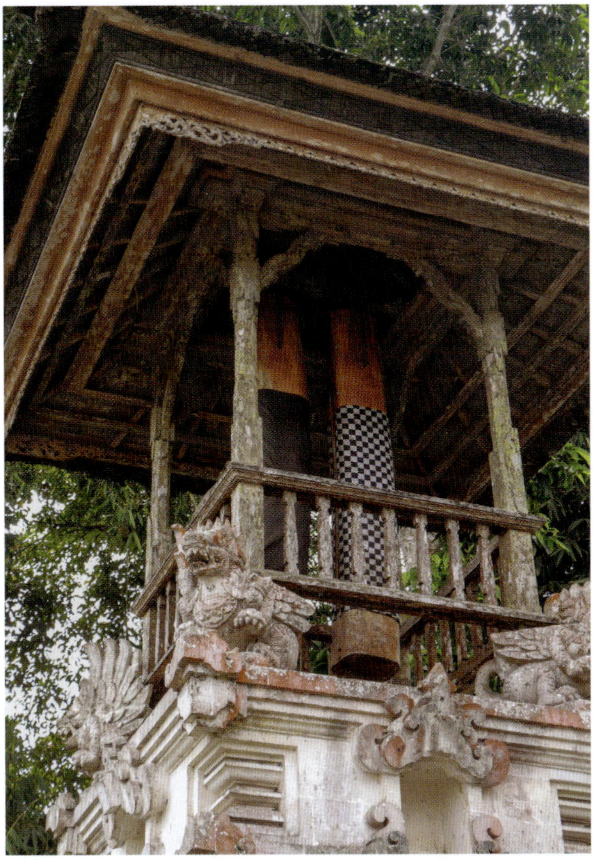

Kulkul **wooden drums tower in the village of Penglipuran, Bangli. The noise of each of these kulkul has a distinct function. It might be to call villagers for duties, inform them of a death in the village, or warn them of danger, such as fire.**

In the olden days in Bali, the wooden signal slit drum (*kulkul*) of the community, often set in a special, centrally located tower, used to be struck to mark the daytime dauh and the striking of the drum, known as *dedauhan*, was also the call to perform corvée labor for the king.

However, counting by dauh is a relatively complex process, since the dauh units are fractions of a whole that vary in duration rather than being units of fixed duration. To complicate matters even further, the day and the night are each divided into two cycles of dauh: the *panca dauh*, with five units, and the *asta dauh*, with eight units. The panca dauh is the most commonly used, whereas the asta dauh is mainly reserved for divination purposes.

In the daytime panca dauh system, five dauh are counted for the day and five dauh for the night. As the duration of night and day changes from one season to another, the daytime dauh are always different from the night-time dauh. Their median duration is two hours and 24 minutes. In the asta dauh cycle, the eight daytime dauh and eight night-time dauh have a median duration of 90 minutes.

There is no precise means of knowing which dauh one is in. So how does one manage? Traditionally, by approximation, that is, by guessing the dauh from the position of the sun or its shadow: approximately dauh IV, when it is *seng kauh*, inclined toward the west; dauh III, when it is *jejeg matanaine*, high noon; dauh I or II when itis *seng kangin*, toward the east; and dauh V when it is *lingsiran*, or late afternoon. In the past, these approximations were assisted by sun dials of Javanese Muslim origin, although no contemporary traces of these dials are to be found. The visible phases of the moon are similarly used to compute the night-time dauh.

It would help if the order of the dauh, day and night, were parallel. But the order is symmetrical: daytime dauh go from one to five, or one to eight, whereas night-time dauh are counted in reverse from sunset to sunrise. Supposing that the day and the night have an equal duration of 12 hours each, with sunrise and sunset at 6:00 a.m. and 6:00 p.m., respectively, then the panca dauh and asta dauh would correspond to clock time as follows:

Panca Dauh

For daytime:
Dauh pisan (I), from 6:00 a.m. to 8:24 a.m.
Dauh ro (II), from 8.24 a.m. to 10:48 a.m.
Dauh tiga (III), from 10:48 a.m. to 1:12 p.m.
Dauh pat (IV), from 1:12 p.m. to 3:36 p.m.
Dauh lima (V), from 3:36 p.m. to 6:00 p.m.

For night-time, in reverse order:
Dauh lima (V), from 6:00 p.m. to 8:24 p.m.
Dauh pat (IV), from 8:24 p.m. to 10:48 p.m.
Dauh tiga (III), from 10:48 p.m. to 1:12 a.m.
Dauh ro (II), from 1:12 a.m. to 3:36 a.m.
Dauh pisan (I), from 3:36 a.m. to 6:00 a.m.

Asta Dauh

For daytime:
Dauh pisan (I), from 6:00 a.m. to 7:30 a.m.
Dauh ro (II), from 7:30 a.m. to 9:00 a.m.
Dauh tiga (III), from 9:00 a.m. to 10:30 a.m.
Dauh pat (IV), from 10:30 a.m. to 12:00 noon
Dauh lima (V), from 12:00 noon to 1:30 p.m.
Dauh nem (VI), from 1:30 p.m. to 3:00 p.m.
Dauh pitu (VII), from 3:00 p.m. to 4:30 p.m.
Dauh kutus (VIII), from 4:30 p.m. to 6:00 p.m.

For night-time, in reverse order:
Dauh kutus (VIII), from 6:00 p.m. to 7:30 p.m.
Dauh pitu (VII), from 7:30 p.m. to 9:00 p.m.
Dauh nem (VI), from 9:00 p.m. to 10:30 p.m.
Dauh lima (V), from 10:30 p.m. to 12:00 midnight
Dauh pat (IV), from 12:00 midnight to 1:30 a.m.
Dauh tiga (III), from 1:30 a.m. to 3:00 a.m.
Dauh ro (II), from 3:00 a.m. to 4:30 a.m.
Dauh pisan (I), from 4:30 a.m. to 6:00 a.m.

In his *Island of Bali* (1937), Miguel Covarrubias wrote that according to R. Friedrich, a mid-19th-century observer, there used to be a special kulkul in a 'clock tower' in Badung, the present-day capital city of Denpasar, on which the Balinese dauh hours were struck. Moreover, according to I Gusti Nyoman Darta, the dauh time was still struck in Ubud until the 1960s. Today, however, the dauh system is not commonly used except for ritual purposes, although in some mountain villages, dauh time (*panca dauh*) is still struck by a kulkul.

Water Clocks and Winks: Other Measures of Time

Despite the sophistication of their calendars, the Balinese never developed a clock to measure and display the hours of the day. However, they did invent various devices to measure brief lapses of time, often ritual situations. For example, they sometimes used a kind of hourglass or water clock, the *ceeng*, half a coconut shell filled with water that drips through a hole in the bottom of the shell. The time it takes for the water to finish dripping out is the duration of a cockfight.

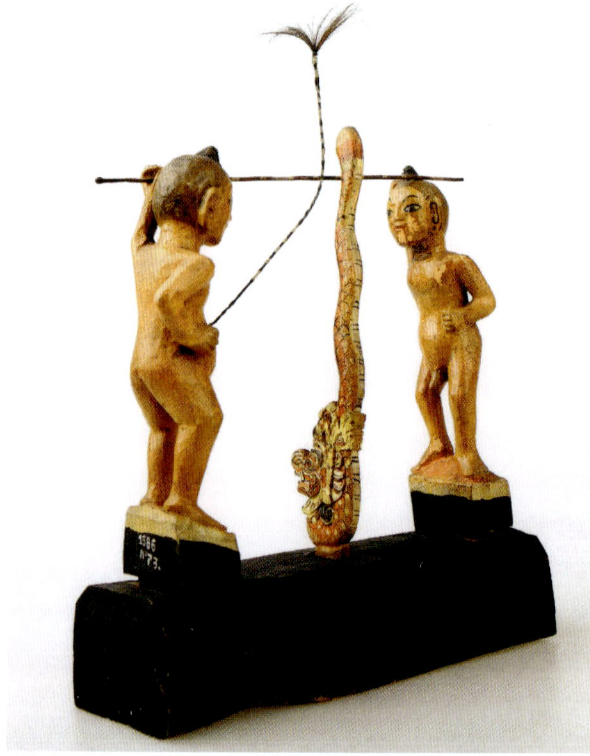

BALINESE 'WATER CLOCK' TIMEPIECE: A timepiece depicting a man and a woman, both naked, playing in some kind of tournament. The man's right hand and woman's left hand hold the ends of a red-colored, gilded iron rod, from which hang eight iron wires. The man's left hand rests on his hip, and the woman's right hand holds an iron staff ending in a tuft of human hair. Between these two human figures is a crowned *naga* serpent (possibly Basuki or Anantaboga) with a high raised tail with red, white, black, and gilded scales. All three figures are mounted on a black-colored wooden base. This timepiece was used as a mnemonic device, together with a half coconut shell (*ceeng*) or copper bowl with a hole in its bottom, to form a 'water clock'. To mark the passage of each of the eight time units (*asta dauh*) into which the Balinese day is divided, one of the eight iron wires suspended from the rod was shifted along. This occurred after the ceeng had emptied three times. The ceeng itself is not illustrated here, but for a depiction of the ceeng in use, see the illustration opposite.

30 x 26 x 8 cm.
19th century.
Collection of Wereldmuseum Leiden, The Netherlands—the National Holland Museum of Ethnology, Leiden (Inv. 1586-73).
Collected by W. O. J. Nieuwenkamp in Banyuning, Buleleng in 1906.

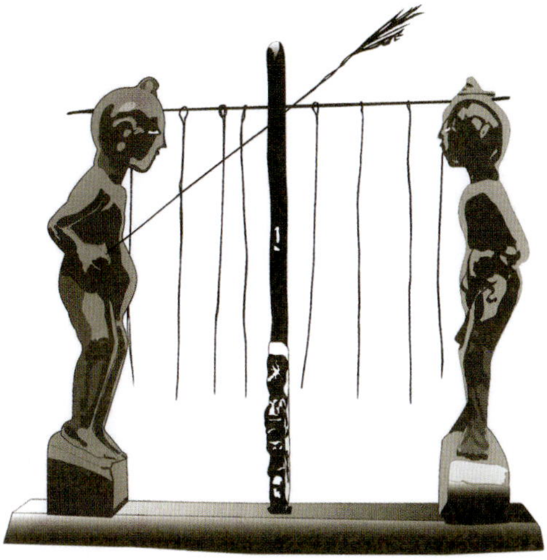

Drawing of the same Balinese 'water clock' timepiece showing the hanging wires.

A similar type of water clock was used, together with a kulkul, to keep time during meetings of the banjar neighborhood association. Covarrubias also wrote that laborers working the earth for communal purposes in the 1930s were paid on the basis of a time unit recorded by water clocks similar to those used in cockfights.

Brief time lapses are referenced by analogy to particular actions. For example, *akejep* is 'the time for a wink'. A short while is called *apakpakan base*, 'the time it takes to chew a wee bit of betel', and a long while is *apanyakanan*, 'the time it takes rice to cook'. However, beware of someone asking you to wait for *akejepan barong*, 'the time it takes the Barong to wink', since the Barong is a mask and, therefore, cannot wink! You may well have to wait forever.

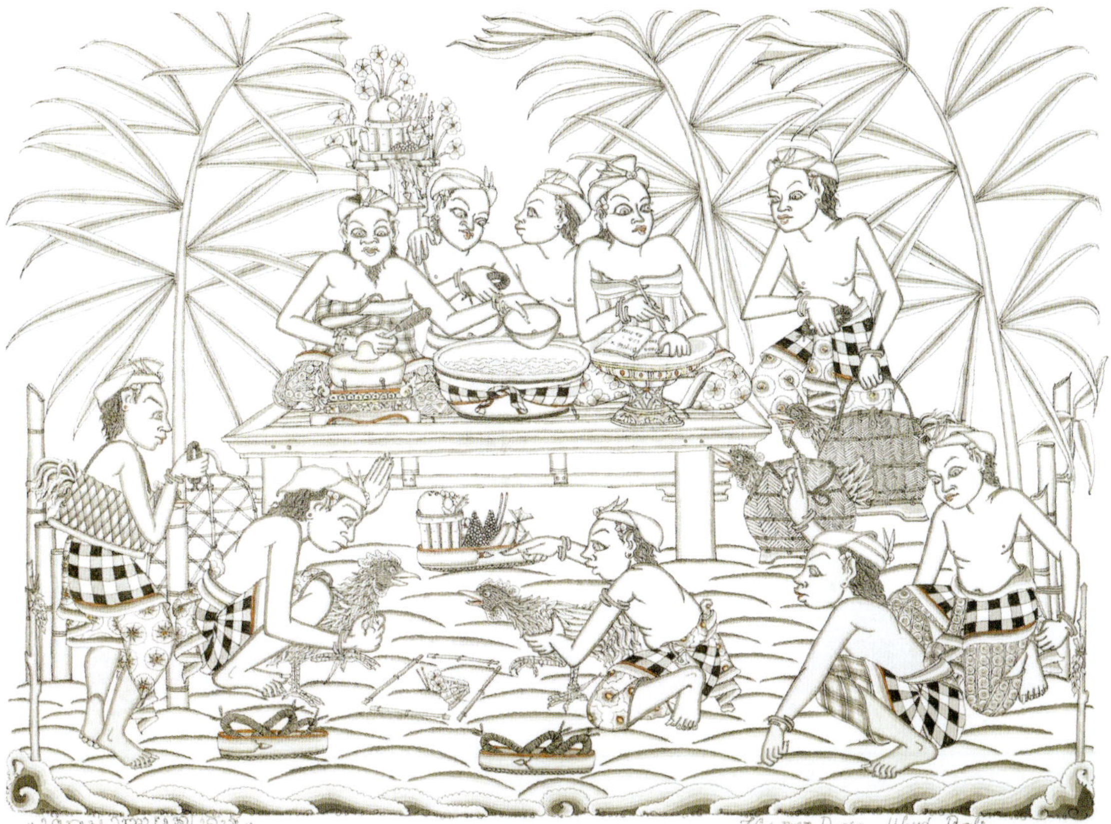

COCKFIGHTING: The scene of a cockfight, with its various actors. Sitting on the platform are the officials directing the fight. The man in the middle is preparing the *ceeng*, which consists of half a coconut shell with a small hole in the bottom, to be placed in a basin of water and left to sink. The sinking time of the ceeng gives the unit of time for the fight. The man on the left is about to hit a small gong (*kempul*) to begin the fight, while a third is recording the bets. Offerings have been made and the two cock owners are ready to start the fight under the watch of the referee (*saya*), shown squatting at front right.

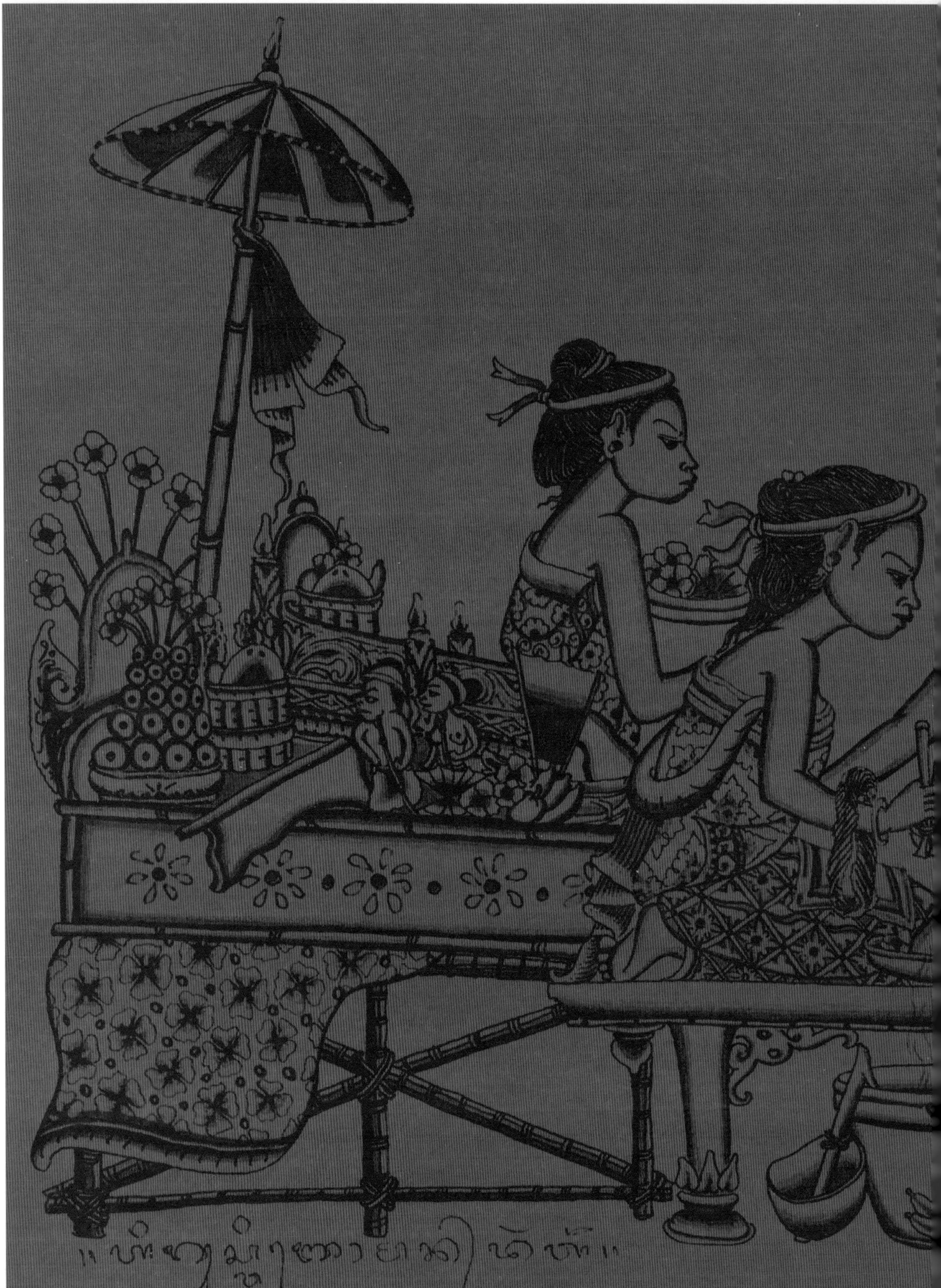

PART TWO

RITES and FESTIVALS

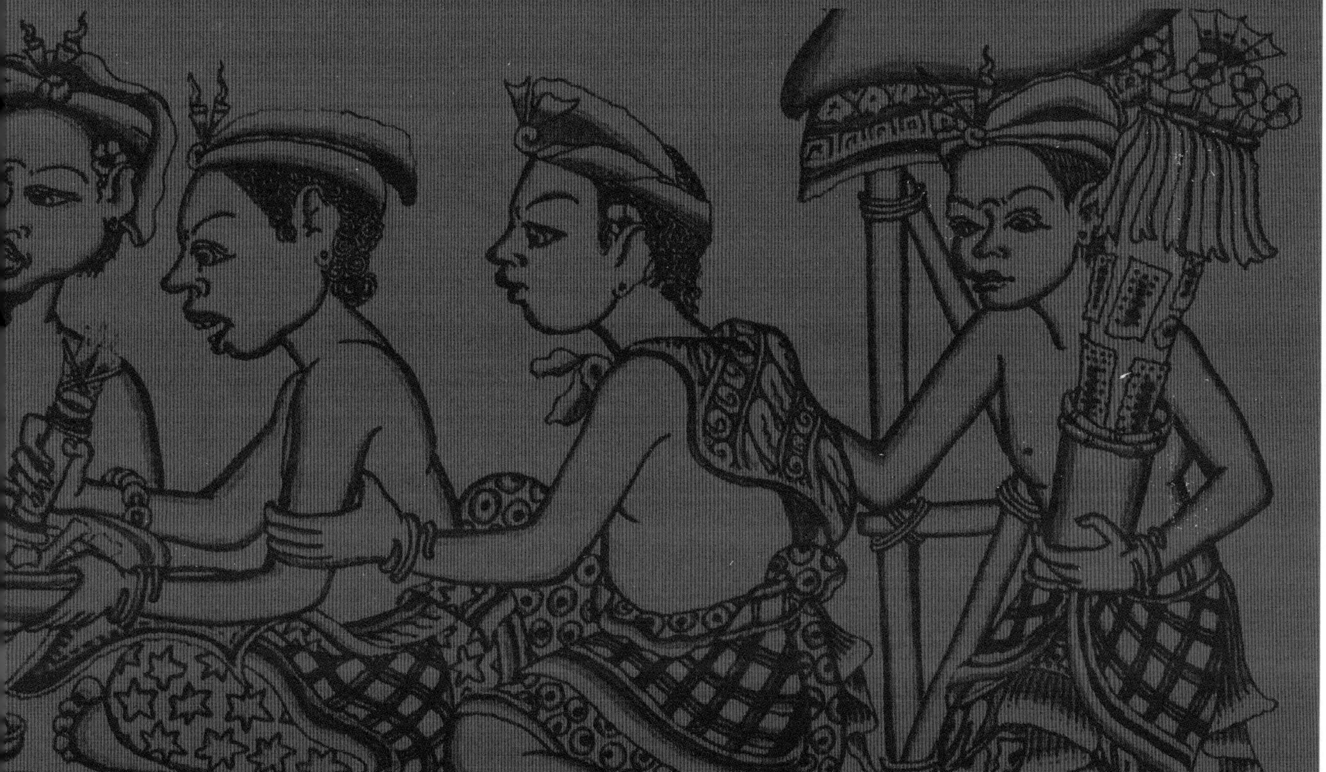

CHAPTER 5

HOLIDAYS AND HOLY DAYS

As discussed in Chapters 1 and 3, the notion of holy days is relative in Bali: all days are charged with varying degrees of demonic and divine power. Life is the realization of a cosmic order. The calendars provide the orientation for arranging one's life in accordance with this order. They thus regulate a wide range of sacred rites and festivals.

Most of these festivities fall on days that correspond to conjunctions of certain days from the various *wara* or 'weeks' (*wuku*) of the 210-day cycle of the Pawukon calendar. Others are determined by moments in the lunar cycle of the 12-month Saka calendar, such as the New Moon (Tilem), Full Moon (Purnama), or days preceding or following them.

Among the calendar-based holy days, the *rerainan gumi* are considered major and are thus celebrated island-wide. Others correspond to the *odalan* (anniversaries) of specific temples. Still others are celebrated across the island, but are not considered rerainan gumi.

Celebrations in the Pawukon Calendar

Conjunctions of Triwara and Pancawara Days

The intersection of Kajeng, the last day of the three-day week (Triwara) and Kliwon, the last day of the five-day week (Pancawara), is called Kajeng-Kliwon. It occurs every 15 days, 14 times during the Pawukon calendar cycle.

Even though rituals linked to this day occur across the island, Kajeng-Kliwon is not considered a major island-wide holy day. It is simply an auspicious day for occult forces. Offerings that are larger and more elaborate than the usual daily offerings, are made to all of the cardinal directions in houses and in temples. On the thresholds of these places, incense is lit and burned in coconut shells (*pasepan*) to ward off negative forces.

Numerous temple festivals and other religious ceremonies also occur on Kajeng-Kliwon, always doubling with other conjunctions. Examples include Anggarakasih Kulantir, which falls on Kajeng-Kliwon-Enyitan during Wuku Kulantir (wuku 4) on the 24th day of the calendar cycle; and Tumpek Kuningan, which falls on the Kajeng-Kliwon-Kuningan conjunction day during Wuku Kuningan (wuku 12). Anggarakasih Kulantir and Tumpek Kuningan are discussed later in this chapter.

Conjunctions of Pancawara and Saptawara Days

Every 35 days there are recurrences of 'strong' conjunctions of particular days in the seven-day week (Saptawara) and the five-day week (Pancawara). This 35-day cycle is sometimes called a Pawukon or wuku 'month' (sasih Pawukon or sasih wuku). These important conjunction days include:

— Buda-Kliwon: the conjunction of Buda (Wednesday) and Kliwon;
— Tumpek: the conjunction of Saniscara (Saturday) and Kliwon,
— Buda-Cemeng: the conjunction of Buda and Wage,
— Anggarakasih: the conjunction of Anggara (Tuesday) and Kliwon.

These four conjunctions succeed one another every 35-day cycle in the following fashion. Ten days after a Buda-Kliwon, a Wednesday, there is a Tumpek, on a Saturday. This is followed four days later by a Buda-Cemeng, on another Wednes-

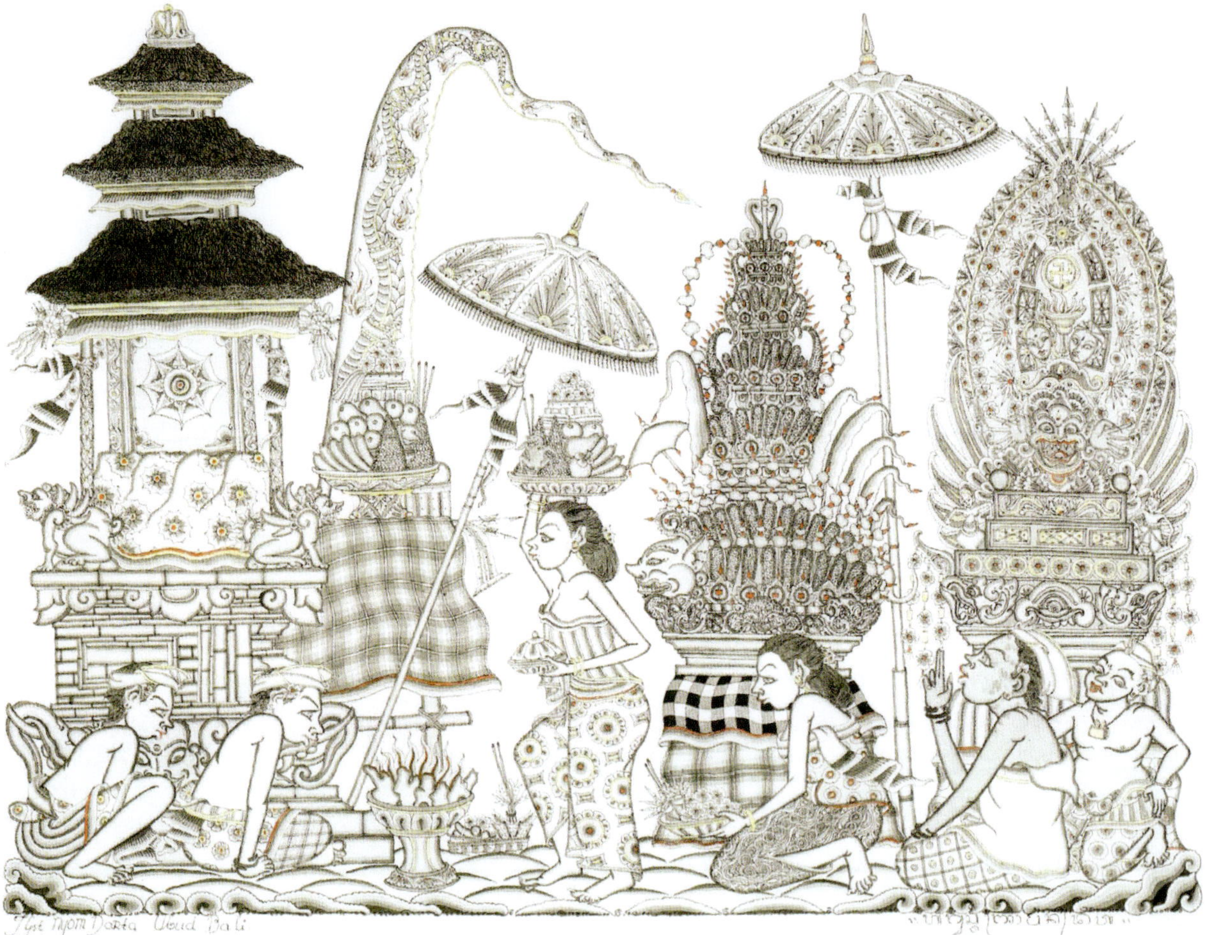

AN ODALAN TEMPLE ANNIVERSARY CELEBRATION: **This illustration shows the atmosphere of a temple during an *odalan* festival. The principal shrine is to the left, whereas to the right are two huge offerings, a *sarad* to the right and a *sate tunggal* to the left. These offerings symbolize the cosmic mountain, hence the world. On their lower parts one can see the cosmic tortoise Bedawang Nala. The higher levels correspond to the godly. Notice the Hindu swastika to the right. The woman in the middle is bearing offerings that she will later take back to be consumed at home. The people seated on the right are singing a sacred religious song (*kidung*).**

day, which is, in turn, followed six days later by an Anggarakasih, on a Tuesday. A new Buda-Kliwon occurs 15 days later.

For a visual illustration of these intersections in the 35-day month, see the *pelelintangan* charts in Chapter 7.

During the course of the 210-day Pawukon cycle, only one such conjunction happens in any particular wuku. There are six occurrences each of Buda-Kliwon (on wuku 1, 6, 11, 16, 21, 26); of Tumpek (on wuku 2, 7, 12, 17, 22, 27), of Buda-Cemeng (on wuku 3, 8, 13, 18, 23, 28), and of Anggarakasih (on wuku 4, 9, 14, 19, 24, 29) per the Pawukon cycle, or once every five weeks.

The dates of the odalan of most of the main temples on Bali are also based on these conjunction days. They also are the occasions for the important pan-Bali holy days, rerainan gumi, in the case of the six Tumpek, as well as Buda-Kliwon in Wuku Sinta (which is the holy day called Pagerwesi), and Buda-Kliwon in Wuku Dungulan (which is the holy day of Galungan). More information on these major holy days follows in the next section of this chapter.

Important temple festivals, however, are also celebrated on the morrow of these conjunction days, called (U)manis, except for Buda-Cemeng, which is not followed by a (U)manis day.

This does not, however, preclude the possibility of other dates. Some temple festivals are held on different auspicious conjunction days, such as Wrespati-Wage during Wuku Tolu (wuku 5) or Soma-Paing during Wuku Warigadian (wuku 8). Moreover, some holy days occur on conjunctions of other days of the Saptawara and Pancawara together with a certain day of the six-day week (Sadwara). For example, on the first day of Wuku Sinta (wuku 1) the holy day of purification called Banyu Pinaruh falls on a day that is a conjunction of Redite (from the Saptawara), Paing (from the Pancawara), and Tungleh (from the Sadwara).

Temple Festivals

Balinese temples are open stone structures designed as microcosms of the universe. Their inner sanctum (*jeroan*) contains the main shrines, which are always located *kaja* (toward the mountain) and *kangin* (toward the east). In the most sacred corner stands the *padmasana*, the empty 'lotus seat' of Acintya the Sublime (Siwa). From this corner, shrines for the deities run east–west, while shrines for the ancestors are aligned mountain–seaward.

Odalan and Pujawali for the Pawukon, or Usaba for lunar ceremonies, bind together the community, ancestors, and the divine. These festivals exist at every level of Balinese social structure, from rice field and kinship shrines to village temples, and eventually to the great Sad Kahyangan or Dang Kahyangan—the six or nine 'pillar' temples of the island. The sheer number of temple types, each with anniversaries on different dates, explains the almost constant symbolic flowering of the island.

The dates for most festivals follow the 210-day Pawukon calendar, alternating between an *odalan alit* (small) and an *odalan ageng* or *nadi* (great) festival. Most occur on significant days, such as Anggarkasih, Buda Kliwon, Buda Cemeng, or Tumpek. Other festivals, particularly in the highlands and the east, follow the Purnama (Full Moon) and Tilem (New Moon) of the Saka lunar calendar.

Festival preparation demands months of communal labor (*ngayah*) under the direction of the *kelian* (village head) and the *sarati* (offering specialists). The resulting *banten* are symbol-laden structures of palm leaves, rice cakes, and fruits—physical vessels for the divine 'presence'.

As the deities will reside temporarily in the temple's *palinggih* (shrines), these stone structures are wrapped ahead of the visit in colored cloths (red, white, yellow, and black) of symbolic cosmic meaning. This signals that they are no longer mere buildings but 'living seats' ready to be occupied. However, before the gods can dwell in the temple, the *pratima* (sacred symbols and statues) must be purified. This is the function of the Melasti procession to a *petirtan* (sacred water source) or the sea, to wash away the *mala* (impurities) of the human world. Accompanied by the clanging of the Gamelan Beleganjur, this is a visual highlight of the odalan, representing a return to the holy 'source' to recharge the ritual power of the temple.

For major ceremonies, holy water (*tirta*) is gathered in a process known as *nunas pekuluh*. Emissaries are sent to the great pillar temples across Bali to request water from the highest sources. This process effectively gathers the key deities from across the island into a supreme hydraulic unity, thus turning the ancestor and holy mountain cult into an encompassing pantheism.

The key moment arrives when the *pemangku* (priest), ringing his bell and wafting incense, calls the gods to descend (*tedun*) and dwell within the purified pratima. It is usually then that the Jero Tapakan (or Jero Dasaran) is 'entered' by the ancestors. Through these mediums, the ancestors may formulate demands or express satisfaction with the community's conduct.

Once the gods have arrived, they are entertained with ritual dances such as the Rejang and Baris. Women bring their offerings, sometimes in procession, to the temple to be 'consumed' by the gods, before being returned home to be eaten. Yet, the 'seal of the blessing' between the divine and the faithful is the collective prayer and the distribution of the gathered tirta.

The faithful are given tirta to drink from their cupped hands and are sprinkled with this holy water; they also receive *bija* (consecrated raw rice grains) to stick upon their foreheads and throats. This is the physical 'receipt' of the blessing, a tangible sign that the connection between the human and the divine has been successfully re-established.

After several days and nights of performances (during a nadi festival), the gods are thanked and ceremonially sent back (*nyineb*) to their mountain abode. The cloths are removed and the temple returns to its quiet, stony vigil, save for the occasional visit of people requesting the blessing of the temple's holy water.

Holy Days in the Pawukon Cycle

The Pawukon calendar comprises many pan-island holy days, or rerainan gumi. All of these days are determined by various conjunctions of the wuku and wewaran systems.

The two most important cycles of holy days are that of the Pawukon 'New Year' and that of Galungan-Kuningan. To these should be added the most important days for temple festivals, including Buda Kliwon, Tumpek, Buda Cemeng, and Anggarakasih conjunctions in particular wuku, as well as certain days consecrated to a particular divinity of the Hindu-Balinese pantheon.

This section describes all of the rerainan gumi and major conjunction days in order of their occurrence in the 210-day cycle, beginning with those related to the Pawukon 'New Year'.

The Pawukon 'New Year' (wuku 28–wuku 1)

The Pawukon 'New Year' comprises a series of ceremonies that begin at least one week, and arguably two weeks, before the end of the Pawukon cycle and continues until at least the third day of the new cycle.

The symbolism of the festival of Saraswati, as the day that marks the separation of the son and the incestuous mother, has already been discussed in the analysis of the myth of Watugunung in Chapter 2 and in the outline of the Pawukon calendar in Chapter 3.

As we shall see now, the ceremonies surrounding the Pawukon 'New Year' follow, step-by-step, the process of purification and enlightenment experienced by the hero of the Watugunung story: from original purity, through purity defiled by incest, to defeat and punishment, enlightenment, and finally, purity restored.

Wuku Kulawu (28): A state of original purity

The state of original purity is found on Wuku Kulawu, which is under the protection of Sedana, who is the god of material welfare and a manifestation of Wisnu.

On Wednesday—Buda-Wage-Kulawu—the god Sedana is worshipped, and no business many be conducted on this day.

Friday—Sukra-(U)manis-Kulawu (also a Kajeng day)—is consecrated to Sri, the goddess of rice. No rice may be processed or sold on this day.

Wuku Dukut (29): The defilement of purity

The incestuous defilement and insult to the gods, Wisnu, in particular, occurs on this week, during which no important celebrations are held.

Wuku Watugunung (30), days 1–3: Defeat and punishment

Watugunung's defeat and punishment are recalled during the first three days of Wuku Watugunung:

Sunday—Redite-Kajeng-Kliwon-Watugunung—is called Pamelastali Labuh Watugunung, meaning 'the day of the fall of Watugunung'.

Monday—Soma-(U)manis-Watugunung—is called Sandung Watang, meaning 'the day when the body is thrown to the ground'.

Tuesday—Anggara-Wage-Watugunung (also a Kajeng day)—is called Paid Paidan. It refers to the day when Watugunung's body is dragged on the ground.

During these three days, Bali is in a state of maximum impurity. Sexual intercourse is forbidden. It is also forbidden to sweep the floor or to tower above anything, for fear of offending the gods. On the Tuesday, women are also forbidden to comb their hair, probably a reference to the scene with the comb from the Watugunung story.

Wuku Watugunung (30), days 4–6: Toward enlightenment

The next three days of this week are focused on the process leading to Watugunung's enlightenment:

Wednesday—Buda-Pon-Watugunung—is called Urip, meaning 'life'. It refers to the 'return to life' when Siwa resuscitates Watugunung after Wisnu has killed him.

Thursday—Wrespati-Wage-Watugunung—is known as Penegtegan, which means 'confirmation'. It refers to the time that Siwa once again brings Watugunung back to life after Wisnu has killed him yet again.

Friday—Sukra-Kliwon-Watugunung—is called Pangeredanan, meaning 'illumination' or 'enlightenment'. It refers to the time when Watugunung worships Siwa.

Wuku Watugunung (30), day 7: Illumination and enlightenment—the worship of Saraswati

Saturday—Saniscara-(U)manis-Watugunung—is called Saraswati Day, and relates to the day when Watugunung achieves full enlightenment or illumination. It is the last day of both Wuku Watugunung, as well as the whole calendar cycle. It is also the day when the goddess of knowledge, Saraswati, as well as all the other gods, descend from their celestial abode and visit every temple in the island.

On Saraswati day, offerings are made to books and manuscripts, and worshippers also visit the priests and healers they may have consulted during the year and present them with ritual offerings. It is a day for the consecration of knowledge.

Wuku Sinta (1), days 1–4: Purity restored

On Sunday—Redite-Paing-Tungleh-Sinta—the first day of Wuku Sinta, as well as the first day of the new Pawukon cycle, falls the holy day Banyu Pinaruh. Literally, Banyu Pinaruh means 'separation by water' or, according to a variant source, 'water of knowledge'. In both cases, the reference to purification is clear.

On this occasion, the Balinese go en masse to the sea or to designated water holes for a purification bath. The new start of the calendar demands the purification of the soul.

Monday—Soma-Pon-Sinta—the second day of the new cycle, is called Soma Ribek, meaning 'full Monday'. Offerings are presented in the rice storehouses (*lumbung*) to the goddess of rice, Sri. It is also prohibited to sleep during the daytime on Soma Ribek.

According to R. Goris in his article on "Holidays and Holy Days" (1984), on this day "the person who does homage with his face turned to the west will make a profit in business. Whoever turns his face to the northwest will find good fortune; to the east, misfortune and illness threaten him; to the southeast, he will experience pleasant things; to the south, he will be robbed; to the southeast, he will acquire health."

Tuesday—Anggara-Kajeng-Sinta—is called Sabuh Mas, perhaps meaning 'gilded gold'. Offerings are presented to the protector gods of riches, in particular Sri's consort, Sedana. The protector of the gold and riches is Mahadewa, the guardian of the west.

Wednesday—Buda-Kliwon-Sinta—is called Pagerwesi, meaning 'iron gate', and marks the definitive closure of the cycle of purification. Offerings are presented to all the gods in their shrines, in particular to Paramesti Guru, the Supreme Teacher. Offerings are also presented to ancestral graves.

Goris says that on Pagerwesi, "The *pedanda* pay homage to the *linggam* as the symbol of Siwa." He interprets this as a prayer for fertility, but Siwa as *guru* and *lingam* may well be a reminder of the incest and a warning against it. This makes sense since this day also marks the end of the period of celibacy imposed at the beginning of Wuku Watugunung.

On the *tika* (calendar charts) examined in Chapter 3, we saw that the first four days of the new cycle and of Wuku Sinta correspond to the four repeated Dangu days of the nine-day week. As noted before, this anomaly underlines the importance of the break with the impurity of Wuku Watugunung. Dangu, meaning 'the time of origin', confirms that this break, accomplished through the separation of the incestuous mother and son, is the origin of human order and consciousness.

The various celebrations and rites of the Pawukon 'New Year' thus confirm the interpretation of the myth given here. The process of purification of the island thus parallels, through the enactment of the rites and taboos prescribed on these weeks, the process experienced by the culture hero Watugunung.

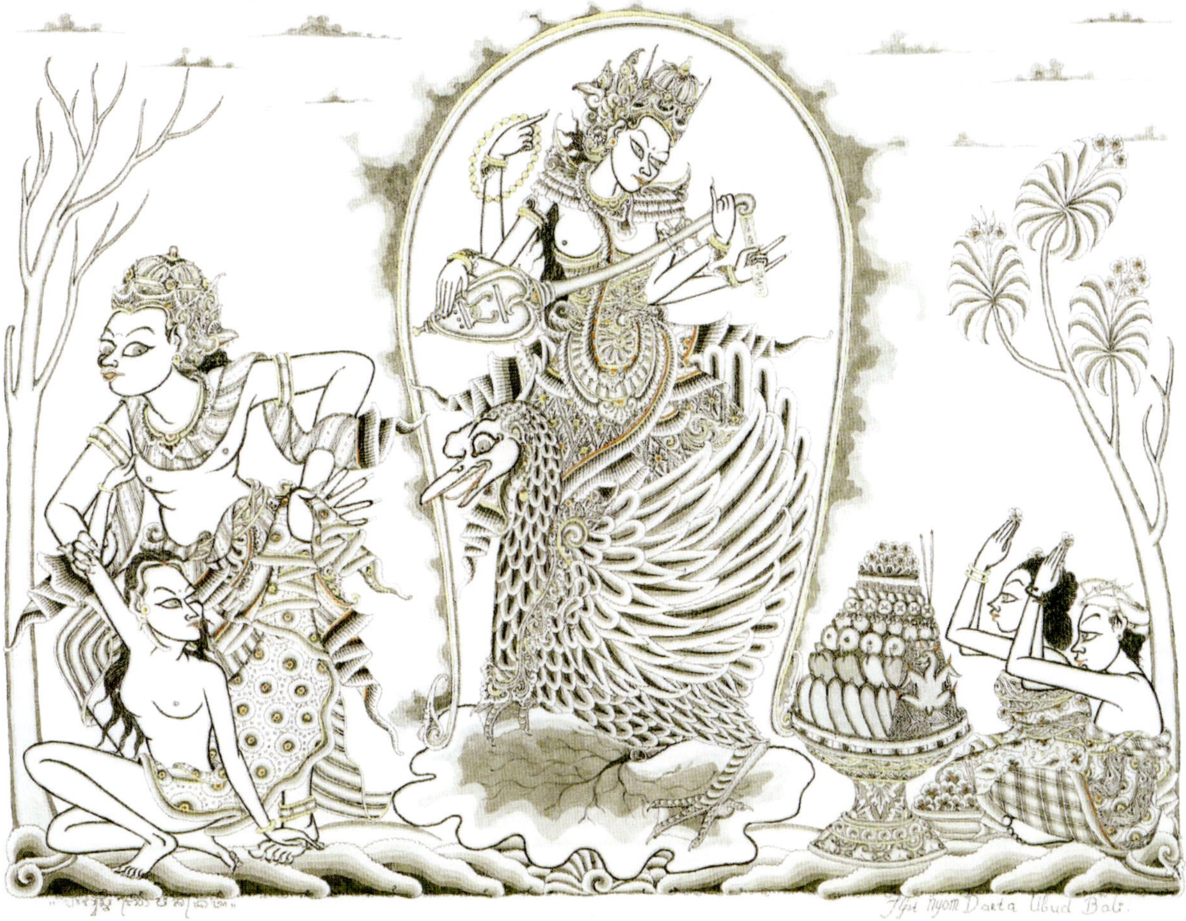

THE ENLIGHTENMENT OF WATUGUNUNG BY SARASWATI: This drawing depicts the life of Watugunung and Sita before (at left) and after (at right) their enlightenment and restoration to purity by Saraswati, goddess of knowledge and consciousness (center). There are many representations of Saraswati. In offerings she is sometimes symbolized by a small lizard (*cecak*) reputed to be able to talk to humans. There is also a more modern, Indian-influenced iconography in use, representing her as a beautiful woman with various attributes, as shown here. She holds a string of prayer beads representing infinite knowledge; a stringed instrument (*rebab*) representing music, and a *lontar* representing literature. The goose, her vehicle, symbolizes her aptitude for knowledge; and the lotus, her base, is a classical symbol of the cosmos.

The last week of the calendar cycle is all about Watugunung's humiliation, defeat, and enlightenment. He is thrown to the ground and then put to death, again and again, by Wisnu before being resuscitated, again and again, by Siwa and various other gods, and finally appointed master of the calendar by Siwa.

Moreover, at the beginning of Wuku Watugunung, sexual abstinence is required, a taboo that lasts until the fourth day of the new calendar cycle, Pagerwesi. Mother and son, having been separated, there is a general prohibition of sexual relations for 11 days.

Interestingly, when Watugunung is finally resuscitated on the last day of the calendar cycle, it is the day of Saraswati, Brahma's consort and the Balinese goddess of knowledge. When Siwa brings Watugunung to life, it indicates the hero's apotheosis and enlightenment by knowledge. Siwa makes him understand that in being appointed master of the calendar, Watugunung becomes the master of time, of the rituals, and of culture.

As for human beings, by celebrating rituals that re-enact the process of defilement and ultimate illumination of their culture hero, they partake in his enlightenment and are purified by it.

Major Holy Days between 'New Year' and Galungan (wuku 2–9)

During the next seven weeks of the cycle (wuku 2–8), there are a variety of holy days on special conjunction days (Buda-Kliwon, Tumpek, Buda-Cemeng, and Anggarakasih), along with days consecrated to the worship of a particular deity.

Wuku Landep (2): Tumpek Landep

Saturday—Saniscara-Kliwon-Landep—is Tumpek Landep, a day dedicated to objects made of metal. The word *landep*, which is also the name of Watugunung's stepmother, means 'sharp'. This is a very important day for blacksmiths, or *pande*. Offerings are presented to *keris*, spears, and other traditional weapons, as well as to vehicles and modern appliances. On this day, no sharp objects may be used. Special worship is addressed to Siwa in his manifestation as Pasupati.

Wuku Ukir (3): The Worship of Batara Guru and Batari Sri

Sunday—Radite-(U)manis-Ukir—is a day of worship to Batara Guru, who is also seen, according to Goris, as one's father. Ukir is the Giriswara of the Watugunung story and, according to one informant, Watugunung's lost father. As Ukir opens the next 26 wuku down to Watugunung, its location here could also symbolize, besides fertility (the mountain), a barrier to incest by the father. Offerings are presented to Batara Guru on this day at the family's shrine of origin.

Friday—Sukra-(U)manis-Ukir—is a day of worship to Sri, the goddess of rice and protector of agriculture.

Wuku Kulantir (4): The Worship of Mahadewa

On Tuesday—Anggara-Kliwon-Kulantir—yellow offerings are addressed in the family shrine to Mahadewa, the god of Gunung Agung, Bali's highest and holiest mountain.

Wuku Wariga (7): Tumpek Uduh

Saturday—Saniscara-Kliwon-Wariga—is Tumpek Uduh (also called Tumpek Pengatag or Tumpek Pangarah), a day dedicated to plants, particularly trees, which are dressed in sarongs, hats, and even keris daggers, while offerings are presented to them on small bamboo shrines. Worship is addressed to Siwa in the form of Batara Sangkara, the lord of all crops. The words *uduh*, *atag*, and *arah* all mean 'announce', and on this day one notifies one's crops that Galungan will be celebrated in 25 days' time.

Wuku Warigadian (8): The worship of Brahma

On Monday—Soma-Paing-Warigadian—prayers are addressed to Brahma, the creator. This is done with offerings symbolizing the *paibon*, or Mother Earth Pertiwi.

The Galungan Ceremonial Cycle (Wuku 10–12)

The ceremonies of the Galungan-Kuningan cycle are, to modern Balinese, the most important of the Pawukon cycle. They span 19 days between Buda-Pon of Wuku Sungsang (wuku 10) and the Tumpek in Wuku Kuningan (wuku 12). From Galungan, which falls on the Buda-Kliwon of Wuku Dungulan (wuku 11), down to Tumpek Kuningan, all the ancestral divinities come and visit their descendants. They are welcomed and celebrated in their 'residences' in family temples and village temples.

The Galungan-Kuningan ceremonial cycle runs as follows:

Wuku Sungsang (10): Sugihan

Wednesday—Buda-Pon-Sungsang—is called Sugihan Pengenten, meaning 'the awakening of prosperity'. On this day, the tutelary protectors of the villages, known as Barong (see the illustration opposite) begin *nglawang* (door-to-door tours) of their villages to placate negative influences.

On Thursday—Wrespati-Wage-Sungsang—offerings are made to ensure prosperity throughout the world. The name of this day is Sugihan Jawa, meaning 'prosperity of Java' since Java was traditionally considered to represent the larger world or macrocosm.

The ancestors are invited to come down to Bali. They are addressed in this way: "Mai jani mulih. Uba yang ngaenang banten. Mai delokin damuh?

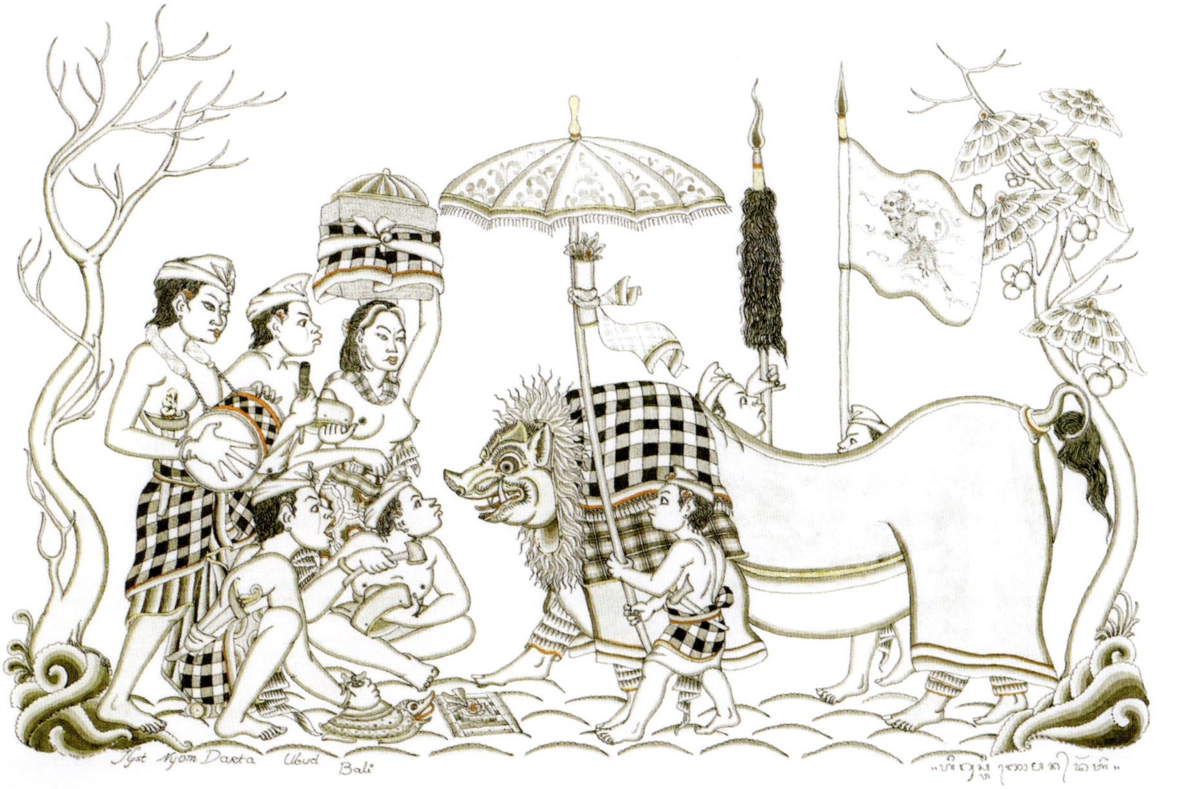

GALUNGAN: Between the Galungan and Kuningan holy days, the Barong, tutelary protector of the village, is taken around to cleanse the land of destructive influences. There are several types of Barong. The most common is the Barong Ket, inspired by both the tiger and the lion. It is said to be Raja Banaspati, or 'lord of the forest'. The Barong represented in this illustration is the pig-headed Barong Bangkung or Barong Celeng, which has a similar function to that of the Barong Ket. It usually stops to perform from door to door (*nglawang*). A woman carries on her head a basket containing a mask of Ratu Sakti, the Barong's eternal foe, who is none other than the witch Rangda, a manifestation of Durga.

Damuhe!", which is Low Balinese meaning "Come! come! I have prepared offerings for you. Come and visit your descendants."

This call is addressed to the liberated souls, that is, those who, after cremation have gone through the purification cycle and have become ancestral deities. Offerings must also be made to other souls who are still hovering around the cemeteries, in order to placate them.

The next day, Friday—Sukra-Kliwon-Sungsang (also a Kajeng day)—is called Sugihan Bali. It is dedicated to the purification of Bali in preparation for when the ancestors will come down to visit their kin.

Wuku Dungulan (11): Galungan days

The first three days of Wuku Dungulan are dedicated to preparations for the festival of Galungan proper, which falls on the fourth day. These three days are of special importance because Kala Tiga, or 'three demons', are thought to be visiting and may disturb the proceedings underway. During this wuku, the days Kala of the eight-day week and the days Jaya of the four-day week are repeated three times in a row. This warns that one must avoid the influence of the three demons of Galungan.

The first day, Sunday—Redite-Paing-Dungulan—is called Penyekeban, meaning that the demons are descending. Unripe bananas are burned in earthenware containers with some coconut as offerings. The bananas will also be used later as offerings during the festival.

The second day, Monday—Soma-Pon-Dungulan—is called Penyajahan Galungan, meaning 'preparation of the offerings'.

The third day, Tuesday—Anggara-Wage-Dungulan—is called Penampahan Galungan, meaning

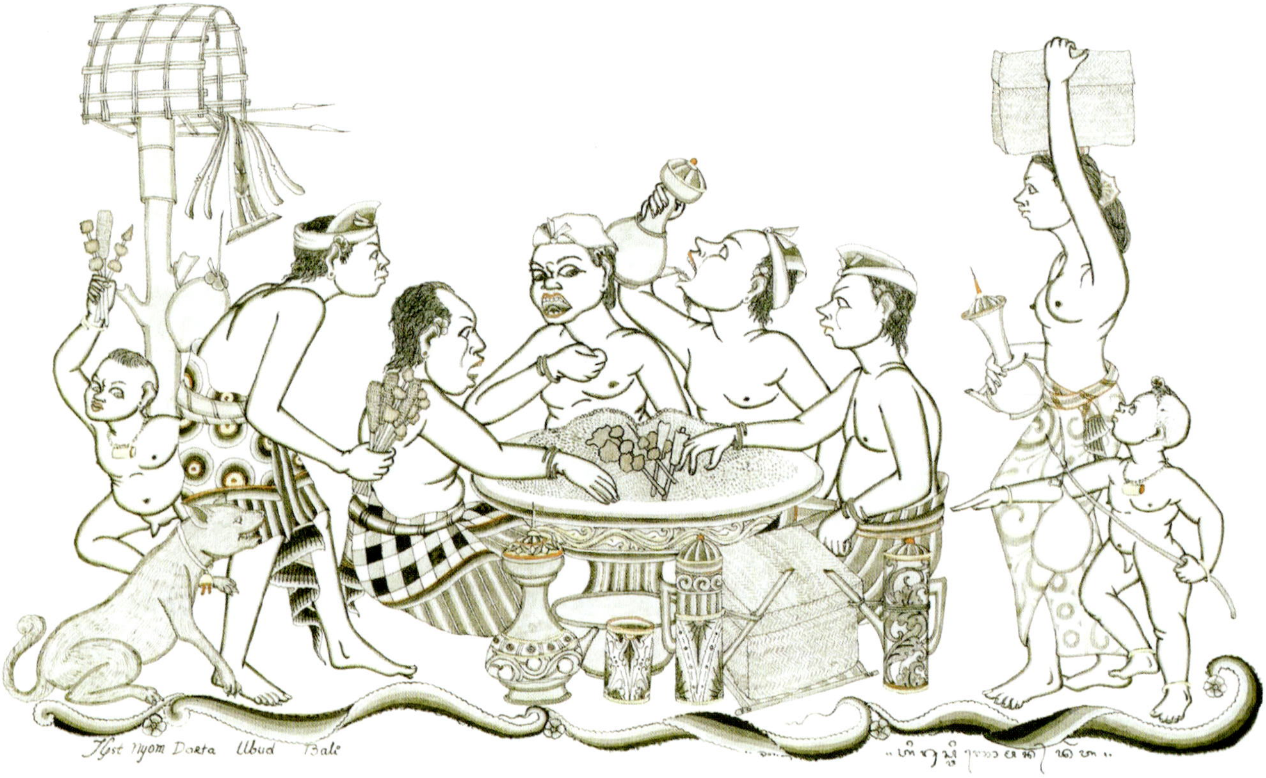

MEGIBUNG: During important holy days, such as Kuningan, the Balinese hold big collective feasts. In some villages, like the one shown in the illustration, they share food on large platters. Notice the bamboo shrine (*sanggah saksi*), at upper left, seat of the Sun god, the ultimate witness (*saksi*).

'slaughter', as pigs are slaughtered. *Penjor*, long bamboo poles hung with elaborate palm-leaf ornaments symbolizing the cosmic dragon Anantaboga, are prepared and erected in front of house gates, and the shrines in the temples are decorated with pieces of cloth of various colors, each symbolizing a different god.

These three days are marked by intense activity. Most of the work is done by women. They are responsible for preparing the ritual food, weaving the numerous plaited offerings out of coconut palm leaves, and organizing the three types of offerings that will be presented to the divine visitors: for gods (*dewa*), for humans (*manusa*), and for demons (*buta*). But the men do not stay idle as they must prepare the penjor, as well as build the small altars (*sanggah cucuk*) that go with the penjor. They also clean the streets in the village.

Wednesday—Buda-Kliwon-Dungulan—is the day of the festival of Galungan proper. All Balinese and their families visit the temples to which they are ritually affiliated and present their offerings. Offerings are presented with a short prayer and then taken back home and eaten by the worshippers. In fact, the gods only demand the 'essence' of the offerings.

In the ten days between Galungan and Kuningan, during which the gods are in residence in the temples, there is a succession of other important days, such as Thursday—Wrespati-(U)manis-Dungulan—a day to visit family and friends.

Saturday—Saniscara-Pon-Dungulan—is called Pamaridan Guru, the day for worshipping Batara Guru (Siwa) and the removal of the last Galungan offerings.

Wuku Kuningan (12): Kuningan

Sunday—Redite-Wage-Kuningan—is called Ulihan Jawa, meaning the day when 'the ancestors from Java go back home'.

Monday—Soma-Kliwon-Kuningan—is called Ulihan Bali ("Ancestors from Bali go home") or Pamecekan Agung ('great nailing'). This holy day closes a period of danger. Offerings are made to placate the three demons of Galungan, which are literally 'nailed' (*pacek*).

On Wednesday—Buda-Paing-Kuningan—the god Wisnu is worshipped.

Friday—Sukra-Wage-Kuningan—is called Penampahan Kuningan, meaning 'slaughter (of pig) ahead of Kuningan'. Pigs are slaughtered both for offerings and food for the following day.

Saturday—Saniscara-Kliwon-Kuningan—which is known as Tumpek Kuningan, is the last day of the Galungan-Kuningan cycle. On this day, it is time to send the ancestors who have been celebrated back to the invisible world where they belong. They are told to proceed with no delay: "Mangkin mantuk ke kedituan!" (Go back to where you belong!'). On this day, a great many festivals are held in temples around the island.

Wuku Langkir (13): Manis Kuningan

The following Sunday—Redite-(U)manis)-Langkir—is called Manis Kuningan even though it falls during Wuku Langkir. This is another day for visiting relatives and friends.

The Meaning and Importance of the Galungan-Kuningan Cycle

How do we interpret the Galungan-Kuningan cycle of festivals? What do they mean, and why are they are so important to the Balinese?

Based on the classical text *Usana Bali*, translated by W. Warna and J. B. Murdha (1986), it is often said that these festivals consecrate the victory of the forces of Good over the forces of Evil. This interpretation is based on a story of the primeval struggle between a Balinese king called Maya Danawa and the gods of the Hindu-Balinese pantheon. The following is an abridged version of the tale:

Once upon a time, in the kingdom of Bedahulu, ruled a king by the name of Maya Danawa, strong and famous, the descendant of the seer Kasiapa and the goddess of the Lake, Dewi Danu. But Maya Danawa was full of arrogance and conceit. He said that the truth lay within the self and, thus, within himself. He would not heed the calls to prayers and offerings issued by Sang Kulputih, the holy priest of Siwa who resided in Besakih on the slopes of Mount Agung.

Because Maya Danawa had forbidden temple festivals and offerings, problems and evils were afflicting Bali at an alarming rate. Failing crops and raging epidemics were proof of the gods' growing vexation. Eventually, Sang Kulputih asked for the gods' assistance to defeat Maya Danawa. And so, the gods, summoned from Jambudwipa by Pasupati (Siwa), came to Bali to attack the evil king, accompanied by their troops. All the gods were there: Wisnu, the Green Lord of the South; Mahadewa, the Yellow Lord of the West; and lswara, the White Lord of the East. All had been summoned to destroy the evil king, under the orders of Indra, the king of the gods.

Maya Danawa was assisted by troops from all over Nusantara, including regiments of Sasak, Bugis, Sumbawan, and Madurese soldiers. But despite their valor, there was not much they could do against the superior force of the gods. After their fierce encounter in battle, the king had to flee. In flight, he had further adventures that explain the names of the present-day villages and landmarks located along his mythical escape route.

Several interpretations of the story of Maya Danawa are possible. The common modern Balinese interpretation is that it is about the fight against the neglect of religion and wickedness. A few Balinese, however, interpret it as a story about the historical fall of Buddhism as the dominant political and religious power of the island, and of the Buddhist emphasis on individual enlightenment over the blind practice of presenting offerings to the gods.

However, completely different stories may also be invoked to explain the origins of Galungan-Kuningan. For example, in another part of *Usana Bali*, the foundation of Galungan is attributed to the mythical king Jayakusunu, who is said to have established these festivals to placate evil influences that were causing Balinese kings to die before their due age.

Yet, none of these stories satisfactorily explain why the Galungan-Kuningan cycle seems to be more important than the 'New Year' cycle. In answer to this question, Goris (1984) speculates that the Galungan-Kuningan festivities once marked the end of the calendar cycle and ushered in a new cycle that began with Wuku Langkir.

In support of this theory, he also notes that the ancestors descend to earth and reside in their shrines before returning to heaven, in four phases, each of which begins with a Kliwon day. Further, the first days of the three most important wara (Saptawara, Pancawara, and Sadwara) all fall on the first day of Wuku Langkir, right after Kuningan, whereas none occur on Banyu Pinaruh, the first day of the current 'New Year'.

This theory is debatable. Why emphasize, with Goris, the role of the Pancawara, Saptawara, and Sadwara rather than that of the Wuku 'New Year', as we do, especially since the first day of Wuku Sinta corresponds to the beginning of the cycles of six wara (all except Ekawara, Dwiwara, Pancawara, and Daswara); and Wuku Sinta is also the occasion for the highly symbolic calendar adjustments discussed earlier (the four Dangu of the Sangawara)?

Indeed, the word *langkir* is often associated in Balinese tradition with the idea of the mountain. One of the ancient names of Mount Agung, the largest and holiest mountain in Bali, is Tolangkir, the 'Man of the Mountain'. This may refer to the ancestor-cum-mountain cult, which holds that the mountain is the residence of the gods and the ancestor-deities. Every Balinese room is provided with a *pelangkiran*, a shrine set up just below the ceiling in the eastern-mountainward corner (*kaja*) of the room. Through this shrine offerings are regularly made to the gods and ancestral deities. Should we also relate this to Ukir and Wuku Langkir? It is perhaps too far-fetched.

Goris misses the key role of the incestuous union and separation of Watugunung and Sinta as the foundation for the Pawukon calendar. As seen in our earlier discussion of the Pawukon 'New Year', the incestuous union is an act of natural, and thus demonic fertility, which is then 'humanized' by the introduction of the incest prohibition and human consciousness of time, which are then regulated by the ritual and agricultural calendar.

Both the Pawukon 'New Year' and the Galungan-Kuningan cycle are important moments of the calendar. To us, however, the primacy remains with the 'New Year', even if the Galungan-Kuningan ceremonies, owing to their positive connotations of welcoming home the ancestors and praying for prosperity, have become more important than the ceremonies of the 'New Year', tainted as it is by the ambiguity of the incest phenomenon.

The desire of the Balinese to attain prosperity may be fulfilled through the Galungan-Kuningan cycle of rituals only after the incest defilement has found its proper resolution through purification and enlightenment, as celebrated in the 'New Year' cycle of the calendar.

The Six Tumpek

Every 35 days, on the crossing of the Saturday (Saniscara) of the 7-day week and the Kliwon of the 5-day week, recurs a Tumpek ritual day, in which an important aspect of Balinese life is celebrated at the end of the corresponding week. There are six Tumpek, the celebration of which is the object of many temple festivals throughout the island:

- To metallic implements and weapons on Tumpek Landep, on the 2nd wuku week;
- To plants on Tumpek Uduh (or Wariga), falling on the 7th week;
- To ancestors on Tumpek Kuningan, on the 12th week;
- To art and music on Tumpek Krulut, falling on the 17th week;
- To domestic animals on Tumpek Kandang, on the 22nd week; and finally, to cosmic forces, through the *wayang* puppet show theater on Tumpek Wayang, falling on the 27th week of the 210-day Pawukon cycle (which consists of 30 wuku weeks).

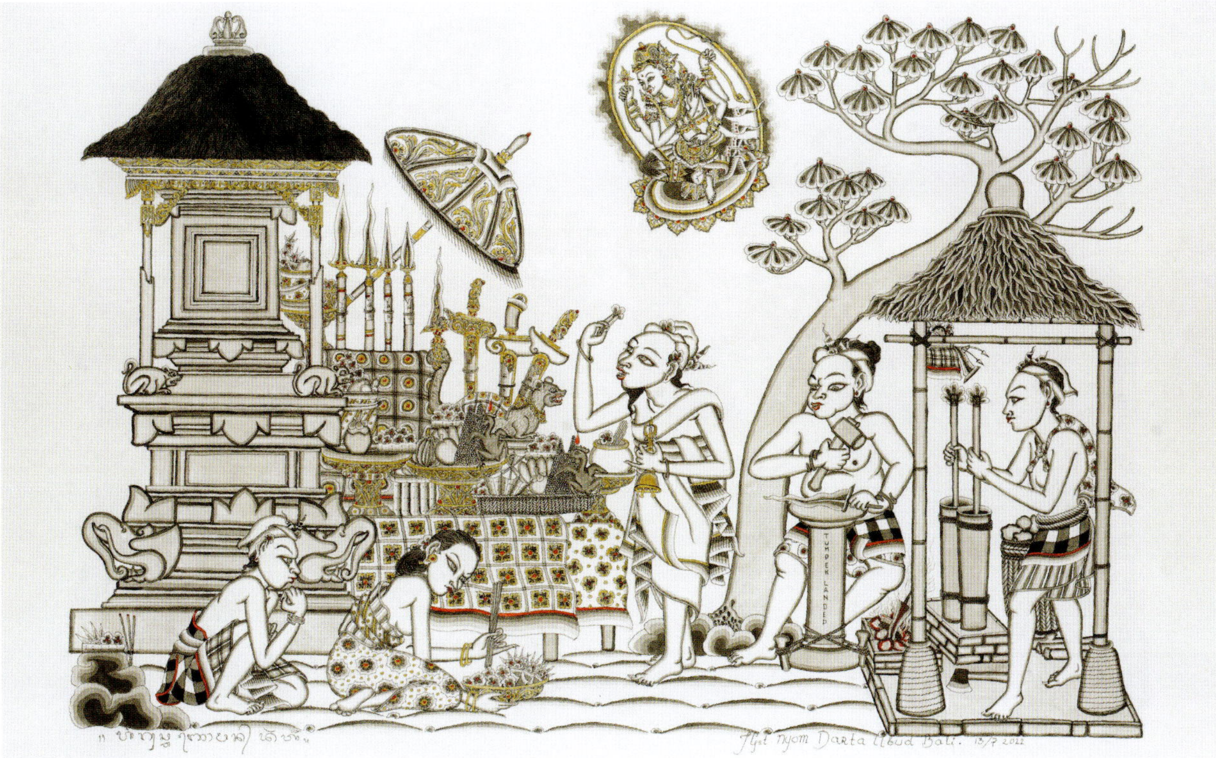

Tumpek Landep

Honoring metal objects and tools (especially weapons, vehicles, and work instruments) as symbols of sharpness of mind and skill.

Falling on the second wuku week of the Balinese 210-day Pawukon calendar, Tumpek Landep is the day reserved by the Balinese for paying homage to all metal objects and tools. These comprise daily objects, agricultural and other implements, and weapons. These objects, in particular weapons, are presented with offerings that aim to *nguripang* or 'activate their power'. Modern objects made of metal, like cars, motorbikes, and machines, are included and are also presented with offerings, often to the surprise and pleasure of visitors to Bali. *Landep* means 'sharp' in Balinese, and Tumpek Landep is said to celebrate the sharpness of the intellect.

Typically, the ritual sequence is that the objects are first cleansed and then decorated with *janur* coconut leaves (sometimes shaped as *sampian*) or tricolor (*tridatu*) thread symbolizing the three sacred colors of red, black, and white. A ritual offering (*puja*) is performed in the family temple (*merajan*) or work space, and then holy water (*tirta*) is sprinkled onto the objects.

The illustration above represents the Tumpek Landep as celebrated in the morning by the kinship group most concerned with metal working—Bali's famous blacksmiths (*pande*). One of them is using a *penglamusan*, a traditional forge bellows consisting of two wooden cylinders within which are two wooden pistons that are activated up and down in order to suck and expel the required volume of air to continuously blow air to the red metal waiting in front of the penglamusan. The second blacksmith is seen shaping the metal with a hammer. Standing next to him is a priest (*mangku*), a bell (*kleneng*) in hand, sprinkling holy water onto the various objects produced at the workshop: four types of *keris* daggers in front and four spears up the ladder in front of the family shrine.

In front of the priest is a yellow-husked coconut (*nyuh gading*) used to hold holy water. Meanwhile, the seated couple on the lower left have presented offerings (*ayaban*) on the ground. Overlooking the situation, in a divine aura, is Siwa as Pasupati.

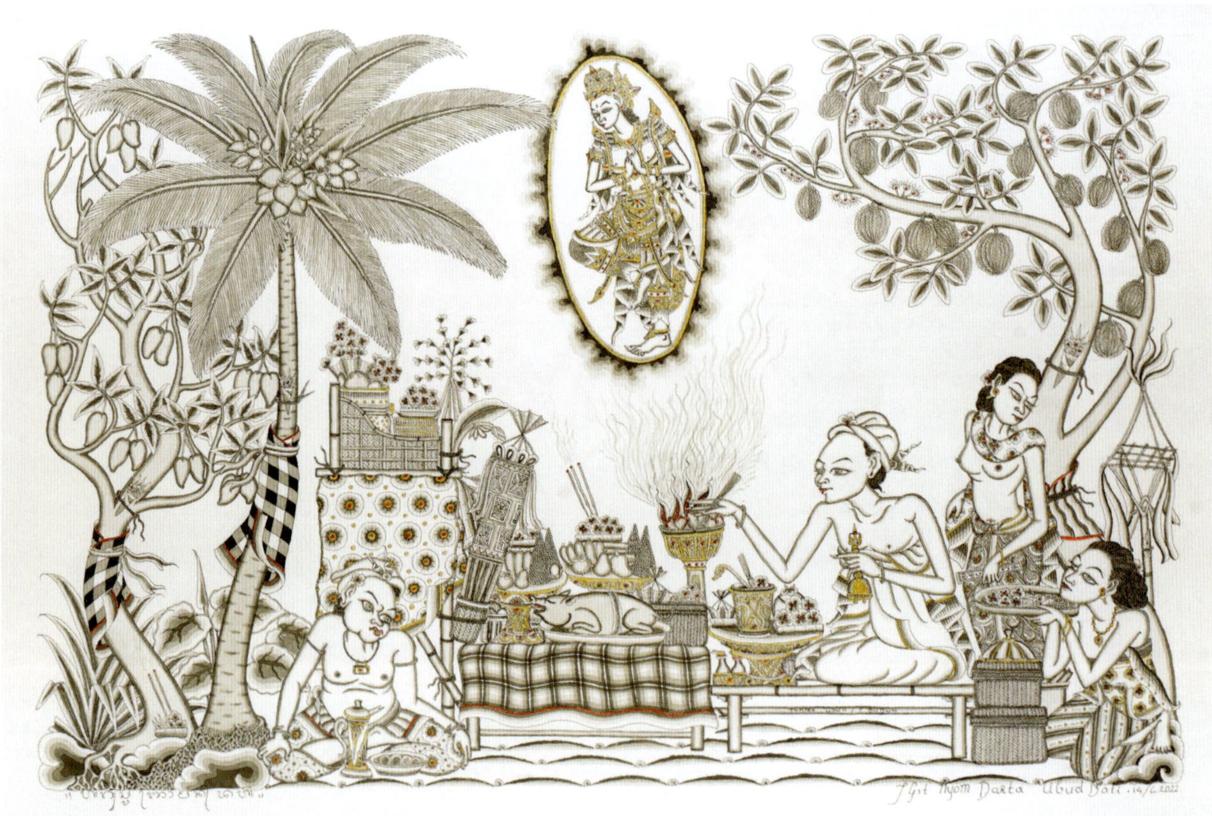

Tumpek Wariga (Tumpek Pengatag)
Honoring plants and trees, asking for fertility and blessings for crops.

The Tumpek Wariga, also called Tumpek Uduh or Tumpek Pengatag, falling on the 7th wuku week of the Pawukon calendar, is dedicated to plants: trees, crops, forests, in short, all vegetation. It falls 25 days before Galungan on the crossing of the Saniscara (Saturday) of the 7-day Saptawara week with the Kliwon of the 5-day Pancawara week during the Wuku Wariga.

Plants are celebrated because they are said to have *eka pramana*, one of the three elements (*tripramana*) of living nature: the *bayu* principle of power; they grow. Only humans have the three elements of life: *bayu* (growth), *sabda* (voice), and *idep* (thought). Animals, however, have only two.

The illustration is a good representation of what takes place. Notice that the trees are 'dressed' with black and white checkered cloth (*poleng*), causing them to be animated by living power. On the trees next to the woman's head the minuscule *kwangen* offering tied to the trunk is said to symbolize the *Ongkara*, the sound symbol (*Omkara*) of God throughout the Indianized world. To the left, the priest is presenting a set of offerings, including a roast suckling pig and a sophisticated offering (*jrimpen*). The god protecting the event in the aura in the middle is Wisnu. To the right, behind the women, is a small woven shrine (*sanggah cucuk*) for exorcism addressed to Pertiwi, Mother Earth. Tirta mixed with roasted coconut and rice may be sprinkled on plant roots, symbolically 'feeding' them. Community offerings are also presented at rice field *subak* temples.

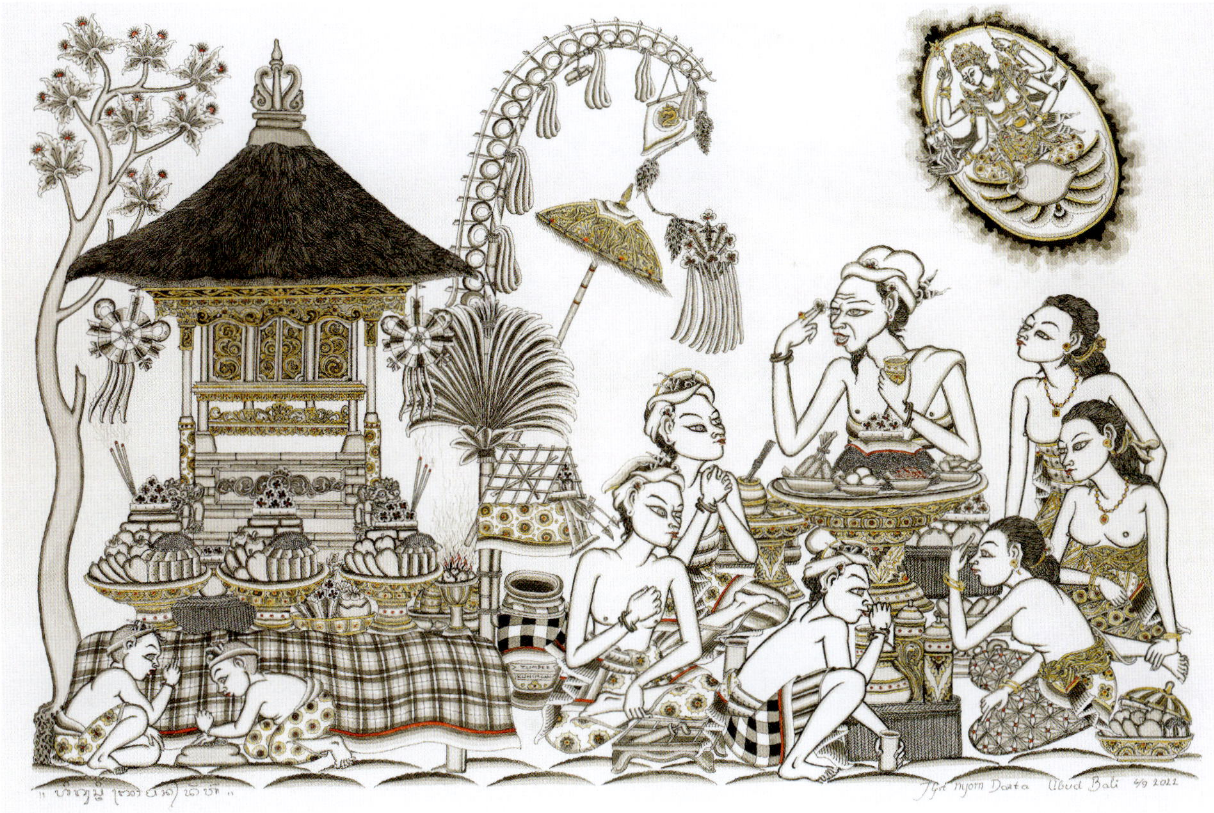

Tumpek Kuningan

The closing day of the Galungan-Kuningan cycle, dedicated to the ancestors.

Dedicated to the ancestors, which are at the core of the Balinese belief system, the Tumpek Kuningan, which falls on the Wuku Kuningan (the 12th week of the Pawukon calendar), closes the 10-day Galungan-Kuningan cycle of ceremonies. All the ancestors in Bali, who have come down for a visit on Galungan, now take leave to go back to their abode on Kuningan.

The image is self-explanatory. It shows the three-door ancestral shrine (*pelinggih*) set within the Balinese *sanggah kemulan/mrajan* temple, with the central guru in the middle. Special Kuningan offerings, prepared the previous day, are presented with prayers before midday, lest demonic *buta* forces interfere with the ritual. One can see ordinary Kuningan offerings, banana and other fruits, flanked by incense sticks. Children play in front of the shrine, while other family members share a collective dish. The god overlooking the situation above right is Sanghyang Paramesti Guru, a manifestation of Siwa as spiritual teacher who is also linked to ancestral spirits (*pitara*), represented by the two small figures in his hand.

Offerings are presented in all the main points of the household: beside the sanggah kemulan above, at the various *bale* pavilions, in the kitchen, and in the rice barn. Other offerings are taken to the clan temple and the main village temples, all before noon.

Most interesting is the way people address their ancestors, as if they were living guests, with the appropriate level of language: "Grand-Ma, Grand Pa, who are still in the ancestral shrine, here is food (offering) which I present you as my thanks to you. May you provide our family with happiness and prosperity."

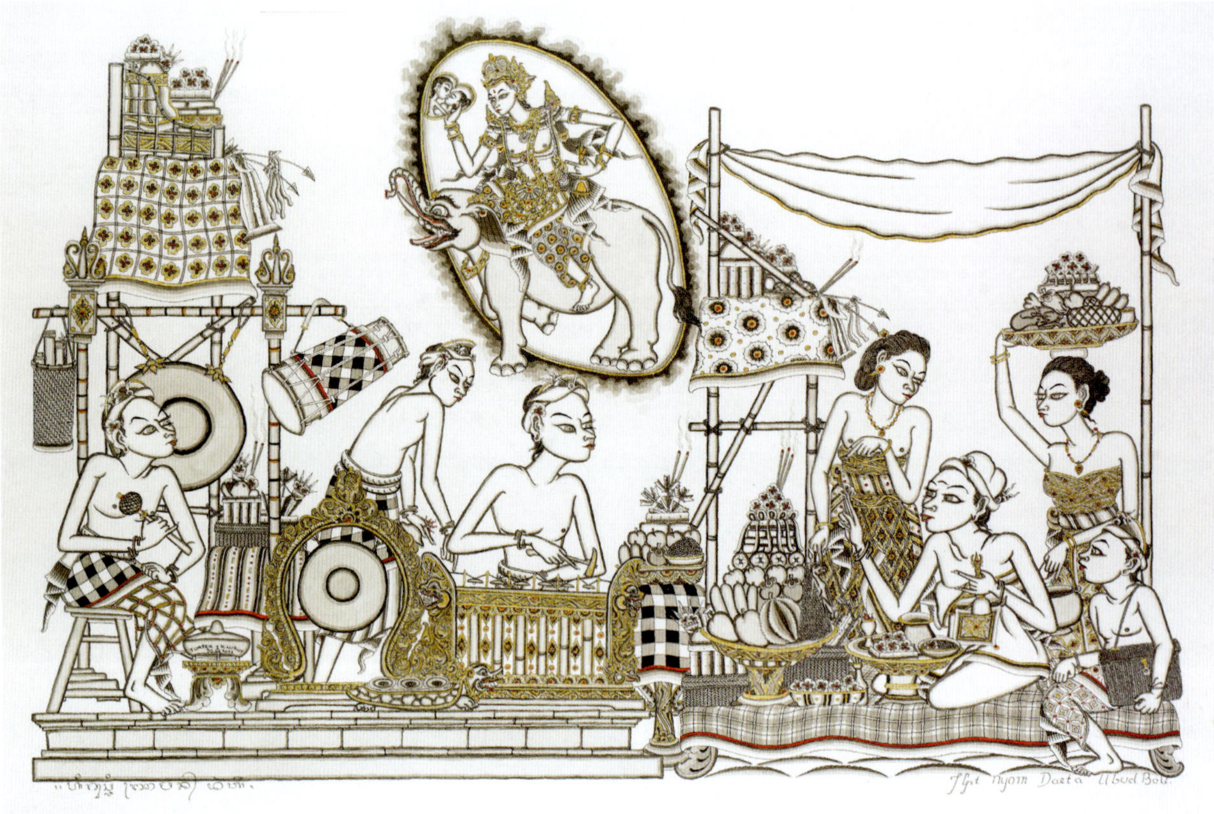

Tumpek Krulut

Honoring the arts, music, and culture, especially instruments like the gamelan.

Tumpek Krulut, also called Tumpek Gong, falls on the Krulut wuku week (the 17th of the Pawukon calendar) and is dedicated to traditional arts, music, and dance.

Here, the celebrant on the right, bell in hand, is presenting offerings to a complete set of musical instruments and performance-related objects: gamelan sets, dance masks, costumes, etc. Overseeing the scene is the god Iswara. Offerings are made in private to one's musical and performance implements, if any, but also to any place or temple holding such instruments. Iswara holds two lovers in his hand.

In the illustration, the offerings are presented on bamboo altars, but in reality they may be directly placed on gamelan sets, dance costumes, masks, etc. The offerings are accompanied by prayers addressed to Iswara or any other god, along with a request for protection: "Today on this Krulut day, I am presenting you with these offerings of mine so that you, Oh God, bearer of the Word, guarantee the power of my word, the charm of my voice, the beauty of my art works, and grant us cohesion in our performances."

The importance of Tumpek Krulut is in line with the role played by art performances as 'offerings' accompanying the presence of the visiting gods during temple festivals and other ceremonies.

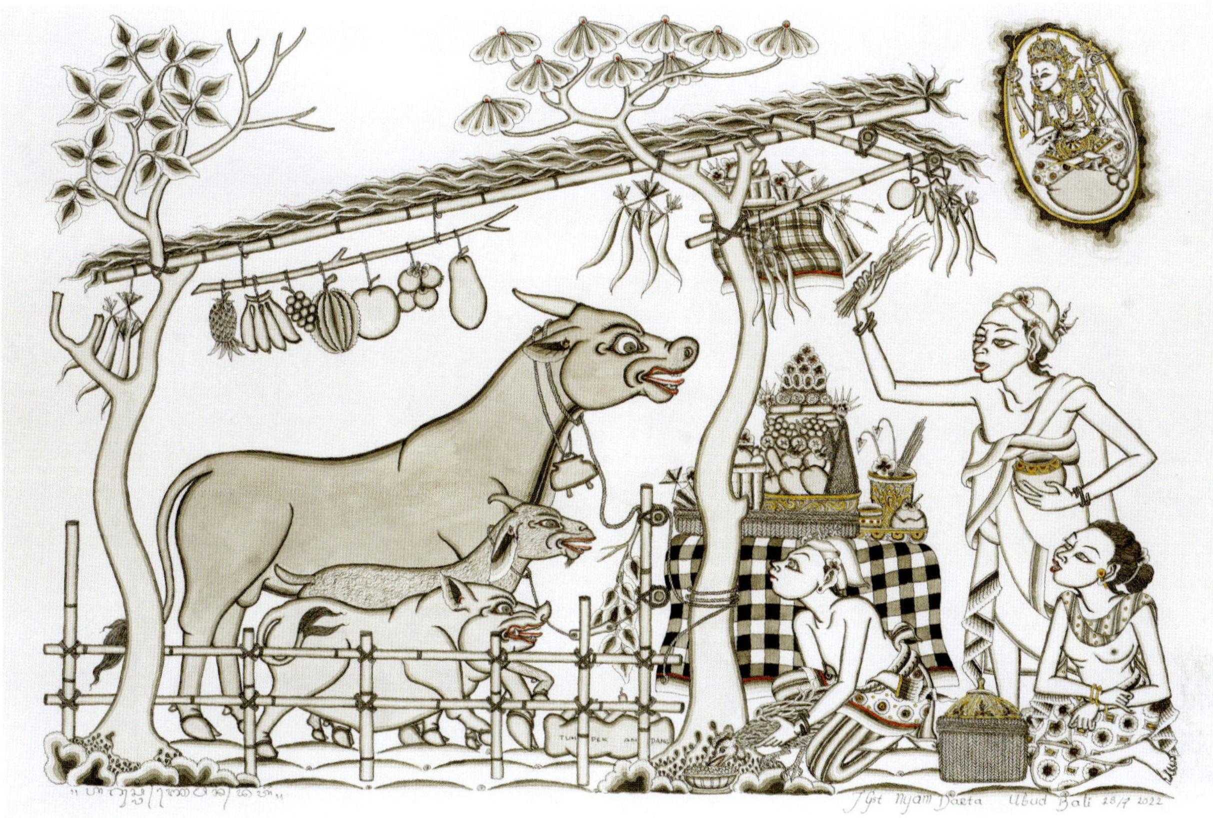

Tumpek Kandang (Tumpek Uye)
Honoring animals, especially livestock, for their role in human life.

The Tumpek Kandang, also called Tumpek Uye, which falls on the Uye wuku week (the 22nd of the Pawukon calendar), is dedicated to domestic animals. While humans possess three principles of life (*Tripramana*) consisting of *bayu* (life/energy), *sabda* (voice), and *idep* (thought), animals have two (life and voice), and must therefore be honored as well. As seen above, plants also have their own Tumpek (Tumpek Uduh), because they have one principle (Eka Pramana: life/energy).

The image shows the priest sprinkling water with a 'wand' (*lis*) made of *ilalang* grass held together by a three-color sacred thread bracelet (*tridatu*.) He gets his holy water from a young, tender coconut (*nyuh bungkah*). The ilalang grass symbolizes immortality, whereas the three-color *tridatu* symbolizes the Hindu Trimurti of Brahma, Wisnu, and Siwa. The god overlooking the scene, in the aura top right, is Siwa.

Usually, it is only women, or more precisely housewives, who are involved in the Tumpek Kandang rites, as they are responsible for looking after pets, hens, and cattle and thus feel it is their obligation to look after the welfare of their animals. Yet, for big-scale Tumpek Kandang holy days, which occur every ten years or so, only a temple priest (*pemangku*) or a shaman (*balian sesonteng*) has the authority to 'send up' the offerings to the gods, whereas when modest offerings are concerned, ordinary housewives may do the job.

The scale of the rites depends on the number of animals owned by the family. The more a family owns, the grander the ceremony. The most important ceremonies are found in the mountainous areas, whereas elsewhere a simple ceremony with few *bebanten* offerings, crafted from natural elements, will suffice.

The ceremony usually opens in the morning with a set of offerings addressed to Rare Anggon, the godly herdsman, a manifestation of the god Siwa. However, the rites and offerings dedicated to cows and pigs (*Ngotonin sampi wiadi celeng*) are performed in the evening. At 4:00 p.m., when the sun begins to glide down to its 'royal bed' in the west, the offerings are ready. The pigs and cows have been washed in the river and are therefore ready to be presented with their offerings, which vary according to the animals, whether they are cows, pigs, or pets.

Once the offerings have been presented to the deity, people may eat them, but this does not go without restrictions. For example, only women are allowed to eat the leftovers (*surudan*) of the offerings dedicated to pigs. According to Balinese belief, if the leftovers are eaten by boys (and men, in general), they will become lazy and stupid and even lose their prestige or authority. Yet, the leftovers of the offerings dedicated to cows may be eaten by both men and women after they have been sacrificed to the other animals.

There is, of course, a hierarchy of sorts between animals. Grilled/barbequed pork (*babi guling*) is included in the offerings sacrificed by those who raise only cows. On the other hand, those who raise only pigs just dedicate modest offerings, whereas those who raise chickens, ducks, and other poultry dedicate yet smaller offerings (*mewadah tamas*).

An interesting anecdote is that people may have pledged to make an offering to a female pig (*bangkung*) if this animal gives birth to many piglets. Once the vow has been uttered, the owner must fulfill his/her pledge. He/she will slaughter a piglet and dedicate it to the bangkung herself on the next Tumpek (K)Andang, together with *otonan* offerings such as those normally given for the return of the tumpek after a full Pawukon year. In preparing the offerings, the owner has to perform a strange ceremony: to cut a little part of the piglet's toenail, the tip of its snout, the tip of its tail, the tip of its ears, and a little bit of its hair. Then the female piglet is to be served with the hair and the toenail cut by its owner as a symbol that he or she has fulfilled the vow he/she once made.

Tumpek Wayang

Honoring *wayang* (shadow puppetry) and requesting protection from calamities; often includes rituals for children born on this day.

The Tumpek Wayang, which falls on the closing day of the Wayang wuku week (the 27th of the Pawukon cycle), is considered the birthday of the *wayang*. This day is dedicated to the wayang puppet show theater and related instruments. As such, it is a key ritual day most of all for the puppet master (*dalang*), who makes offerings to his set of puppets, especially to the most sacred ones, the godly buffoons Delem and Sangut, representing the negative and positive sides, respectively. He usually has a shrine in his family temple through which he addresses the 'spirit' of his talent, or *taksu*, that inhabits him during his performances, and through which he communicates with forces from the intangible world.

On Tumpek Wayang, the dalang does not play ordinary stories but a cosmos-dimensioned story, Sapuh Leger, that brings people born during the Wayang Wuku in risky contact with the unfurling of cosmic forces, specifically the vengeful Batara Kala, the god master of time. The playing of Sapuh Leger symbolically produces the water of immortality (*tirta*) needed to cleanse babies under risk born during the Wayang Wuku week.

The origin of this ritual is mythological. It is believed that it goes back to the story of the birth of Batara Kala from a drop of semen fallen into the sea after his father was repelled by his wife Uma. As Siwa feared the consequences for the world of the bad temper of his demonic son, he asked him to cut his canines and thus control his demonic temper. Kala accepted, but on one condition: that he may devour those children born like him on Tumpek Wayang. Siwa accepted. Alas, fate had decided that Siwa's wife was to give birth to another son born on Tumpek Wayang—Dewa Rare Kumara—the god protector of children. When he heard about it, Kala claimed his due: he should be allowed to eat his brother. Siwa and Uma begged him to delay this since Kumara was still a baby. But after he had grown up, there was nothing they could do to prevent their demonic son from going after his prey. Before he could be caught, Dewa Rare

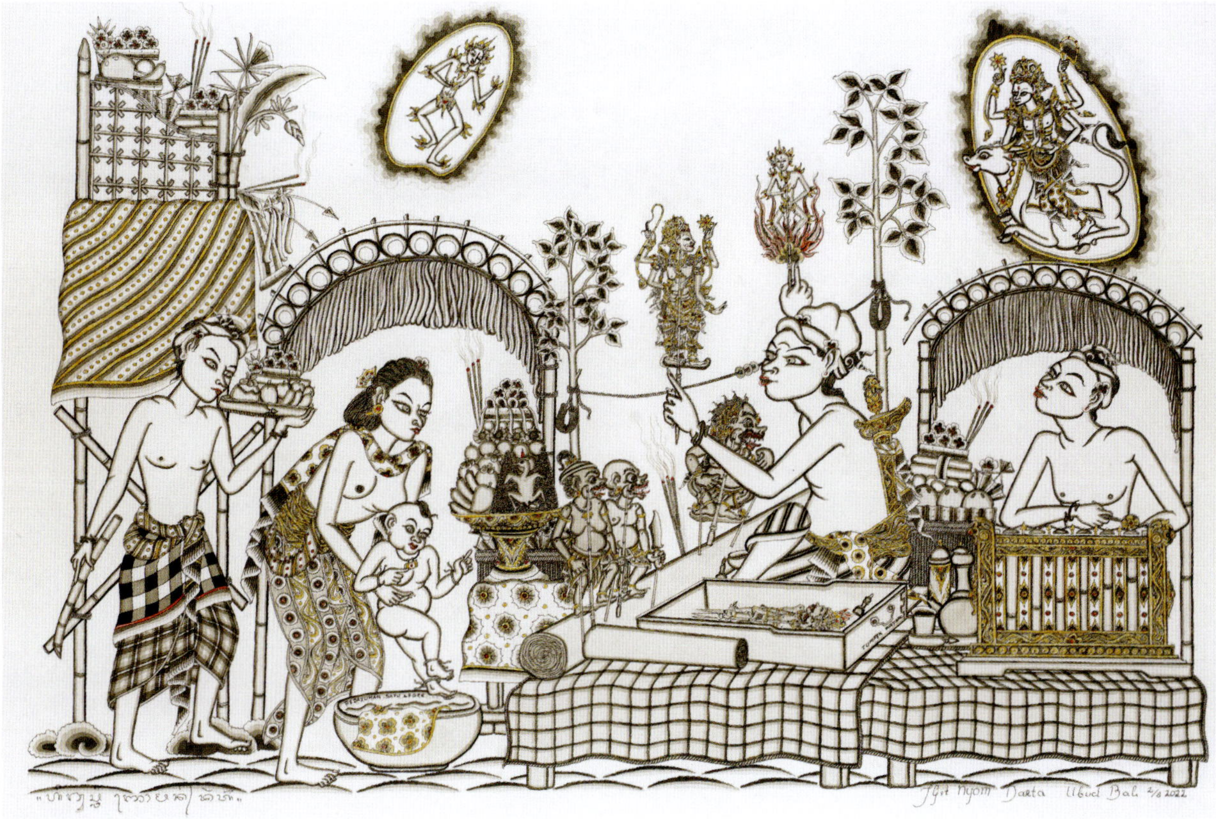

Kumara had fled and taken refuge among humans. Furious, Batara Kala pursued him all over the middle world, wreaking havoc along the way. He was on the verge of catching him when his brother hid in a gamelan, just as the shadow master was performing a cleansing ritual. Seeing offerings there, the hungry Kala carelessly swallowed them. But he had eaten what was not his by fiat of the gods. The dalang was furious and asked for something in return. Ashamed, the demonic god accepted that he give up trying to devour his brother. Since those days gone by, Dewa Rare Kumara is the protector of children. But Kala, the Balinese Chronos, is still the 'devouring' Lord of time and of people (especially children), but he only devours those who are not respectful of ritual requirements. He is at his most dangerous during the 'joints' (*sandi*) of the day: dawn, midday, and sunset. He is also a danger to all those born during the wayang week. To ward off this danger, people who have a child born during this week usually make a vow to hold a Sapuh Leger wayang performance, which tells the story of Kala depicted above, and thus cleanse (*ngruwat*) the child of all danger.

The illustration shows a young couple taking their newly born baby to the dalang so that, in his priestly function, he may cleanse the child, which he does by plunging him in tirta holy water produced by the Sapuh Leger performances. He thus wards off the threats facing the newly born. The dalang is shown performing the Sapuh Leger with a musician behind him. For this particular cleansing performance, no screen is used. Instead, it is replaced by a simple thread. He holds a puppet of Siwa in one of his hands, and in the other he brandishes the mythical puppet of Acintya, the androgynous Sublime One. In front of the puppet master, next to the offerings, are the puppets of the clowns Delem and Sangut. Above the scene, in the aura to the right is the God Siwa, and to the left Acintya. A bamboo shrine laden with offerings is visible on the left.

Major Holy Days between Kuningan and the End of the Cycle (Wuku 16–30)

Wuku Pahang (16): Pegat Uwakan

Wednesday—Buda-Kliwon-Pahang—which is called Pegat Uwakan, formally closes the Galungan-Kuningan cycle of ceremonies begun in Wuku Sungsang. Sang Hyang Tunggal, the One Supreme God, is worshipped on this day. The last offerings are made to the still-hovering deities, and the *penjor* are taken down from the fronts of houses and then burned. The ashes will be used as fertilizer for the next crop, confirming the link between agricultural prosperity and the cult of ancestral divinities. Meanwhile, the Barong, who have wandered for several weeks around the villages, go back to their temple residences for a long rest.

Wuku Krulut (17): Tumpek Krulut

Saturday—Saniscara-Kliwon-Krulut—is Tumpek Krulut, a day dedicated to protecting and honoring musical instruments, masks, costumes, and other items of the Balinese theater often stored in temples as sacred objects. On this day, they are taken out of storage, cleaned and presented with offerings.

Wuku Merakih (18): Rambut Sedana

Friday—Sukra-(U)manis-Merakih—is dedicated to the divine couple Sri and Sedana as manifestations of Wisnu and protectors of fertility and wealth. Some manuscripts also associate this day with the god of love Kamajaya as the divine inhabitant of the shrine of origin (*sanggah kemulan tiga sakti*) in family temples.

Wuku Uye (22): Tumpek Kandang

Saturday—Saniscara-Kliwon-Uye—is called Tumpek Kandang and is dedicated to cattle and other livestock. Cattle are bathed and cleansed with holy water. Men make special offerings for their game cocks and women for the pigs.

Wuku Wayang (27): Wara Cemer and Tumpek Wayang

Sunday—Redite-Wage-Wayang—is called Wara Cemer, meaning 'the dirty day', as well as Kalapaksa, or 'belonging to Kala'. Both names refer to the fact that this day opens the dangerous Wuku Wayang, during which Siwa's son, the demonic god Kala, comes to life and threatens to devour children. During this day, it is forbidden to cut hair or to bathe.

To avoid Kala's wrath, children born during Wuku Wayang have to be purified by a Sapuh Leger shadow puppet performance usually held on a Friday—Sukra-Wage-Wayang.

Saturday—Saniscara-Kliwon-Wayang—is known as Tumpek Wayang or Tumpek Ringgit. Offerings are made to shadow theater puppets, musical instruments, costumes, and masks. Tumpek Wayang is sacred for shadow puppeteers (*dalang*), who may not perform on this day. Prayers are addressed to the god Iswara.

Wuku Kulawu (28), Wuku Dukut (29) and Wuku Watugunung (30)

Because the holy days during the 28th, 29th, and 30th wuku announce the coming of the new Pawukon cycle and are tightly linked to the phases of the Watugunung story arc, they are described above, at the beginning of this section, under the heading The Pawukon 'New Year' (wuku 28–wuku 1).

Celebrations in the Saka Calendar

The celebrations of the Saka calendar are regulated by the waxing and waning cycles of the moon, as determined by the lunar month (*sasih*) system. While the nights of every Full Moon (Purnama) and every New Moon (Tilem) are occasions for ritual offerings and prayer, some are more important than others, as described below.

Nights of the Full Moon (Purnama)

On Purnama, people present offerings to the gods at their village temples, at their temples of origin, and at their family temples. Important temple festivals, usually related to agriculture (*usaba*), are held on Purnama Kapat during Sasih Kapat (fourth month), and on Purnama Kadasa, during Sasih Kadasa (tenth month) of the Saka year.

Purnama Kadasa (full moon of the tenth month): Batara Turun Kabeh

On Purnama Kadasa, a great festival takes place in the mother temple of Besakih, called Batara Turun

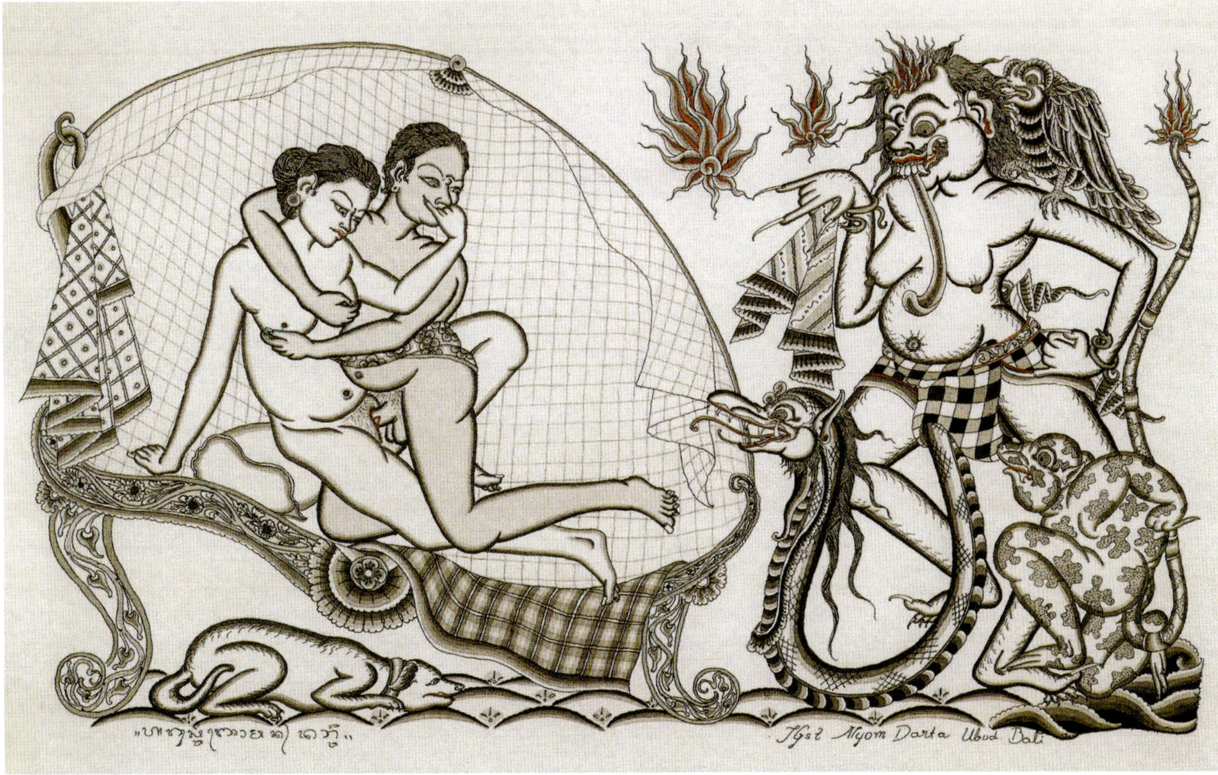

LOVERS SUFFER THE WRATH OF THE GODS: The two lovers are making love when they should not be, as it is the night of the full moon. Thus, Siwa's son Kala, the god of time, shown here with his demonic companions, an owl, a frog and a snake, subjects the couple to his wrath. The flames are signs of his anger.

Kabeh, meaning 'All the gods come down to visit'. It is indeed the biggest ceremony to take place in Bali every year. The Batara Turun Kabeh ceremony is linked to the Tawur Kasanga 'cleansing' of the world that takes place fifteen days earlier on the dark moon of the ninth Saka month, just before the Nyepi New Year (see more on this below). Batara Turun Kabeh focuses on the central Padma Tiga shrine of the Besakih temple, which is dedicated to the three manifestations of Siwa as lord of the upper, middle, and lower worlds, respectively (Parama Siwa, Siwa, and Sadha Siwa). The ceremonies of both Batara Turun Kabeh and Tawur Kasanga feature an extraordinary pageantry of rites, processions, and dances.

Nights of the New Moon (Tilem)

New moon nights are times dedicated to occult forces. Offerings are made at the temple of death (Pura Dalem) found in each customary village. Many temple festivals are also held on this day throughout the island, often featuring performances in which the performers go into collective trances. The new moons of Sasih Kapitu (the seventh month) and Sasih Kasanga (ninth month) are particularly important.

Tilem Kapitu (new moon of the seventh month): Siwa Ratri

Tilem Kapitu, the evening of the new moon of Sasih Kapitu (the seventh month, which usually falls in January or February), is the shortest new moon night of the Saka calendar year. This night is called Siwa Ratri (or Siwa Latn), meaning 'the night of Siwa'. It is a night of meditation aimed at cleansing personal impurities. People who participate stay awake the whole night. They pray, meditate, and discuss holy texts in the temple of

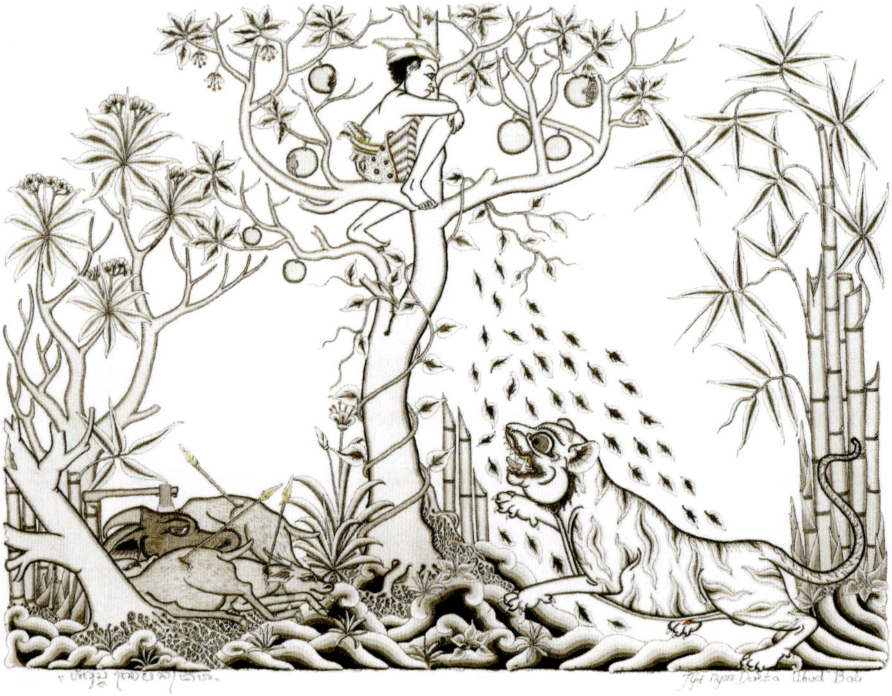

SIWA RATRI: The illustration shows the hunter Lubdaka threatened by a tiger in the middle of the night. He picks *bila* leaves and throws them on the ground until they accumulate to form a lingam, the symbol of Siwa. To the left are the animals the hunter has killed—sinful deeds for which Siwa will cleanse Lubdaka, rewarding him for his night-long vigil of worship.

death (Pura Dalem) or temple of origin (Pura Puseh) of their village.

Barely known until 20 years ago, Siwa Ratri is now one of the most popular holy days in Bali. Siwa Ratri is inseparable from the story of the hunter Lubdaka, which is the principal object of reading sessions. The story, known as *Siwaratri Kalpa*, goes as follows:

A hunter called Lubdaka lost his way in the forest just before dark on Tilem Kapitu. As the sun was setting, he was obliged to take refuge in a *bila* tree overlooking a lake. Tigers and other wild animals lurking at the foot of the tree would be sure to kill and eat him if he were to fall asleep and tumble down from the tree. To stay awake and pass the time, Lubdaka plucked the leaves of the tree, one by one, and threw them into the lake. A big lingam, symbol of Siwa, emerged in the middle of the lake. Although it was unintentional, Lubdaka had inadvertently worshipped Siwa in his all-night vigil. The god Siwa was pleased by the hunter's devotion, and Ludaka survived the dangerous night unharmed.

In other variations of the story, the leaves fall on the ground, rather than into a lake, or, unbeknownst to Lubdaka, there is already a lingam shrine to Siwa under the tree where he takes refuge, and Siwa assumes that the leaves the hunter showers on it are offerings.

After Lubdaka died, Siwa granted him ultimate enlightenment instead of sending him to hell as he deserved to be punished for his sins as a hunter who had killed innocent animals for his own pleasure. Lubdaka had been cleansed of his sins by his involuntary meditation on the shore of the lake.

Tilem Kasanga (new moon of the ninth month): Tawur Kasanga and Ngrupuk

On the eve of the New Year of the Saka calendar, that is, the new moon that ends Sasih Kasanga, the ninth month, people hold purification ceremonies to cleanse themselves of impurities accumulated during the past year.

A few days before year's end, effigies of village deities are taken to the sea or to a confluence of

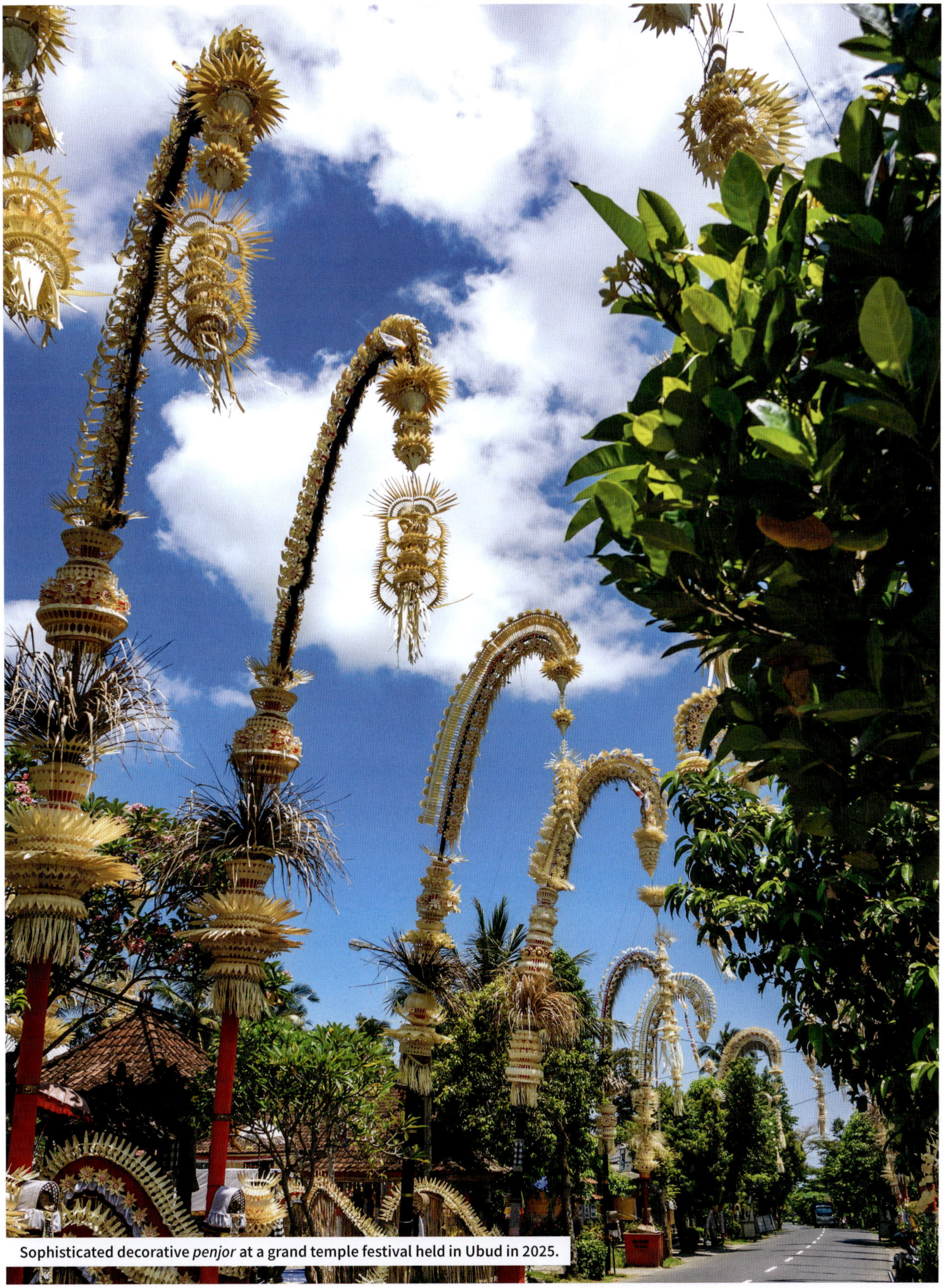

Sophisticated decorative *penjor* at a grand temple festival held in Ubud in 2025.

two rivers for ritual bathing and purification (*melasti*), then brought to the village temple (Pura Desa) to rest. On the last day, Tilem Kasanga, a major exorcism occurs at the main crossroads of each village. This exorcism, known as Tawur Kasanga, is officiated by a Siwa priest to address the gods in the heavenly world, a high priest (*buda*) to address humans in the middle world, and an exorcist priest (*sengguhu*), to address the demons (*buta kala*) in the netherworld. All the effigies may then return to their respective temples, and families make small exorcism ceremonies in their own compounds.

At nightfall, the demons to be placated are entertained. Hundreds of *ogoh-ogoh*, huge demon puppets artistically crafted by several groups in each village youth over the past several weeks, now fill the roads. The monsters are mounted on bamboo scaffolding. Men and youngsters carry these bamboo palanquins on their shoulders, swerving and twirling and making a great deal of noise. This is the Ngrupuk parade, most impressive in the streets of Denpasar. (See illustration: 'Sasih Kasanga' in Chapter 3). Eventually, after circling the village many times and meeting in mock battles at the crossroads, the monsters are paraded to the village cemeteries and burned. Now cleansed of all demons, the community is ready for Nyepi, a day of total silence.

Every hundred years or so, the festival of Tawur Kasanga takes a far more dramatic dimension in the festival called Eka Dasa Rudra, which was last held in the Saka year 1900 (the spring of 1979). The aim of this ceremony is the purification of the world so that the balance between 'good' and 'evil', or Siwa and Rudra (a demonic form of Siwa), may be restored worldwide.

Sasih Kadasa (tenth month): The Saka New Year

The following day is the first day of Sasih Kadasa and, hence, the first day of the new Saka year. Called Nyepi, it is the most important holy day of the Saka calendar. In sharp contrast to the noise of Ngrupuk, Saka New Year's day is a day of complete silence.

The silence of Nyepi is very serious. Starting at sunrise, all activities must cease. Hence, the mandatory and tightly enforced prohibitions: no pleasure, including sex (*mati/elangon*), no traffic (*mati lelungan*), no fire (*mati geni*), and no work (*mati pekaryan*). So there is no road traffic and lighting is kept to a strict minimum. Satellite television broadcasting is temporarily interrupted. Foreigners who happen to be staying on the island are kindly, but firmly, requested to stay put in their hotels and must cope with minimum service. No planes are allowed to land or take off at the airport. The whole day is simply filled with the barking of a few dogs, the shrill of insects, and a long quiet. On the following day, called Ngembak Geni, life in Bali resumes its normal course, beginning at sunrise.

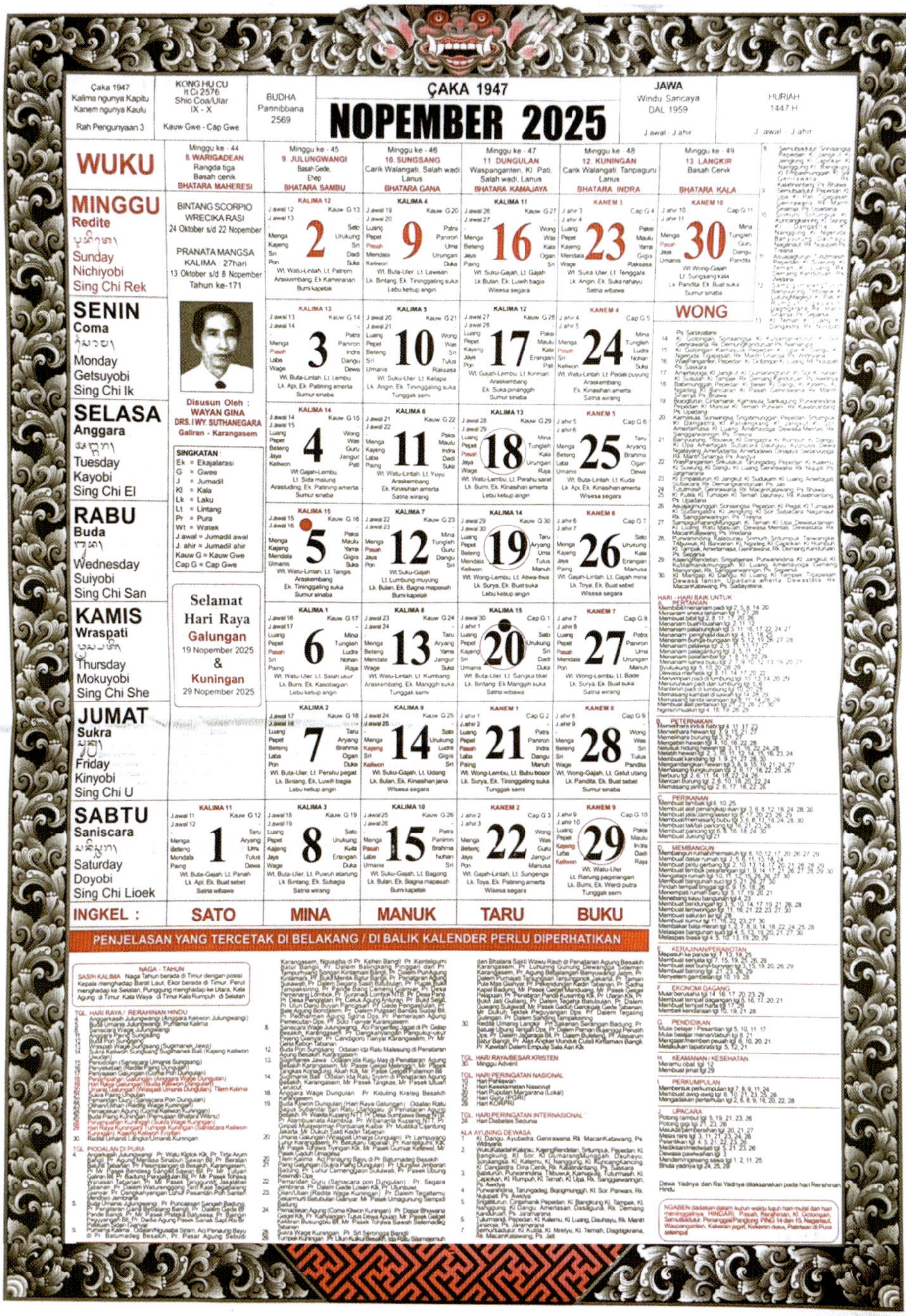

The Introduction of modern time by the Dutch, instead of simplifying things complicated it for the Balinese. There was a new type of time to take into account. The Dutch, however, introduced printing and 'the rational approach'. This monumental shift in Balinese time-keeping was the work of I Ketut Bangbang Gede Rawi (1910–89), a renowned scholar and specialist in *wariga* (the traditional science of determining auspicious dates). Before his intervention, the 'science of the days' was the guarded domain of the priesthood. Bangbang Gede Rawi translated this celestial complexity into a visual language for the common man. His contribution was not just the printing of a calendar, but the democratization of Balinese time.

Bangbang Gede Rawi's calendar comprises, in the left-hand vertical column, the days of the week in Indonesian, Balinese (writing), English, Japanese, and Chinese. Along the top are the *wuku* of the months. Below, in each square, are the days with their characteristics (especially *wewaran*), and below them the *ingkel* unauspicious characteristics applying to *sato* (animals), *mina* (fish), *manuk* (birds), *taru* (vegetal), and *buku* (bamboo), and at top right *wong* (people). In the right-hand column are the auspicious and inauspicious characteristics of any day, and at the bottom of the chart the festivals around the island, which may change from one calendar to another.

CHAPTER 6

RITUALS IN THE CYCLE OF LIFE

As noted in Chapter 1, according to Balinese beliefs, each human being is a microcosm, literally a small world (*bhwana alit*). Since human beings are made of the same material and divine components as the macrocosm (*bhwana agung*), they should live their lives in accordance with principles of cosmic order. Only then can they reincarnate and their souls eventually achieve, after many reincarnations, the condition of *moksha*—blending into the Sublime Soul of the World (Paramatma) or God—whereas their bodily components blend into the Five Cosmic Elements of matter (Panca Maha Bhuta).

Incarnation requires sex and love. These are not abstract concepts in Bali, where the human microcosm is a duplicate of the universe. Human love is the meeting field of cosmic forces. The god of love, Batara Smara, and the goddess of the moon, Batari Ratih, are both believed to be at work within the individual, making possible the encounter of the forces of the macrocosm within the microcosm. The act of love is also spurred by the god of flirtation, Sang Hyang Deleng (from *deleng*, or 'glance').

When a man and a woman have sexual intercourse, they physically unite 'the red and white elements of desire' (*kama bang* and *kama petak*), symbols of the male sperm and female ovum, respectively. This act is accompanied by the descent (*numadi*) of an ancestral soul. The soul comes, according to different interpretations, either straight out of the mouth of hell, or down from the 'Old Country', the abode of both gods and ancestors, high above Mount Agung. From this fecundation process originates the *bhwana alit*, a human being who is a discrete cosmic unit, a combination of spirit and matter in time.

All phases of life, from conception to birth, birth to death, and death to the afterlife, are paralleled by rites of passage. The main functions and purposes of these rites are, successively, to fasten the soul into the body; to welcome it to the world; to take it harmoniously along the various stages of life, and finally, upon death, to help it cast away all earthly bonds and rejoin the 'Old Country' of its origins, where it waits to come down again in a new incarnation, or merges in moksha with the Sublime Void of the World, Sang Hyang Embang, one of the many names of the Supreme God.

Let us start with the early stages of life. The sexual meeting and merging of the two *kama* beget Sanghyang Jabang Bayi (meaning 'Godly Fetus'). The divine status of the fetus is due to the fact that the soul originates from the heavenly world. It will keep this attribute under changing names beyond birth. Hence, newborn infants are often called 'little gods' (Dewa Alit).

Upon the seventh month of pregnancy, a ceremony of 'housing the soul' (*magedong-gedongan*) is held to formally welcome the soul in the womb of the mother. Then, directly following birth come a whole set of other 'welcome' ceremonies (*penyambutan*): the birth rites proper, the burial of the four siblings (*nyama* or *catur sanak*, which corresponds to four elements of the afterbirth), and a ceremony on the fifth or seventh day of life for the fall of the umbilical cord (*kepus pungsed*).

After that come ceremonies at 12 days old (*ngrorasin*), one month or 35 days old (*mulanin*), 42 days old (*abulan pitung dina*), three months or 105 days old (*nelubulanin*) when the child's feet touch ground for the first time, and six months, or

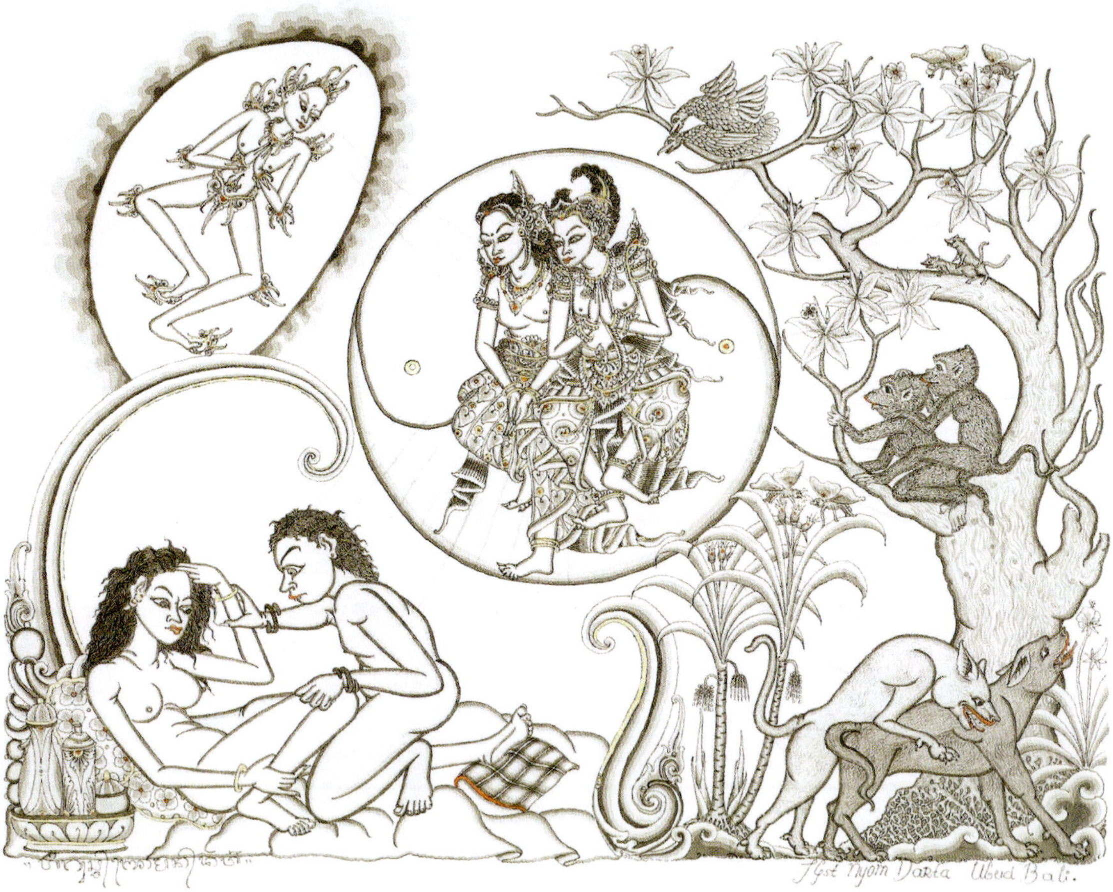

CONCEPTION: This illustration shows that love-making at the level of the middle world, inhabited by the human couple and nearby animals, is directed by cosmic forces, symbolized here in a bubble showing the god of love Asmara/Kamajaya, the moon goddess Ratih, and Acintya, and the Supreme inconceivable god (top left), representing Siwa in hermaphroditic form as witnesses to the process.

210 days old, a complete Pawukon cycle (*otonan*).

Upon the arrival of such a divine being as a baby, the parents try to identify its origins, to find out who it is which ancestor is incarnating. For that purpose, usually at the time of the 12-day ceremony, the parents consult a medium who summons the baby's soul of origin.

It may be that more than one soul is incarnating a newborn. Sometimes two or more ancestors show up, each with their own pasts, names, and features. It is commonly believed that, when this happens, there should ideally be at least one male and one female soul, symbolizing the unity of opposites that make up a human being.

The incarnating souls may come from several generations back, each with one or more highly specific requests. As families want their children to grow up healthy and unimpeded, they go to great lengths to fulfill the requests of these souls. These range from requests for a yellow shawl (*saput kuning*) to requests for a shadow puppet show (*wayang*), or another sacred performance to be given at a specific stage of the child's development.

The Rites of Life and Death

The series of drawings that follow illustrate the rites of life and death which all Hindu Balinese expect to go through. The scenes depicted are based on practices found in the Ubud area of Central Bali.

Actual rites may, and do vary, as the Balinese say, due to *desa mawa cara* (customs vary from village to village). They also vary due to the fact that modernity compels change. People are now usually born at a medical facility rather than at home; plastic objects are used to prepare rites, replacing bamboo, earthenware, and other natural implements shown in the drawings; and the burning of corpses at cremations is accelerated by using a gas burner.

In spite of these innovations, the rites of birth, childhood, adult life, and death still constitute the basic framework for the religious life of the people of Bali. And while the main life transitions (conception/birth/puberty/death) are determined by biological constraints on which the calendar has no direct bearing, the ceremonies related to these events are determined by calendar computations, largely based upon the 210-day Pawukon calendar. Only the cremation ceremony is influenced by the Saka calendar, in which Sasih Karo (the second month) is deemed propitious for cremations.

Finally, it should be noted that all Balinese rites are accompanied by offerings. However, offering is a generic term, which fails to account for the vast technical and symbolic complexity of these offerings. There are hundreds of different types, all with their own names, each endowed with a specific ritual purpose and laden with a special meaning.

From Conception to Marriage

Although love-making is not a ceremony in the strict sense of the term, it should take into account the auspiciousness of the time when it occurs. For example, it is considered taboo to engage in sexual intercourse during the last week of the Pawukon cycle (Wuku Watugunung) and the first three days of the new cycle (up to Pagerwesi). If a couple want a male child, intercourse should take place on even days; if they want a female child, it should take place on odd days (both *panglong* and *penanggal*) of the lunar Saka months.

The love-making brings together in an embryo the woman's 'red desire' (*kama bang*) and the man's 'white desire' (*kama petak*). The embryo receives the ancestral soul coming out of the Balinese hell or field of sorrow (*tegal penyangsaran*). Although it has been cleansed for some period of time, the reincarnating soul is one that has not yet fulfilled the conditions to achieve moksha, and is still bound to earth by an imperfect *karma* (the sum of its past life deeds).

Also descending are various cosmic forces, in particular the 108 protective spirits (*nyama bajang*) and four siblings (*kanda mpat* or *catur sanak*): Anggapati, Prajapati, Banaspati, and Banaspatiraja.

The Pregnancy Ceremony

The *magedong-gedongan* ceremony takes place when the embryo has given way to a Jabang Bayi, a foetus with a full human form, deemed to be solidly 'installed' in its mother's womb (*gedong* means 'building'). The ceremony usually takes place six 35-day Pawukon months following conception, the precise day being chosen after consultation with a calendar specialist.

This ceremony is addressed both to the child and its spiritual guardians or siblings, the *kanda mpat*, who have also now taken a physical shape: Anggapati has become the amniotic fluid, Prajapati the blood, Banaspati the vernix caseosa, and Banaspatiraja the placenta. These protective beings will spiritually accompany the child and then the adult throughout life.

They also correspond to various gods, deities, and demonic beings who inhabit nature, the human body and, more generally, the cosmos. Their names change according to the age of the person they protect. Addressing offerings to them aims not only to obtain a happy future life but also to maintain the proper balance between the human-to-be microcosm and the larger macrocosm.

If the mother has a miscarriage and the embryo already resembles a baby, it must be immediately buried lest it bring bad luck to the family. The burial does not require any ceremony other than the presentation of a simple offering (*canang sari*). However, the impurity lasts 42 days for the mother and 12 days for the father.

The Birth and Welcome Ceremony

Today, birth usually takes place at a hospital or midwife's clinic. Until 25 years ago, it took place at the parents' compound, typically in the part of the compound symmetrically opposed to the temple. Until the 1960s, most midwives were male (*balian manakan*), sometimes assisted by an elderly woman. However, it was taboo for a male midwife to bring a baby into his own family.

Before the arrival of modern medicine, giving

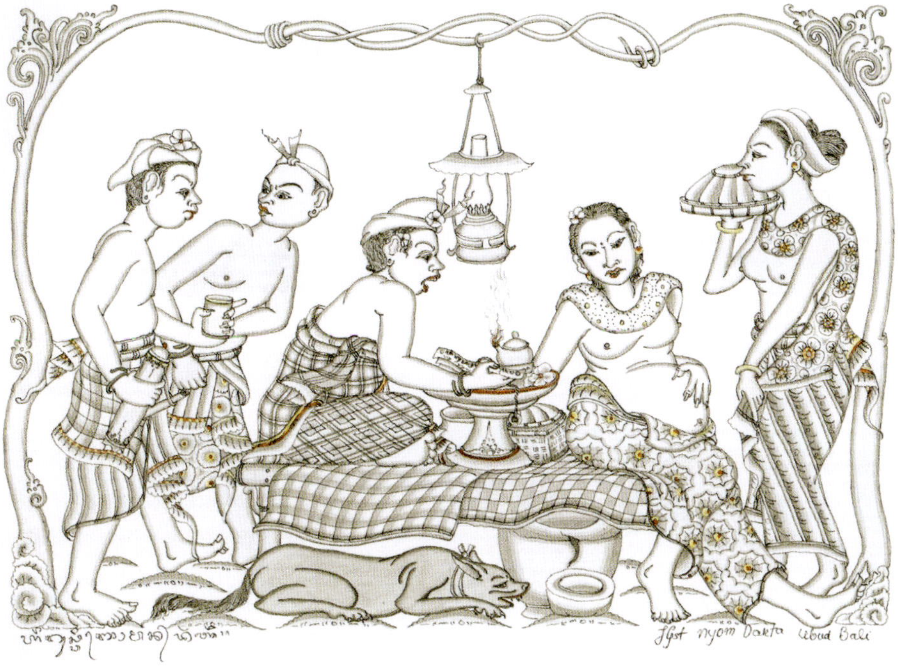

THE PREGNANCY CEREMONY: This drawing shows a scene from a *magedong-gedongan* ceremony. A *lontar* is read, accompanied by a notification offering (*pejat*) to bless the pregnant mother and unborn baby. The small oil lamp between the couple signals the presence of Brahma, god of fire.

birth was a painful ordeal. However, the balian manakan had his own remedies. If the woman had an excessive discharge of uterine liquid before birth (*beling ngemuh yeh*), she was given a concoction of vinegar and sour lime to drink. If, on the contrary, the discharge was insufficient to smooth the birth path, the balian gave her an amalgamation of young hibiscus leaves (*loloh don pucuk putih ane nguda-nguda mabejek*).

Women were not allowed to lie on a bed because their uterine discharge, containing blood, was believed to bring further impurity (*leteh*). Instead, they lay on the floor beside the bed. The unclean discharge was left to run onto a wide sheath of sugar palm leaf. The

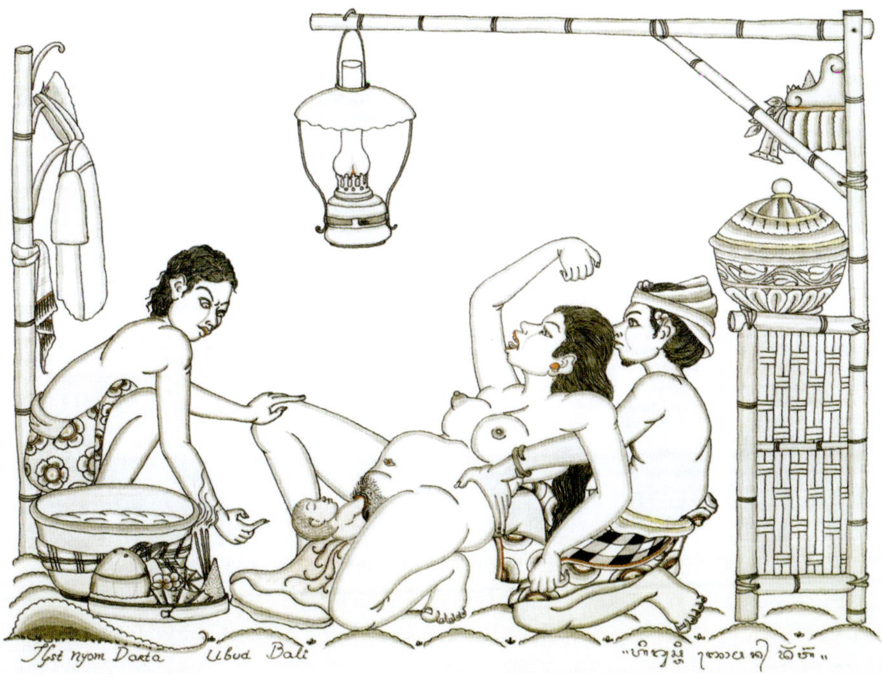

THE BIRTH AND WELCOME CEREMONY: This drawing depicts a traditional birth scene, facilitated by a male midwife. The basin on his right is used to wash the afterbirth. The *pejati* notification offering lies nearby. At upper right is a *canang* offering signaling that the ancestors are witnessing the event.

waste was later washed away using a container especially allocated for this purpose.

Often a woman would go through long hours of labor. The normal treatment given by the balian in this case was very simple: palm oil, which had previously been used for frying a frisky kind of fish called *julit*, was taken orally. If this medication failed to speed up the birth, the ultimate step was taken: the woman was moved onto the bed and the baby was believed to be the reincarnation of an ancestor who refused to be born on the floor, probably, people said, because the baby was the reincarnation of a holy person (*ane mapawayangan anak marage suci*). After the baby finally made its entrance into the world, the balian cut the umbilical cord and then applied, on the severed end, an ointment—*paya misi uyah macacak*, a mixture of bitter, green, squash-like vegetables and salt—to ward off infection and pain.

After this step, today as in the past, the father washes the remaining placenta (*ari-ari*) and places it with offerings and the other afterbirth materials (physical embodiments of the kanda mpat) into a coconut shell or clay pot. After being inscribed with the proper holy letters and wrapped in cloth or coconut fiber, this small container is buried in front of the entrance of the north pavilion (*bale daja*) in the family compound, on the right side for a boy, or the left side for a girl.

A black stone is then placed over the spot where the ari-ari is buried and a small pandanus is planted nearby. Over the next 42 days, an incense stick or candle will remain lit on the site. A small bamboo shrine (*sanggah cucuk*) is also erected and dressed for the purpose of presenting regular offerings to various spirits (*buta*) and to the kanda mpat, who will be the guardians and witnesses of the incarnated human for the rest of his or her life.

As for the woman, after giving birth, her belly is softly massaged to restore it to its normal condition, but she has to rest in a sitting position, traditionally on the floor, for three days. During this period, she also has to eat from a split coconut shell instead of a normal plate. She has also to remain confined to the house compound for 42 days, during which she has to eat alone, apart from other members of the family. She cannot take part in other rites. Her husband and the house are also considered impure (*leteh*).

The Fall of the Umbilical Cord

A week or so after birth, the umbilical cord (*pungsed*) dries and falls off. It is then wrapped in a cloth and put in a small container. The dried cord is deemed to have healing power, and can later be crushed and soaked for use as a medicine when the child is sick.

The ceremony proper consists of an ordinary offering to the earthly forces (*mabiakala*) and to the kanda mpat. The child is deemed 'clean' and separated from its kanda mpat siblings. Other offerings are addressed to the god Hyang Kumara, protector of children, for whom a special shrine is set in the *kaja-kangin* (upstream east) corner of the room. Hyang Kumara will protect the child until its first teeth appear.

The mother holds the baby and ties cotton threads as protective bracelets around its wrists

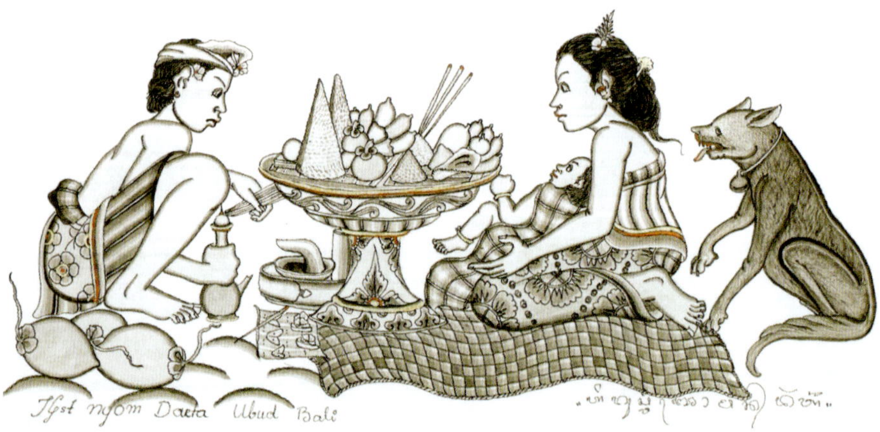

THE CEREMONY FOR THE FALL OF THE UMBILICAL CORD: In the center of the drawing is a tray with a welcome offering containing an egg, rice cones, three sticks of incense, and fruits. The man holds a Balinese water jug, which he will use together with the nearby stone grinder to crush the umbilical cord.

and feet. The father, whose ritual impurity lasts only until the fall of the umbilical cord, may address the god with a mantra that means "Oh you, the One without eyes, without mouth, without nose, without desire, I beg you to cleanse all the impurities and demonic influences that cling to the body and send them back to their proper abode."

When the child is still a newborn, its fontanel, called *Siwa dwara* (Siwa's door), is not fully closed. Considered as the point of entrance into the body of divine forces as well as demonic forces, the fontanel is protected by applying a herbal paste (*loloh*) to it.

The first days of life are considered highly dangerous. Indeed, newborn infant deaths were frequent until 20 years ago. The baby is said to be subject to both temptations and attacks by all sorts of otherworldly beings. If the child dies very young, before 42 days, it is said to have remained untouched by the five senses (*panca indra*) and is therefore buried in a children's cemetery (*setra bebajangan*) instead of undergoing a cremation ceremony. Despite this, proper offerings must be made lest the child's soul becomes a deranged or lost soul (*atma kesasar*).

The Twelve-day Ceremony

The *ngerorasin* ceremony held 12 days after birth is of particular importance. The child is thought to have survived its most dangerous period, when it was at risk of falling victim to some evil spirit (usually an illness). Its soul is now well bonded to

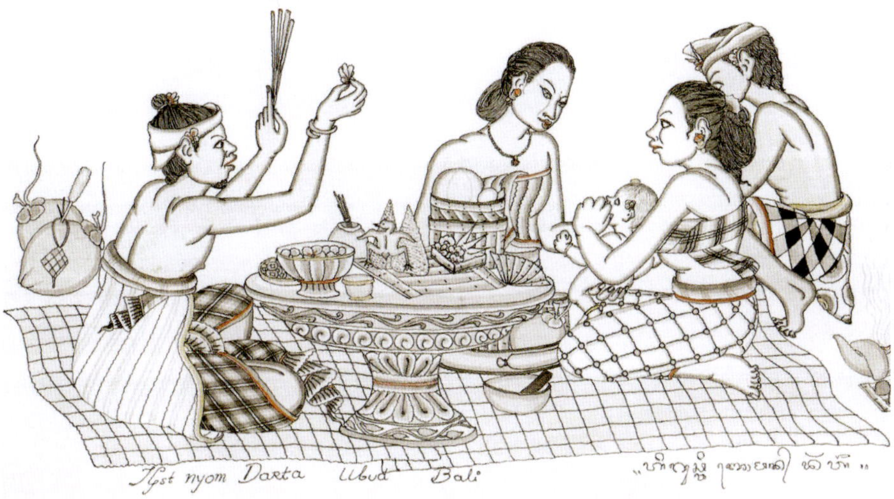

THE TWELVE-DAY CEREMONY I: A priest faces the baby's parents while sprinkling holy water with a bundle of coconut leaf shafts (*lis*) and a frangipani flower. The offerings on the tray include a young coconut, a small bowl of holy water, and a grilled chicken. On the ground behind the couple lie two offerings addressed to the earthly forces. The first (*segehan*) consists of ritual food, the second (*api tekep*) of two pieces of burning coconut crossed over one another as a form of cleansing by fire.

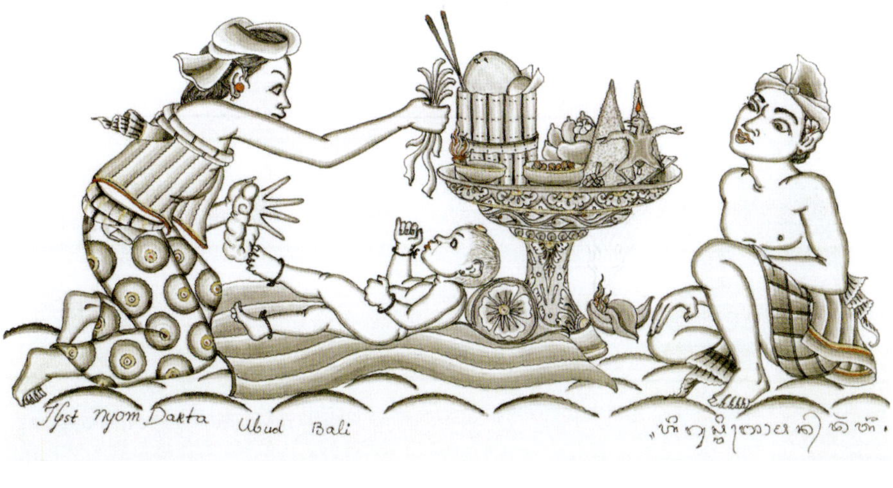

THE TWELVE-DAY CEREMONY II: This shows a mother putting thread bracelets on her child's ankles and wrists. A *penyambutan* welcome offering is on a tray with rice, fruits, and a chicken, while an api tekep offering lies on the ground to cleanse the baby of negative influences.

its body. The ceremony usually begins near the kitchen fireplace with the preparation of holy water. A simple *canang sari* offering is presented to Brahma, god of fire, accompanied by these words: "Oh, god Brahma, I ask of you this holy water (*tirta*), so that this baby may be happy, safe, and have a long life."

Following this, another rite is performed near the well, the abode of Wisnu, and then the child is sprinkled with holy water in the family temple (*sanggah* or *merajan*). The ceremony is performed by a third party, usually a balian or priest, because the parents are still considered impure. The purpose of the event is to cleanse the mother and her baby of the impurities of the birthing.

Until the 12th day, the child has no name, as if its incarnation were not yet final. Now, it may be named. The parents can choose the name themselves, seek the advice of a calendar specialist, or select it on the basis of the information given by the shaman or medium, known as a *balian tetakson*, who is also usually consulted on the 12th day.

The parents of the baby usually consult with a balian tetakson who lives in a different village and presumably does not know the family. After receiving the offerings the parents bring, the balian enters a state of trance to find out which ancestor or ancestors are reincarnating (*numadi*) and what their demands are, if any.

Some ancestors, speaking through the balian's voice, may ask for specific requirements to be met at the child's three-month or six-month ceremony, or to be offered a dance when the child reaches adulthood. Others might suggest a name for the child. The parents may accept the shaman's suggestions, or if they are not convinced, reject them and consult another balian.

The Role of the Balian Tetakson

The balian tetakson, male or female, is a key figure in the Balinese indigenous tradition, acting as a navigator of the unseen world. While the High Priests manage the cosmic laws of the Indianized aspect of Balinese culture, the balian tetakson manages the ancestral circulation of the Balinese soul. The name is derived from *caksu*, meaning the 'cosmic eye,' granting the balian the unique ability to locate a soul as it wanders through *niskala* (the intangible) space.

The balian's expertise is vital for finding an *atma kesasar*, an erring or lost soul, and providing the necessary guidance to set it back on its proper

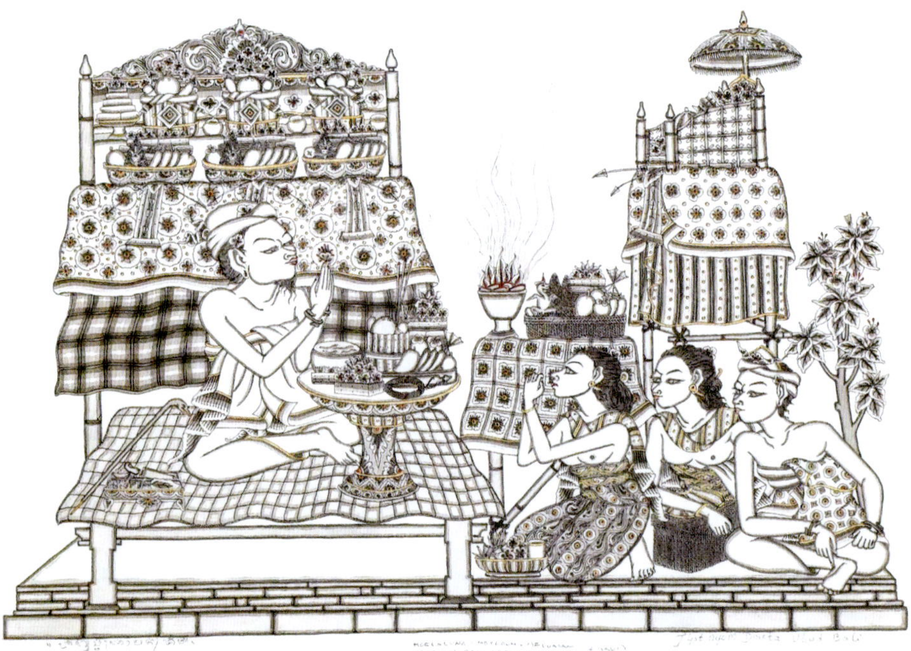

THE ROLE OF THE BALIAN TEKAKSON: While the High Priests are in charge of the cosmic laws, the *balian tetakson* manages the personal and ancestral geography of the Balinese soul.

path. Beyond this, the balian officiates at two critical junctures of the life cycle:

Reincarnation (*The 12th Day Post-Birth*): Approximately 12 days after a child is born, the parents visit a balian to ask if he can identify the specific ancestor who has incarnated into the infant. He sometimes provides a clear and startlingly accurate depiction of that ancestor's identity, but most of the time remains vague.

The Transition after Death: Following a death, the balian can locate the soul on its journey toward the ancestral realm. Most importantly, the balian acts as a medium, communicating the soul's final requests or concerns to the living family, ensuring that no spiritual loose ends remain.

The Forty-two-day Ceremony

The *tutug kambuhan* ceremony takes place 42 days after birth—one Pawukon 'month' of 35 days, defined by the crossing of the five-day week (Pancawara) and the seven-day week (Saptawara), plus another seven-day week.

The purpose of the tutug kambuhan ceremony is to thank the 108 *nyama bajang*, or protective spirits, who have accompanied the kanda mpat guardians from conception through birth. Now, after 42 days, their role is fulfilled and they must return to where they belong lest they threaten rather than protect the child. They are symbolically replaced by animals that may not be slaughtered since they are there to protect the child.

The tutug kambuhan rite comprises a complex set of offerings addressed to earthly forces (*buta*) and gods (*dewa*) alike. A cleansing (*mabiakala*) is followed by an 'invitation' to the kanda mpat and nyama bajang to thank them for having protected the child and let them leave. The child's head is then shaved. The ceremony is completed by prayers accompanied by the sprinkling of water of immortality (*tirta*) on the mother, father, and child.

This completely cleanses the impurities associated with birth. After the tutug kambuhan, the mother may once again enter temples and participate in ceremonies. The ceremony usually takes place in the kitchen, the symbolic abode of Brahma. It can also be held in the yard, facing downstream. On the occasion of this ceremony, a shrine is placed next to the infant's cot with offerings addressed to Dewa Kumara, the deity who will protect the infant until its first tooth appears. When the baby's first tooth appears, another small ceremony (*ngempugin*) is held. A similar ceremony (*dapetan*) is also held when the child loses his or her first tooth.

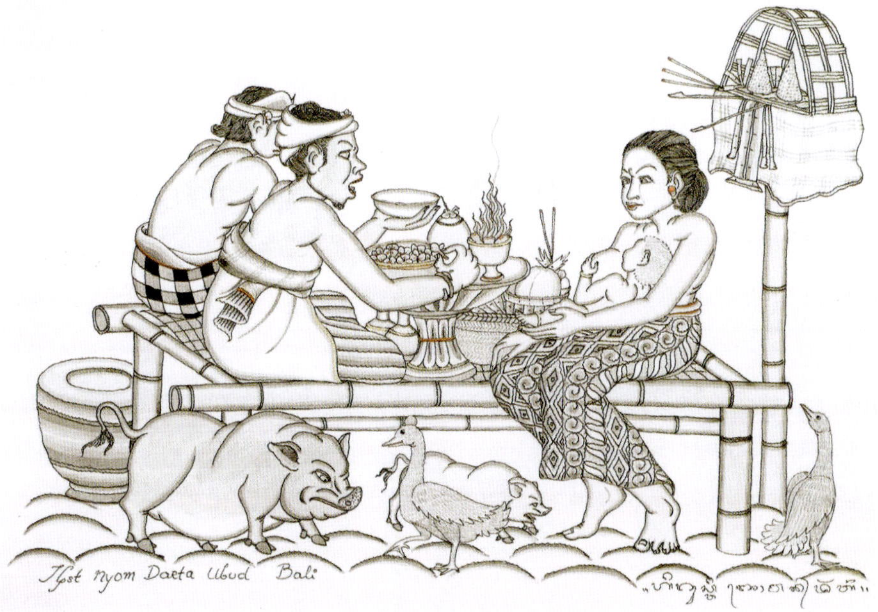

THE FORTY-TWO-DAY CEREMONY: Sitting on a bamboo platform, the *pemangku* is presenting a set of *penyambutan* welcome offerings. Behind the woman stands a bamboo shrine on which offerings are made to the *kanda mpat* protective guardians. Notice the hens and pigs. In former times, a pair of animals, either a hen and cock, or sow and male pig, had to be stolen but could not be slaughtered afterwards because they had become the child's guardians.

The Three-month Ceremony

The *nelubulanin* ceremony is conducted 105 days after birth. It corresponds to half a Pawukon cycle or 'year' based on the crossing of the three main types of week: Pancawara, Saptawara, and Triwara (5 x 7 x 3).

The nelubulanin ceremony is another in the series of post-birth purification rites, only much bigger than the previous ones. It may include entertainment and visits by family and friends bearing gifts. Upon the nelubulanin, the child is definitely entering the world. Any remaining impurity clinging to the child is cleansed. The ceremony is directed by an ordinary priest (*pemangku*) or balian, or if the family can afford it, a high priest (*pedanda*). If there are impediments, though, part of these rites may be postponed until the six-month or 210-day ceremony.

The most impressive part of the ceremony is the ritual bathing of the child, usually in a large clay container, which represents the primal ocean or the river Gangga. In this container are put items that symbolize aspects of the child's future life: a palm-leaf manuscript (*lontar*) inscribed with Balinese script, representing intelligence and wisdom; Chinese coins (*kepeng*), representing the acquisition of wealth; grains of rice, representing daily work, and jewels, representing the burden of desire.

Before the child is bathed, the parents have to perform a short ritual addressed to the kanda mpat. The father, holding in his hands symbols of the kanda mpat, followed by the mother holding effigies of these same four guardians, and a relative holding the child, half-run counter-clockwise around the house yard three times. Each time they pass the container, water is sprinkled on the child and the effigies.

Then the mother takes the baby, saying, "My child is not that young any more, it is time he/she becomes a fully human person," and immerses the

THE THREE-MONTH CEREMONY: This drawing shows a child being bathed in an earthenware basin set on top of a big stone mortar. The child will grope for the items put in the basin. To the right, the mother is holding a budding banana (*pusuh*), symbol of the baby, which she will dispose of in front of the house, thus signifying that the child is changing status.

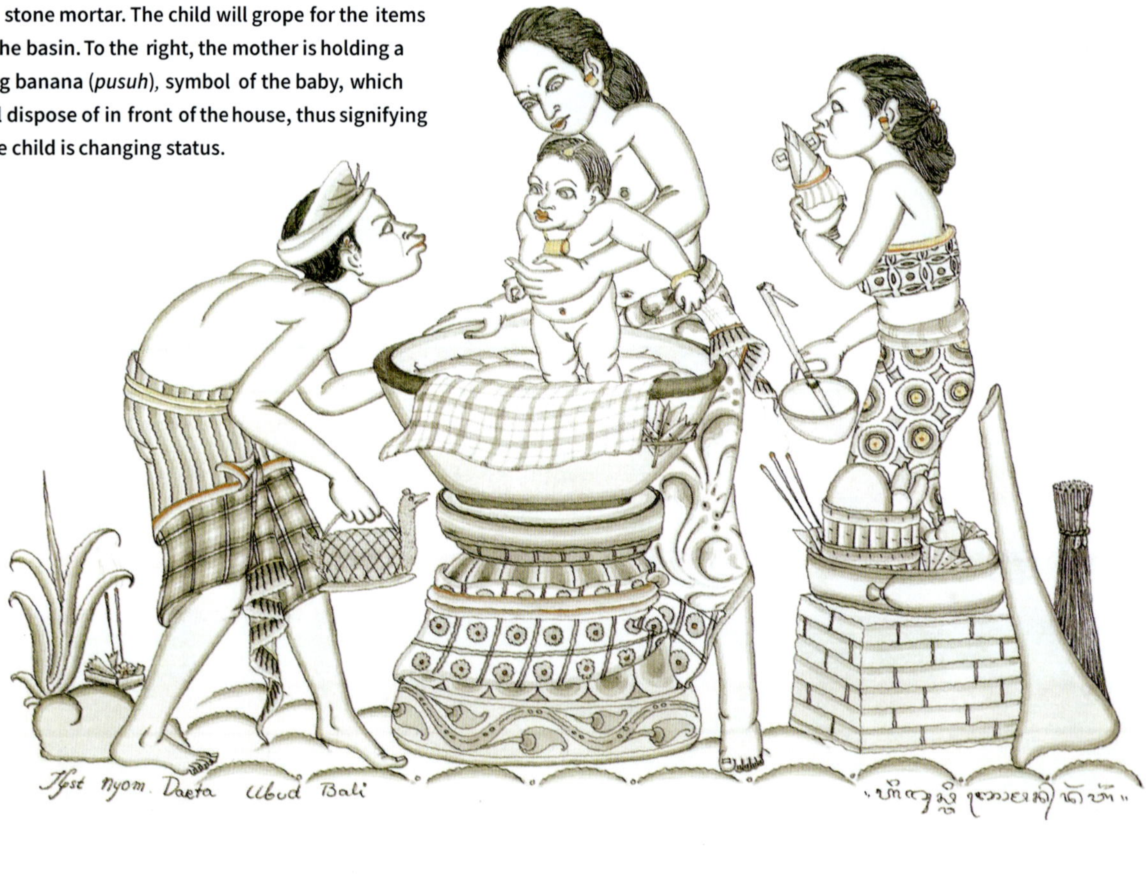

baby in the container. The surprised baby's hands grope for anything they can find. People say that what the baby picks up will determine the child's future activities. On this occasion, the thread bracelets that were put on the baby's hands and feet at the time of the fall of the umbilical cord are replaced by silver bracelets. A token meal of rice is also fed to the child, this being the first time he or she is given solid food.

It is usually during this ceremony that the child is also given his or her formal name. This name, though, which often sounds like a Sanskrit name (Darmayasa, Sudirta, Wibawa, etc.), is rarely used. People prefer being called by the name of their order of birth (Wayan or Putu, Made, Nyoman, Ketut), or a nickname (Kocong, Dolar, Luweng, etc.), or a caste title such as Agung (for those of the Ksatria caste) or Bagus (for those of the Brahmin caste). Once people have a child, they are commonly called Pan Agus (Agus's father) or Men Kocong (Kocong's mother).

There are many local variants of this ceremony, part or all of which might be shifted to the 210-day ceremony.

The Touching the Ground Ceremony

In this ceremony, the child is allowed to touch the ground (*napak stiti*) for the first time, accompanied by the following mantra: "Oh, baby, come down, come down and touch the ground, gold, money and all sorts of wealth are waiting for you." By these words the child asks to be blessed by Mother Earth (Hyang Pertiwi). Sometimes, to underline the fact that the birth and post-birth processes and rites are over, and while the child is touching the ground for the first time, a bamboo-slat cock cage is put over the child for a moment before being withdrawn.

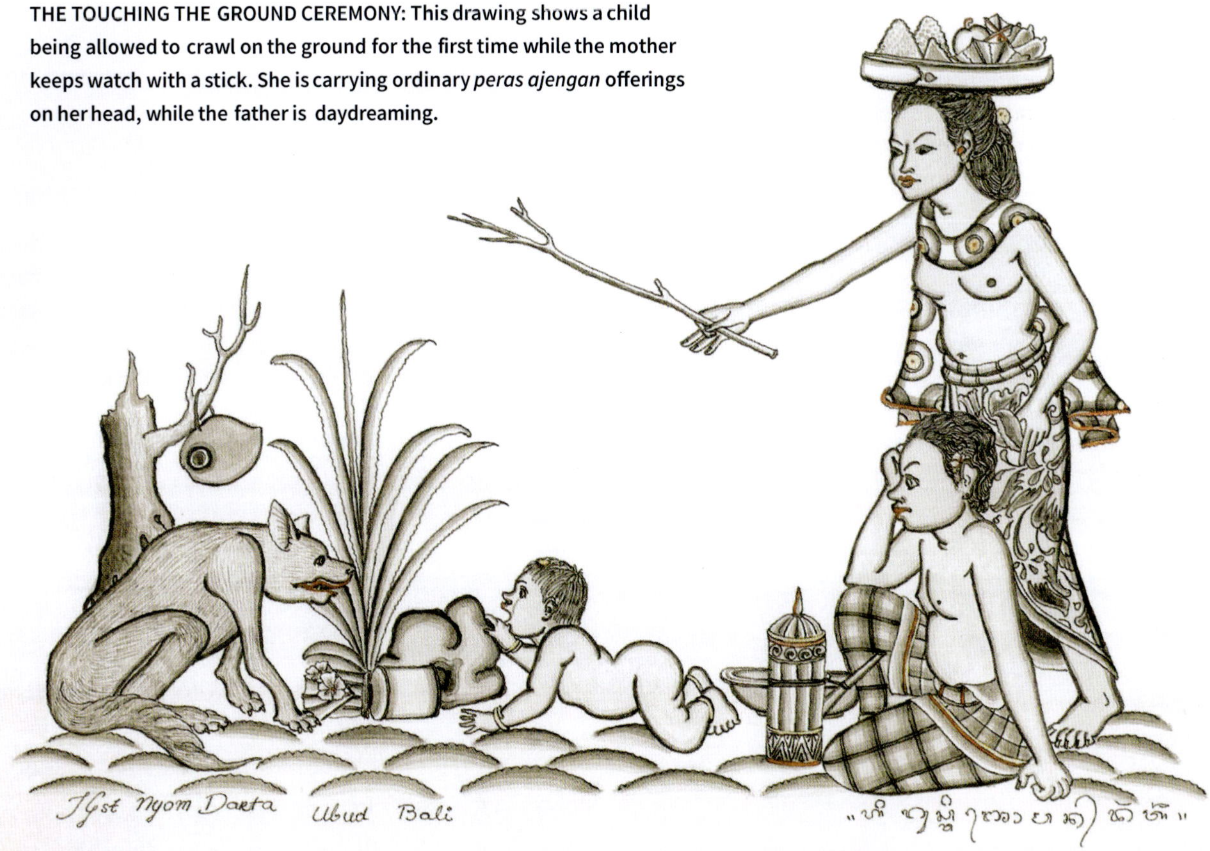

THE TOUCHING THE GROUND CEREMONY: This drawing shows a child being allowed to crawl on the ground for the first time while the mother keeps watch with a stick. She is carrying ordinary *peras ajengan* offerings on her head, while the father is daydreaming.

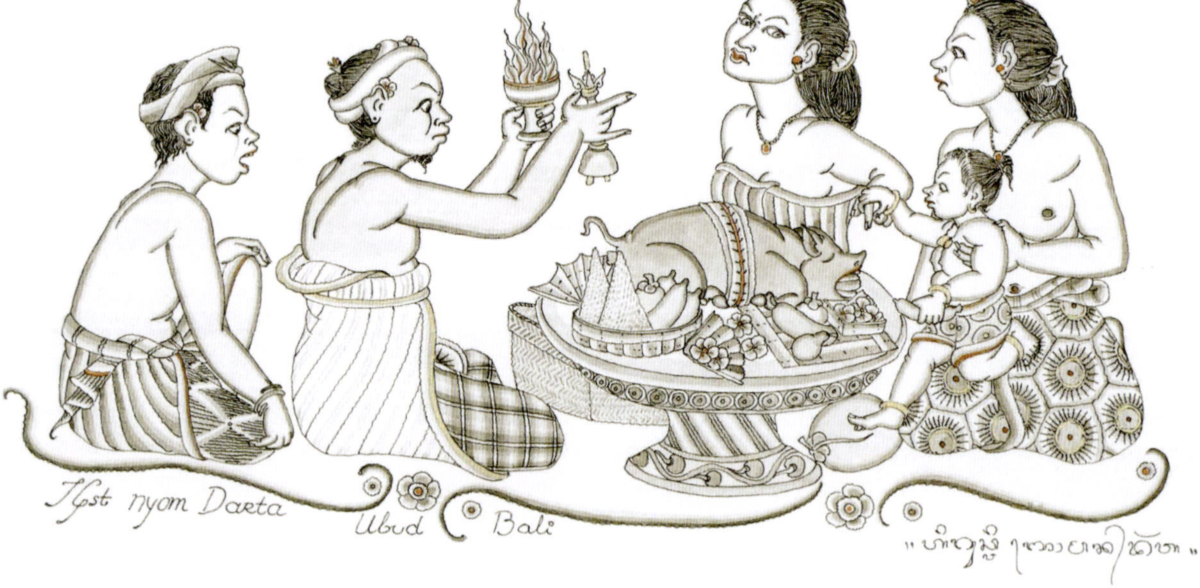

THE 210-DAY CEREMONY: In this illustration of activities at a child's first *otonan*, a *pemangku* (low priest) officiates, welcoming (*mapag*) the child into the realm of full-fledged humans. He holds a *genta* bell and a *pasepan* fire. The offering is a roast suckling pig.

The Napak Pertiwi rite usually takes place either on the occasion of the three-month ceremony or, in some villages, the six-month ceremony (*otonan*). The celebrant is often a family priest, even though well-to-do families may engage the services of a reputed balian or high priest.

The 210-day Ceremony

Two-hundred and ten days is the full length of the Pawukon cycle, made of 30 individually named weeks, or *wuku.* It is also the amount of time it takes for the particular day when a person was born to repeat, that is, the same conjunction of days of the seven-day, five-day, and six-day weeks on a given wuku.

Thus, if someone is born on Soma (Monday of the seven-day week), Paing (of the five-day week) during Wuku Menail, then this same combination will recur every 210 days. This day, Soma-Paing-Menail, which is the closest equivalent to a birthday in the Pawukon calendar, is that person's *oton.* Therefore, the ceremony performed to celebrate it is called an *otonan.* The word *oton* comes from *wetu*, which means 'to come out'.

Every Balinese knows which days of the various weeks their oton falls on, as well as the auspicious and inauspicious traits associated with it. Yet, they usually do not know the true date of their Gregorian birthday, and in villages, at least, are often at wit's end when it comes to guessing their age.

Of all the otonan a person will go through, the first is the most important. It is through this ceremony that the semi-divine child definitively rejoins the human world. Accordingly, it is also the moment when the child is formally introduced to the neighborhood community (*banjar*). It is often accompanied by a great feast to which representatives of all households in the community are invited. They come bearing contributions of rice, coffee, sugar, and incense, and leave bearing portions of pork sate and other food to take home.

The Hyang Kumara shrine is pulled down, a sign that the child, after a final mantra addressed to the child god, will lose his semi-divine status and protection. From now on, all rites and ceremonies for the child will go through the ancestors' shrines in the family temple.

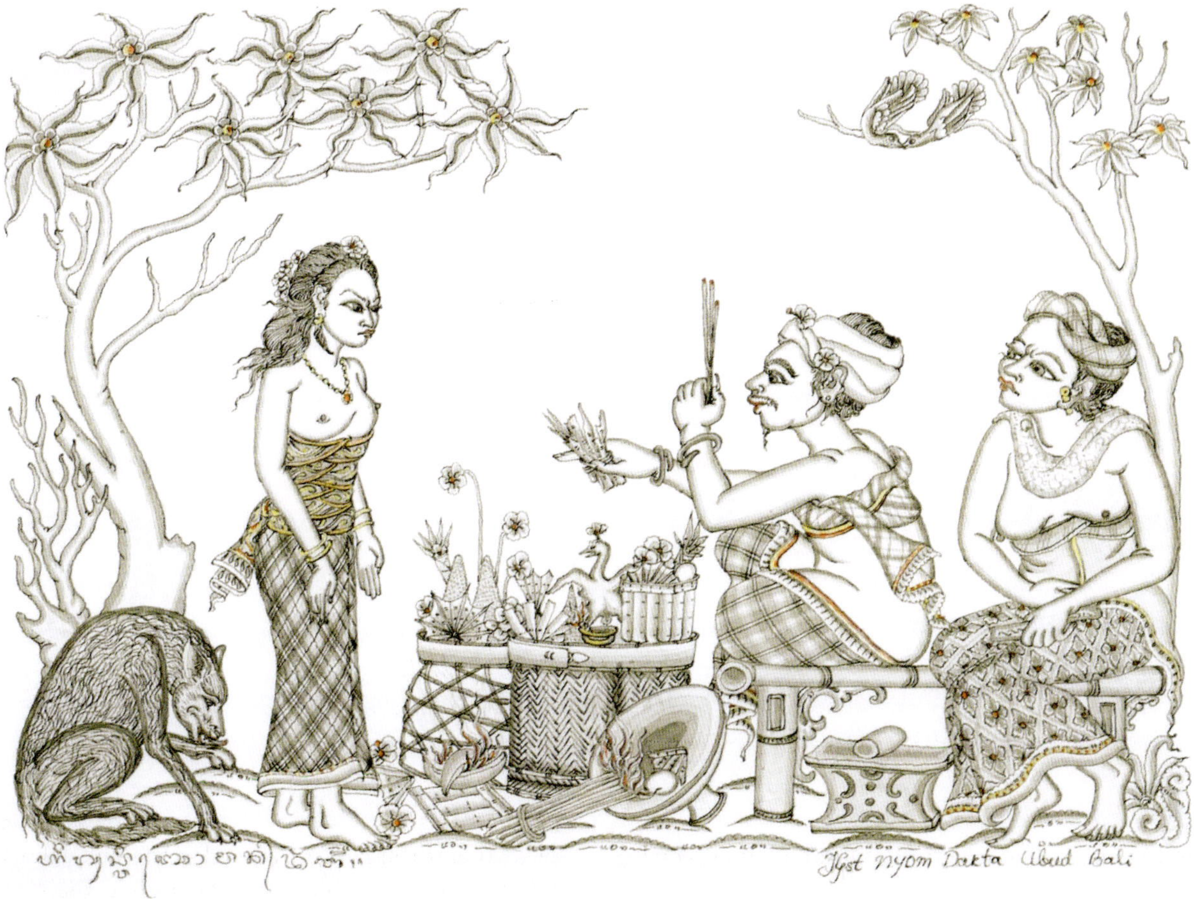

THE PUBERTY CEREMONY: This drawing depicts a priest performing a *mabiakala* cleansing rite for a pubescent girl. He holds in his hands a small vegetal holy water sprinkler (*lis*). Between him and the girl is a set of offerings comprising rice cones (*tumpeng*) and *pejati* notification offerings. These offerings lie on a kind of basket (*sok*) which the girl is going to kick, thus symbolically repelling the demonic forces that will tempt her with the coming of adolescence.

Other mantras are recited to fully 'separate' the kanda mpat from the fully incarnated human, and to send them to the directions of the compass to which they belong. Thus, Anggapati will go east, Rajapati south, Banaspati west, and Banaspati Raja north.

The Puberty Ceremony

This ceremony celebrates puberty, marked for the girl by her first menstruation, and for the boy by a change in his voice. Following this introduction to adolescence, boys and girls become members of the community youth associations (*seka teruna/teruni*) through which they will manage their onward passages into adulthood. The ceremony indicates that as an unmarried virgin (*bramacari*) the young person is prepared to submit to the cosmic influence of the gods Semara and Ratih, the male and female symbols of love and sexual union. The offerings differ for girls and boys: the girl's main offering refers to the letting of blood (*tabuh rah*), while the boy's emphasizes his potency (*ngraja singa*).

Since the young girl's menstrual blood is considered impure (*leteh*), she must undergo a short period of seclusion. In some cases, her mother has her taste 'seven ritual flavors' that constitute a symbolic initiation to the pleasures of adult life.

The Tooth-filing ceremony

The *metatah* or *mesangih* ceremony involves the filing of six teeth in the upper jaw, namely the two canine teeth and four incisors. It is believed that pointed teeth connote animal and demonic character. This is associated with the story of Kala Tatwa.

Kala, the lord of time, was born when the semen of interrupted sexual intercourse between Siwa and his consort Uma fell into the sea. Siwa agrees to recognize Kala as his son only after he has cut his canine teeth. Thus, access to God is possible only for those who control their animal nature. The ceremony is also related to the story of Siwa burning the god of love Semara and the moon goddess Ratih.

Tooth-filing is said to give people proper control over six private enemies (*sad ripu*): desire (*kama*), greed (*loba*), anger (*kroda*), intoxication (*mada*), confusion (*moha*), and jealousy (*matsarya*). In theory, tooth-filing should be carried out before marriage, but may in practice be delayed. Nowadays, because of the great expense involved, the tooth-filing ceremony is usually done collectively by an extended family group, most often on the occasion of a wedding or a post-cremation ceremony (*nyekah* or *mukur*).

After prayers in the family temple and purification, the young people, hair freshly cut, and dressed in beautiful new white and yellow attire,

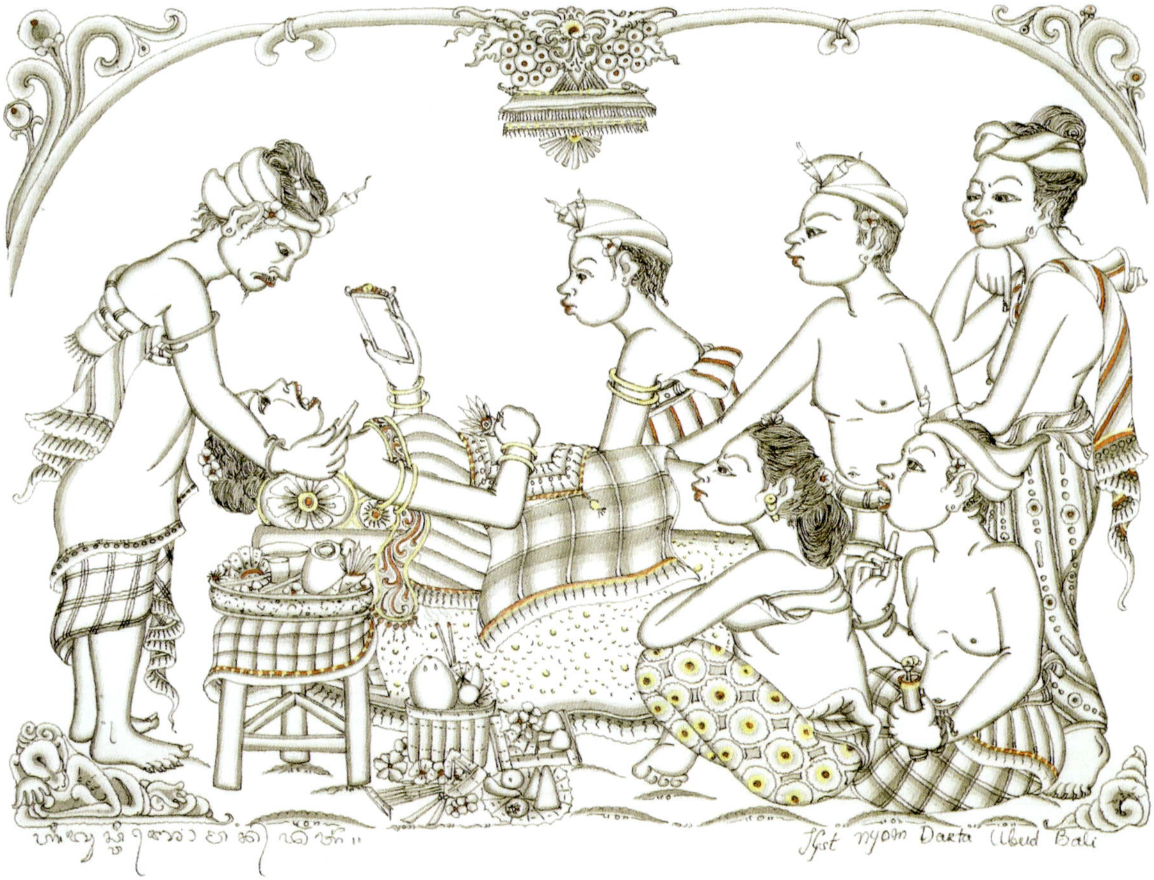

THE TOOTH-FILING CEREMONY: The drawing shows a young woman looking in a mirror at her filed teeth. The *sangging* priest who has just finished the filing, still holds the file in his right hand. On a stool next to the woman's head are some of the other implements used during the ceremony: a water bowl, a coconut with its upper part chopped off, for spitting into, several files, and a triangular *kwangen* offering whose shape and color symbolize the Hindu trinity (*trimurti*) and lords of the directions of the compass. The woman holds another kwangen in her hands. On the ground is a *penanjung* offering to keep evil influences away during the tooth-filing rite.

lie down on the cots specially prepared for the occasion in the ceremonial pavilion of the selected family compound. Their head pointing upstream, they lie on a symbolic representation of the god of love Semara and his consort Ratih as a sign that the time of sexual union is approaching. They may not move from their cots before the ceremony is over, lest 'danger' ensue.

The 'patients' are handled one by one. The rite begins with sacred *rajah* letters being written on the body—teeth, chest, forehead, navel, and thigh—by the *sangging* priest in charge. He uses a red ring for this purpose. The patient's mouth is held wide open with a piece of sugar cane. Then the filing takes place, following which the patient bites hard on a betel leaf. Spitting is forbidden, except into a coconut provided for this purpose, which is usually held by the mother.

Once the filing is done, the youths are handed a mirror so they can look at what has become of their teeth, although the filing is usually superficial. They are also given six flavors to taste, a sign that they have now entered adulthood. Another set of prayers completes the ceremony.

The Wedding Ceremony

Marriage marks the passage of the young man and woman to the second stage of life (*grahasta*)

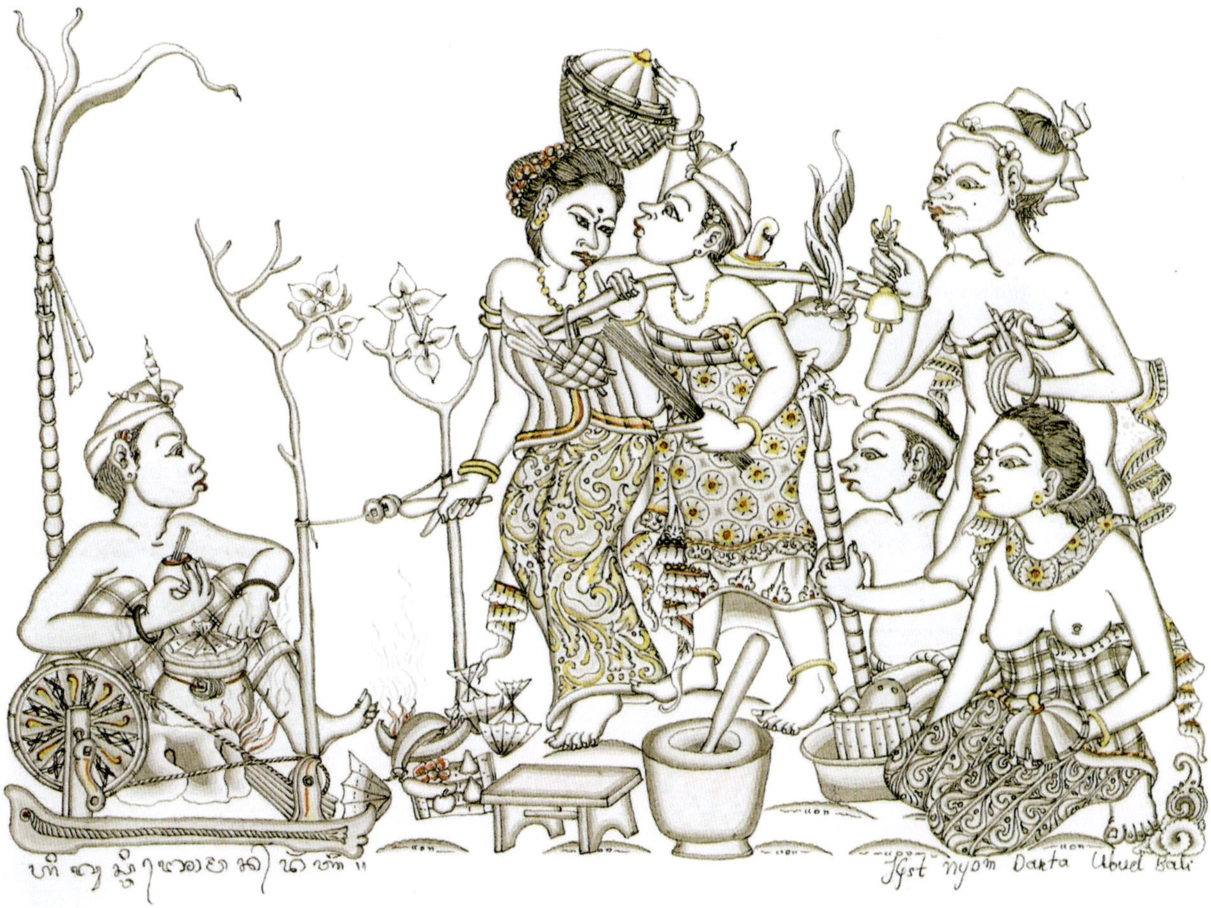

THE WEDDING CEREMONY: In the wedding scene shown in this drawing, the groom, in the center, carries farm produce, while the bride carries a basket containing things she is going to sell at the market. The groom holds a short broom, ready to beat his wife should the need arise. Meanwhile, she gets ready to cut the thread, thus releasing money. A spinning wheel, a small stool, and a mortar are in wait for her; Balinese women are never idle. One can also see a tekep api offering—two crossed half-coconuts—below the thread. In the rear, a priest stands jingling his bell.

during which they will try to find a new balance between the three goals of life (*triguna*): desire (*kama*), wealth (*artha*), and virtue (*dharma*). They will fall under the influence of kama, but try to control it through dharma, so as to properly accumulate the wealth needed to raise a family. Only in the next stage (*wanaprasta*), the 'forest stage', will they fully focus on dharma.

There are several ways to enter into a marriage (*pawiwahan*). In the first (*mapadik*), the marriage is organized by the family, who always tries to find their son or daughter a spouse from the proper caste and kinship group. In this case, there is a complex set of social procedures to follow before the wedding proper takes place: a proposal or request to marry (*mepadik*) leading to an engagement; the fetching of the woman (*mejauman/ mulih nelok*) at her house, where she takes leave of her ancestors (*mepamit*), and the wedding ceremony proper (*mesakapan*), during which the bride is introduced (*mapiuning*) to her husband's ancestors in his family temple.

More common today is *ngerorod* or *merangkat*, the elopement of the girl, chosen either to circumvent the girl's family's objections, or to marry at cheaper cost. In this case, a respected intermediary informs the parents of the elopement. In the face of a fait accompli, they usually relent. The girl then takes leave of her ancestors only after the actual wedding ceremony.

Another traditional type of marriage is *meglandang*, or forced elopement. It has been banned by the authorities since Dutch times, but in the case of *ngejuk* (taking), it cannot be totally ignored. This is when, after forcing a girl to have sex—in effect, raping her—the youth takes responsibility for his act and asks her to marry him. She may refuse to accept her fate. Otherwise, shame and social pressure, accompanied by the proper mantras and the help of a reputed balian, compel the girl to yield to a marriage that often ends up in divorce or infidelity.

Yet another type of marriage is the *nyentana*, through which a family without any male heir (*sentana*) adopts the son-in-law as their son. The adopted groom must give up his bonds to his natural ancestors to look after those of his wife.

The actual wedding ceremony begins with a series of *mabiakala* offerings placed on the ground at various points in the house compound. These offerings are specially addressed to the earthly forces (*buta*). Then the bride and groom mimic several aspects of their future life as husband and wife. The symbols mainly relate to the loss of virginity and to fertility, as well as to marriage as an economic institution.

As prayers are intoned, the newlyweds circle clockwise three times around a group of offerings, the groom carrying goods hung on a shoulder pole, the bride goods in a basket on her head. As they walk, they break through a thread stretched across their path, and the bride stomps on a coconut. Then they enact a mock market scene in which the bride, squatting on a coconut, 'sells' food and cloth to the groom in exchange for Chinese kepeng coins. Then they eat together, feeding each other in public.

After this, the bride and groom retire to bathe and change into new clothes. In the past, this involved bathing in the river and throwing away their old clothes. The second part of the ceremony then unfolds. The priest blesses the couple on the ceremonial pavilion, and they go into the family temple to pray and receive the blessings of the ancestors.

The Kanda Mpat: The Individual's Cosmic Siblings

The Kanda Mpat are an individual's 'four cosmic siblings'. They symbolically express the Balinese concept of macrocosm and microcosm (Bhuana Agung and Bhuana Alit), linking the elements of the universe to the elements of the self. These siblings are present from the moment of conception, suggesting that even in the darkness of the womb, a human being is already a microcosm of the entire universe. From one phase of life to the next, they evolve and change names as the person grows and ages. Upon death, they transform once more, eventually dissolving back into their macrocosmic origin. Their presence illustrates how the individual is but a microcosmic component of a macrocosmic whole, emerging from the source only to eventually return to it.

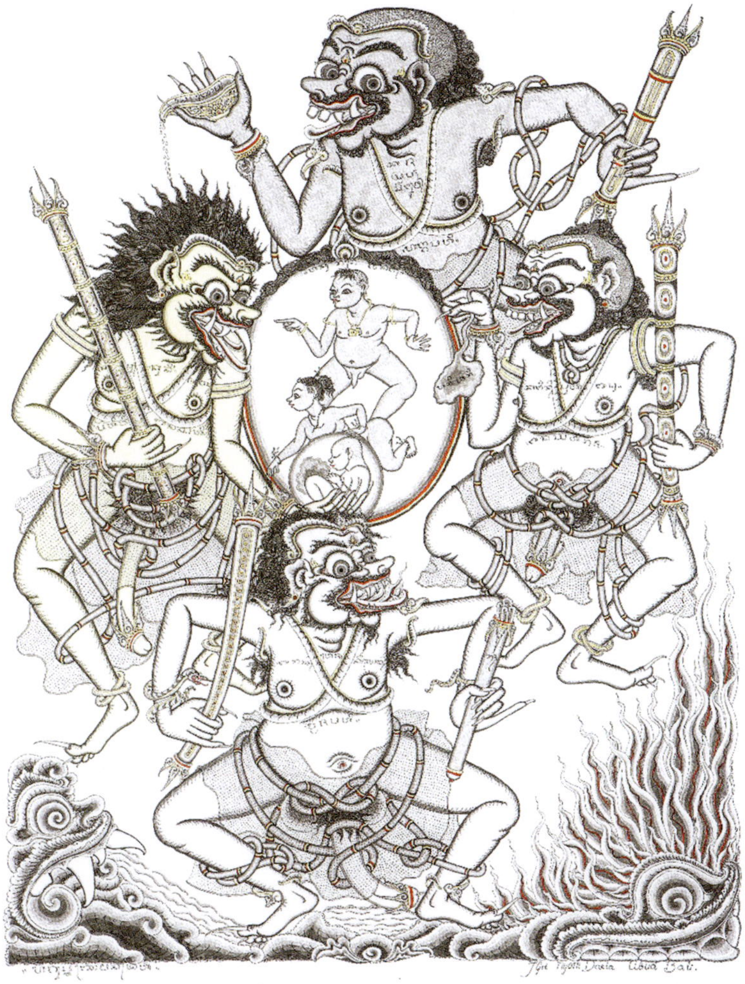

The Kanda Mpat represent at birth the cosmic forces such as they accompany the human being at birth and with different names, through life and after death.

The Multi-dimensional Link to the Cosmos
The correspondence between the micro- and macro-cosmos is mapped onto the Balinese *pangider-ider* (the cosmic rose of the winds). The siblings correspond, under their changing names, to the following elements:

Category	East (Purwa)	South (Daksina)	West (Pascima)	North (Uttara)	Center (Pancer/Space)
Birth Element	Yeh Nyom (Amniotic)	Ari-ari (Placenta)	Getih (Blood)	Puser (Cord)	The Infant (Self)
Life Name	Anggapati	Rajapati	Banaspati	Banaspati Raja	I Jati/The Self
Element	Air (Bayu)	Fire (Teja)	Water (Apah)	Earth (Pertiwi)	Ether (Akasa)
Physical Link	Breath/Nerves	Heat/Vitality	Metabolism	Flesh/Bone	Consciousness
Psychological Role	Guardian of Mind	Guardian of Form	Guardian of Senses	Leader/Protector	The Witness (Ego)
Deity (Dewa)	Lord Iswara	Lord Brahma	Lord Mahadewa	Lord Wisnu	Lord Siwa
Demon (Kala)	Kala Petak	Kala Bang	Kala Jenar	Kala Ireng	Kala Tattwa
Symbolic Color	White	Red	Yellow	Black	Polychrome
Afterlife Duty	Guarding the Grave	Fire of Change	Guide of the Soul	Gatekeeper	Unity with Source

Conclusion: The Eternal Balance

In this system, the Pancer (The Center) represents Ether or Space, the container for all other elements. This teaches that health and happiness depend entirely on balance. When you honor your 'siblings' through mindfulness and right action, they protect you as Gods (*dewa*). However, when you live in greed or anger, they manifest as the demons (*buta kala*) of your own psyche.

You are the conductor of this cosmic quartet, orchestrating the energy of the universe within your own body. The Kanda Mpat and their related offerings (*banten-segehan*) are the practical application of Balinese spiritual philosophy. They represent the method used to maintain Life Balance: the transition of these forces from their 'wild' demonic state into their 'protective' divine state, a process called Somya, the turning of chaos into harmony.

Note: The Kanda Mpat are the same regardless of one's gender.

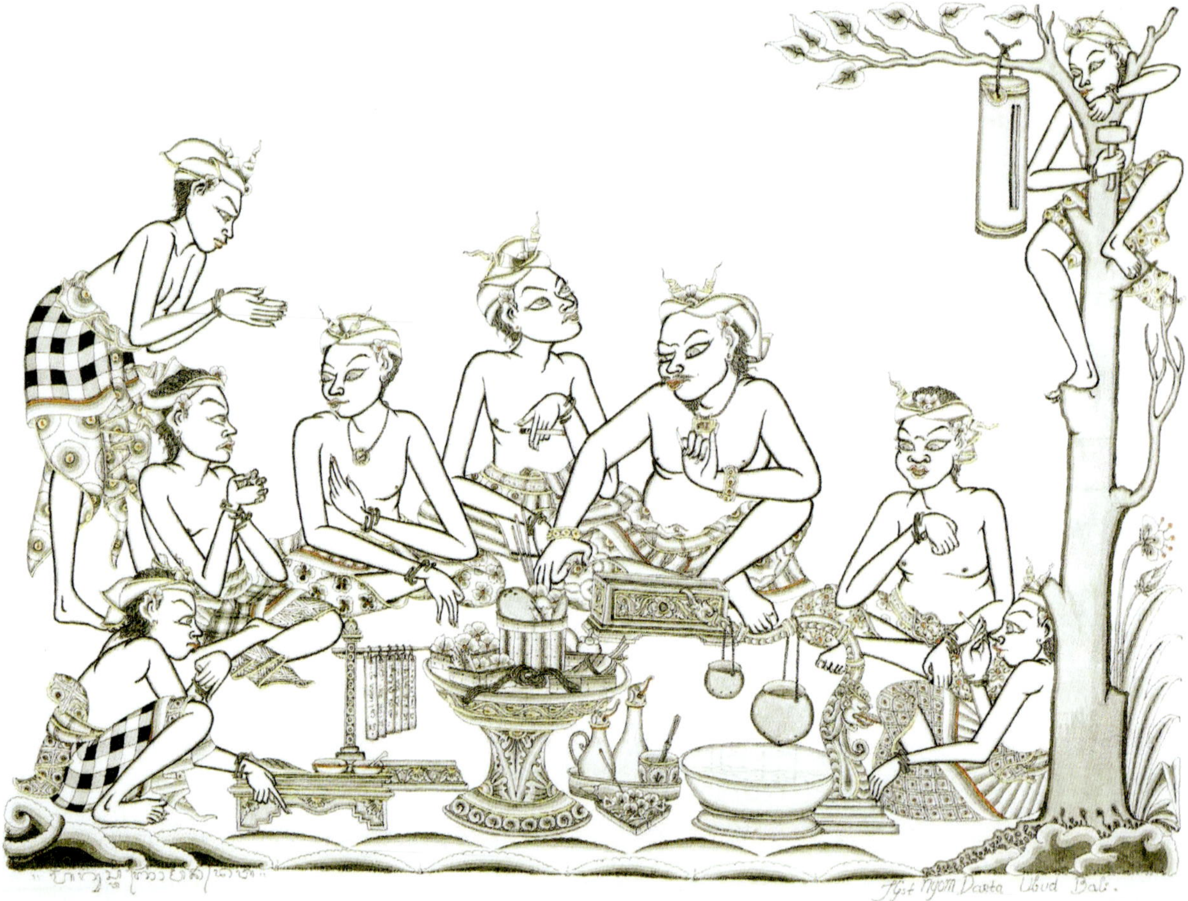

A BANJAR MEETING: Perched in a tree on the right, a man strikes a wooden slit drum (*kulkul*), 'tong', then hits the opposite side, 'ting', followed by quickly repeated but weakening 'tong-tong-tong-tong'. These sounds summon the married male villagers to attend the meeting. They come one by one, each hanging their lontar-leaf summons (*urak*) on a decorated wooden hanger (lower left). After most urak are in place, the banjar leader (*klian*), seated behind the betel box, fills two pierced coconut shells (*ceeng*) with water. When no more water drips from the hole of the smaller ceeng, latecomers will pay half a fine (*dosa*); those who arrive after the big ceeng is empty, will pay the full fine. The meeting is inaugurated by untying the knot of the rope on the platter in the middle, which lies next to some offerings addressed to the gods, as well as a betel set. Offerings to the earthly forces (*buta kala*) are on the ground. Upon closure of the meeting, the klian will store the urak in a box, visible in the center, and disband the meeting while the men chew the betel.

Adult Life and Ritual Obligations

Just as Balinese individuals are considered to be fully incarnated humans only after their first *otonan*, they become fully adult only upon marriage. They then become 'old' (*tua*), as people used to say, and as such, full members of a household (*pekurenan*), through which they also become full members of the village community (*kerama desa*).

A pekurenan is the union of male (*purusa*) and female (*pradana*), in conformity with the Rwabhinneda principle of generalized cosmic dualism—spirit/matter, day/night, male/female, tangible/intangible, good/bad.

Bali is a patriarchal society, so when it comes to the distribution of roles between the couple and within the village, power rests with the male. Only men participate in the meetings of the *banjar* (sub-village level neighborhood community), usually held once every lunar month or once every 35 days, according to the calendar of reference.

At banjar meetings, community issues are discussed, mainly but not only pertaining to customary ritual matters. The work decided during these meetings is then divided up to be carried out by male and female work units, respectively. The men cut the wood and bamboo needed to make platforms, bamboo walls, and other ritual implements. They also slaughter animals and prepare ritual kebabs and food and offerings made of meat. In contrast, the women are entrusted with the preparation of all the other offerings, both those plaited of coconut leaves and those made of colored rice flour dough, which accompany every ceremony.

The activities decided by such meetings occupy a large proportion of available time. Further, all Balinese are part of interlocked communities that constitute as many congregations, each with its own temple and ritual paraphernalia. Banjar members are typically not only members of a larger village (*desa*) community consisting of two or more banjar, but also at least three, and sometimes more village temple congregations.

Additionally, villagers may also be members of an irrigation community (*subak*) if they own land, and a kinship organization (*merajan gede, dadia*), and other royal and territorial temple congregations, such as *pura penataran.* They are enmeshed in a web of social relations and obligations that frames, but also extends well beyond the fields of their economic activities.

This web of social links entwines the Balinese pekurenan in an unending cycle of ritual duties (*ayahan*) and other social duties. No week passes without a husband and wife participating in the preparation of a village temple festival here, being on call to the banjar to give a hand at a princely cremation there, or being a guest at a tooth-filing or other extended family ceremony somewhere else, not to mention having to prepare a village exorcism (*rsi gana*). In their own homes, they also must take care of daily offerings: full moon, new moon, and Kajeng-Kliwon offerings every 15 day, and *adalan* ceremonies in their family temples every 210 days.

As time passes, the married couple have children, for whom they conduct all the relevant rites of passage: birth rites, otonan, tooth-filing, and weddings. At marriage, daughters 'take leave' of their fathers' ritual networks and are received into their husbands'. They lose all rights to their fathers' properties as well. Male heirs, on the other hand, carry on with their fathers' networks and duties as well as inheriting from the latter. People tend to spoil their male children, who will be the ones to finance and undertake their parents' cremations.

Neighborhood Obligations

During adult life, the Balinese have to participate in numerous collective activities, called *ayahan.* The most important take place at the level of the banjar.

The *ayahan banjar*, or 'neighborhood working-bee', corresponds to a broad range of demands. Sometimes the banjar community initiates the duty. An example could be when cleaning and security duties are needed. At other times, a working session will be held at the request of a member who needs help for a cremation or a kinship temple festival.

It may also originate at the village level, for example, when the different banjar provide the work units needed for the preparation of the

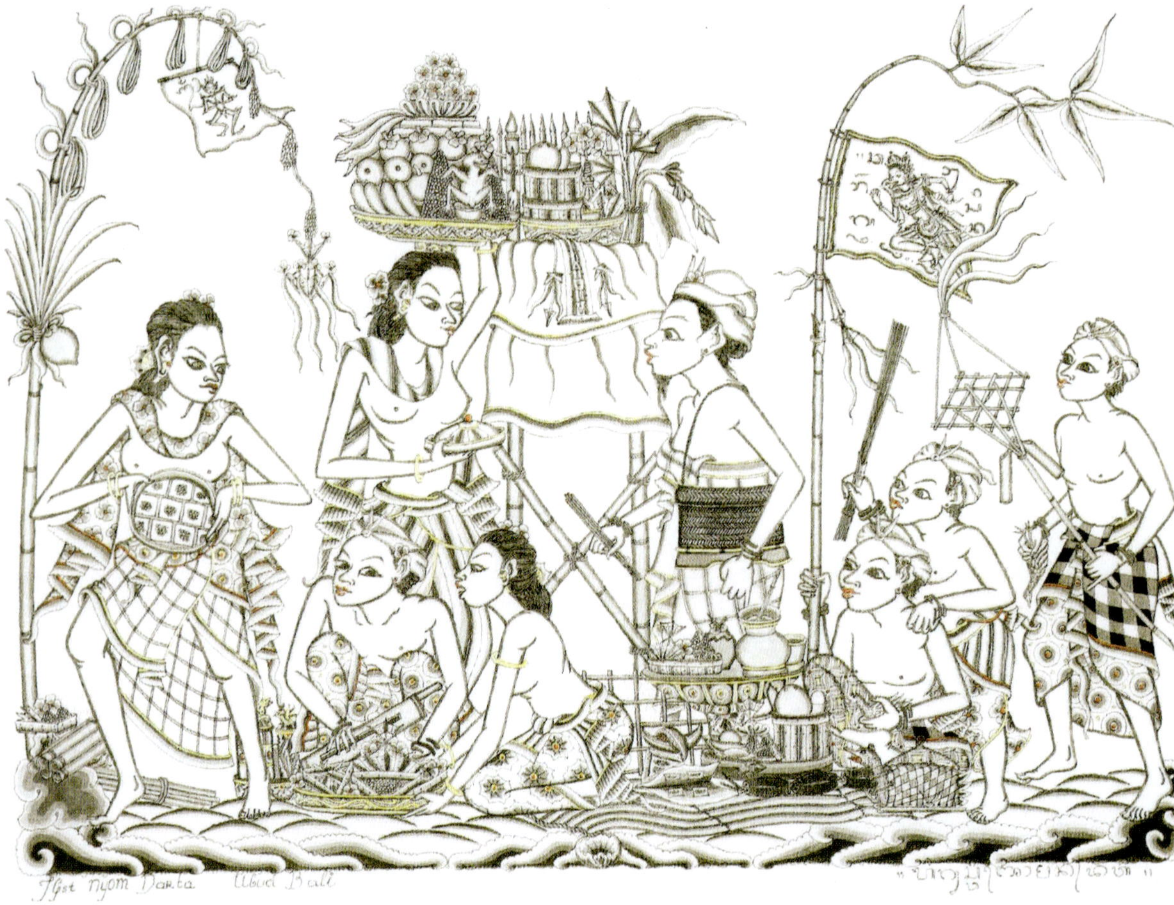

A RSI GANA EXORCISM: This drawing depicts a purification ceremony in a Rsi Gana exorcism, which usually takes place after an unexpected catastrophe or death, or other events attributed to intangible (*niskala*) forces. The god invoked for his wisdom and protection at this purification is Gana, Siwa's elephant-headed son by the goddess Durga. Gana is better known in the West under his Indian name, Ganesha. Gana is drawn on the flag to the right, and an image of the Supreme God Acintya (Siwa in a protective function) on the flag on the left. Offerings addressed to the chthonian forces are on the ground (right), while offerings to the Sun god Surya are on the bamboo shrine (middle). The standing woman (middle) carries a *pejati* notification offering to present to the gods. Another woman (left) holds a daily *saiban* offering basket. By her feet are three bamboo sticks that will be struck to scare away demons. The man squatting between the women strikes a bamboo bell. Other men (right) hold bamboo sticks, a broom, and a *sanggah cucuk* bamboo structure with a similar purpose. A high priest (*pedanda*) would normally lead the rite, but is not visible here. The people will turn three times around the shrine counter-clockwise while striking bamboo and singing "Budal kala ngrauhang sesari" (Go back home, demons, enter the offerings).

village temple festivals, as the banjar members are also members of the main village temple congregations: the *pura desa* (village temple), the *pura puseh* (temple of origin), and the *pura dalem* (temple of the dead). Finally, the ayahan working-bee may also be called up by the authorities for purposes such as the building of a road or attendance at a speech on family planning. The working groups are suited to the importance of the task. For events such as cremations, the whole banjar is involved, but for minor occasions only sections of the banjar, called *tempekan*, are called up.

A big or regular ayahan is usually discussed in the meetings, which the banjar community holds every month of the Balinese wuku calendar system, that is, every 35 days. The call to meet is announced by the beating of the *kulkul* wooden slit drum.

"Ida dane sareng sami!" (Gentlemen!) begins the *klian dinas* (official head of the banjar as a village government unit), "We have here a request from the district head to participate in the making of a mud road between the hamlet of Dauh Tukad and the market of Ambengan Kauh. He asks us to supply ten men for fifteen days. As Indonesian citizens and supporters of economic development, we cannot refuse this request."

Then it is the turn of the *klian adat* (head of the banjar as a customary law institution), to speak: "We have also received a request from the families of the Kebon Tubuh clan. The bodies of their dead have been waiting for a long time in the cemetery and they believe the souls are still enslaved by Batari Durga, *Kari ngaturang ayah ring Batari Durga.* We have been asked to help in the preparation of their collective cremation, which will take place on the day Manis Kajeng of Wuku Ugu, two months from now, as decided by the high priest.

"That is not all. As you are already aware, eight days from now, our young men will be called up to 'throw away' (*ngutang*) the body of the *anak lingsir* (elder) from the palace of banjar Ambengan. The cremation tower is going to be nine tiers high. Five banjar will participate so it should not be too much work. We owe our respects to the old man because of our position as *panjak* (serfs), and because of the fact that he fought for us during the Revolusi (war of independence)."

Once the discussion is over and decisions are reached by consensus, smaller meetings (*paum*) follow to discuss in great detail the implementation of the various projects, particularly in relation to the quantity and type of labor requested.

Sometimes, only men's work (*ayahan muani*) will be called up while at other times women's work (*ayahan/uh*), will be requested. Often, couples are involved (*ayahan/uh muani*). Unmarried people, who are not yet full citizens of the village, do not normally take part in the work, except for limited purposes, such as dance, welcome, etc.

The ayahan banjar is not always a scheduled event. Emergencies such as death are unpredictable. Banjar customary laws (*awig-awig*) have stipulations for all contingencies, and each banjar citizen knows exactly what to do as a matter of habit.

Emergencies are announced by the pounding of the kulkul drum. The accelerated pounding (*kulkul bulus*) means that there is great danger, like a fire, murder, or someone running amok. All the men come out with their swords or *keris.*

Upon the repeated three-beat striking of the wooden drum, people know that a fellow banjar member has died. A messenger will follow, bringing news of who it is. Men get ready with their machetes, saws, and other woodcutting tools, while women prepare rice, white cloth, and sometimes, money.

Next, they all go to the deceased's house to work together. The work itself varies according to the family's decision of whether the corpse is going to be buried, cremated right away (*mekingsan di api*), or preserved with chemicals while awaiting a later cremation.

The ayahan work, which is implemented under the direction of the klian, is often physical. Some men dig, while others cut and split wood, preparing the many provisional shrines, fences, or other wood and bamboo implements. Yet others prepare the vegetables and meat needed for the food. The women prepare the offerings under the guidance of a Brahmin woman or another specialist.

Everyone, with the exception of the high priest, is expected to participate in the collective work and be willing to dirty their hands, although some duties are light, such as assignments involving dance, music, and security. The duty is allocated according to a person's talents whenever possible.

If, for example, a high priest is needed, the banjar member considered to have the best command of High Balinese will be entrusted to visit the holy man and beg him to 'descend' (*tedun*) and visit his followers.

Participation in ayahan duties is obligatory, although it is possible to have oneself replaced by a family member, or by payment. Attendance is a serious matter. When ayahan work is taking place, the klian checks who is present or absent (*ngetos*) and who is misbehaving. He will air his findings in public during the next collective monthly meeting. Fines will be announced. While these fines are never big, the shame can be unbearable, especially if one is reputed to be indolent, or even worse, dishonest.

"I Made Kiul," the klian may say, "was caught eating the *lawar* food he was cooking. Fined Rp. 200! Ketut Dollar stole Rp. 1000 which was destined to buy a lamp. He is fined five times the amount, Rp. 5000."

This goes on, taking up the first half of the banjar meeting. Such respect of discipline is strongly advocated by its members, particularly the poorest ones and those belonging to the lowest caste groups. Even if the customary law is not formally broken, banjar members do not easily forget or forgive lapses in acceptable behavior, particularly in relation to ayahan work for death rituals.

Those who are too often replaced or fined had better beware. When it is the turn of the 'negligent' member to need the help of the others, they may not show up, or even worse, in the case of a death, they may 'accidentally' drop the body in a roadside gutter. The only way to compensate for neglecting banjar duties is by a show of over-generosity in repairing temples, paying for dances, and the like.

Ayahan participation exacts a cost but also entails privileges, particularly in relation to food. Villagers bring uncooked rice, coconuts, and other implements, but they expect food and polite treatment in return. The 'higher' the family receiving help, the higher the expectations, although there is a minimum that is defined by banjar customary law.

The banjar members do not so much judge the food as the family who is putting on the ceremony. If the family is high caste, with a reputation for stinginess, it is in for trouble as the banjar members may start looking for faults. This is one of the reasons why powerful families are especially tense during big ceremonies, such as cremations. They can put on a big show only with the help of their fellow villagers, but by doing so, they also put themselves at their mercy. They had better be generous and behave, or else!

The banjar, the Balinese say, is an association for the sharing of *suka* (joy) and *duka* (pain). The ayahan working-bee sees to it that the banjar serves as a tool for social harmony and conformity.

Growing Old Wisely

When people grow old, they often remain participants of community working-bees as long as their health allows. Yet, when they weaken, they know when to withdraw from active life and hand over their social responsibilities to their heirs. They then enter the *wanaprastha* period of 'withdrawal into the forest', meaning that they focus on religion and holy texts, sometimes to become priests. They often take up residence in the ceremonial pavilion of the family compound (*bale dangin*).

All this time, however, they may remain engaged in domestic activities, making household items or participating in jobs such as coconut-oil making, chicken and pig breeding, or vegetable growing. Old age in Bali signifies power rather than decrepitude. Instead of being 'ruled' by the younger members of the family, they 'rule' everybody and their commands are absolute.

As everywhere throughout the world, the main function of Balinese grandfathers and grandmothers is to look after their grandchildren, teaching them good manners and telling them educational stories. This is good for both generations. The children need instruction, while the elders long for communication.

Rites of Death

Death engages a new phase in the cycle of the soul. The two types of components of the person—the five elements, on the one hand, and the incarnated soul, on the other—which once merged in lovemaking, have now to return to their respective origins. They have to be separated. The physical body (*stula sarira*) will end up in the lower part of the world, in the sea, to eventually merge into the five elements. The soul (*sukma sarira*) is expected to rejoin the spiritual forces, gods, ancestors, and accompanying deities who symbolically dwell above the mountainous heights.

The ceremonies of death are complex, and of many varieties, either due to local traditions or to different statuses and circumstances. Thus, upon death, the corpse may be preserved in wait for the cremation, which is what high-status families usually do. Or it may be buried; burned without a ritual cremation; or have disappeared. The cremation will take place with or without a corpse,

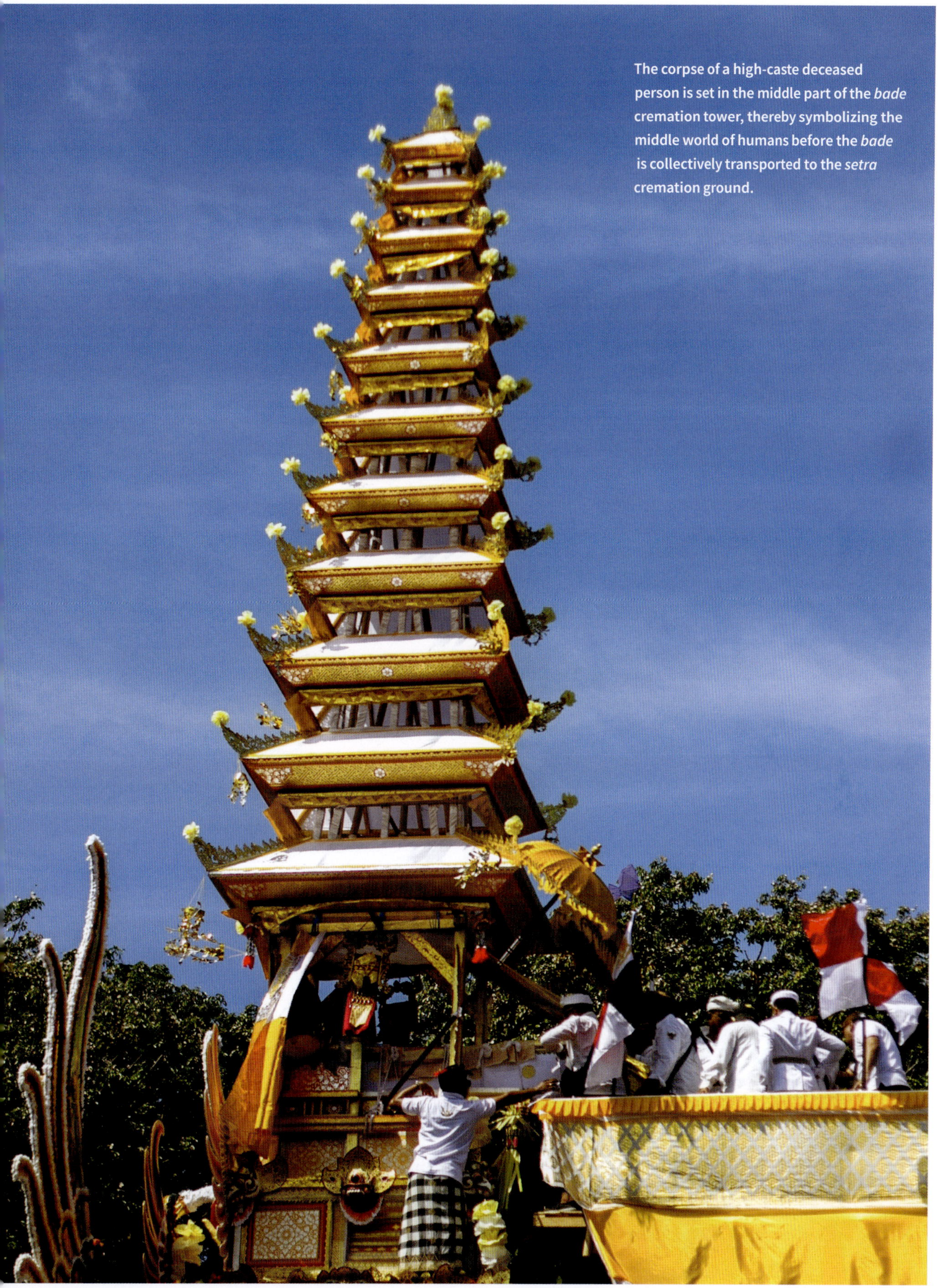

The corpse of a high-caste deceased person is set in the middle part of the *bade* cremation tower, thereby symbolizing the middle world of humans before the *bade* is collectively transported to the *setra* cremation ground.

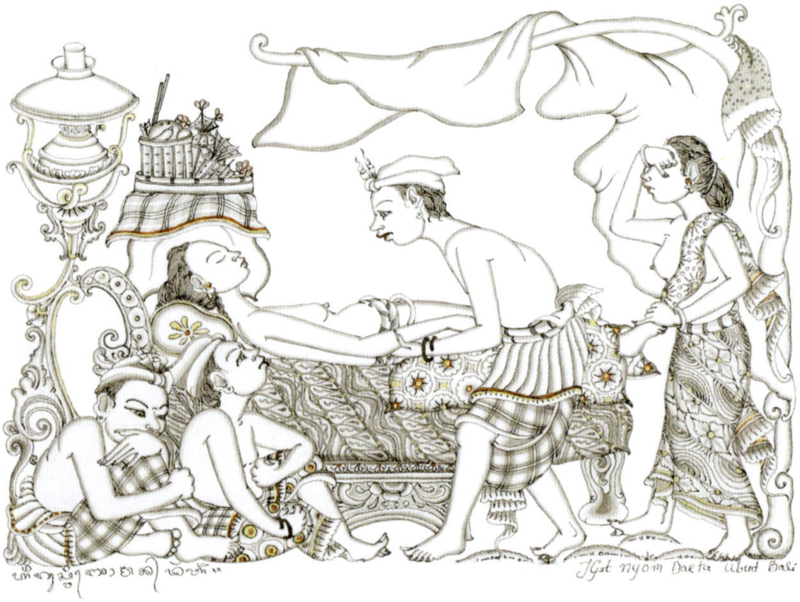

DEATH RITES: A woman has just passed away. Her relatives are grieving even though they may not cry, lest it disturb her soul. Her soul is still hovering in the vicinity of the corpse, and a *sanggah urip* is set next to the body as its symbolic seat. In the presence of death, no grief should be manifested. As one saying goes, "Da kanti yeh peningalan kena ked ke sawa, sang pitra/akar nemu jalan ane belig." (Don't let tears touch the corpse, lest the deceased find the road to heaven slippery.)

accordingly. In the first instance, the remains will be dug up, in the others the body will be represented by an effigy.

When someone dies, not only will the family members consult with one another to determine the type of ceremony to take place, but more importantly they will also consult the newly deceased through a medium (*nunas di baos*). The dead person, whose soul is still deemed to be around, will usually make demands pertaining to the grading of the upcoming cremation: superior (*utama*), medium (*madia*), or modest (*nista*). Or they may make a particular demand to be fulfilled during the cremation, such as a set of clothing. "Cening, yen cening lakar ngabenang pekak, baang pekak sarwah putih saperadeg." (Oh, my children, if you want to hold a cremation for me, buy me a set of white clothes.)

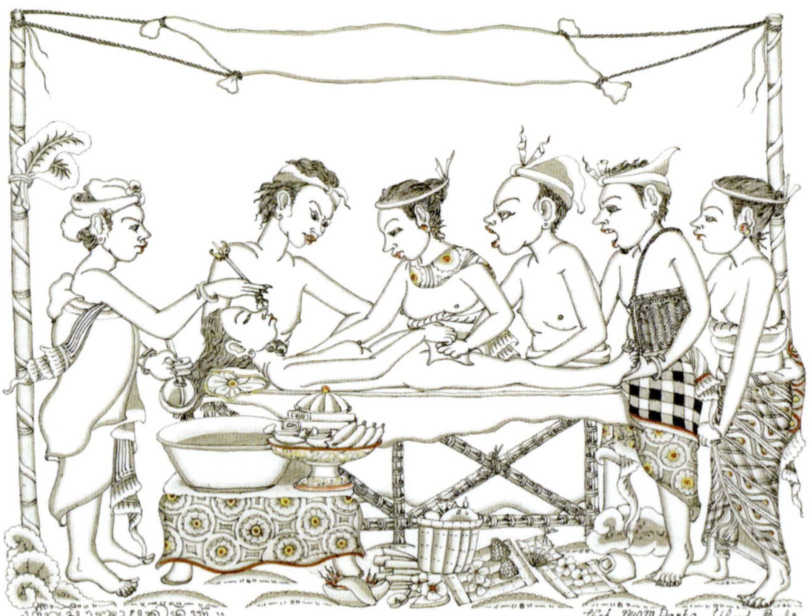

BATHING THE CORPSE: The corpse is bathed using a basin of water in which flowers have been scattered. Next to it is the symbolic food for the deceased which, at the end of the rite, will be put on the ground since the body will eventually rejoin the earth goddess, Pertiwi. Two offerings addressed to the *buta*—a burning *tekepan* coconut husk and a *segehan* offering—are also laid on the ground. To the left of the corpse, an unordained Brahmin priest (*wulaka*) officiates. He sprinkles holy water on the face of the deceased while uttering a mantra. A piece of cloth with holy syllables on it is placed over the genitals of the deceased. If the latter is a woman, this is done by a female relative; if a man, by a male relative. The cloth hanging above the scene is the *leluhur* symbol of the ancestral world that the soul is going to rejoin.

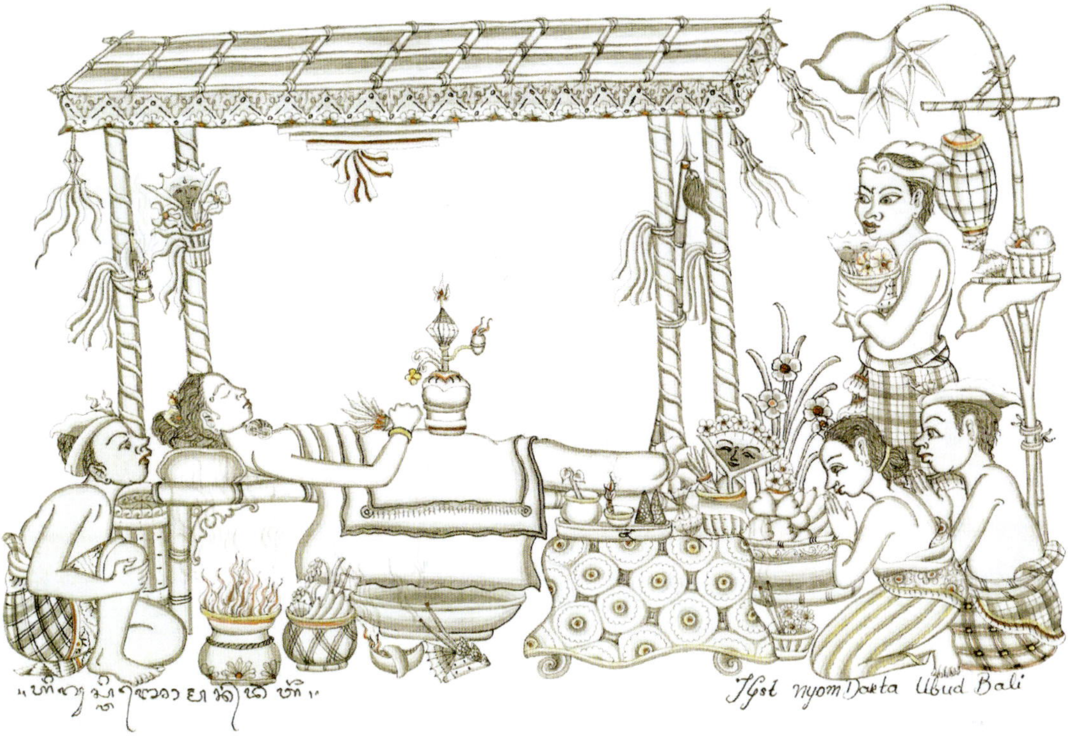

LYING IN STATE: This drawing depicts the normal situation when a body lies in state. The lampion, visible on the extreme right, is set up outside the compound. On the body, with a small oil lamp inside an empty egg shell, is the *angenan,* which symbolizes the presence of the soul. The oil is obtained from a priest. The *pengawak* symbol of the body is held by the man standing on the right; it will later be put next to the body. Beside the angenan and pangawak are a number of other offerings and implements, each with their own function. On the lower left, a *tabunen* fire has to be kept alive throughout the time the corpse lies in state. Close to it is a basket of fruit to symbolically feed the deceased. Next to the fruits a coconut *tekepan* fire is burning, with two sticks of a *segehan* offering abutting it. Below the bed is a big basin containing rice; this rice absorbs the liquid that drips from the decomposing body. In some mountain villages, this rice is eaten by the relatives of the deceased. Near the feet of the corpse are clothes and other implements symbolically related to the deceased, who is treated as if he or she were still alive. The offering attached to the pillar above the woman's head is the 'residence of life' (*sanggah urip*).

In the event, the grief of the family and kin will be handled, and thus softened, by a multiplicity of ritual activities. It is usually only upon completion of the rites of symbolic release (*nyekah* or *mukur*), when the dead person has become a deified ancestor (*dewa pitara* or *dewa hyang*), that the expression of emotions is allowed.

Bathing the Corpse

The first rite to which the deceased is subjected is bathing (*manyusang*), which is undertaken by the close relatives of the deceased, assisted by a priest. All first-degree relatives are expected to participate in washing, massaging, dressing, oiling, and perfuming the body, and more distant relatives and friends who feel moved to do so can join in as well.

Not all the dead undergo a cremation right after death. The richest families, as well as the members of some high-caste groups, may postpone the cremation until a propitious day. This might be months after the death. In the meantime, the body is kept lying in state.

Lying in State

After the bathing ceremony, the body is laid in state facing the impure western-downstream (*delod-kauh*) direction. The cremation, with all its ritual paraphernalia, might take place in a few days, or it might be postponed for months or years. If the body is not disposed of immediately, it is kept (*mesekeh*) in the ceremonial pavilion (*bale dangin*) and preserved in formalin.

Meanwhile, to prevent it from 'running wild', the soul is neutralized by offerings in the nearby

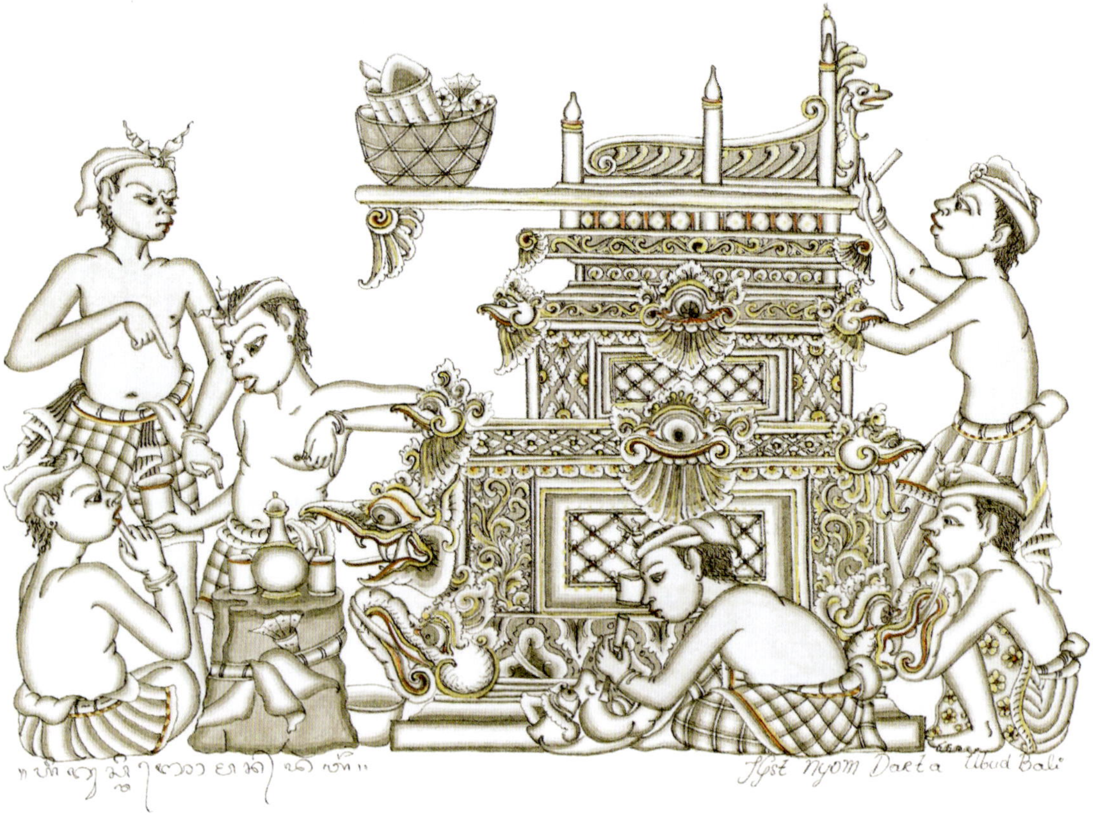

PREPARING THE BADE: The drawing depicts a scene of men at work on a very simple, single-level *bade*. On top of the palanquin is the bed-like platform on which the corpse or effigy of the deceased will be laid. A *santun penjejer* offering, signaling the ritual work in progress, is visible at its foot. At the head of the palanquin appears the beak of a goose. This animal symbolizes wisdom because it can feed itself from muddy waters, like a wise person does in life. Other elements of the illustration are the decorative motifs, which represent the life forms of the middle world: the elephant head motif (*karang asti* or *karang gajah*), the crow's head motif (*karang guak*), and the fern leaf motif (*karang simbar*).

shrine for the non-purified dead (*sanggar pitra*). When the time comes to begin the cremation rites proper (*ngwangun karya*), a sort of lampion (*damar kurung*) is set up outside the compound in which the death rites will take place. All this requires offerings, rituals, and often great expense.

Temporary Burial

Although some families may directly cremate the corpse, most bury the corpse (*makingsan di bumi*) or burn it provisionally (*makingsan di api*), waiting for a collective cremation to take place at the level of the banjar or kinship group (*warga*).

The burial, even though provisional, cannot be done without proper ceremony. This would invite the soul to turn into an erring soul (*atma kesasar*), a cause of illness and disorder. Before the burial, the family goes first to the Prajapati temple of the dead to present a 'notification' offering (*piuning*), entrusting the soul to the goddess of death whom it will faithfully serve (*ngaturang ayah*) while waiting for the exhumation of the body.

After the body has been ritually bathed and dressed, it is taken in procession to the cemetery to be entrusted to the custody of the goddess of the earth, Pertiwi, under the watchful eyes of the guardian of the cemetery (*sedahan setra*), Surya the sun god, as Ultimate Witness, and many others. There, the body will rest for months, or even years, until it is awakened and unearthed to be cremated.

This is the purpose of the awakening ceremony (*ngendag*), which is followed by the ritual opening of the grave (*ngagah*). The remains of the corpse are then collected, washed (the flesh taken away), and accompanied by an effigy, 'reconstituted' to make it suitable to be cremated. This is an ordeal

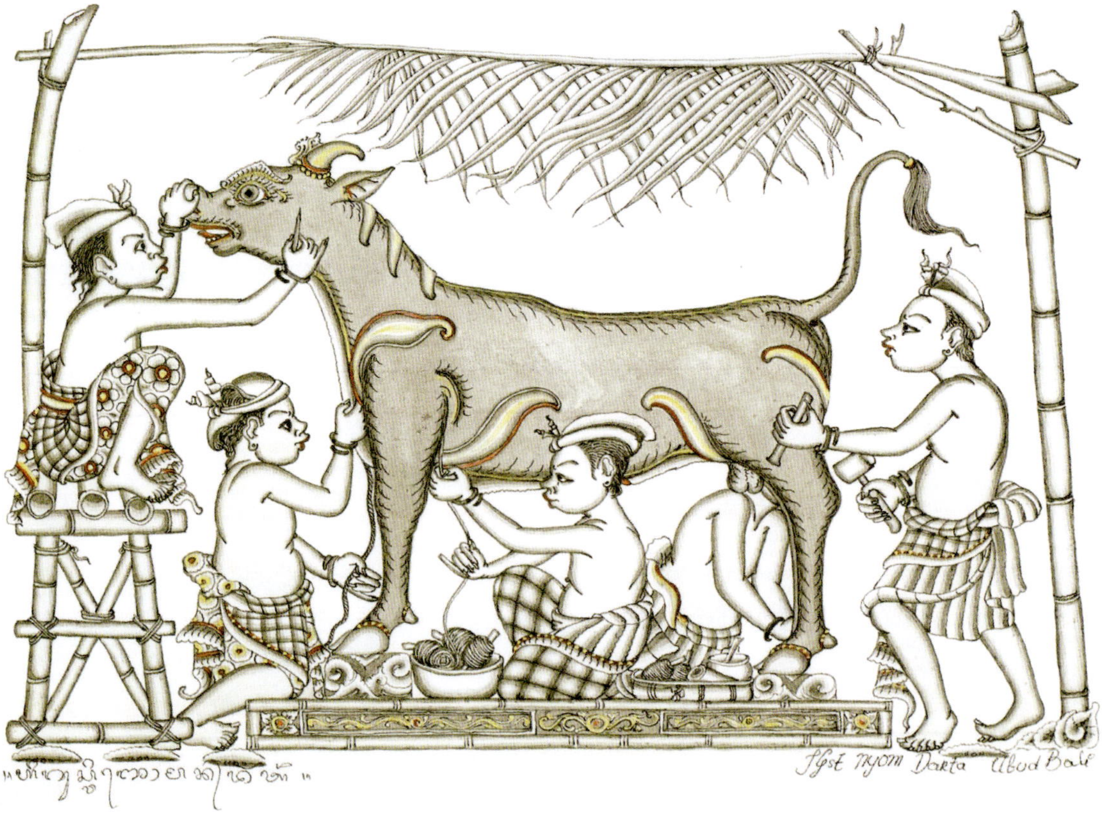

PREPARING THE SARCOPHAGUS: This illustration shows a group of relatives preparing a bull sarcophagus which is going to be the vehicle of the high-caste person being cremated.

for family members, many of whom today prefer to replace the unearthed corpse with an effigy.

Preparing the Bade

The *bade* (pronounced ba-day) is the structure used to carry the corpse from the compound of the deceased to the cremation grounds. It might be a simple palanquin, or an 11-tiered tower in the case of cremations for members of the nobility.

The size of the bade is determined using measurements based on the body of the dead person, according to the principles of cosmic harmony stated in the *Asta Kosala Kosali*, a Balinese system of architectural rules similar to Feng Shui.

The type of bade made will depend on the grading of the cremation to take place and the status of the deceased. The higher the caste, the taller it is and the more tiers it has, always an odd number (3, 5, 7, 9, 11). The pagoda-like structure of the bade symbolizes the structure of the world. Its tiers represent the heavenly world (*swah loka*), its base the earthly/demonic world (*bhur loka*), and its middle part the middle world of humans (*bhwah loka*). The corpse will be laid on a platform on this middle part. Various materials are used for the bade: bamboo, wood, papier-mache, and silk or cotton cloth.

Preparing the Sarcophagus

Relatives must also prepare the sarcophagus (*wadah* or *petulangan*) in which the body will be burned, sometimes with the help of a specialist (*sangging*). The wadah is made of the light, easy-to-carve wood of the trunk of an Albizia tree (Mimosa tree), and provided with a removable cover to allow the corpse to be inserted by banjar and family members upon arrival at the cremation grounds. The wood structure is wrapped in velvet cloth and adorned with paper filigree decorations in gold and other colors.

The type of sarcophagus depends on the status of the deceased: Most take the form of a bull (Lembu)—the sacred vehicle of Siwa—though they may also take the form of a lion (Singa), an elephant-fish (Gajah Mina), or a simple wooden box (Wadah). The animals are intricately detailed down to their very

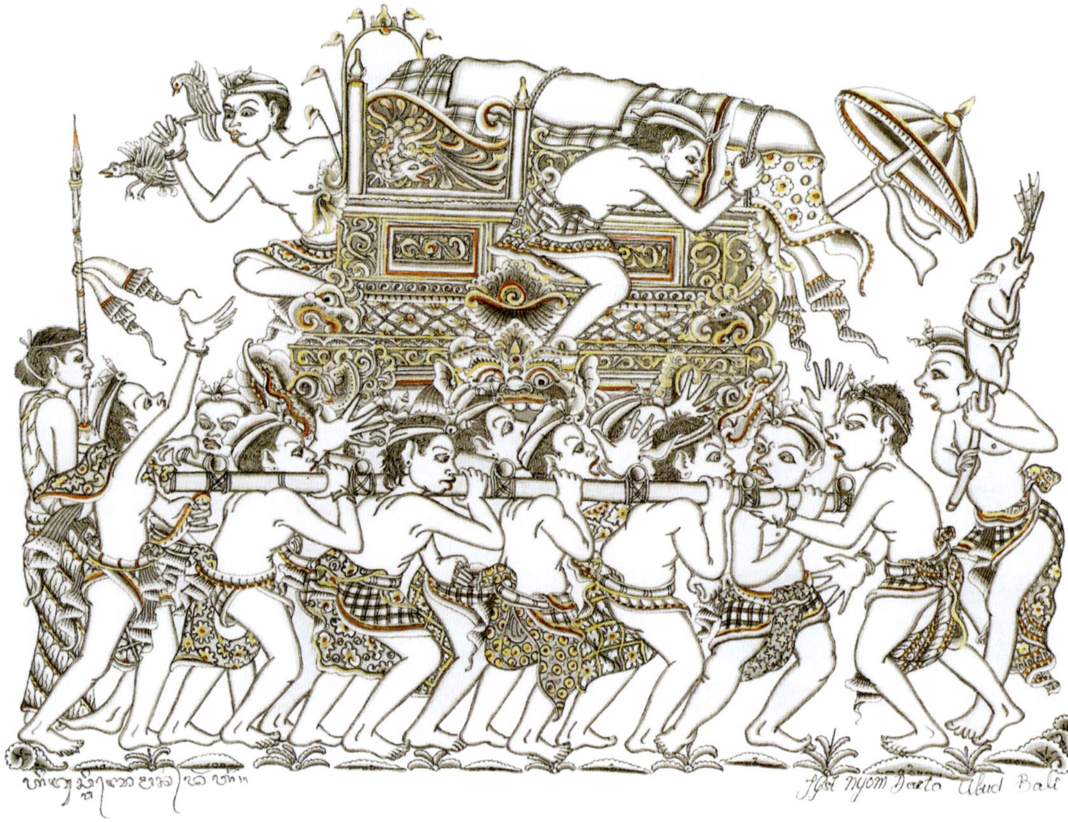

'THROWING AWAY' THE BODY: This drawing shows a simple sarcophagus (*wadah*) carried by banjar members. On the left, a woman is holding a sort of spear (*tulup*) to open the road to the dead person's release, and against her bosom she carries a *pangawak* symbol of the body. The tulup usually leads the procession. On the bade, a relative, who is a legal heir of the deceased (*sentana*), is holding a stuffed bird of paradise, symbol of heaven, and releasing a chicken. Another man stands next to the corpse. On the right, a roast suckling pig is shown pierced from end to end. Notice the clothes hanging next to the umbrella. Usually a long white cloth (*lancingan*) is unfurled from there, and held on its sides by the long line of relatives of the dead.

explicit genitalia; sometimes they are equipped with a movable penis. The bases are also decorated with ink drawings of scenes of the tortures of hell, also quite frequently laden with sexual connotations.

The relatives, banjar and clan members, are kept busy for weeks, especially if it is the cremation of a powerful person or a collective cremation. Apart from the tower and the sarcophagus, they also have to prepare several effigies and a great variety of offerings and other implements to accompany the dead on their voyage to the 'Old Country' of the ancestors (bamboo structures, clothing, agricultural implements, *ukur* effigies assembled out of Chinese coins, and *adegan/pangawak* effigies). Almost all the elements used are made of plant materials, particularly bamboo and coconut (plaited leaves, chiseled shells, and fibers).

But those called up also have other, no less important duties, such as contacting the priest, fetching the different holy waters to be used from particular springs and temples, as well as preparing food for workers and guests. Not to be forgotten is finding the right people to play ritual gamelan music and recite holy manuscripts in song. Everything proceeds following a tightly defined division of labor and schedule determined by the banjar and the clan. Meals are freely and generously distributed to participants and guests, hence the tremendous costs of the cremation.

'Throwing away' the Body

Pengutangan, or the moment when the body is brought to the cremation ground, is the most visible, spectacular, and best-known phase of the cremation ceremony. It may involve a crowd of anywhere from one hundred to one thousand participants and spectators. Big or small, the basic principles and steps are similar.

The body (or unearthed remains, ashes, or effigy of the body), kept until then in the ceremonial pavilion (*bale dangin*), is transferred to the bade by male members of the family after a short 'leave-taking' ceremony. After installing it in the bade, they lay on it a magical drawing inscribed with holy letters (*rurub kajang*). It then passes under the control of banjar members, who collectively carry it to the cemetery (*setra*), the least pure part of the village, where it is to be burned. There, the family take charge again to perform the final rites with the help of a priest.

This trip to the setra is accompanied by a procession of other people carrying all the offerings and implements—the petulangan (and *naga* for very high-ranking individuals), ritual clothing, various effigies—which will all be discarded in the setra. This takes place with the musical accompaniment of a mobile orchestra of musicians playing portable gamelan instruments. Whenever the bade and petulangan reach a crossroads, and upon arrival at the cremation grounds, they are made to circumambulate three times counter-clockwise to symbolize the earthly trajectory of the body.

The villagers carrying the bade are, in fact, 'throwing away' a mass of impure dead matter and its accompanying demonic buta. Hence the name given to the event: *pengutangan*, or 'throwing away'. This gives the villagers total control. They can treat, or mistreat the corpse (or effigy) according to their mood and their opinion of the deceased and his or her family. Carried by men in trance, the body may be shaken and the cremation tower toppled.

We heard of an incident 20 years ago when a corpse was thrown on the roadside and stabbed in the groin through its shroud. The deceased man had been accused of raping a young girl a few years earlier. It would be difficult for him to attain the expected release after such treatment. Thus, death is an occasion for the exertion of social control. The living are told to 'watch out and beware'. On rare occasions, the roads of the village and to the cemetery might be 'closed' to the dead person. The body then rots in the family compound until the family makes amends and pays the required fines.

Burning the Corpse

On their way to the setra, the bade and procession turn counter-clockwise at each crossroad and upon arrival at the cremation ground. The

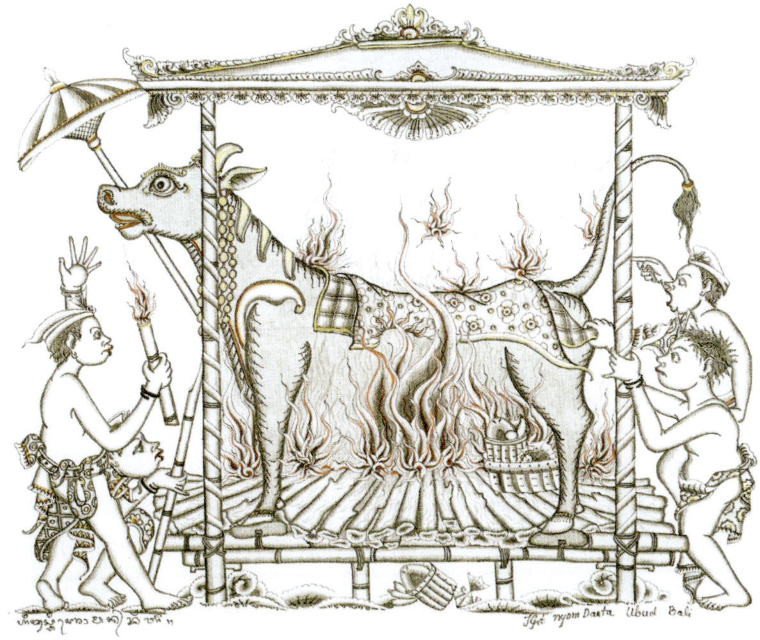

BURNING THE CORPSE: This drawing shows the moment when the *sentana* sets fire to the bull. The offering addressed to the goddess of the earth Pertiwi, is just below the bull.

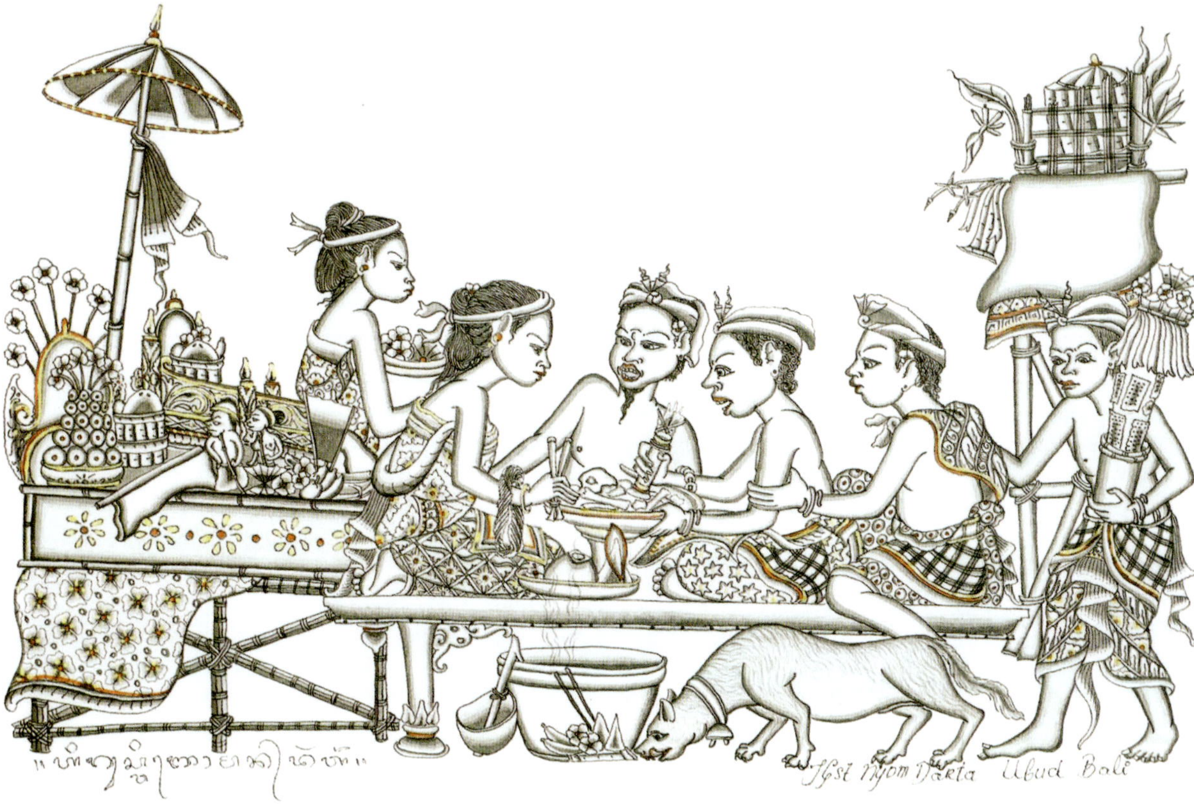

CRUSHING THE BONES: In the middle of the drawing, a male heir is crushing the bones remaining from the cremated body, assisted by two women relatives. Below the bench where they are sitting is the basin that has been used to cleanse the bones. The water is gone, though, and in its place an *api tekepan* offering and incense sticks have been lit to ward off negative influences. The bamboo structure on the right is a *sanggar tawang*, addressed to the sun god Surya as witness of the ceremony. To the left of the two seated women are a *pemerasan* offering and two small figurines that represent a male and female pair of sailors with a small wooden boat. They will accompany the soul and its remains to its new abode in the realm of the dead. The boat containing the ashes will be released to the sea or a nearby river. In Balinese lore, it is said that the soul, not yet released, is entrusted to the god of the sea, Baruna. Many also say that it is at sea that the tortures of hell take place. (No illustration is given here of this ceremony, but a very similar one is illustrated in *Releasing the Sekah into the Sea* on page 121.)

sarcophagus, or *petulangan*, meanwhile, has been set under a special bamboo structure, the *bale basmian.* The sarcophagus is cut open and the corpse (or effigy) transferred into it from the bade by the relatives.

Next, a cloth wrapping (*ulantaga*) containing ten sacred letters corresponding to different parts of the body is unfolded and laid upon the head of the deceased or the effigy. Then, all the holy waters (*tirta*), kept in small earthenware pots, are poured one by one onto the body (*tirta pengembak*), that have been fetched by a legal heir of the deceased (*sentana*) from a three-branching stream: *tirta penglukatan*, to cleanse the body of impurities; *tirta pengentas*, to facilitate the passage into the netherworld; then the remaining holy waters from the family temple, the clan temples, the various village temples, and the Prajapati shrine of the guardian of the cemetery.

After this, the *pangawak*, symbolizing the body and the symbolic residence of the soul (*angenan*), as well as holy drawings (*kajang*), are all laid on the body along with many pieces of cloth and bounteous provisions. The sarcophagus is then closed and a burning torch, prepared by the high priest, is handed over to a sentana, who sets fire to the whole structure. Also present are offerings addressed to Mother Earth Pertiwi and a set of *peningkeb* offerings to activate the fire.

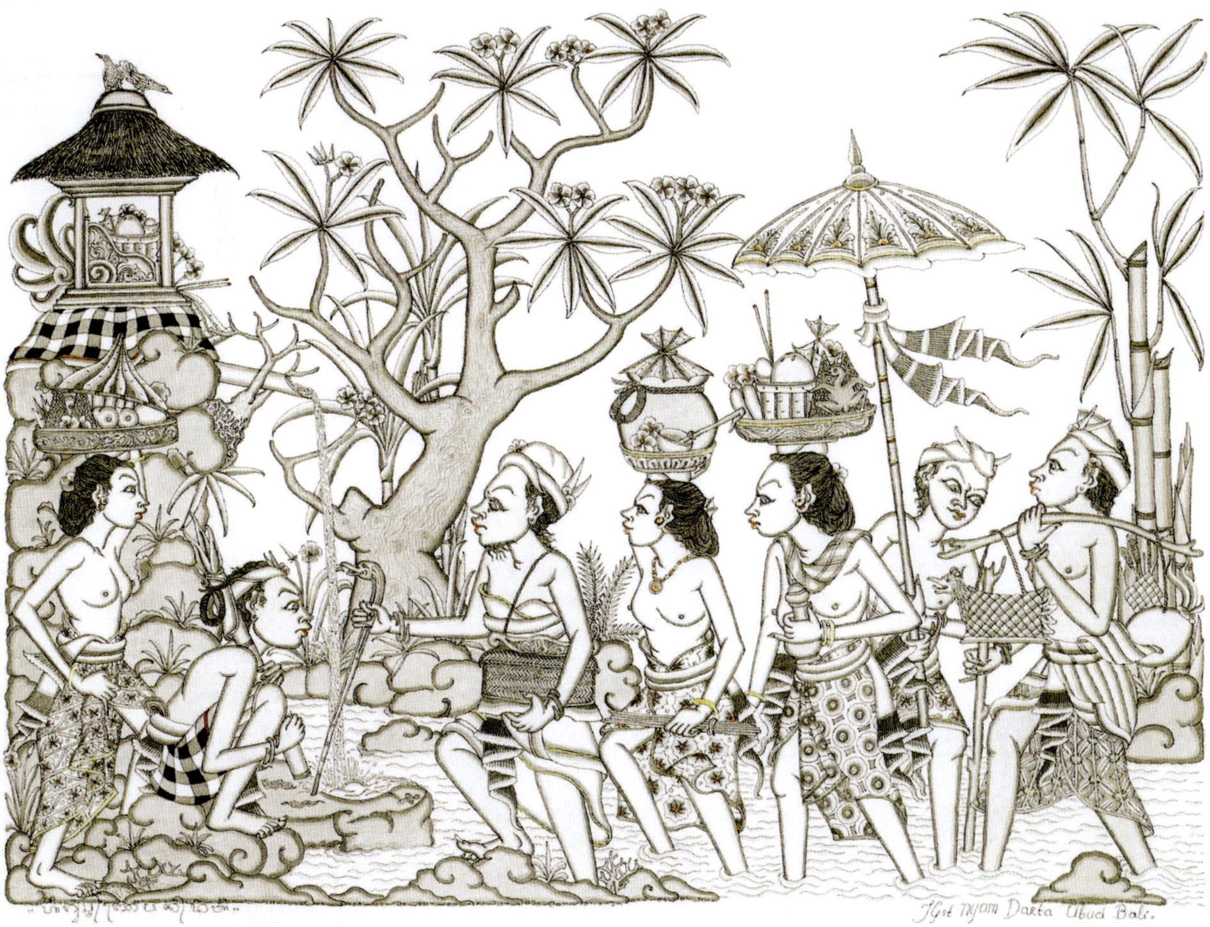

FETCHING HOLY WATER: **This drawing depicts a group of people, headed by a *pemangku* temple priest, fetching the *toya ning* (pure water) spouting from the rocks to the left. The temple sits next to the river. The pemangku, recognizable by his cane and headdress, will perform the *anteban* prayer that accompanies the fetching of water for the upcoming post-cremation ceremony. The two women behind him carry *ajuman* and *pejati* notification offerings. Interestingly, the man on the right is carrying coins inserted in the long bamboo pole on his back as compensation to the gods, in case any offerings are missing. In front of him, the head of a duck protrudes from a basket. It symbolizes the mythical Garuda bird's flight in search of *amerta*, the water of immortality.**

Crushing the Bones

Once the body, or its effigy, has been burned, the bones or effigy leftovers are collected and washed, then arranged in such a way as to make up a simulacrum of the body (*pangrekan*), with a head, torso, feet, and hands. This figure is then thoroughly crushed by each family member who take turns to perform the act. The remains are collected using a ritual spoon (*sidu*) and inserted into a young yellow coconut (*bungkah nyuh gading*) in preparation for the journey to the sea or river, where they will be discarded.

Fetching Holy Water

For the cremation ceremony and various post-cremation rites, all sorts of *tirta* (holy waters) are required, which are prepared and 'blessed' in their own ritual way. For many of these, the actual water originates from a small river temple (*pura beiji*), usually located on a river gorge or on the lower slope of a valley where a pure water (*toya ning*) spring spouts. It is only upon completion of a blessing rite, performed by a *balian*, temple or high priest, that toya ning is turned into tirta of many types: *tirta pengembak*, *tirta pengentas*, etc.

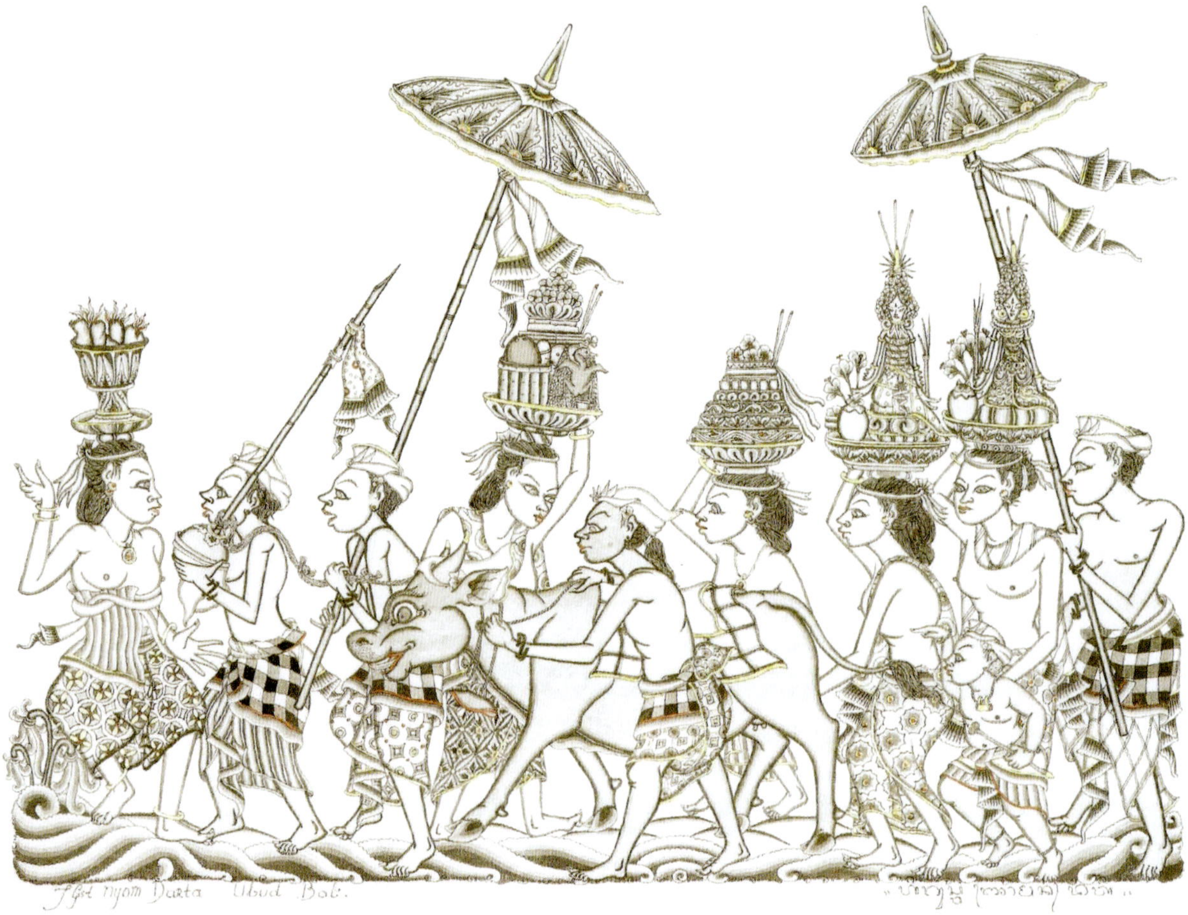

POST-CREMATION CEREMONY: This drawing shows the circumambulation rite as it takes place in royal families. This bull is white, a reference to Nandini, the sacred vehicle of the god Siwa. It is for this reason endowed with golden horns. At the head of the procession is a *sentana* relative who holds a bamboo spear (*tulup*) said to open the way to heaven (Sunialoka). A three-color (*tridatu*) rope, symbol of the Hindu trinity, links the procession's participants to one another. The young boy holding the reins of the bull symbolizes the godly herdsman, Siwa's incarnation in the classical Balinese story, *Rare Angon.* The bull and the herdsman are guiding the soul toward its new status of *dewa pitara* or *dewa hyang*. The *sekah* effigies proper, several of which are shown here, are carried by the two women at the rear of the procession.

Post-cremation Ceremony

The post-cremation disposal of the ashes into the river or the sea is not the end of the death rites. What disappeared into the sea were only the remains of the physical body (*stula sarira*) made of the five material elements of the world, or Panca Maha Bhuta. The soul, even though it has been entrusted to the lord of the sea Baruna, is not yet fully released. In its own way, it still sticks in the water to its material envelope. Thus, to fully complete the separation, a new series of rites is undertaken: *nyekah*, also called *mukur* (or *meligia* for royal families). This ceremony usually takes place 12 days after the cremation, or on another appropriate day decided by a priest or medium (*balian tetakson*).

The nyekah process is a sort of repetition of the cremation process: call back the soul to inhabit an effigy, burn the effigy, collect the ashes, and throw them into the sea or river once again. The ceremony is usually done collectively, except by royal families. It is also common for a large number of commoners to *ngiring* (accompany or join) a nyekah ceremony undertaken by aristocrats.

The rites begin at the beach or river where the cremation ashes were released. The soul is literally called back (*ulap*) and made to symbolically enter an

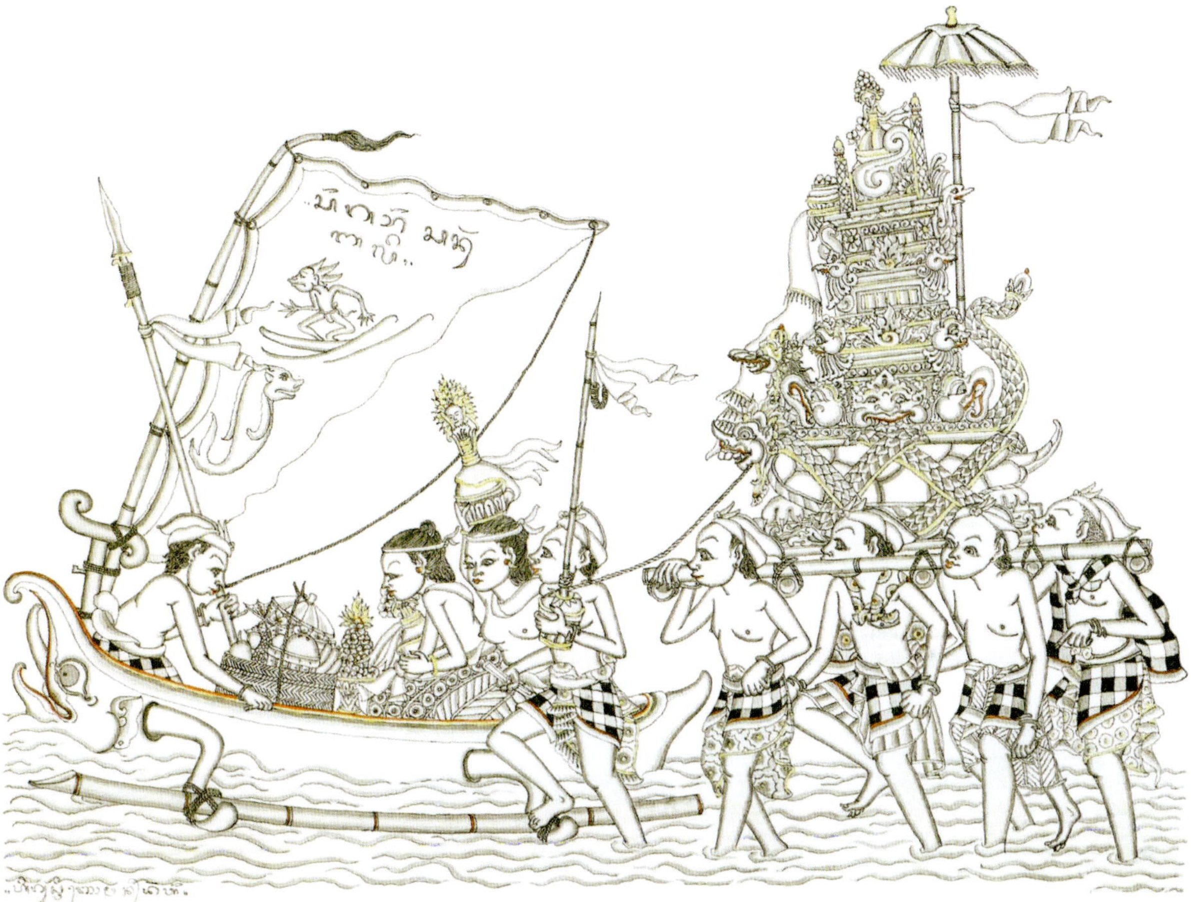

RELEASING THE SEKAH INTO THE SEA: In this *nyekah* scene, one can see three *sekah*. Two are already in the boat, one set on a plank and one carried on a woman's head, while the third appears on top of the bamboo tower structure (*bengku*). This reminds us that the nyekah is usually a collective event. The bengku is decorated with symbols similar to those found on the cremation tower: the cosmic turtle, the naga dragons, and the figure of Bhoma. Notice the offerings and the *tulup* spear carried by a man. The scene takes place in Sanur, as indicated by the Balinese writing on the sail.

effigy (*pratima*) where the soul will dwell temporarily. The making of this effigy is itself an interesting ceremony, called *ngangget don bingin*. It is prepared by a priest using leaves from the waringin tree (*Ficus benjamina*), the tree of life of Indian mythology and one of the key symbols of the Indonesian state.

Using a bamboo pole, at the extremity of which is attached a knife that cleanses impurity (*sudamala*), and accompanied by music, the leaves are ceremoniously made to fall onto a mat. The leaves that fall facing the ground will be used to make male effigies while those that fall facing the sky will be used to make female effigies. More leaves are employed for men than for women (66 compared to 54).

Back at the ceremonial compound, with the help of bamboo frames and other implements, the leaves collected are plaited into effigies, called *sekah/puspalingga*, each of which becomes, through prayers from the priests and the sprinkling of holy water, the provisional residence of a soul of the dead. The peak of the rite comes three days later, when the effigy is circumambulated clockwise (*mapurwadaksina*) three times around the *bale peyadnyan*, a symbol of the world.

This clockwise procession represents the upward movement of the soul toward the gods; it is the opposite of the downward path followed by the counter-clockwise circling of the cremation tower. Accompanied by priestly mantras, it symbolizes the imminent change in status of the soul, from the soul of an ordinary dead person (*pitara*) into a divine soul (*dewa pitara* or *dewa hyang*).

This is still not the end of the rites, however. A paper lamp (*damar kurung*) is installed to mark the living presence of the soul. Ritual food is presented to it. A fully ordained priest (*pandita*) then reads mantras to release it to its new status (*muput karya*). The families involved pray to the gods and Widhi the Supreme for the desired transformation to take place without any problems. *Pendet* and other dances are performed. Eventually, the sekah effigy is burned, thus symbolically separating the spiritual and material components of the deceased once more.

Again, as in the cremation, the ashes of the effigies are gathered and recomposed into yet another effigy to serve as the physical residence of the divine soul to be. This effigy consists of a coconut shell on top of which is set a small figurine (*makastun*) wrapped in a cloth. The effigy will then be ceremoniously released into the sea, usually the day after the circumambulation.

Releasing the Sekah into the Sea

The ceremony of release into the sea (*nganyud*) is very similar to the one that takes place immediately after the cremation, except for the bamboo tower structure (*bengku*) on which the sekah is carried. The relatives of the deceased, wearing white headbands, carry the sekah to the beach and throw it into the sea.

Hell or Paradise?

In Balinese lore, it is during the journey of the soul into the sea toward release (after the cremation and nyekah) that it spends time in hell or paradise. Upon arrival at the gateway to the place where the dead sojourn, the fate (*karma*) of each soul is decided by the judge of souls, Sang Suratma. According to the sins accumulated during the person's life, which are written on a lontar carried by Sang Suratma, his or her karma will differ, and harsh or light punishment will be meted out accordingly. The torturers of the dead (Cakrabala)

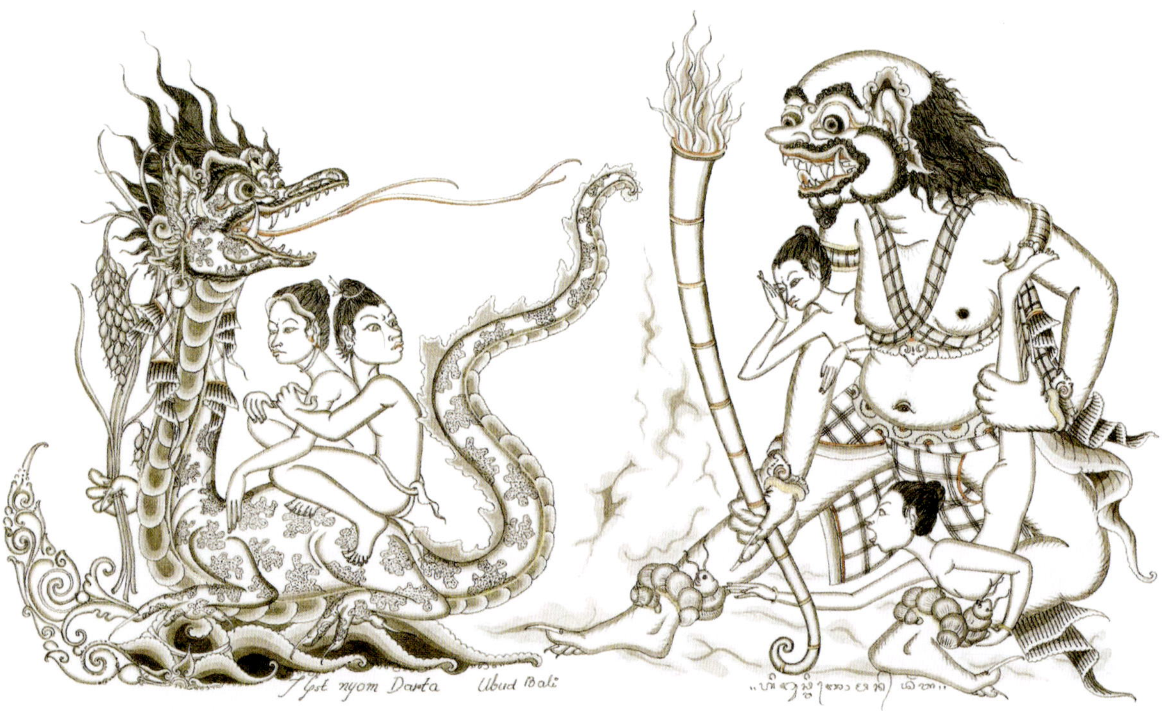

HELL OR PARADISE?: This drawing shows two souls on the left escaping the tortures of hell by riding away on a *naga* dragon. However, two others on the right have a less enviable fate. They are in the hands of a Cakrabala demon, one of the minions of the god of hell, Yama, who prevents them from riding the dragon to heaven.

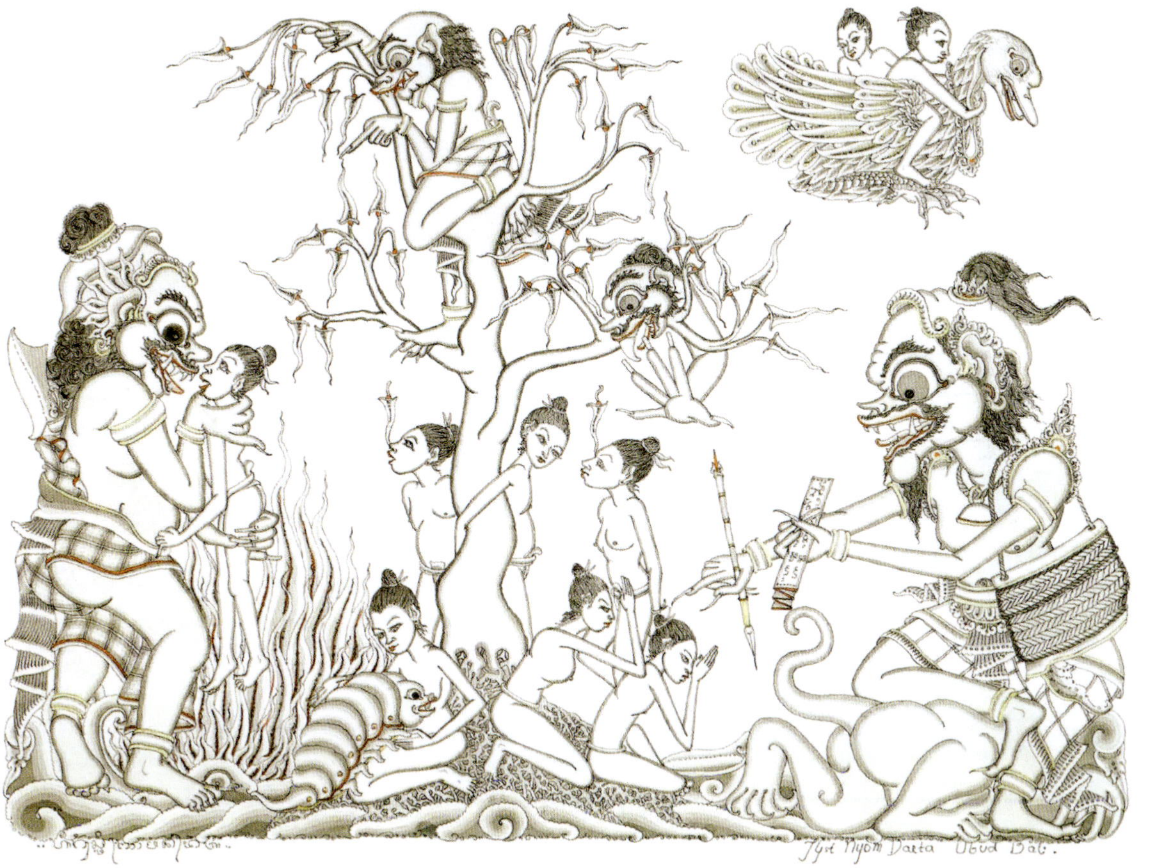

THE TORTURES OF HELL: This drawing represents the Balinese hell and its tortures (*atma prasangsa*). The demonic character to the right is Sang Suratma, the guardian of hell. Written on a *pandanus* leaf manuscript are the sins of the dead who present themselves to him, pleading for mercy. He punishes them according to their faults during life: lightly if their karma is light, harshly if they are sinners and criminals. Traditional illustrations always show women as the preferred target of the demonic Cakrabala; Bali is indeed no women's paradise. On the left are two of the most common tortures inflicted on sinners: those who have spoken ill of others during their life are showered with *keris* daggers as they pass under the keris tree. A woman is breast-feeding a giant worm. Her sin is to have borne no children.

are the minions of Sang Hyang Yama, the lord of hell.

The nyekah is not the last ceremony to which the souls of the dead are subject. For the soul to achieve ultimate release, three important ceremonies remain to be implemented.

The ceremony of *nyegara-gunung*, as its Balinese name suggests, involves the two poles of traditional economic and ritual life: the sea (*segara*) and the mountain (*gunung*). Close family members (*sentana*) perform on this occasion a ritual 'notification' visit, with the required offerings, to a temple that embodies the meeting of these two elements, usually Goal Lawah temple a few kilometers east of Klungkung, even though they may also go to Tampak Siring or to Pura Gunung Lebah in Ubud, temples located at the meeting points of a hill and a river. They carry an effigy of the dead (*daksina lingga* or *puspa lingga*) to which the soul of the dead, already cleansed, has been symbolically called back (*ulapin*) from the sea to inhabit.

Upon completing the nyegara-gunung rites, and using the same effigy, the relatives must make a final tour to all the temples to which the family is ritually linked through kinship and other local affiliations. This is called *mendak nuntun.* Most important to visit are the Pedharman clan temple and other shrines from the Besakih complex: the Dalem Puri temple; Titi Gonggang, a symbol of the bridge souls must cross during their sojourn in hell; the Tegal

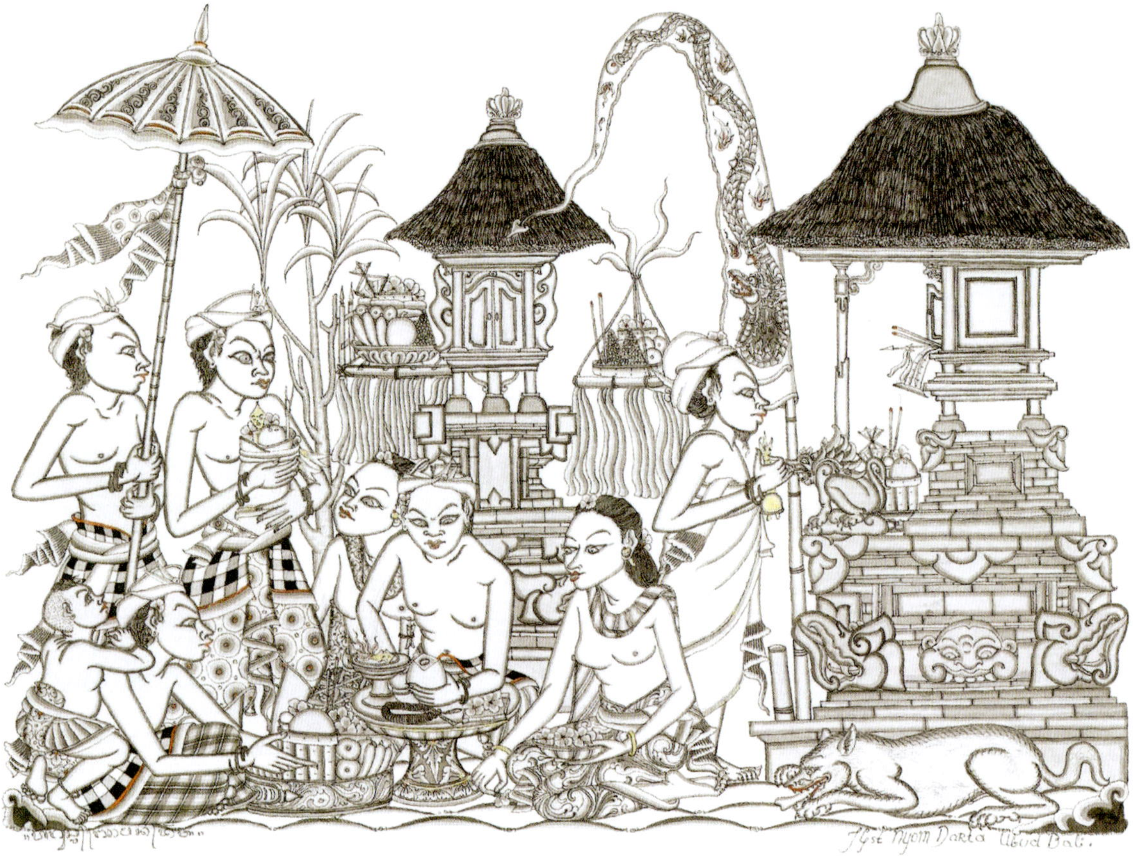

ENSHRINING THE ANCESTORS: This drawing illustrates the ritual process of enshrining an ancestor. Two shrines are clearly visible. To the right is the main ancestor shrine (*rong telu*) composed of three chambers that correspond to the male, female, and androgynous principles as well as to the Hindu trinity of Brahma, Wisnu, and Siwa. It is also the seat of Batara Guru, one of the names of God the Supreme, who is also the Father. The other shrine is the *kamulan taksu*, through which one connects with one's cosmic soul. To this shrine is affixed a bamboo structure made to receive the offerings. Between the rong telu and taksu shrines is a bamboo *sanggah cucuk* shrine, the provisional residence of the witness god Surya. A priest is addressing prayers with mantras and a bell in front of the rong telu, while a *sentana* relative, standing to the left, prepares to bury the sacred effigy he holds (*daksina pelinggih*) behind the rong telu.

Penangsaran, a symbol of the hellish 'field of tears'; the Marga Tiga, a three-way crossroads; the Ulun Kulkul, as a sign that a new soul is presenting itself for judgment; the Goa Raja; and the Pura Besukian, resting place of the cosmic dragon Besuki.

It is only after visiting this series of shrines, each time presenting a pejati offering and praying, that the family members, having fulfilled their duty at their mother clan temple, can symbolically forward the soul of the deceased to the abode of his or her origin. They return home, but not directly to the house and family temple (sangah) of the dead person. They first visit their village and local clan temple(s), again with offerings and prayers.

Back home, the ultimate and most important task awaits them: *ngelinggihan dewa pitara*, the enshrinement of the soul of the deceased in the ancestor shrine (*rong telu*) of the family temple, males to the right, females to the left.

Requests to the Ancestors

After the soul is enshrined in the family temple, it becomes an ordinary ancestor and is henceforth addressed with all the ritual offerings related to ancestor worship during temple festivals (the 210-day anniversary of the family temple),

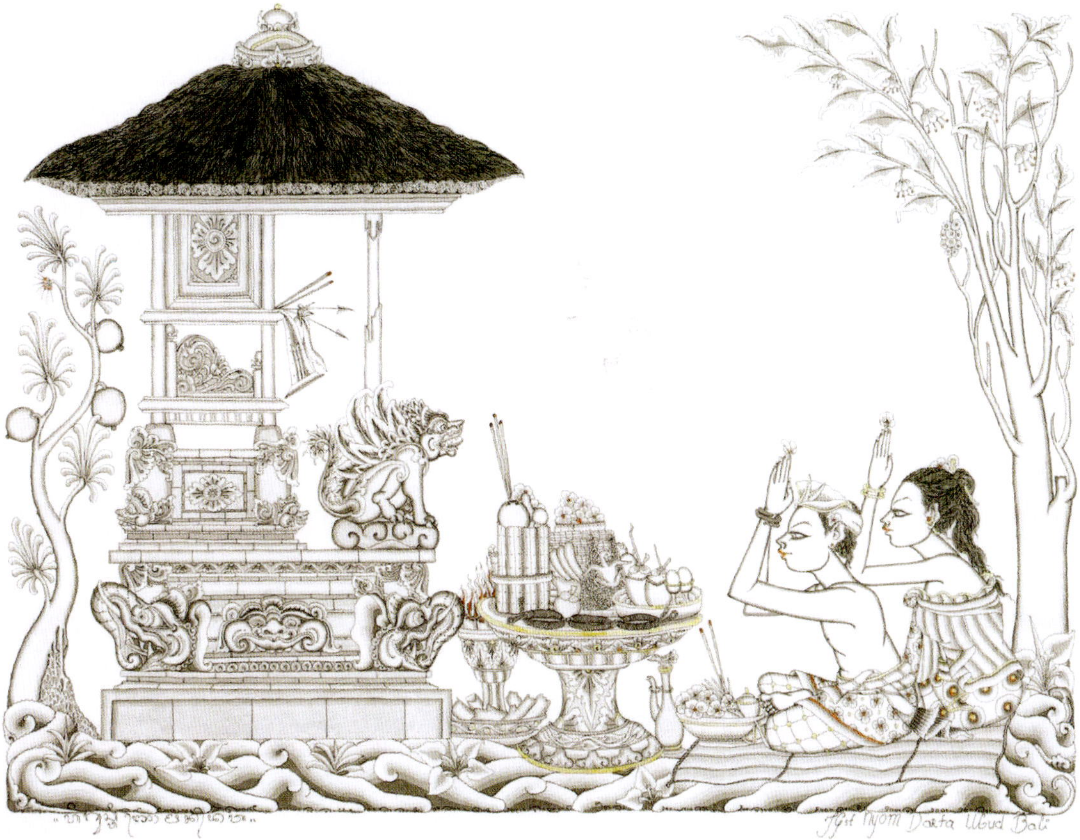

NAKTI: The illustration shows the couple saying their prayers before taking leave. One can see sets of Chinese *kepeng* coins on the offering tray. These coins are a ladder to the gods, as is the smoke rising from the offering. Visible within the smoke are ancestral souls ready to come down and incarnate. The two eggs, symbols of the male semen and female ovum, will be eaten at home along with the two coconuts.

ancestors' visits during Galungan-Kuningan, and so on.

It may happen, however, that people, usually a barren couple, address offerings and prayers to the rong telu or *kamulan taksu* to ask the ancestors to come down and incarnate in the beseeching woman's womb. Examples of such requests, known as *nakti*, are found in classical literature, such as in the opening verses of the famous poem, *Sutasoma.* It is still a common practice today, demonstrating the enduring nature of the belief that the transmigration of souls takes place within the same kinship group.

The nakti proper is always preceded by the presentation of a *pejati* offering to the family's rong telu, the three-part shrine that is the seat of Batara Hyang Guru, from which the two supplicants take holy water to sprinkle on themselves. Their request for a child follows, in approximately these words: "Ratu Batara Batari, melarapan peswecan Ida Batara Guru, titiang nunas mangda prasida Dewa Hyang titiang meteja ring dewek titiang, mangde titiang medruwe perti sentana, angge penerus kahuripan." (Oh male and female ancestors of ours, through the blessing of Batara Guru, we beg you to bequeath to us your light (soul) so that we may have an heir as a continuation of our life.)

A sign is expected to appear if the request is granted. The couple take leave after saying their parting prayers to the sun god, to Sang Hyang Widhi the Supreme God, and to Batara Guru. Upon completion of the nakti, the couple are expected to return home and make love after again addressing proper prayers to Batara Hyang Guru and the ancestors. Hence, the cycle of life is enacted at two levels at once: procreation and reincarnation.

CHAPTER 7
DIVINATION AND HOROSCOPES

As we have seen, the traditional Balinese calendar system plays a crucial role in regulating what happens in Balinese life. The calendar system is very complex, and the body of knowledge about it, known as Wariga, is correspondingly esoteric. Before scheduling any important event, people will generally consult a Wariga expert well-versed in the art and science of calendar-based divination, to find the best possible date for the undertaking concerned.

Divination is based on the values attributed to the different units of time, or temporal elements, in the Pawukon and Saka calendars, as well as the day cycle, and to the intersections of these many elements with each other.

The value attributed to each element depends on the numerical value (*urip*) and other characteristics—gods, *wayang* puppet characters, demons, trees, and other elements of nature—corresponding to it, as defined by its position on the *pangider-ider* compass rose. Each element may be classified as either mainly auspicious (*dewasa ayu*) or mainly inauspicious (*dewasa ala*).

The main purpose of a calendar-based divination session or reading is to choose the most auspicious date for an undertaking. An auspicious date will warrant its success, whereas if the date is inauspicious, the individual must be dissuaded from proceeding. Once again, the cosmic order is not to be disturbed.

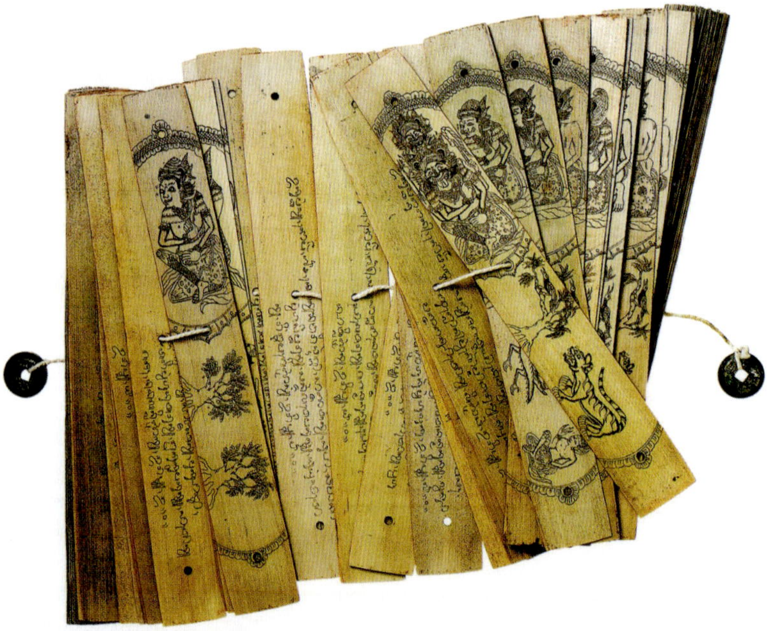

WARIGA LONTAR MANUSCRIPT
Unknown artist.
27.5 x 3.5 x 2.5 cm.
Ubud, ca. 1970.
Private collection.

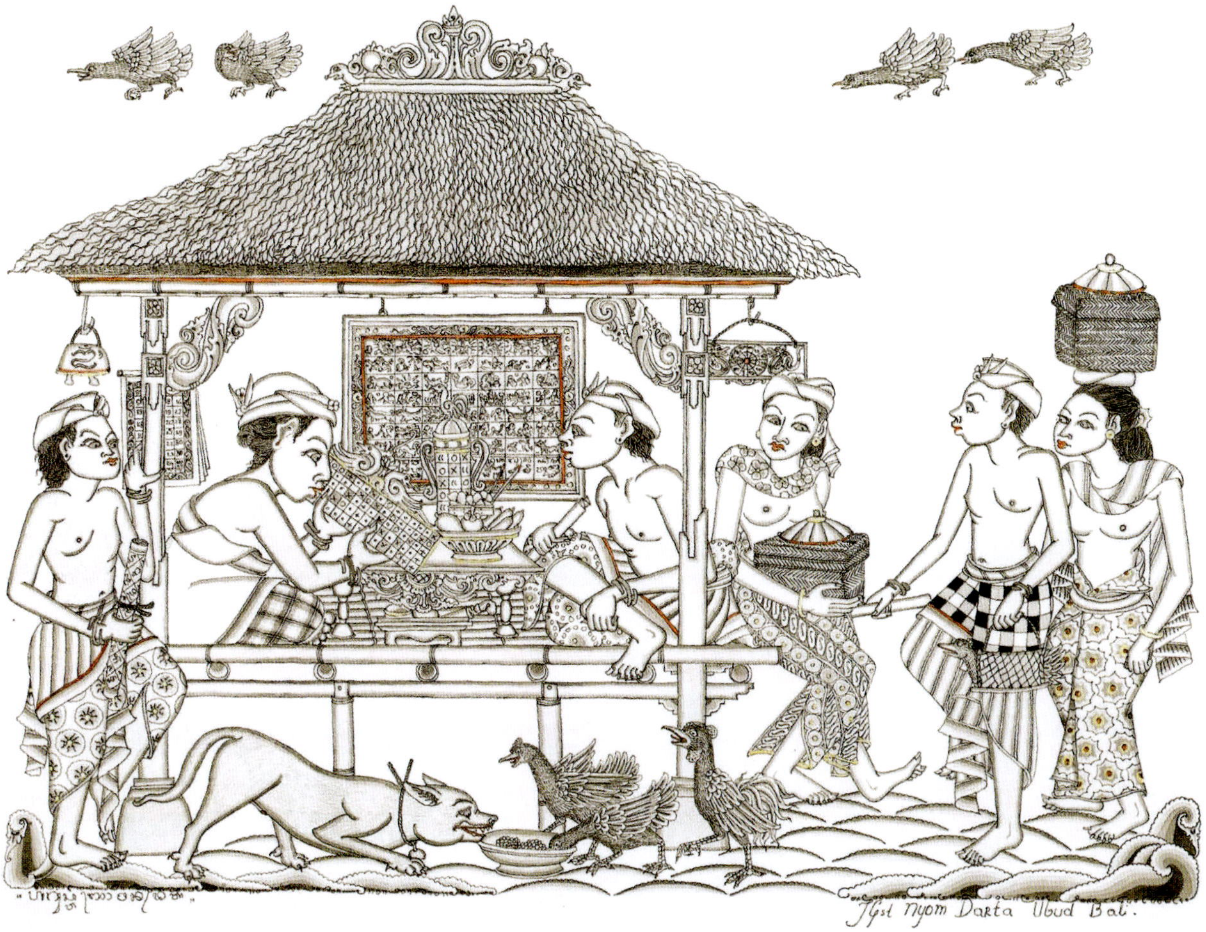

CONSULTING A CALENDAR EXPERT: **This drawing shows a family consulting a priest about the most propitious time to hold a ceremony. The priest, seated left on the pavilion, holds a wooden *tika* chart in his hands, while a painted *pelelintangan* chart hangs in the background. Another tika is visible behind the head of the seated woman, while a modern printed calendar hangs to the left. A set of *pejati* offerings, made to ask the goddess of knowledge to guide the priest, stands on a platter between the two men.**

The kind of reading made depends on the relative importance of the event, task, or activity to be scheduled.

To determine good days to conduct ordinary daily activities, it may be enough to consider the auspicious or inauspicious qualities of the *wuku* (seven-day weeks named after the wuku or nobles of the Watugunung story) and of the urip of the days of the five-day week (Pancawara) and seven-day week (Saptawara), whose intersections make up each 35-day wuku month.

These variables give a general indication of how auspicious or inauspicious a particular date may be, and how to behave accordingly. It is possible to glean such information by reading the modern, printed Balinese calendar found in every home and office.

However, these indications are highly sensitive to multiple influences. The value of a particular date changes according to the days from the other different-sized weeks that intersect it. The value of a date according to the Pawukon calendar may also be accentuated or mitigated by its value in the Saka calendar.

In addition, no day or moment is fully auspicious or inauspicious, absolutely holy or absolutely ruled by demonic forces. The same day that is auspicious for a temple community to hold a festival or cleansing ceremony may be inauspicious for an irrigation community (*subak*), and it may be auspicious or inauspicious for different individuals depending on what day they were born.

Therefore, for more important events, such as a cremation, all of the variables associated with all of the time units at play must be taken into account. This includes the quality of the wuku and the quality of the day in all of the concurrent cycles of the *wewaran* (week) system; the qualities of the *tithi* (lunar day), the *penanggal/panglong* (days in the cycle of the waxing and waning moon, respectively), and the *sasih* (lunar month) of the Saka calendar; not forgetting the units of the 24-hour day cycle (*dauh*), to determine the right time of day or night for specific activities during the event. People consult a calendar expert to sort out this kind of information.

It is usually impossible to find a perfectly auspicious moment. The global quality of the moment chosen is defined by weighing all the elements against one another, in the following order of priority:

The value of the wuku is stronger than that of the wewaran days; the panglong/penanggal position is stronger than that of the wuku; the sasih lunar month is stronger than the panglong/penanggal position; and the dauh moment of the day is stronger than the sasih.

Finally, people say, the *ning*, or 'void', is stronger than the dauh, meaning that nothing is ever completely certain: all circumstances are dictated by intangible (*niskala*) forces, so no outcome can ever be entirely predicted.

Calendar-based divination is also used to forecast a child's likely character attributes and future, to predict whether two individuals will be compatible in romance or marriage, and to specify what offerings should be made to alleviate the sickness or other misfortune that has afflicted someone, based on which day in the Pawukon cycle they were born.

Readings of personal character are commonly based on *pelelintangan* charts, which identify 35 'star signs' based upon the 35-day cycle of the Pawukon month. A pelelintangan reading is similar in function to, and sometimes called, a 'horoscope', even though it is not strictly based on astrology.

When determining auspicious dates for a purely personal undertaking, the person's character attributes will be taken into consideration, in addition to the other variables mentioned above.

It would take volumes to explain the Balinese divination system. Following are some examples of illustrated charts based on the schemes most frequently used as sources for divination, including pelelintangan 'horoscope' charts; charts of lucky and unlucky days for common activities based on the Pawukon calendar; *pelelindon* 'earthquake calendars' and other charts based on the Saka calendar; charts based on the day cycle; and the modern printed calendar.

Two Visits: Fixing a Date with a Pedanda and Reading the Character of a New Born

A Visit to the Surya: The Search for a Propitious Date

"Somprong, I absolutely need your help to go to the *brahmana gria* (Brahmin mansion). As you know, you are the only one who can assist me. You know them well; you are close to them."

Dabdab made his request while sitting with his friend on the single wooden plank of the tea stall. There, amidst heaps of fruit, colorful cookies, and the pervasive scent of incense, they sat every day to gossip about the yellowing of the rice or their collective duties to the gods.

This time, Dabdab was serious. "I cannot even speak their language," he admitted, referring to the *basa halus* (High Balinese) required for such a visit. "But for you, Somprong, it will be easy. You are one of their disciples (*sisia*), aren't you?"

They soon reached the entrance of the gria. From the outside, nothing distinguished it from other village houses except for the two guardian statues flanking the entrance and the relief of a swan, the *angsa*, symbol of the pure soul, carved above the lintel of the gate.

The high priest, the *surya*, was there in the Balai Dangin (East Pavilion), sitting straight-backed among his palm-leaf manuscripts (*lontar*), his silver betel set, and a hand-painted *pelelintangan* cloth that mapped the heavens. Somprong and Dabdab sat silently on the floor at his feet, ensuring their heads remained lower than his.

"I come to you with a man of the village who has a request," Somprong whispered in a refined tone.

The old man raised his eyes. "It is you, my good Ketut," he said, using the childhood name he had always used for Somprong. "But you—who are you?" he asked, addressing the blushing Dabdab.

"I am Kaki Ada's son," Dabdab answered. "I come to beg you to choose a propitious date (*dewasa ayu*) for an important family event, a *mukur* post-cremation. Our clan's fortunes have been uneven, and we fear that our previous undertakings were ill-timed."

The priest's eyes sharpened. Finding a date was not a simple matter of looking at a calendar; it was a complex calculation of time elements. He began to cross-reference the Pawukon cycle with the lunar Saka system.

"A date is not just a day, Dabdab," the priest murmured. "It is a meeting of forces. To find your right *dewasa*, I must see where the *wara* and the *pancawara* meet the influence of the moon. If the earth is 'hot' while the moon is 'dark,' your event will wither like a seedling in a drought."

The priest reached for a specific Wariga lontar—a manuscript dedicated to the science of time. He began his *tenung* (calculations), counting the joints of his fingers in a rhythmic *ngait*. He looked for the intersection of a 'fruitful' hour (*dauh*) and a day that did not clash with the *ingkel*—the taboos of the week. This was no mere performance; the priest was navigating a genuine mathematical and spiritual maze where a single error could invite misfortune.

After a long silence, during which the only sound was the scratching of a long fingernail against the palm leaves, the old man looked up.

"You seek a Wednesday," the priest finally spoke, his finger resting on a line of ancient script. "But not just any Wednesday. It must be Buda Paing in the wuku week of Uye. Why? Because on that day, the numerical value (*urip*), is at its peak. Furthermore, it falls three days after the Full Moon (Purnama). The lunar energy will still be 'rising,' providing a 'cool' shadow for your guests and the ancestors."

He looked at Dabdab. "But beware. Even on a perfect day, the success depends on your 'inner' weather. I have chosen this Wednesday because it is a 'light' day, a day of *melaspas* and beginnings. It will balance the 'heaviness' of your clan's recent misfortunes."

Dabdab remained silent. The priest was clearly aware of his clan's problems.

"Take this date, Buda Paing on the Uye wuku," the priest concluded, closing the lontar with a definitive clack. "The heavens are open on that morning. Do not be late, and don't forget anything, lest the *buta kala* take advantage of it."

Dabdab bowed, his forehead almost touching the floor. He knew better than to expect an immediate confirmation of every detail, but for a ceremony of this weight, the priest's word was the start of a long preparation. He would return in three days with the proper offerings, the *pejati*, to 'seal' this moment of time that had been carved out for the cremation.

The Visit: Character Reading of the Wariga

The family—mother, father, and their young baby—enters the balian's inner sanctum (*jero*) with heavy, deliberate steps. They carry the pejati, the notification offering, as their spiritual passport, with a few banknotes slipped discreetly underneath. Before ascending the stone steps to the pavilion, they pause at the foot of the stairs. The father stoops to place a *segehan* on the damp earth, a small tray of colored rice, ginger, and onion, spilling a few drops of water as a humble bribe to the buta kala and other earthly forces. These restless spirits must be fed so they do not interfere.

They take their place on the balai pavilion outside, joining a row of others waiting in shared silence. When their turn finally comes, they cross the threshold into the inner sanctum. The room is dim. The balian sits before a small shrine, gesturing toward a mat for them to sit in a lotus position. They have already lit the pejati; its blue-gray coils of incense smoke unite with the balian's own offerings and begin to rise, carrying their unspoken petitions toward the mountain gods. Inside the quiet pavilion, shielded from the afternoon heat, the balian acts as the interpreter of the *niskala*, the unseen world.

For any Balinese, and especially for parents holding a newborn, life is indeed not a series of random accidents but a journey largely predetermined by one's birthplace among the wewaran week, wuku months, and other markers of cosmic time. The balian, certain *mangku* priests, and the 'twice-born' are the dedicated readers of this Pawacackan, or character-reading system. Consulting a balian at all critical junctures of life is of the utmost importance to discern what might be about to happen. Whether facing a sudden professional collapse, a mysterious ailment, or, most pivotally, the arrival of a new family member, the Balinese turn to the Wariga. Through it, they discover the 'why' of their circumstances and the 'when'—the *dewasa*, or auspicious timing—to counter obstacles through proper rites. Balance is paramount.

The Wariga is the island's intricate system of traditional astrology and spiritual science. By reading its shifting cycles, the balian uncovers the hidden forces at play, revealing whether the path ahead is clear or blocked by unseen obstacles. He does not merely guess; he calculates. He may count days on his fingers, consult a *lontar*, an ancient palm-leaf manuscript etched with ancestral wisdom, or a palelintangan, the astrological cloth chart where stars and gods intersect.

Using the calendar and other details provided by the parents, he identifies the child's patron deity, their protective animal, their magical urip number, and the specific spiritual vulnerabilities where misfortune might enter.

A heavy silence fills the room as the balian's fingers stop at a specific intersection of the calendar. He looks up, his expression somber. The child has been born during Wuku Wayang, the most precarious week of the Balinese year. In the shadow world of Balinese mythology, children born in this week are 'indebted' to the demon god Batara Kala, who has the divine right to devour them.

This means specific rites must be implemented to cast away the illnesses and woes that would otherwise threaten the child's soul. The parents are told to perform a Bayuh 'soul resetting' ceremony, but the most vital demand is for the parents to make a *sesangi* (a sacred pledge). They must vow to perform a Sapuh Leger shadow puppet performance on a future *Wuku Wayang.* This sacred play tells how Kala, the god of time, is tricked by the performance into sparing the child-god Kumara. The ritual produces *tirta*—holy water that cleanses the threatened child of any danger.

The pledge is very formal. The balian instructs the father to hold the incense smoke in his palms and waft it toward his face (*muspa*), then the Balian intones the following:

"Ratu Betara, mangkin titiang ngaturang sesangi. Yan sampun kanti mayusa nem sasih, titiang jagi ngaturang aturan Sapuh Leger mangda pianak titiang selamet, dirgahayu, tur luput saking Batara Kala. Titiang nebus utang ring ajeng Ratu Betara." (O, Divine Gods, I now offer my sacred pledge to You. When my child reaches his/her Otonan, I will commission a Sapuh Leger performance so that he/she may remain safe, enjoy a long life, and be released from Batara Kala's pursuit. Thus, I shall redeem my debt before You, O Gods.)

When the family finally departs, they are no longer in the dark. They know what lies ahead and what must be done. The reading of the wariga has set their child on a well-marked road; the parents are now armed with the rituals necessary to raise their child in harmony with the cosmic laws that govern the island

Pelelintangan 'Horoscope' Charts

The pelelintangan is a chart of personal character based on which of the 35 possible intersections of the five-day week (Pancawara) and seven-day week (Saptawara) in any wuku month coincides with the person's day of birth.

Pelelintangan are generally painted on cloth or drawn on a wooden calendar (*tika*) representing the 35-day cycle. The days of the Saptawara and the days of the Pancawara are laid out in a grid of seven columns and five rows.

On the header row, general attributes for people born on each of the seven Saptawara days are shown: a god, a tree, a letter, a character of the wayang puppet theater, a bird, and an animal. On the footer row are represented seven demons (*buta*) corresponding to the Saptawara. In be-

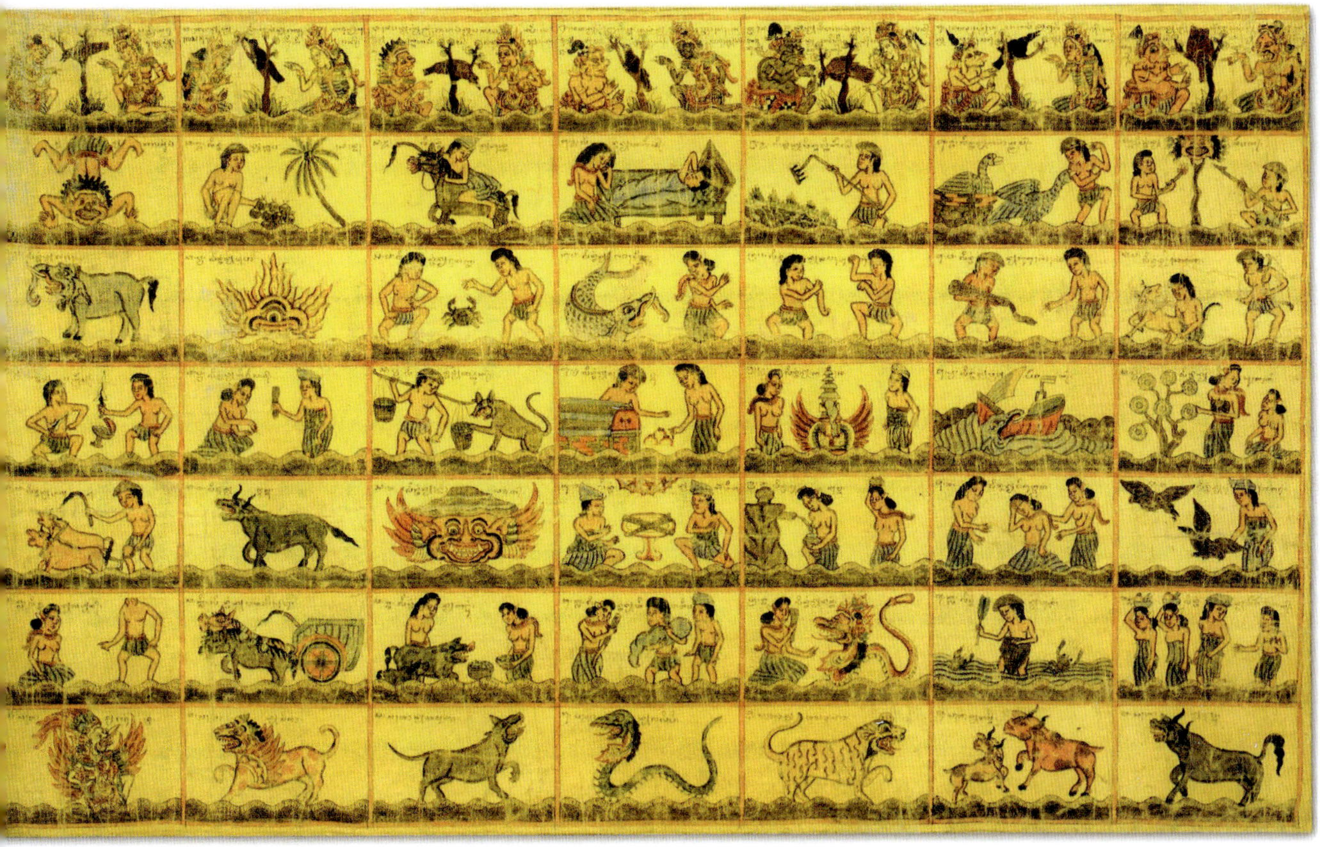

PELELINTANGAN
Paint on canvas.
Artist: Pak Dita, Gianyar school.
130 x 170 cm.
Third quarter of the 20th century.
Private collection.

tween are the 35 intersections of the wuku month with the seven days of the Saptawara running horizontally left to right, and the five days of the Pancawara running vertically from top to bottom.

Each square of the pelelintangan is given a 'star sign' (*lintang*), with a corresponding illustration. The character of a person is defined by the interpretation of these attributes along with the corresponding value of the urip of the Pancawara and Saptawara days that intersect on the square concerned. No matter what date, month, or year you were born according to the Gregorian calendar, your day of birth will match one of these 35 options.

How to Read a Pelelintangan

Listed below are the general attributes associated with each Saptawara day, and the star signs for each of the 35 Saptawara-Pancawara conjunction days typically depicted in pelelintangan, along with brief summaries of common interpretations of these signs. The number after each conjunction day indicates the position of the corresponding square in the pelelintangan charts shown in the illustrations. The numbers proceed from the second row to the sixth row in each column, with one column for each day of the seven-day week, moving from Sunday on the left, to Saturday on the right.

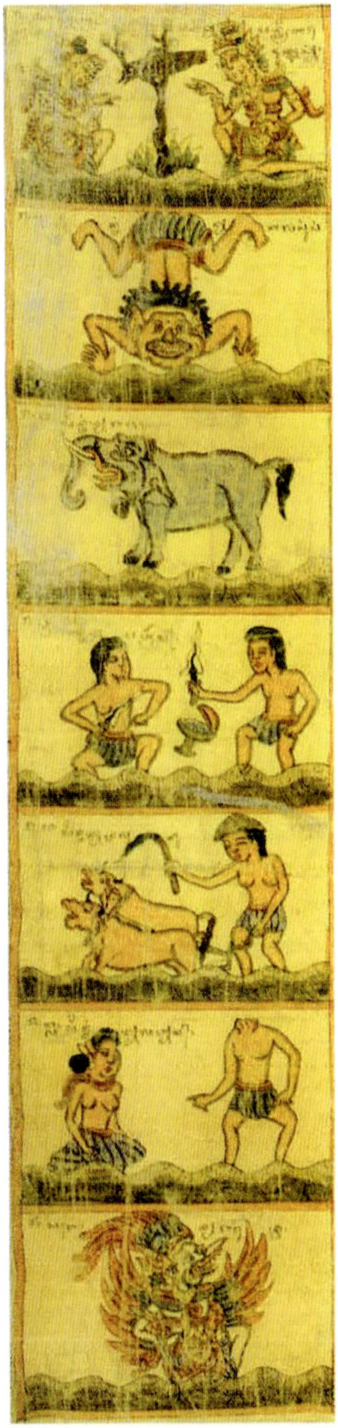

Sunday—*Redite*

God: Indra
Wayang character: *mantri* (minister)
Tree: *ambulu* (*Ficus infectaria*)
Bird: *beo* (*Gracula religiosa*)
Animal: garuda (mythical bird)
Demon: elephant

Redite-Umanis (1): The sign is an upside-down demon (*kala sungsang*). Does not heed advice, and contradicts his or her guru's opinions. Should not be entrusted with important tasks. Stubborn but helpful.

Redite-Paing (2): The sign is an elephant. Courageous, dedicated, and hard-working. Has many children and gets wealthy quickly. Might appear arrogant or opinionated. Congenial, has many friends but also many enemies.

Redite-Pon (3): The sign is a dagger (*patrem*). Argumentative, but also a diplomat, appreciates luxury. Conscious of being gifted. Carries a risk of unnatural death (*salah pati*). Cannot succeed in important tasks. Stubborn but helpful.

Redite-Wage (4): The sign is a plough (*tenggala* or *wuluku*). Gifted farmer. Likes meditating, is generous. Gets richer with time.

Redite-Kliwon (5): The sign is a headless corpse (*laweyan*). Small in height, a gambler, and rough-tempered. Difficult to get along with.

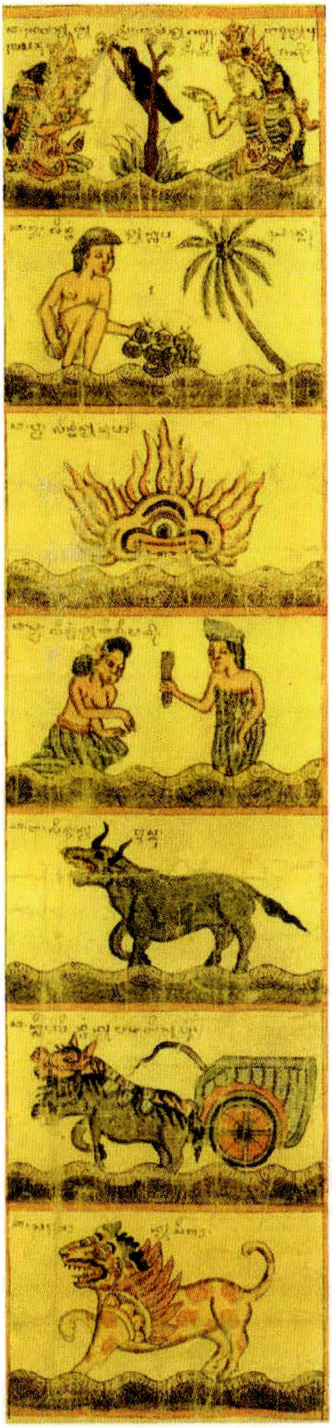

Monday—*Soma*

God: Sri
Wayang character: *galuh*, princess
Tree: *pule* (*Alstonia spectabilis*)
Bird: dove
Animal: lion
Demon: dog

Soma-Umanis (6): The sign is a coconut tree (*kelapa*). Gets rich from the products of coconuts. Keen farmer, patient and honest, likeable. Lacks wit, which causes problems.

Soma-Paing (7): The sign is a comet (*kukus* or *dupa*). Gets rich quickly and poor equally quickly. Has difficulty finding a spouse; if successful, one of the spouses dies. Good farmer, patient, honest, but lacks wit.

Soma-Pon (8): The sign is sadness (*kiriman* or *akikirim*). Suffers due to the faults of others. A good farmer, patient, honest, appreciated by others. Very stupid, which makes him or her sad.

Soma-Wage (9): The sign is a cow (*lembu*). Seldom happy, poor since childhood, often sick. Dedicated to and precise in his or her work. A good farmer, patient, honest, sensitive, appreciated by others.

Soma-Kliwon (10): The sign is an empty cart (*pedati puyung*). Gets rich easily but is often a victim of burglary. Faithful to family and friends, easy speaker, friendly. A good farmer, patient, honest, appreciated by others. Lacks wit, which is a hindrance to his or her undertakings.

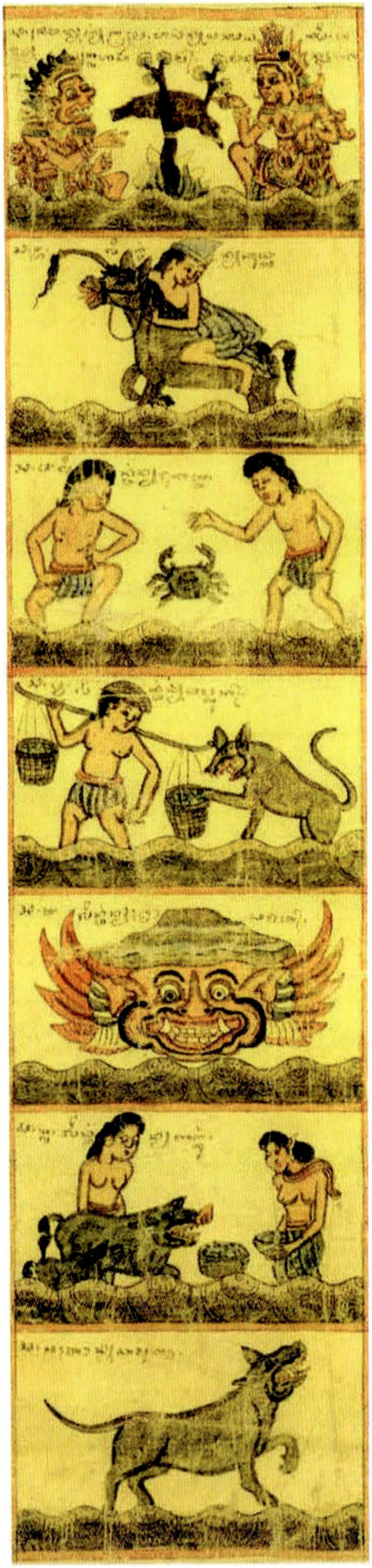

Tuesday—*Anggara*

God: Brahma
Wayang character: a giant (*Yaksa-yaksi*)
Tree: *rendu* (*Eriodendrum anfractuasum*)
Bird: raven
Animal: wolf
Demon: horse

Anggara-Umanis (11): The sign is a horse (*kuda*). Open-minded and ambitious. Slanderous and does not mind his or her own business. Must take care not to upset people. May earn a good living but also loses a fortune due to bad health.

Anggara-Paing (12): The sign is a crab (*yuyu*). Bad-tempered, knows how to get organized, wealthy throughout life. Must pay attention to undertakings, though a hard worker. Likes to help people but with strings attached.

Anggara-Pon (13): The sign is a dog (*asu*). Hard worker, audacious, heroic, and wise. Gains people's confidence, makes many friends, is appreciated by people in high places. Must pay attention when dealing with other people so as not to upset them.

Anggara-Wage (14): The sign is a heavily loaded junk (*jung sarat*). Likes to study and is a hard worker, temperamental, easily upset, lends money but does not know how to get it back. Not to be entrusted with complicated tasks because it might provoke his or her displeasure.

Anggara-Kliwon (15): The sign is a wild boar (*depat* or *sidamalung*). Pleasant to deal with; if a woman, may die giving birth, if a man, may die of unnatural causes. Is interested in conversation but full of reproach for other people.

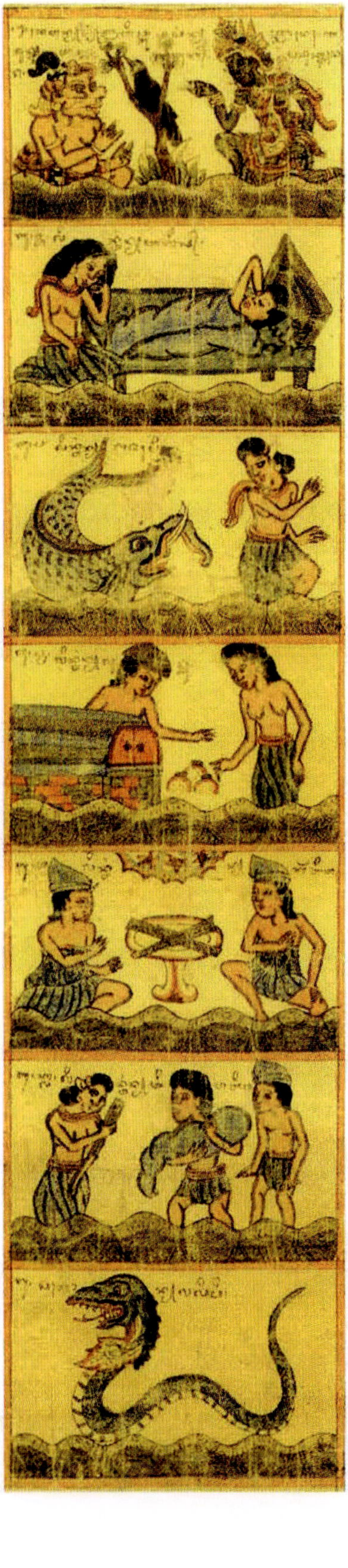

Wednesday—*Buda*

God: Wisnu
Wayang character: Merdah
Tree: *ancak* (*Ficus religius*)
Bird: pigeon
Animal: snake
Demon: raven

Buda-Umanis (16): The sign is sadness (*lintang ngeling*). Lives a simple life and likes to help other people, is just and wise, but often resents other people's malice, struck by bad luck.

Buda-Paing (17): The sign is an elephant fish (*gajah mina*). Has a happy and prosperous life, is an extremely wise person, but does not interfere with other people's business, sometimes arrogant and vindictive.

Buda-Pon (18): The sign is a rice barn (*lumbung muyung*). Can get rich if he or she heeds divine words, is sensitive to flattery and likes to show off. Likes to parade his or her riches, is polite and moderate, somewhat vindictive.

Buda-Wage (19):The sign is the Kartika star (*lintang Kartika*). Appreciated by other people, relatively well off and likes to show it, polite, obstinate, and vindictive. Stingy but acts wisely.

Buda-Kliwon (20): The sign is the cremation of corpses (*atiwa-tiwa*). A glib talker, polite, gets angry easily. Happy in his or her family life, but the children will die and this causes family disputes.

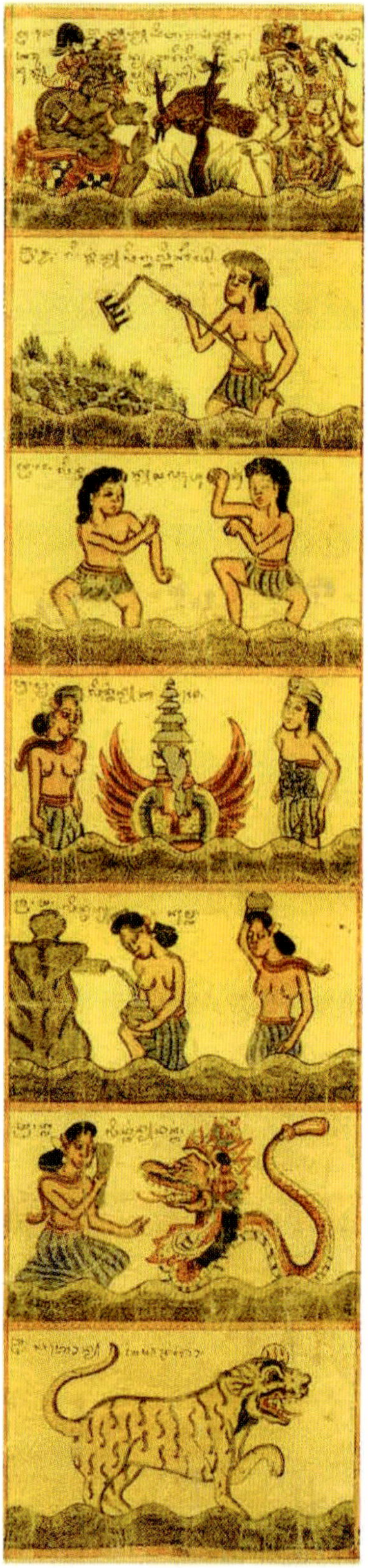

Thursday—*Wrespati*

God: Siwa
Wayang character: Twalen
Tree: banyan (*Ficus indica*)
Bird: peacock
Animal: cat
Demon: man

Wrespati-Umanis (21): The sign is a broken hoe (*sangka tikel*). Born under bad luck: whatever he or she uses, it does not work or it breaks. Social but likes flattery, does not interfere with other people's business, absent-minded.

Wrespati-Paing (22): The sign is a measurement mistake (*salah ukur*). Indifferent, stubborn, ambitious, spendthrift, and clumsy with other people.

Wrespati-Pon (23): The sign is a cremation tower (*bade*). Open and ambitious, likes to show off, is just but hard. Poor during childhood and may die young.

Wrespati-Wage (24): The sign is a water jug (*kumbha*). Ambitious, intelligent, and hard-working, wise, sensitive to flattery, gets easily upset.

Wrespati-Kliwon (25): The sign is a dragon (*naga*). Very ambitious, a know-all, gets easily upset, can be offensive, spendthrift.

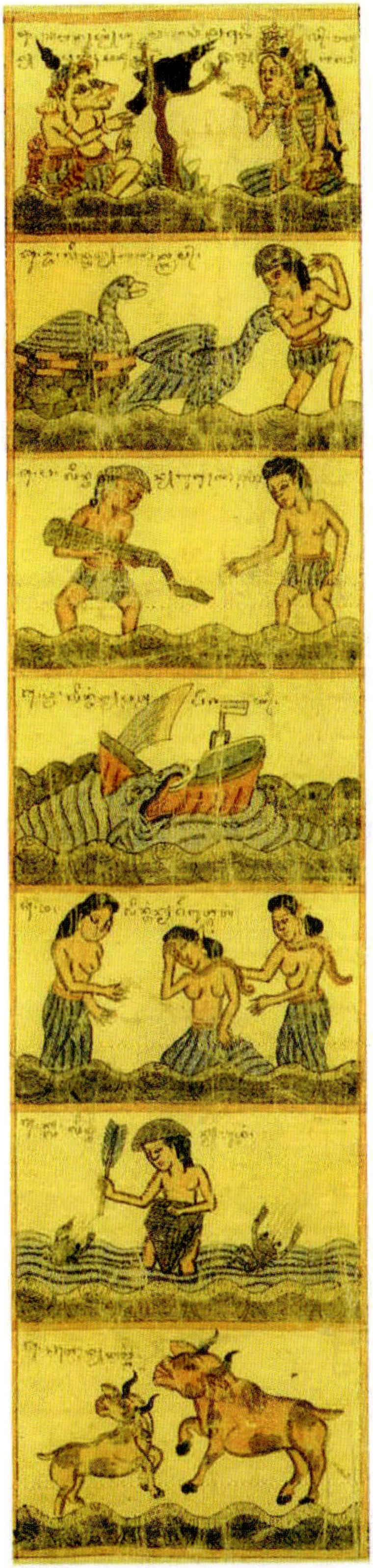

Friday—*Sukra*

God: Uma
Wayang character: Sangut
Tree: *kayo putih* (*Mangifera indica*)
Bird: egret
Animal: goat
Demon: cow

Sukra-Umanis (26): The sign is the hatching goose *(angsa makeem)*. Honest and likes to help other people, successful, spendthrift but too generous at times, gets easily upset when contradicted.

Sukra-Paing (27): The sign is a torn net (*bubo bosor*). Courageous, amiable, honest, appreciated by other people, bad-tempered. Becomes rich but loses these riches through illness.

Sukra-Pon (28): The sign is a broken boat (*prahu pegat*). Irregular and inconsistent in work habits and ideals, unsteady, hesitant, often sad or worried, yet kind and gentle towards others. Tends to gamble, likes to show off his or her possessions.

Sukra-Wage (29): The sign is 'debt-ridden' (*gelut utang/ magelut*). Bad-tempered and lacks flexibility, generous and ready to sacrifice himself or herself for other people, but poor and ridden with debts.

Sukra-Kliwon (30): The sign is a shrimp (*udang*). Intelligent, glib talker, has a good heart and pleasant nature. Suffers during childhood but becomes rich as he or she gets older.

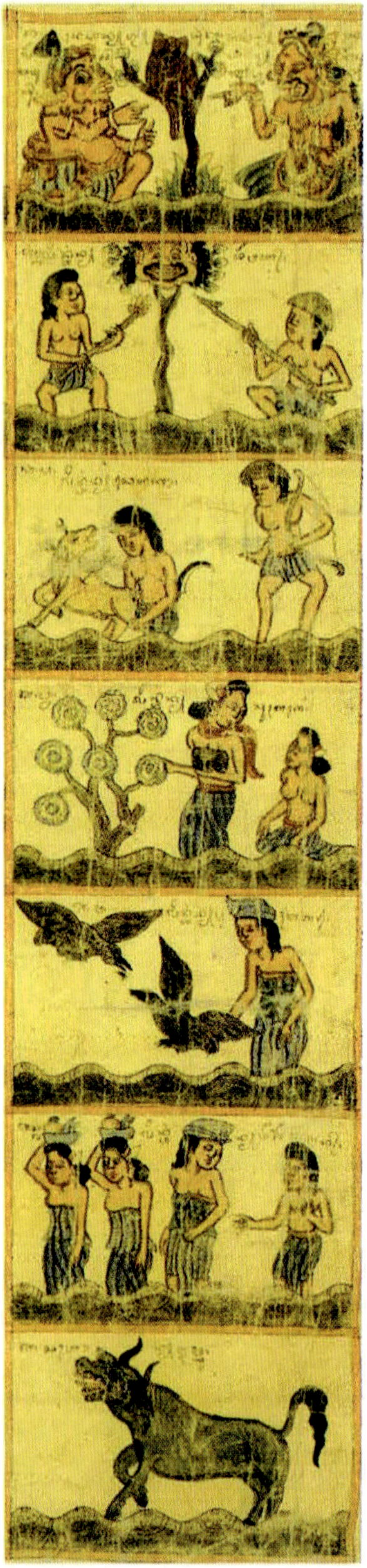

Saturday—*Saniscara*

God: Durga
Wayang character: Delem
Tree: a variety of *randu* or kapok
Bird: owl
Animal: cow
Demon: buffalo

Saniscara-Umanis (31): The sign is a comical giant (*Begoong*). Knows how to appreciate other people's qualities, likes a life of luxury and minds other people's business. Whatever his or her intentions, is often accused of wrongdoing.

Saniscara-Paing (32):The sign is an arrow (*ru*). Courageous and feared by people, polite, gets easily upset.

Saniscara-Pon (33): The sign is a sunflower (*sungenge*). A good person, appreciated in high places, likes luxury, shows off his or her superiority.

Saniscara-Wage (34):The sign is quarrelling quails (*puwuh atarung*). Sometimes stiff in demeanor, likes to contradict and create disorder. Likes to show off his or her superiority, may become rich but is stingy.

Saniscara-Kliwon (35): The sign is a gaze (*pangelangan*). Amiable and polite, glib talker, wise. After marriage, often falls ill. Protects other people.

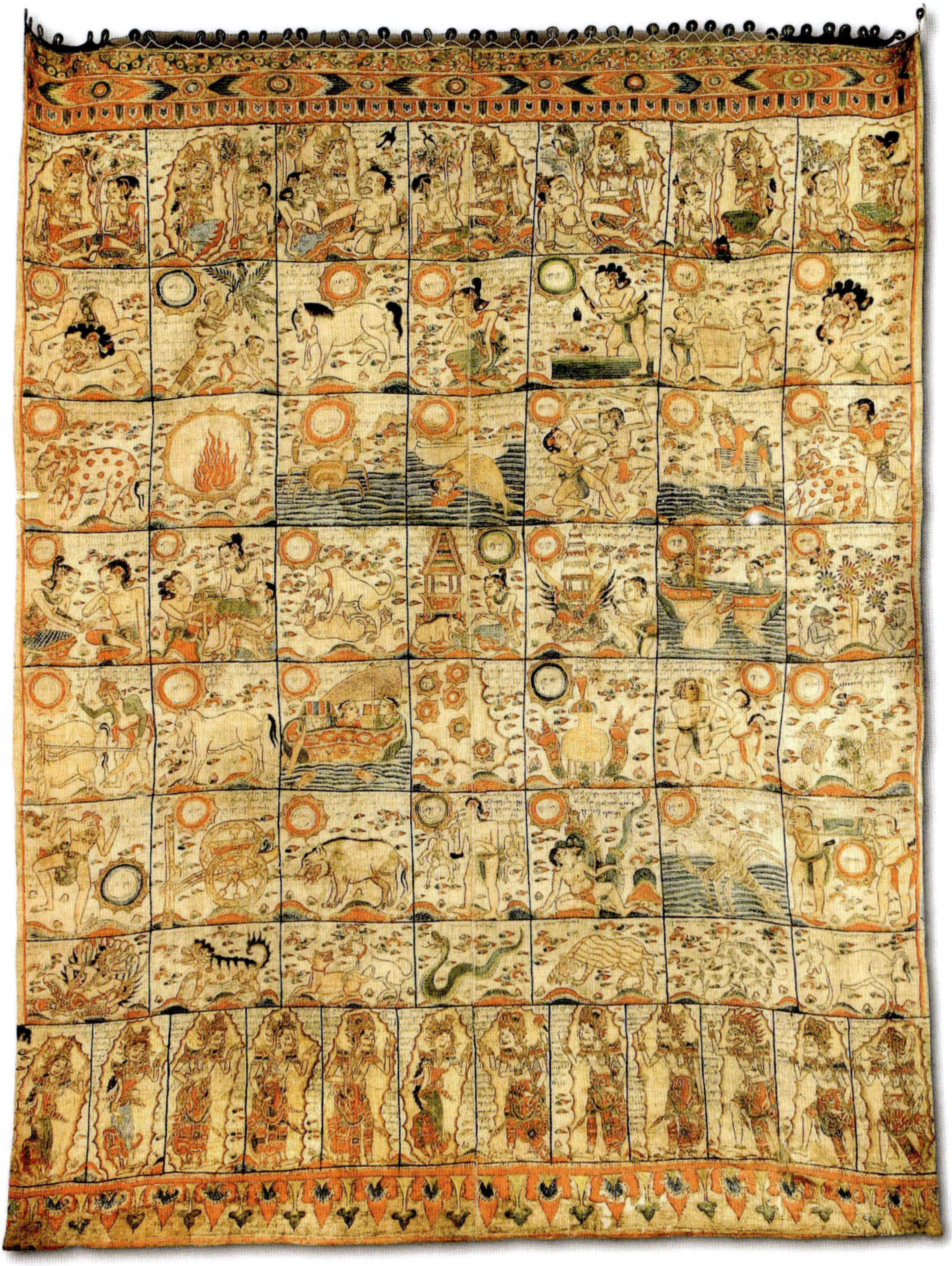

PELELINTANGAN

Langse (curtain), paint on cotton cloth.

240 x 192 cm.

ca. first quarter of the 20th century.

Collection of the National Museum of Ethnology, Leiden (Inv. 4491-81).

Collected by Th. A. Resink in the 1930s.

Note that this pelelintangan has an extra row on the bottom showing 12 deities, one for each Saka month, who influence those born in each particular month.

Personal Character According to the Wuku of One's Birth

1. ***Sinta*:** Jealous, hot-tempered but good, amiable, protects other people, young-looking, serious and organized in his or her work. May face danger when of mature age.
2. ***Landep*:** Likes to meditate, intelligent, good-looking, hard in his or her orders but correct, generous, protects those in need, appreciated by the powerful. May be injured or killed by a falling tree.
3. ***Ukir*:** Generous and good, good-looking, can do anything, delicate, polite, likes to show off, appreciated by his or her boss, likes the good life, does not like to be dominated. May be tortured.
4. ***Kulantir*:** Hot-tempered, spends his or her time sleeping, likes the good life, dishonest, likes a fight, cannot protect other people, does not know how to save money, skilled at seducing other people.
5. ***Tolu*:** Audacious, wise, glib talker, quick in his or her work, does not sleep a lot, happy in old age. Risk: Being gored by a buffalo.
6. ***Gumbreg*:** Honest, true to his or her word, expresses him or herself softly, protects his or her family, appreciated by high-ranking officials, talkative, big income earner, generous. Risk: Drowning.
7. ***Wariga*:** Jealous, sometimes nasty, unsociable, has a difficult life but is liked by other people. Risk: Being implicated in a scandal.
8. ***Warigadian*:** Strong-willed, likes pleasure, has a lot of responsibilities to face, good, knows how to get on in life but does not follow up. Risk: Being the victim of black magic.
9. ***Juluwangi*:** Likes to debate, people trust him or her, speaks softly, appreciated by other people, generous to those who obey him or her, favored by fate. Risk: Being the victim of wild beasts.
10. ***Sungsang*:** Confused, full of hesitation, good-tempered, good worker, greedy towards other people's property, spendthrift, accepts tasks of dubious morality. Looks generous, but this is only a facade. Risk: Being killed by a sharp weapon.
11. ***Dungulan*:** Ready to help other people, sophisticated in language and character, not easily troubled, skilled at surmounting difficulties, greedy towards other people's property, often in a quandary, not very intelligent, does not succeed. Risk: Quarrels with other people.
12. ***Kuningan*:** Proud, intelligent, glib talker, hard worker, likes to be on his or her own, sometimes stingy. Risk: Falling into a rage.
13. ***Langkir*:** Ill-tempered, stubborn, noisy, creates problems for other people. Risk: Being the victim of other people's nastiness.
14. ***Medangsia*:** Gets angry on all occasions, likes worldly pleasures, refined in his or her speech, fears other people, protects poor people, wealthy, thrifty, wise with riches. Risk: Being the victim of fire.
15. ***Pujut*:** Quiet, sensitive, knows how to master his or her anger, good-looking, ambitious. Risk: Being the victim of slander.
16. ***Pahang*:** Talkative and always wants to have the last word, boastful, imprudent in his or her actions, helps people in need. Risk: Being tortured.
17. ***Krulut*:** Likes any task entrusted to him or her, does not speak much, chivalrous, pure in spirit, likes family and friends, branded with the seal of fortune. Risk: Being poisoned.
18. ***Merakih*:** Tolerates suffering, pure in spirit, knows how to tempt fate, shows respect to the ancestors, runs into danger while traveling. Risk: Being drowned.
19. ***Tambir*:** Talkative, depressed, cannot protect his or her family, envious, slanderer. Risk: falling victim to black magic.
20. ***Medangkungan*:** Opinionated, true to his or her word, likes water, can get rich. Risk: Being stabbed.

21. ***Matal*:** True to his or her word, good-looking, talks softly, liked by people in high places, favored by fortune, has many friends. Risk: Too many arguments with people.

22. ***Uye*:** Arrogant and jealous, not always chivalrous, liked by other people, prudent in actions, does not hesitate to sacrifice him or herself for loved ones, lives to a ripe age, favored by fortune. Risk: Falling victim to other people's nastiness.

23. ***Menail*:** Proud but knows how to make friends, prudent, hard worker, sober, does not seek honor. Risk: Being stabbed.

24. ***Prangbakat*:** Strong-willed, shy, chivalrous, obeyed by others, lives to a ripe old age, hard worker, favored by fortune, rather arrogant. Risk: Injury from falling.

25. ***Bala*:** Always creates trouble, likes nasty people, approached by people in high places, rich but proud, socially ill at ease. Risk: Being poisoned.

26. ***Ugu*:** Stingy and selfish, unsociable, easily hurt, quiet, humble but jealous. Risk: Getting bitten by a snake.

27. ***Wayang*:** Prudent, handsome, speaks softly, gets troubled, appreciated by other people, his/her orders are apparently easy to follow but pose problems. Risk: Falling victim to slander.

28. ***Kulawu*:** honest, credible, easily moved, knows how to please, lives to a ripe old age, favored by fortune but does not know how to keep his or her riches, not jealous. Risk: Being poisoned.

29. ***Dukut*:** Audacious and strong-willed, understands quickly, appreciated by important people, prudent in his or her actions, and may become rich. Risk: being the victim of war.

30. ***Watugunung*:** Ambitious, self-confident, not talkative, easily scared, very jealous, keen to live like a hermit. Risk: Being tortured.

Other Pawukon 'Horoscope' Schemes

Panca suda

The *panca suda* is a scheme consisting of seven categories of birth traits issuing from the overlaps of the five-day (Pancawara) and seven-day (Saptawara) weeks.

- ***Wisesa Segara*:** 'The power of the sea' relates to Anggara Umanis, Redite Paing, Buda Paing, Saniscara Pon, Soma Wage, and Sukra Kliwon. People born on these conjunction days are influenced by other people's mistakes but readily forgive them.
- ***Tunggaksemi*:** 'The flower stem' relates to Soma Umanis, Sukra Paing, Wrespati Wage, and Saniscara Kliwon. People born on these days are rather proud, not very congenial, and are always ready for a fight.
- ***Satria Wibawa*:** 'The powerful warrior' relates to Wrespati Umanis, Saniscara Paing, Anggara Pon, Redite Wage, and Buda Wage. People born on these days are chivalrous, honest, and live in luxury.
- ***Sumur Sinaba*:** 'The full well' relates to Redite Umanis, Buda Umanis, Soma Pon, Sukra Wage, and Anggara Kliwon. People born on these days get easily angry, despair of everything, but help other people.
- ***Bumi Kapetak*:** 'The white earth' relates to Saniscara Umanis, Soma Paing, Redite Pon, Buda Pon, and Wrespati Kliwon. People born on these days dislike traveling, are hard workers, and like to meditate.
- ***Lebu Ketiup Angin*:** 'The dust to the wind' relates to Wrespati Paing, Sukra Pon, Anggara Wage, and Redite or Buda Kliwon. These people are of unsteady opinion, and difficult to please. They live in poverty.
- ***Satria Wirang*:** 'The humiliated warrior' relates to Sukra Umanis, Anggara Paing, Wrespati Pon, Saniscara Wage, and Soma Kliwon. These people get easily angry, and are obsessed by their problems. Their good intentions sometimes have disastrous consequences.

Pawukon Charts of Lucky/Unlucky Days

Lucky Days of the Wuku

You can identify lucky days for agricultural activities and weddings in each wuku by adding the male, female, and hermaphrodite qualities associated with each day of the five-day, six-day, and seven-day weeks, as shown in the table below.

Pancawara (five-day week)	**Sadwara** (six-day week)	**Saptawara** (seven-day week)
Umanis: female	Tungleh: hermaphrodite	Redite: male
Paing: hermaphrodite	Aryang: female	Suma: female
Pon: hermaphrodite	Urukung: male	Anggara: hermaphrodite
Wage: female	Paniron: hermaphrodite	Buda: hermaphrodite
Kliwon: male	Was: female	Wrespati: male
	Maulu: male	Sukra: female
		Saniscara: female

A given day of a wuku is considered lucky if it features one of the following three combinations:

- One male, one female, and one hermaphrodite
- One male and two females
- Three females

As an example, for Wuku Sinta:
Paing + Tungleh + Redite: two hermaphrodites and one male, considered unlucky.
Pon + Aryang + Soma: two females and one hermaphrodite, also considered unlucky.
Wage + Urukung + Anggara: one of each gender, considered lucky. And so on....

Ingkel Days

Some days in the Pawukon calendar are considered inauspicious for certain, mainly agricultural, undertakings. There are two types, called *ingkel awuku* and *ingkel adina.*

The ingkel awuku cover the entirety of a seven-day week, from Sunday through Saturday, appearing in this order: activities applying to people (*wong*), livestock (*sato*), fish (*mina*), poultry (*manuk*), plants and trees (*taro*) and bamboo (*buku*).

The *ingkel adina* only last a single day and they run in a different order and have three similar and three different names: *mina, taro, sato, patra* (related to plants and trees), *wong* and *paksi* (related to poultry and/or birds).

These ingkel adina days follow a cycle parallel to the cycle of the six-day week, starting with *mina* on the Sunday of Wuku Sinta. During this week, it is recommended not to conduct rituals or to indulge in economic activities related to any of the above-mentioned entities.

Auspicious Days of the Wuku

Tika charts mainly deal with auspicious days for weddings and agricultural undertakings.

1. Sinta:	Tuesday, Thursday
2. Landep:	Sunday, Saturday
3. Ukir:	Wednesday, Friday, Saturday
4. Kulantir:	Monday, Thursday, Friday
5. Taulu(Tolu):	Monday, Friday, Saturday
6. Gumbreg:	Thursday, Saturday
7. Wariga:	Sunday, Monday, Tuesday, Thursday, Friday, Saturday
8. Warigadian:	Sunday, Monday
9. Julungwangi:	Tuesday, Wednesday, Saturday
10. Sungsang:	Monday, Thursday
11. Dungulan:	Sunday, Monday, Wednesday
12. Kuningan:	Monday, Friday
13. Langkir:	Sunday, Friday
14. Medangsia:	Sunday, Monday, Saturday
15. Pujut:	Thursday, Friday, Saturday
16. Pahang:	Tuesday, Thursday, Friday
17. Krulut:	Sunday, Saturday
18. Merakih:	Wednesday, Friday, Saturday
19. Tambir:	Monday, Thursday, Friday
20. Medangkungan:	Monday, Friday, Saturday
21. Matal:	Thursday, Saturday
22. Uye:	Sunday, Monday, Tuesday, Thursday, Friday, Saturday
23. Menail:	Sunday, Monday
24. Prangbakat:	Tuesday, Wednesday, Saturday
25. Bala:	Monday, Thursday
26. Uhu:	Sunday, Monday, Wednesday
27. Wayang:	Monday, Friday
28. Kulawu:	Sunday, Friday
29. Dukut:	Sunday, Monday, Saturday
30. Watugunung:	Thursday, Friday, Saturday

Lucky/Unlucky Days According to Watek Catur and Watek Panca

If the urip of the day in the five-day week and in the seven-day week are added, then divided by four, one gets the *watek catur* according to the remainder, as follows: if the remainder is 1, then the day is *lelipi*, or snake, and you should avoid planting vegetables or fruit trees; if it is 2, then the day is *gajah*, or elephant, a propitious day for animal husbandry; if it is 3, then the day is *sampit*, or cow, a propitious day for cattle breeding; if it is either 4 or 0, the day is *lintah*, or leech, a propitious day for the cultivation of creeping plants.

If the urip of the day in the five-day week and in the seven-day week are added, then divided by five, one gets the *watek panca* according to the remainder obtained, as follows: 1 = *gajah*, or elephant, propitious for husbandry; 2 = *watu*, or stone, propitious for building; 3 = *buta*, or demon, propitious for ceremonies addressed to underworld or earthly forces; 4 = *kaki*, or foot or man, propitious for erecting a wall or a stable, but unlucky for making marriage proposals.

Other Important Days for Divination

There is a multiplicity of other intersections and computations that generate days with particularly auspicious or inauspicious value in the Pawukon cycle.

- The conjunctions of Pancawara and Saptawara days may give a positive or negative quality to a day according to the sum of their urip. For example, Kala Gotongan days, always three in a row, are obtained when the sum of the two urip is 14. We find this combination every 35 days in the Pawukon cycle (see Tika Chart II, page 35). Kala Gotongan days are good for beginning a business, but no cremation should be held. Semut Sedulur, meanwhile, corresponds to those days whose urip sum is 13. These days are propitious for meetings, but no cremation or burial should ever take place on them. We also find this combination every 35 days (see Tika Chart II).
- Conjunctions of a certain wara day and wuku also give important days: for example, the day Taliwangke (see Tika Chart II), which falls on the following conjunctions: Wednesday in Wuku Landep, Thursday in Wuku Wariga, Friday in Wuku Kuningan, Saturday in Wuku Krulut, Monday in Wuku Uye, and Tuesday in Wuku Wayang, thus, every 36 six days (6 x 6) except once, between Saturday Krulut and Monday Uye, when the interval is only 30 days. These days are propitious for the making of ropes and barriers related to agricultural work. They are not, however, propitious for the making of ropes for cattle or for washing or weaving. The conjunction may also be unique. For instance, the conjunction of Wednesday of the seven-day week and Wuku Kulawu produces Kala Awu, a day that is propitious for making a plough, but unpropitious for erecting a building.
- Other days of importance are those combining a certain Pancawara–Saptawara conjunction with a certain day of the Saka lunar calendar. For example, the conjunction of Soma Wage with penanggal 1 and the conjunction of Buda Pon with penanggal 7 are called Amerta Bumi and are deemed propitious for a wedding, regardless of the month.
- The wuku and lunar month combination may also be taken into account. For example, the conjunction of the Wednesday of Wuku Parangbakat with penanggal 12 in the Katiga, Kapat, and Kalima lunar months also produces an Amerta Bumi day that is considered lucky for exorcisms and hair cutting, and indicates good health for anyone born on that day.

Divination According to the Saka Calendar

Character Attributes of the Sasih Lunar Months

1. Kasa: illness
2. Karo: poverty
3. Katiga: simultaneous happiness and misery, numerous children to those born in this month
4. Kapat: wealth, numerous children
5. Kalima: prosperity
6. Kanem: correct situation
7. Kapitu: ripe old age
8. Kawulu: not enough food
9. Kasanga: unhappiness
10. Kadasa: happiness
11. Desta: misery and shame
12. Sadha: illness

Pelelindon: Earthquake Calendars

Pelelindon (or *pelindon*), often called 'earthquake calendars', are painted divination charts based on the 12 lunar months of the Saka calendar. They forecast in words and pictures what can be expected if an earthquake strikes during a given lunar month, and in some cases, during each of the days of the seven-day week as well.

Each month is associated with a god or goddess from the Hindu pantheon (although not all pelelindon agree on which god goes with which month). The painted scenes for each month illustrate and expand upon written predictions (possibly adapted from *lontar* texts). The predictions are generalized, and not necessarily negative; they clearly pertain to human health and agriculture.

Most pelelindon take the form of *tabing*—square paintings designed to be hung on walls as a backdrop for offerings, or stretched on ceilings above the raised platforms on which offerings are placed. The 12 months are typically arranged around the edge of the square, counter-clockwise, with an open space in the center divided into nine areas, symbolic of the nine sacred directions, or *nawa sanga*, often used to illustrate predictions for the seven days of the week, plus a god and a demon.

In rare cases, they may be directly incorporated into the architecture of an important building, giving the artist a large space to use for depicting the various predictions. This is the case with the pelelindon on the ceiling of Kerta Gosa, the Hall of Justice in the ancient capital of Klungkung, which was painted by Pan Semaris from Kamasan for the renovation of the building in 1960. Each of the 12 months, along with its associated deities and predictions if an earthquake happens during the month concerned, is depicted in a series of rectangular panels along the fifth tiers of the inside lower portion of the roof. The panels cover all four sides of the open-air pavilion, with three months per side, running clockwise.

Qualities of the Penanggal/Panglong Days

Each lunar day (*tithi*) of the waning (*panglong*) or waxing (*tanggal/penanggal*) moon has a corresponding attribute (object/plant/animal) and quality, defined by its position from 1 to 15. When there is a *ngunalatri* (compression of two days into a single day to adjust the length of the month), the number of the second day is the reference used.

For the tanggal days of the waxing moon: 1 = horse; 2 = deer; 3 = tiger; 4 = cat; 5 = cow; 6 = buffalo; 7 = rat; 8 = dust; 9 =dog; 10 = dragon; 11 = goat; 12 = palm tree stem; 13 = elephant; 14 = lion, and 15 = fish.

For the panglong days of the waning moon: 1 = candle; 2 = eagle; 3 = coconut tree; 4 = buffalo; 5 = ghost; 6 = palm tree; 7 = shrimp; 8 = sea; 9 = the Southern Cross; 10 = honey; 11 = demon; 12 = snake; 13 = rice; 14 = worm, and 15 = the fiber of the palm tree leaf.

The qualities associated with these days are named in Old Javanese, as follows:

For the penanggal days: 1 and 15 = *awidya*; 2 = *jaramerana*; 3 = *jati*; 4 and 5 = *upadana*; 6 = *tresna*; 7 = *wedana*; 8 and 9 = *sparsa*; 10 = *sedayatana*; 11 = *nama rupa*; 12 = *widnyana*; 13 and 14 = *saskara*.

For the panglong days: 1 = *awidya*; 2= *jaramerana*; 3 and 13 = *jati*; 4 and 14 = *bhawa*; 5 and 15 = *upadana*; 6 = *tresna*; 7 = *wedana*; 8 = *sparsa*; 9 = *sedayatana*; 10 = *nama rupa*; 11 = *saskara*.

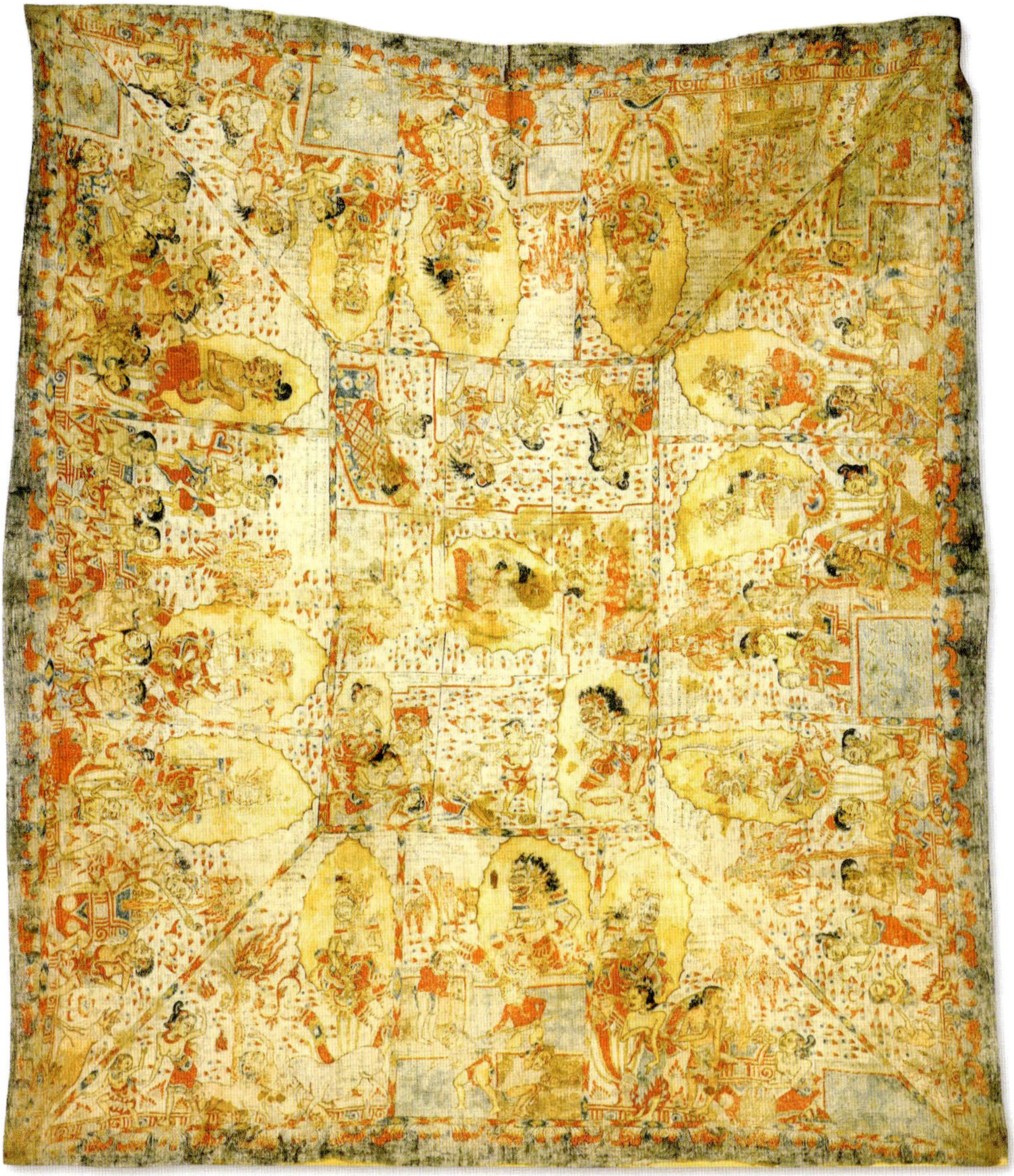

PAINTED CEILING PELELINDON ON CANVAS
Kaki Rambug, Kamasan school.
ca. 1880–1900.
207 x 237 cm.
Private collection.

This is a classic example of a pelelindon designed to be stretched above the raised platform on which offerings are put. The artist has painted the 12 months of the luni-solar Saka year on panels running counter-clockwise around the edge, starting from the central panel on the right side: 1. Kasa; 2. Karo; 3. Katiga; 4. Kapat; 5. Kalima; 6. Kanem; 7. Kapitu; 8. Kawulu; 9. Kasanga; 10. Kadasa: 11. Desta; 12. Sadha. Each panel depicts the deity corresponding to that month and a prediction of what political, agricultural, and/or health consequences can be expected if an earthquake falls on that month. The large central area is divided into nine squares, seven of which illustrate predictions for the consequences of earthquakes falling on each of the days of the seven-day week.

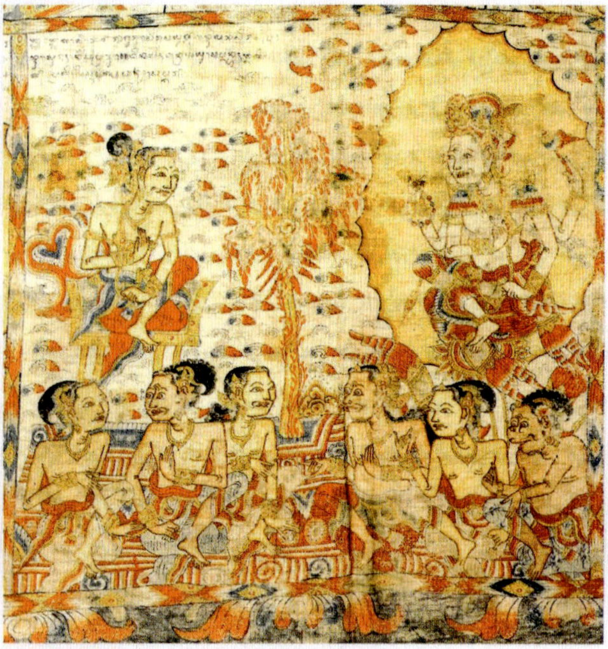

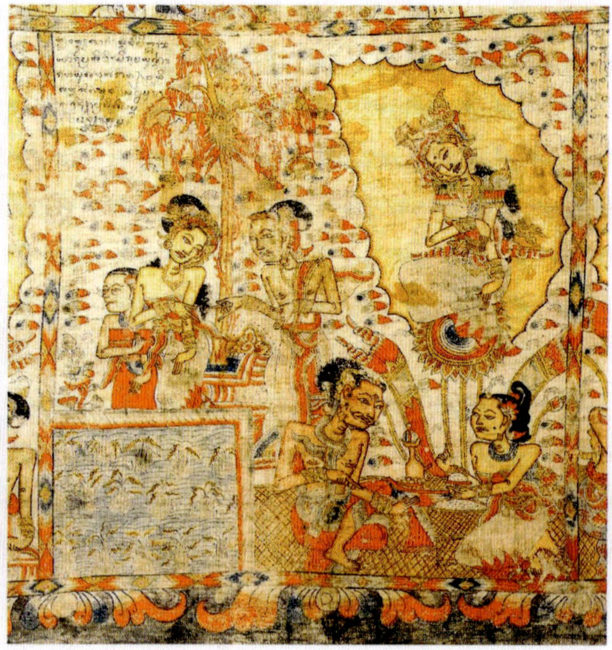

DETAILS OF PAINTED CEILING PELELINDON
(predictions based on Warsika, 1986)
Above left
Month: Sasih Kapitu
Deity: Batara Guru
Prediction if an earthquake happens this month: The government will be in trouble, the population will be confused and will lose trust in the government.

Above right
Month: Sasih Kasa
Deity: Betari Sri
Prediction if an earthquake happens this month: Peace.

Those qualities, derived from the Old Javanese meaning of their names, often with new connotations, may be interpreted as follows:

- *Tresna* (from *tresna* = love): negative to undertake a task, ill-fortune and troubles ahead. A person born on this day is religious and wise, but has many enemies, is poor and generous.
- *Upadana* (from *upadhana* = kindness): neutral—people are ready to give a hand, but there is a tendency to waste energy and money. A person born on this day is amiable, religious, and a spell-binding orator, audacious, generous, but lacks direction; generally happy.
- *Bhawa* (from *bhawa* = behavior, character): negative—a lot of troubles are to be encountered; people who help are not to be trusted. A person born on this day is good-natured, audacious, reliable, but strong-headed, an insomniac, and likes working in the fields.
- *Jati* (from *jati* = true): neutral—people are ready to help, but this does not ensure success. A person born on this day is good-natured, honest, trustworthy, well-liked, audacious, and prosperous.
- *Jaramarana* (from *Jara* = old and *marana* = unhappy): negative—conflict, illness, or perhaps even death ahead; the god Kala is wreaking havoc. A person born on this day is clever, ill-tempered, chivalrous, and loved by his or her family, but has many enemies.

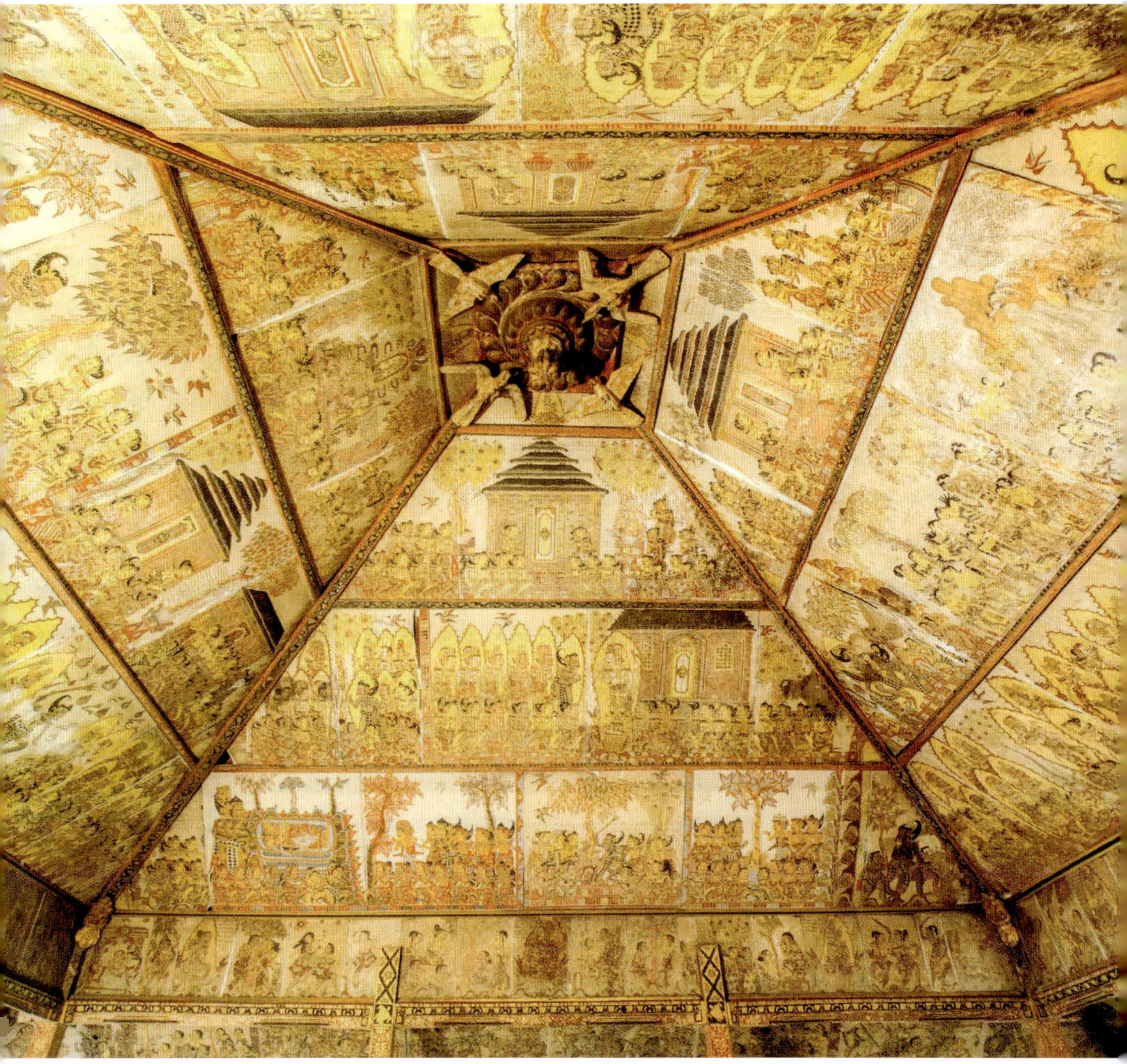

WIDE VIEW OF PAINTED CEILING INSIDE THE ROOF OF THE KERTA GOSA PAVILION, SEMARAPURA, BALI.
The pelelindon/earthquake calendar (fourth row down) shows predictions for the consequences of earthquakes falling on particular months and days. The upper panels depict scenes from the *Bima Swarga* and other stories.

Details of the *pelelindon* painted on the roof of the Kerta Gosa (predictions based on Warsika 1986).

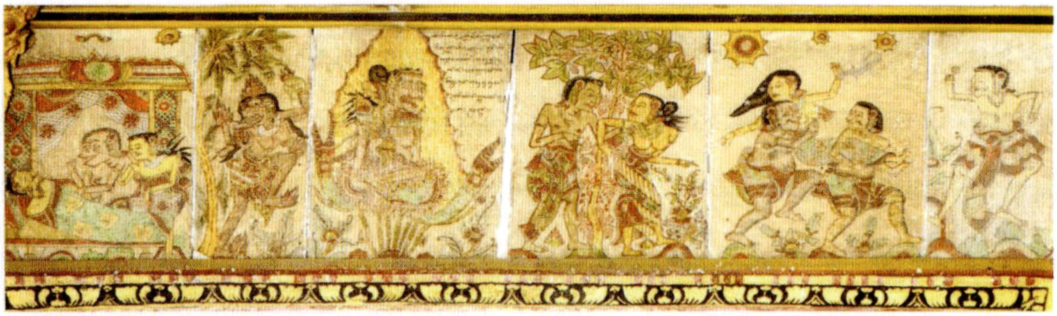

Sasih Kanem (month 6): This panel is located on the south side of the roof. **Deity:** Batari Durga. Prediction if an earthquake happens on this month: There will be an epidemic, especially in densely populated areas.

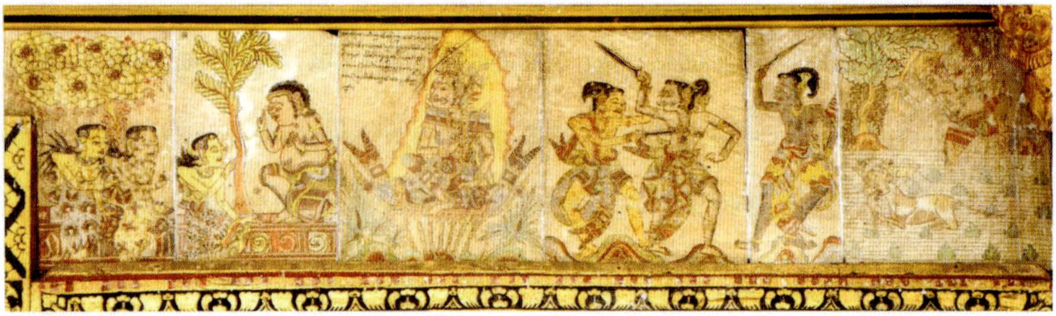

Sasih Kawulu (month 8): This panel is located on the south side of the roof. **Deity:** Batara Parameswara. Prediction if an earthquake happens on this month: No peace and the kingdom will be troubled.

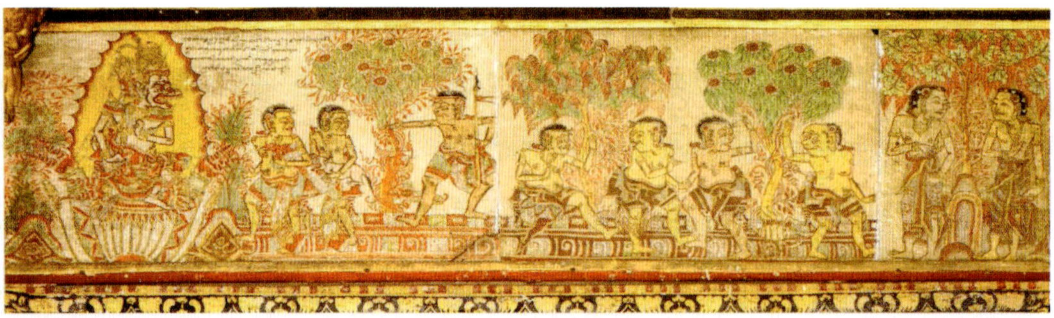

Sasih Sadha (month 12): This panel is located on the north side of the roof. **Deity:** Batara Anantaboga. Prediction if an earthquake happens on this month: Chaos, long drought, agricultural difficulties, bad commercial transactions will happen soon in the kingdom.

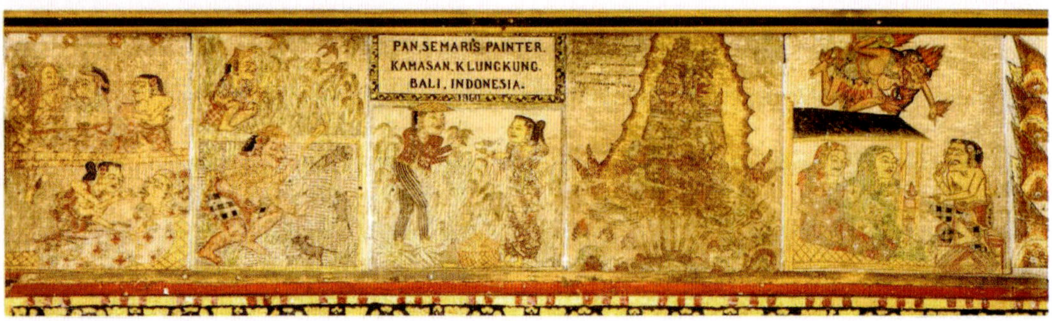

Sasih Kapat (month 4): This panel is located on the east side of the roof. **Deity:** Batara Brahma. Prediction if an earthquake happens on this month: Peace and a lot of rain.

- *Awidya* (from *awidya* = unlearned): positive—happiness and success ahead. A person born on this day is smart and hard-working, a good orator, experiences short stints of unhappiness, but is generally successful, including with women.
- *Saskara* (from *sangaskara* = purification?): negative—all sorts of hurdles are to be encountered, with much sniggering and infighting. A person born on this day is well-off but often encounters all sorts of troubles, is well-liked, gifted at literature and architecture.
- *Widnyana* (from *widyana* = knowledge?): positive—owing to friends, it is easy to get what is needed. A person born on this day is happy, chivalrous, not well-off, but appreciated by priests.
- *Namarupa* (from *nama* = name and *rupa* = form): negative—many troubles ahead, much sadness and embarrassment; other people do not care. A person born on this day is smart and skilled, poor during middle age, but then prosperous; has to wait a long time before having children; is disliked by many.
- *Sadayatana* {?): neutral—people give love and attention, but work does not proceed smoothly. A person born on this day is full of ideas; is jealous and ill-tempered; escapes danger and illness.
- *Sparsa* (from *sparsa* = sense of touch): very negative—troubles erupt everywhere; work is muddled and unfocused; all endeavors end up badly, whatever amount of money is spent. A person born on this day is broad-minded, a good debater, but jealous and evil; may get rich.
- *Wedana* (?): neutral—everyone helps without creating trouble and things run smoothly, but much money is spent. A person born on this day is a skilled worker, well-off, and rather happy, polite, and amiable, full of love towards others.

Panca Dauh Chart

Panca Dauh		Monday	Monday	Tuesday	Wednesday	Thursday	Friday	Saturday
Daytime	**Night-time**							
I. 6:00 a.m. to 8:24 a.m.	V. 6:00 p.m. to 8:24 p.m.	Urip	Gering	Gering	Pati	Urip	Pati	Pati
II. 8:24 a.m. to 10:48 a.m.	IV. 8:24 p.m. to 10:48 p.m.	Pati	Urip	Urip	Urip	Gering	Urip	Gering
III. 10:48 a.m. to 1:12 p.m.	III. 10:48 p.m. to 1:12 a.m.	Urip	Gering	Urip	Urip	Pati	Gering	Urip
IV. 1:12 p.m. to 3:36 p.m.	II. 1:12 a.m. to 3:36 a.m.	Pati	Gering	Urip	Gering	Urip	Gering	Gering
V. 3:36 p.m. to 6:00 p.m.	1. 3:36 a.m. to 6:00 a.m.	Gering	Pati	Gering	Gering	Gering	Urip	Urip

Asta Dauh Chart

Asta Dauh		Monday	Monday	Tuesday	Wednesday	Thursday	Friday	Saturday
Daytime	**Night-time**							
I. 6:00 a.m. to 7:30 a.m.	I. 6:00 p.m. to 7:30 p.m.	○	☼	☼	☼	☼	☼	☼
II. 7:30 a.m. to 9:00 a.m.	II. 7:30 p.m. to 9:00 p.m.	☼	☼	○	☼	☼	○	☼
III. 9:00 a.m. to 10:30 a.m.	III. 9:00 p.m. to 10:30 p.m.	☼	☼	○	○	○	☼	☼
IV. 10:30 a.m. to noon	IV. 10:30 p.m. to midnight	☼	☼	☼	○	○	☼	☼
V. Noon to 1:30 p.m.	V. Midnight to 1:30 a.m.	☼	○	☼	☼	☼	☼	☼
VI. 1:30 p.m. to 3:00 p.m.	VI. 1:30 a.m. to 3:00 a.m.	☼	○	☼	○	☼	☼	☼
VII. 3:00 p.m. to 4:30 p.m.	VII. 3:00 a.m. to 4:30 a.m.	○	○	☼	☼	○	○	○
VIII. 4:30 p.m. to 6:00 p.m.	VIII. 4:30 a.m. to 6:00 a.m.	○	○	○	○	○	☼	○

In divination, the waxing and the waning position of the moon, the urip corresponding to the day, and the quality attributed to the name of the panglong or tanggal are taken into consideration at the same time.

Auspicious Times of Day

The time units (dauh) of the Balinese day (the modern 24-hour day), as defined by the parallel panca dauh (five-unit) and asta dauh (eight-unit) cycles, are also taken into account to determine an auspicious schedule for an event. The two charts on page 149 show the auspiciousness of the dauh in each cycle on each day of the seven-day week.

The codes in the Panca dauh chart are: urip = life (success); pati = death (failure); and gering = illness (difficulty). The codes in the Asta dauh chart are:*= positive; O= negative.

These charts by no means exhaust the dauh divination system. To determine the auspiciousness of a given moment of time, one may combine the information from the two different dauh cycles to come up with moments that are *ala* (negative) or *ayu* (positive) according to both.

Reading the Modern Printed Balinese Calendar

The modern printed Balinese calendar is a regular Gregorian calendar, except that the familiar seven-day weeks are laid out vertically, not horizontally. The header above the column for each seven-day week gives the name and number (1–30) of the wuku and name of its deity. The footer below the column gives the ingkel for that wuku.

Inside each square, the Gregorian date is surrounded by lots of other information, including, the name, number and key characteristic of the Saka lunar day and month; the names of the day in the two-, three-, four-, five-, six-, seven-, eight, nine-, and ten-day weeks; and the day's characteristics based on the intersection of the five- and seven-day weeks, type of ingkel, and perarasan and panca suda schemes.

Outside of the calendar grid proper are a list of dates of major holy days and temple festivals, and a list of auspicious/inauspicious activities (*ala ayuning dewasa*) for each Gregorian date.

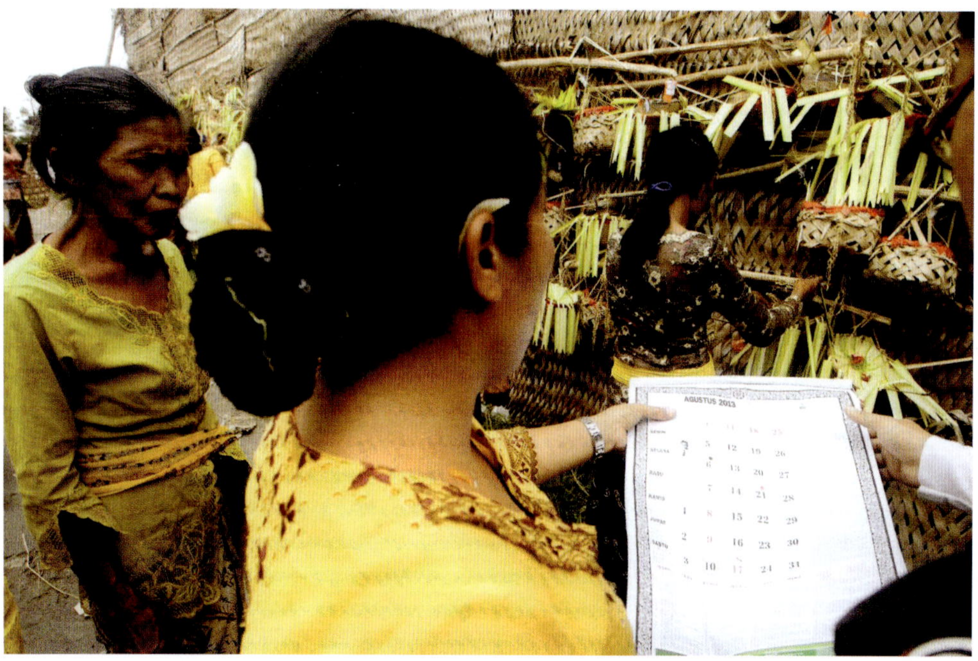

A woman consulting a Balinese calendar.

AFTERWORD
THE SYNTHESIS OF BALINESE TIME

Time as experienced and organized in contemporary Bali is now both cyclical and linear. The Pawukon calendar, which originated in Java, was fundamentally cyclical, but it achieved its current sophistication only after literacy through Indianization and the introduction of the linear Saka calendar enabled a structured formulation of the system.

Today, this complexity must further contend with the linear time of modernity, where units of duration possess neutral symbolic value and concrete economic weight. This shift is most visible in the evolution of speech. Older generations would mark time by reference to upcoming rites or to natural solar movements. They would often know their upcoming *otonan* anniversary on the Pawukon calendar better than their own Gregorian birth date. "Dauh napi?" they would ask about the time of day, referring to the relative position of the sun. Now, one frequently hears "Kali napi?" (What time is it?), meaning specifically what hour and minute.

This linguistic shift allows the Balinese to navigate a world governed by the clock. The seemingly 'endless' time traditionally dedicated to preparing offerings and participating in festivals is increasingly shifting toward a modern, to-the-minute quantified time. Ritual labor now carries an economic price. This shift is challenging the dominance of the ritual cycle. Villagers, now beneficiaries of modern education and employees in the tourism sector, often find their professional duties as guides or waiters at odds with their ritual obligations. Consequently, they must pay fines for absences or remunerate relatives to take over their duties. Similarly, the ability to purchase ready-made offering sets from specialists represents a generalized monetization of what was, until recently, 'free' or voluntary ritual labor.

Furthermore, modern nation-building, systematic planning, and the technological onslaught of the internet are transforming Balinese cultural memory. More and more Balinese are aware that they are residing in a 'global village' where information circulates instantaneously. In this environment, local understandings of time are increasingly marginalized by a global temporal standard.

Does this signal the wane of cultural difference? To an extent, yes. Many Balinese youths have become indifferent to the cultural idiosyncrasies of their society, identifying more with national or global culture. Yet, globalization, especially in an island 'constructed' as a tropical paradise, is also triggering a counter-movement—a crystallization of local identity. Many young Balinese are refocusing on traditional culture and religion as key distinguishing features. Significantly, the traditional calendar has not disappeared; it has been digitized. It is now possible to access 'horoscope' readings or look up auspicious days (Dewasa Ayu) via Indonesian-language websites and apps.

Yet, as 'global time' penetrates the core of society, Balinese time is not necessarily vanishing. Instead, it is being enshrined in a secure niche. From this position, it allows the Balinese to claim that their identity and tradition are not merely surviving, but thriving—continuing to function, albeit in a more marginal and specialized capacity.

I GUSTI NYOMAN DARTA:
THE MAGICAL UBUD MASTER AND THE EKALAYA STORY

From the age of five, I Gusti Nyoman Darta (1951) spent his youth as a *parekan* (attendant) to one of the princes of Ubud, Tjokorde Ngurah of Puri Saren. Within the palace walls, he was not only formally schooled but also initiated into the esoteric knowledge of the court: the art of carving Barong masks and the sacred principles of architecture—building temples in a way that preserves the balance of the surrounding spiritual forces.

The Ubud Palace served as the *axis mundi* of Balinese culture, a central laboratory where sacred ritual met aesthetic refinement. In the 1930s, this royal patronage had merged with the influence of the German artist Walter Spies and the legendary Gusti Nyoman Lempad. Together, they birthed the Pita Maha movement, a revolutionary guild that synthesized ancient palace discipline with a new, individualized expression. While Spies provided a bridge to Western perspectives, the palace remained the vital hearth, allowing Balinese art to evolve into a sophisticated modern movement while remaining rooted in ancestral soil.

Through these palace circles and family ties, Darta was in frequent contact with Gusti Nyoman Lempad (1862–1978), the progenitor of the Balinese 'free-line' drawing style and the island's most celebrated artist. Darta and Lempad shared the same clan rituals; both were 'men of the palace'. Darta would often encounter Lempad when the elder artist visited the Puri to receive royal commissions or to attend poetry readings (*kakawin*) and shadow puppet performances (*wayang kulit*).

An intimate bond formed between the youth and the patriarch. Darta became a silent witness to Lempad's process, learning through visual absorption. Lempad, already over a century old, was past the age of formal teaching. Instead, he offered a cryptic blessing: "Just focus on what you are doing, learn the stories, and you will certainly be able to be as good as me."

Darta took this to heart, identifying with the hero Bambang Ekalaya from the *Mahabharata*. In this wayang episode, Ekalaya seeks to learn archery from the great master Drona. However, Drona refuses to teach him, having promised his favorite pupil, Arjuna, that no one would ever surpass him. Undeterred, Ekalaya retreated to the forest, fashioned a statue of Drona, and meditated before it as if the master were present. Through this total devotion and identification, he miraculously acquired Drona's skills.

When Arjuna discovered that Ekalaya had become the superior archer, Drona was forced to uphold his promise through a cruel trick. He asked Ekalaya for *guru daksina* (teacher's fee), demanding the archer's thumb. Without hesitation, Ekalaya severed his own finger. He sacrificed his status as the world's greatest archer to remain the world's most faithful disciple.

By invoking the myth of Ekalaya, Darta suggests that talent is not merely a matter of DNA or biological descent. Instead, it is something intangible—a magical power transmitted from master to pupil through faithfulness, discipline, and spiritual identification.

Rather than competing for international fame, Darta became a local legend. He is renowned as an *undagi* (traditional architect), an inspired healer, and a master of the ritual culinary arts—

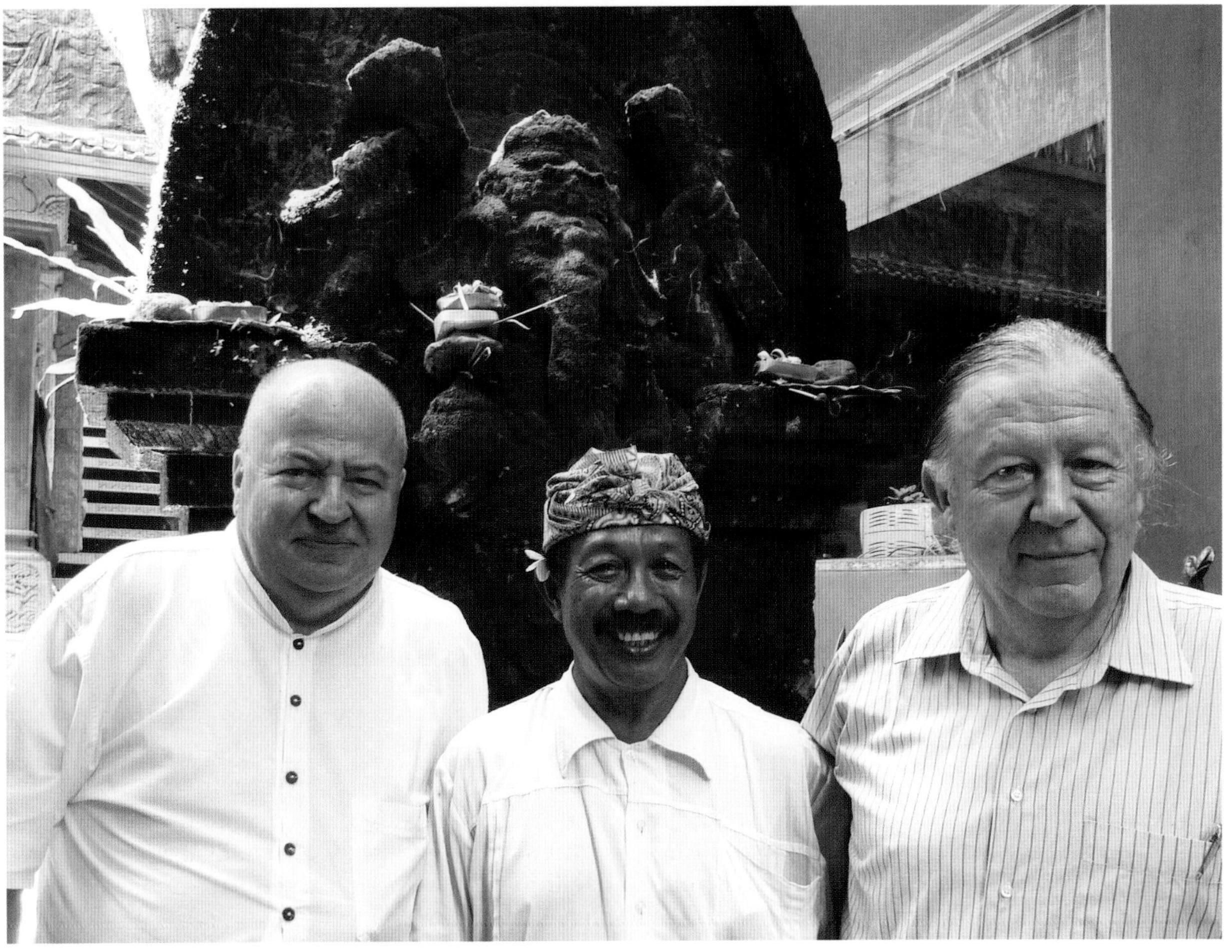

From left **Georges Breguet, I Gusti Nyoman Darta, Jean Couteau.**

skills honed within the Ubud court. He remains part of an elite circle of specialists who travel to temples in Java, Kalimantan, and Lombok to officiate at major festivals.

Darta's evolution as a draughtsman flourished through his encounters with Western connoisseurs. In the late 1970s, he befriended a Swiss gentleman, Gaspard de Marval, and subsequently met Georges Breguet, the visionary behind this project. Breguet commissioned Darta to document the phases of Balinese life. With the later involvement of Jean Couteau who, on top of the general text, undertook a systematic explanation of all the captions, these drawings evolved into a profound study of time and ritual, forming the very foundation of the book *Time, Rites, Art and Magic*. The drawings alone cover a working period of more than 20 years.

SELECT GLOSSARY OF BALINESE TERMS

This list covers those Balinese-language terms related to time, rites, and festivals which recur in the main text or captions in certain chapters of this book and are not redefined on each occurrence. The many other Balinese terms in this book are directly glossed, or discussed in-depth on the page where they occur, or glossed on a previous occurrence on the same page.

Anggarakasih The conjunction of Anggara (Tuesday) and Kliwon of the five-day week, one of the 'strong' conjunction days of the Pawukon calendar on which major temple anniversaries and pan-island holy days occur.

bale Various kinds of raised, open-air pavilions and platforms, including *bale banjar* (the halls in village commons where *banjar* gatherings are held); *bale dangin* (ceremonial pavilions in the eastern part of family compounds); *bale petemu* (meeting halls of the male and female youth associations in Tenganan Pegeringsingan), and Bale Agung (the meeting hall of the Tenganan council of elders).

balian A term covering various types of indigenous Balinese healers, who also play priestly roles in certain rites, including *balian tetakson* (trance mediums who act as intermediaries with gods, spirits, ancestors, and lost souls); *balian usadha* (medicine men who heal using medicinal plant preparations); *balian manakan* (male midwives), and others.

banjar Neighborhood associations, one or more of which comprise each customary (*adat*) village responsible for maintaining 'cosmic order' in the community and for coordinating *banjar* members in fulfilling their community ritual obligations (*ayahan banjar*).

Batara/Batari Terms of address for gods/goddesses, also known as Dewa/Dewi.

Buda-Cemeng The conjunction of Buda (Wednesday) and Wage of the five-day week, one of the 'strong' conjunction days of the Pawukon calendar on which many major temple anniversaries and other ceremonies are held.

Buda-Kliwon The conjunction of Buda (Wednesday) and Kliwon of the five-day week, one of the 'strong' conjunction days of the Pawukon calendar on which major temple anniversaries and pan-island holy days occur, including Pagerwesi, Pegat Uwakan, and Galungan, three of the most important pan-Bali holy days of the Pawukon calendar.

buta kala Demons, low spirits, earthly forces.

buta yadnya Ceremonies addressed to demons, low spirits, or earthly forces.

canang sari The most common, simplest type of offering made and offered daily in Bali, consisting of tiny plaited palm-leaf baskets or trays filled with symbolically significant bits of food, flowers, betel ingredients, and incense.

caru/mecaru Rites of exorcism addressed to demons and earthly forces to cleanse land, buildings, and other environments of unwanted malevolent influences.

daha A term used to designate unmarried women and adolescent girls.

dauh Variable duration time units into which the Balinese day (the modern 24-hour day) was traditionally divided. The passage of time each day and each night is defined by two parallel cycles of five units (*panca dauh*) and eight units (*asta dauh*), respectively, and their duration varies according to natural variations through the year in the time span between sunrise and sunset, sunset and sunrise.

Dewa/Dewi Terms of address for gods/goddesses, also known as Batara/Batari.

Dewasa In Balinese culture, *dewasa* (often referred to as *Dewasa Ayu*) refers to the system of auspicious timing or 'chosen days'. It is the art of determining the most propitiously aligned moment to perform a specific action to ensure it is in harmony with cosmic forces.

Galungan-Kuningan A series of holy days spanning 19 days, which comprise one of the most important ceremonial cycles of the Pawukon calendar, during which all ancestral divinities come to visit their descendants and are welcomed and celebrated in their 'residences' in family and village temples across Bali.

Hari Saraswati An important day to honor the goddess of knowledge and learning, which marks the last day of each Pawukon cycle, and separates the week (*wuku*) of Watugunung, the incestuous son, from that of Sinta, his incestuous mother, thus signifying the dawn of human consciousness of time, and hence, civilized life.

ingkel Days or weeks considered unlucky/inauspicious for certain activities.

Kajeng-Kliwon The conjunction of Kajeng of the three-day week and Kliwon of the five-day week in the Pawukon calendar, which occurs every 15 days. Considered to be fraught with occult power, this is a day of ritual exorcism on which elaborate offerings are made to all of the cardinal directions in houses and in temples and outside their thresholds, to ward off negative forces.

kanda mpat Four spiritual siblings and guardians who protect individuals through their life cycles.

kerama desa All married members of a Balinese village community.

kulkul Wooden slit gong/drum used to notify village members of community meetings, deaths, ceremonial events, catastrophes or crimes, e.g. fire or theft, and also, traditionally, the passing of time during the day (*dauh* time units).

lontar Traditional manuscripts made of dried, treated palmyra-palm leaves incised on both sides with a knife, then blackened with soot to reveal the script, and bound together with string passed through holes in each leaf and knotted at the outer ends.

mabiakala Offerings to demons and earthly spirits.

naga Cosmic mythical dragons, notably including Anantaboga (symbol of water) and Basuki (symbol of earth).

nawa sanga The 'nine sacred directions' and their correspondences, which compose the Balinese 'compass rose of the winds' known as *pangider-ider*.

odalan Festivals held in every Bali-Hindu temple every 210 days, to mark the anniversary of the temple in the Pawukon calendar.

oton/otonan One's day of birth (*oton*) in the Pawukon cycle, which is celebrated every 210 days with a ritual (*otonan*), most elaborately on the first one, when a child reaches 210 days of age.

Pagerwesi Literally meaning 'iron gate,' this is one of the most important holy days and marks the closure of the cycle of purification of the Pawukon 'New Year.'

pangider-ider An indigenous 'compass rose of the winds' or mandala of the universe. The four cardinal directions, four intermediary directions, and center of this compass are each associated with particular sacred numbers (*urip*); deities and their weapons and vehicles; elements of nature; colors of the spectrum; mountains of the island; body parts, and all the components of the calendars.

panglong Days of the waning moon (from the full moon to the new moon) in each *sasih* (month) of the Saka calendar.

penanggal (tanggal) Days of the waxing moon (from the new moon to the full moon) in each *sasih* (month) of the Saka calendar.

Pawukon The 210-day, rule-based Javanese-Balinese calendar that regulates most of Bali's rituals, and consists of a system of overlapping cycles of one-day to ten-day 'weeks' (*weweran*).

pedanda A title for high priests, that is, priests of the Balinese Brahmin caste.

pejati Offerings to 'notify' the gods of and invite their blessings on the ritual being held. Consisting of arrangements of plaited palm-leaf, fruits, meat, rice, and other ingredients, they are larger and more complex than daily offerings and are carried on a tray on the head.

pelelindon (pelindon) Painted divination charts, or 'earthquake calendars,' based on the 12 lunar months of the Saka calendar, which forecast in words and pictures what can be expected if an earthquake strikes during a given lunar month.

pelelintangan (pelintangan) Painted divination charts that depict 35 *lintang* (star signs), based upon the 35 possible conjunction days of the five-day week and seven-day week of the Pawukon calendar, and are used, like horoscopes, to divine a person's character based on which of these conjunction days the person was born.

pemangku Temple or village priests who are not of the Brahmin caste.

pura Bali-Hindu temples, including the temples found in every village, known as *pura dalem* (temple of death); *pura desa* (village temple), and *pura puseh* (temple of origin), respectively.

Purnama The full moon.

rerainan gumi Holy days regulated by the Pawukon calendar that are celebrated island-wide, including but not limited to those in this glossary (Galungan; Hari Saraswati; Pagerwesi; Tumpek).

Saka Name of the Balinese luni-solar calendar, which was diffused from India and dates back to 78 CE. Consisting of 12 lunar months (*sasih*), it regulates a number of important holy days and ceremonies which fall on or around full moons and new moons.

sanggah A term for various kinds of shrines and altars, as well as the walled ancestor temples, filled with shrines, found in Balinese commoner homes; known as *merajan* in high-caste family homes.

sasih Lunar months of the Saka calendar year, consisting of 12 months of 29 or 30 days each, whose names refer to their numerical order, except for the last two months, which have retained names of Sanskrit origin: 1. Kasa; 2. Karo; 3. Katiga; 4. Kaput; 5. Kalima; 6. Kanem; 7. Kapitu; 8. Kawulu; 9. Kasanga; 10. Kadasa: 11. Jyaistha (or Jhista or Desta), and 12. Asadha (or Sadha).

teruna A term used to designate unmarried men and adolescent boys.

tika Charts, carved of wood or painted on cloth, made to visualize and facilitate the reading of the Pawukon calendar. Most *tika* show all 30 weeks of the calendar cycle, using different codes in the individual boxes of the chart to focus attention on important conjunctions and particular patterns of repetition in the multiple, various-sized 'weeks' that make up the calendar.

Tilem The new moon.

tithi The lunar days of the month in the Saka calendar.

Tumpek The conjunction of Saniscara (Saturday) and Kliwon of the five-day week, an important conjunction day that occurs six times in each Pawukon cycle, each dedicated to honoring different things, including cattle and other livestock; musical instruments, masks, costumes, and other theater accessories; metal objects and weapons; trees and plants; visiting ancestors, and shadow puppet theater.

urip Sacred or magical numbers assigned to elements of the *pangider-ider*, including elements of the calendar system.

usaba A generic term for festivals and ceremonies related to agriculture. The term is also used, together with the name of a lunar month, to identify specific ceremonial cycles in Tenganan Pegeringsingan based upon the month in the Tenganan calendar in which the ceremonies fall. For example, Usaba Sambah is a month-long cycle of ceremonies held in the month called Kelima or Sambah.

Wariga A body of esoteric knowledge pertaining to the Balinese calendar and calendar-based divination, inscribed on various palm-leaf manuscripts (*lontar*). This knowledge is held by specialists whom Balinese people consult when planning special events and activities.

Watugunung The main protagonist of the incest myth that accounts for the origin of the Pawukon calendar, and hence, the lord of the calendar and the culture hero of/bringer of civilization to Bali, as well as being the name of the last week of the Pawukon cycle.

wewaran A system of *wara*, or 'weeks,' ranging from one to ten days long, which run concurrently through each 210-day Pawukon cycle: Ekawara (one day); Dwiwara (two days); Triwara (three days); Caturwara (four days); Pancawara (five days); Sadwara (six days); Saptawara (seven days); Astawara (eight days); Sangawara (nine days), and Dasawara (ten days). Each day of each wara has particular sacred correspondences and characteristics, so that their conjunctions on a given day determine its character and auspiciousness.

wuku The title of the royal characters in the Watugunung incest myth that explains the origins of the Pawukon calendar, whose names are also those of the 30 seven-day weeks of this calendar: Sinta, Landep, Ukir (Wukir), Kulantir, Taulu (Tolu), Gumbreg, Wariga, Warigadian, Julungwangi, Sungsang, Dungulan, Kuningan, Langkir, Medangsia, Pujut, Pahang, Krulut, Merakih, Tambir, Medangkungan, Matal, Uye, Menail, Prangbakat, Bala, Ugu, Wayang, Kulawu, Dukut, and Watugunung.

yadnya The ceremonies conducted in all rites of passage and on all holy days, which consist of five categories addressed to different beings and levels of reality, as follows: *buta yadnya* (for demons/earthly forces); *dewa yadnya* (for deities/divine forces); *manusa yadnya* (for living human beings); *pitra yadnya* (for the dead), and *rsi yadnya* (for priests).

SELECT BIBLIOGRAPHY

Ammarell, G., "Sky Calendars of the Indo-Malay Archipelago: Regional Diversity/Local Knowledge," *Indonesia*, 45: 85–104, Ithaca: Cornell, 1988.

Bateson, G., "An Old Temple and a New Myth," *Djawa*, 17: 291–307, Batavia, 1937.

Belo, J., *Bali: Temple Festival*, Seattle: University of Washington, 1953.

Berthier, M. T. and Sweeney, J. T., *Bali, l'Art de la Magie*, Paris: FMVJ Voyagers, 1976.

——— *"Tenung" Le Livre des Explications: Traité divinatoire de la tradition balinaise*, Paris, 1978.

Breguet, G. and Couteau, J., *Un autre temps, les calendriers tika de Bali*, Paris: Le Locle, 2002.

Brinkgreve, F. and Stuart-Fox, D., *Offerings: The Ritual Art of Bali*, Sanur: Image Network Indonesia, 1992.

Buvelot, E., *Bali 50 years of Change: A Conversation with Jean Couteau*, Carindale, Queensland: Glass House Books, 2022.

Couteau, J., *Bali Today! In Search of the "Real Bali,"* North Clarendon, VT: Tuttle Publishing, 2026.

——— *Myth, Magic and Mystery in Bali*, Denpasar: Phoenix Communications, 2018.

——— "Watugunung, inceste et calendrier," *Archipel*, 35: 101–27, Paris, 1988.

Carpenter, B. et al. *Lempad of Bali: The Illuminating Line*, Singapore: Editions Didier Millet, 2016.

Covarrubias, M., *Island of Bali*, New York: Alfred A. Knopf, 1937.

Damais, L. C., *Epigrafi dan Sejarah Nusantara, Pilihan Karangan Louis-Charles Damais*, Jakarta: Ecole Française d'Extreme-Orient, 1995; in particular, "Penanggalan Jawa Kuno": 101–9. [Originally published as "Le calendrier de l'ancienne Java," *Journal Asiatique*, 133–42, Paris, 1967]; and "Tentang Perlambangan Warna pada Mata Angin," 111–64. [Originally published as "Etudes javanaises III: A propos des couleurs symboliques des points cardinaux," *Bulletin de l'Ecole Française d'Extreme-Orient*, 56: 75–118, Paris, 1969.]

Eade, J. C., "Georges Breguet et Jean Couteau: Un autre temps. Les calendriers tika de Bali," *Bulletin de l'Ecole Française d'Extreme-Orient*, 38: 411–15, Paris, 2002.

Eiseman, Jr, F. B., *Bali: Sekala and Niskala. Volume I: Essays on Religion, Ritual, and Art*, Berkeley, California: Periplus Editions, 1989.

——— *Bali: Sekala & Niskala. Volume II: Essays on Society, Tradition, and Craft*, Hong Kong: Periplus Editions, 1996.

——— *Balinese Calendars*, Jimbaran, 2000.

Forge, A., *Balinese Traditional Paintings: A Selection from The Forge Collection of The Australian Museum*, Sydney: The Australian Museum, 1978.

Friedrich, R., *The Civilization and Culture of Bali*, Sisil Gupta, India, 1959.

Gardan, D., "Balinese Wooden Calendars," *Arts of Asia*, 12(2): 142–50, Hong Kong, 1987.

Gaspar, A., Casanova, A., and Couteau, J., *Lempad: A Timeless Balinese Master*, Jakarta: Afterhours, 2018.

Geertz, C., "Person, Time and Conduct in Bali: An Essay in Cultural Analysis," Cultural Report Series 14, Southeast Asia Program, Yale University, New Haven, 1966.

——— "The Wet and the Dry: Traditional Irrigation in Bali and Morocco," *Human Ecology*, 1(1): 29–39, 1972.

Geertz, H., *The Life of a Balinese Temple*, Honolulu: University of Hawai'i Press, 2004.

Gina, W., *PengantarWariga Dewasa*, Denpasar, 1992.

Goris, R., "Holidays and Holy Days," in J. L. Swellengrebel (ed.), *Bali: Studies in Life, Thought and Ritual*, KITLV, Dordrecht-Cinnaminson, 1984. [Originally published as "Bali's hoogtijden," *Tijdschrift voor Indische Taal-, Landen Volkenkunde (TBG)*: 436–52, Batavia, 1933.]

Hägerdal, H., "Candrasangkala, the Balinese Art of Dating Events," University of Växj, Sweden, 2006.

Hobart, A., "Between Things, the Place of the Pandasar in Bali," *Archipel*, 25, Paris, 1983.

Hobart, A., Ramseyer, U. and Leeman, A., *The Peoples of Bali*, Oxford: Blackwell, 1996.

Hobart, M., "The Path of the Soul: The Legitimacy of Nature in Balinese Conceptions of Space," in

G. B. Milner (ed.), *Natural Symbols in South East Asia*, London: SOAS, 1978, pp. 5–28.
Hooykaas, C., "A Balinese Temple Festival," *Bibliotica lndonesica*, KITLV, 15, The Hague, 1977.
——"Cosmogony and Creation in Balinese Tradition," The Hague: Martinus Nijhoff, 1974.
——*Kama and Kala: Materials for the Study of Shadow Theatre in Bali*, Amsterdam: North-Holland Publishing Company, 1973.
Lansing, J. S., "Balinese 'Water Temples' and the Management of Irrigation," *American Anthropologist*, 89(2): 326–41, New York, 1987.
Lefort, J., *La saga des calendriers ou le frisson millénariste*, Paris: Bibliothèque Pour la Science, 1998.
Liefrinck F. A., "Rice cultivation in Northern Bali," in J. L. Swellengrebel et al (eds.), *Bali, Further Studies in Life, Thought and Ritual: Selected Studies on Indonesia*, Vol. 8, pp. 113–73, The Haag: Van Hoeve, 1960. [Originally published as "De rijstcultuur op Bali," 1886/87.]
Lombard, D., "Les concepts d'espace et de temps dans l'archipel insulindien," *Annales ESC*, 6: 1385–96, Paris, 1986.
——*Warisan Kerajaan-Kerajaan Konsentris*, Vol. 3, *Nusa Java: Silang Budaya*, Jakarta 1996. [Originally published as *Le carrefour javanais, essai d'histoire globale III: L'héritage des royaumes concentriques*, Paris, 1990.]
Lovric, B., "Rhetoric and Reality: The Hidden Nightmare, Myth and Magic as Representations and Reverberations of Morbid Realities," Ph.D. thesis, University of Sydney, 1987.
Mershon, K. E., *Seven plus Seven, Mysterious Life-Rituals in Bali*, New York: Vantage Press, 1971.
Ossenbruggen, F. D. E. van, "Java's Mocapat: Origins of a Primitive Classification System," in P. E. Josselin de Jong (ed.): *Structural Anthropology in the Netherlands*, KITLV, Translation Series 17, The Haag, 1977. [Originally published as "De Oorsprong van het Javaansche begrip montja-pat, in verband met primitieve classificaties," *Verslagen en Mededeelingen de Koninklijke (Nederlandsche) Akademie van Wetenschappen, Afdeeling Letterkunde*, Vol. 3, 1918.]
Ottino, A., *The Universe Within: A Balinese Village Through Its Ritual Practices*, Paris: Karthala Editions, 2000.
Picard, M.: *Kebalian: The Construction of Balinese Identity*, Singapore: NUS Press, 2024.
Pigeaud, T.: *Literature of Java*, 3 vols., The Hague: Martinus Nijhoff, 1967–70.
Pringle, R.: *A Short History of Bali: Indonesia's Hindu Realm*, Singapore: Talisman, 2011.
Proutfoot, I., "In search of lost time: Javanese and Balinese understandings of the lndic calendar," *Bijdragen tot de Taal-, Land- en Volkenkunde (BKI)*, 163(1): 86–122, Leiden, 2007.
Ramseyer, U., *The Art and Culture of Bali*, Basel Museum der Kulturen: Verlag Schwabe and Co., 2002. [Originally published as *Kunst und Kultur in Bali*, Fribourg: Office du livre S.A., 1977, 1986.]
Ruggles, C. L. N., *Ancient Astronomy: An Encyclopedia of Cosmologies and Myth*, Santa Barbara: ABC-CLIO, 2005.
Stuart-Fox, D. J., *Pura Besakih and the Eka Dasa Rudra Festival*, Jakarta: Sinar Harapan, Indonesia, 1982.
——"Pura Besakih: Temple, Religion and Society in Bali," *Verhandelingen van het Koninklij lnstitut voor Taal-, Land- en Volkenkunde*, 193, Leiden, 2002.
Vickers, A., *Balinese Art: Paintings and Drawings of Bali 1800–2010*, Tokyo/ Rutland, Vermont/ Singapore: Tuttle Publishing, 2012.
Warna, W. and Murdha, J. B. (eds.), *Usana Jawa; Usana Bali; Teks dan Terjemahan*, Bali: Dinas Pendidikan dan Kebudayan, 1986.
Warsika, G. M., *Kertha Gosa Selayang Pandang—Kertha Gosa at a Glance*, Klungkung: Research-Gate pdf, 1986.
Weck, W., *Heilkunde und Volkstum auf Bali*. Stuttgart, 1937. [Re-edited Denpasar, 1975.]
Zoetmulder, P. J., *Old-Javanese–English Dictionary*, The Hague: Martinus Nijhoff, 1982.

ACKNOWLEDGMENTS AND PICTURE CREDITS

Over the more than 25 years during which we gathered documentation for the various editions of this book, we received help from countless individuals and institutions. There are so many that it is impossible to list them all. Please know that we have not forgotten them, and that we are deeply aware of and grateful for what we owe them. The success of this book is theirs too.

Illustrations/Drawings of I Gusti Nyoman Darta: front cover; back cover; pages 3, 4, 6–7, 13, 14, 15, 16, 19, 21, 25, 28, 32, 44, 45, 46, 47, 48, 49, 50, 51; 52, 53, 54, 55, 58, 63 (below), 64–5, 67, 71, 73, 74, 77, 78, 79, 80, 81, 83, 85, 86, 91, 93, 94, 95, 96, 97, 98, 99, 100, 101, 102, 103, 105, 106, 108, 112, 113, 114, 115, 116, 117, 118, 119, 120, 121, 122, 123, 124, 125, 127, 159, 160. The originals of all drawings by I Gusti Nyoman Darta that appear in this book are now in the possession of the Musée du quai Branly—Jacques Chirac, Paris, France.

Courtesy of Georges Breguet: endpapers; pages 3 (bottom), 131, 132, 133, 134, 135, 136, 137, 138, 145, 146.

Courtesy of Musee d'horlogerie du Lacie (MHL), Chateau des Monts, Switzerland. Photo by Giorgio Savini: pages 27 (top, middle and bottom), 38 (above and below); 39 (below), 40, 43.

Courtesy of Georges Breguet, photo courtesy of BABBOOKS: 37 (above and below), 39 (above)

Courtesy of Wereldmuseum Leiden, The Netherlands, the National Museum of Ethnology, Leiden: pages 62, 139.

Courtesy of Gaspard de Marval: page 126

Drawing courtesy of BABBOOKS: page 63 (top)

Photo of Aimery Joëssel: page 1

Photos by IB Putra Adnyana: pages 147, 148, 150.

Shutterstock photos: pages 2, Mazur Travel; 10, Ann Kapustina; 61, Meniga.id; 87, Imagentle; 111, eTanod.

Periplus Editions (HK) Ltd: page 89.

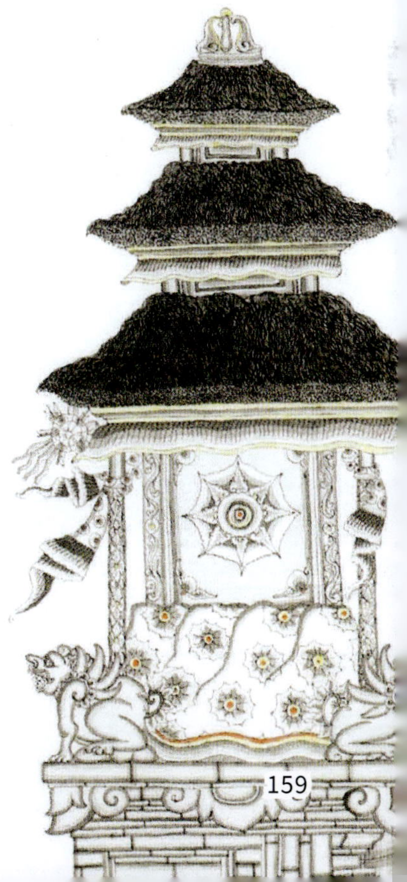

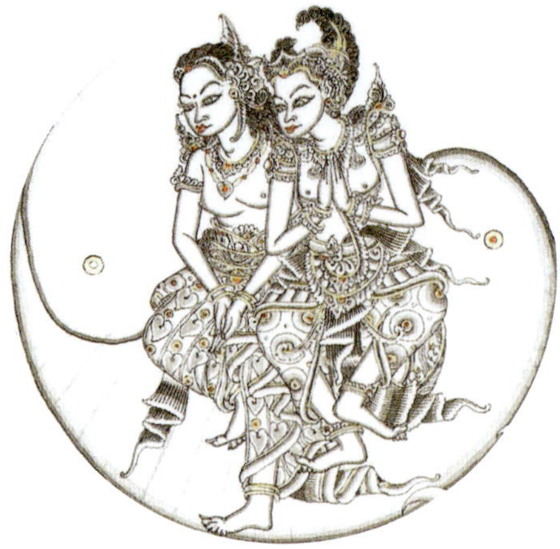

"Books to Span the East and West"

Tuttle Publishing was founded in 1832 in the small New England town of Rutland, Vermont [USA]. Our core values remain as strong today as they were then—to publish best-in-class books which bring people together one page at a time. In 1948, we established a publishing outpost in Japan—and Tuttle is now a leader in publishing English-language books about the arts, languages and cultures of Asia. The world has become a much smaller place today and Asia's economic and cultural influence has grown. Yet the need for meaningful dialogue and information about this diverse region has never been greater. Over the past seven decades, Tuttle has published thousands of books on subjects ranging from martial arts and paper crafts to language learning and literature—and our talented authors, illustrators, designers and photographers have won many prestigious awards. We welcome you to explore the wealth of information available on Asia at **www.tuttlepublishing.com**.

Published by Tuttle Publishing, an imprint of Periplus Editions (HK) Ltd

www.tuttlepublishing.com

ISBN: 978-0-8048-5944-8

Library of Congress Control Number: 2026932926

28 27 26 10 9 8 7 6 5 4 3 2 1
Printed in China 2605EP

GPSR representative
Matt Parsons, matt.parsons@upi2mbooks.hr, UPI-2M PLUS d.o.o., Medulićeva 20, 10000 Zagreb, Croatia

TUTTLE PUBLISHING® is a registered trademark of Tuttle Publishing, a division of Periplus Editions (HK) Ltd.

Distributed by
North America, Latin America & Europe
Tuttle Publishing
364 Innovation Drive
North Clarendon, VT 05759-9436 U.S.A.
Tel: 1 (802) 773-8930; Fax: 1 (802) 773-6993
info@tuttlepublishing.com
www.tuttlepublishing.com

Asia Pacific
Berkeley Books Pte. Ltd.
3 Kallang Sector #04-01
Singapore 349278
Tel: (65) 6741-2178; Fax: (65) 6741-2179
inquiries@periplus.com.sg
www.tuttlepublishing.com

Indonesia
PT Java Books Indonesia
Kawasan Industri Pulogadung
JI. Rawa Gelam IV No. 9
Jakarta 13930
Tel: (62) 21 4682-1088; Fax: (62) 21 461-0206
crm@periplus.co.id
www.periplus.com

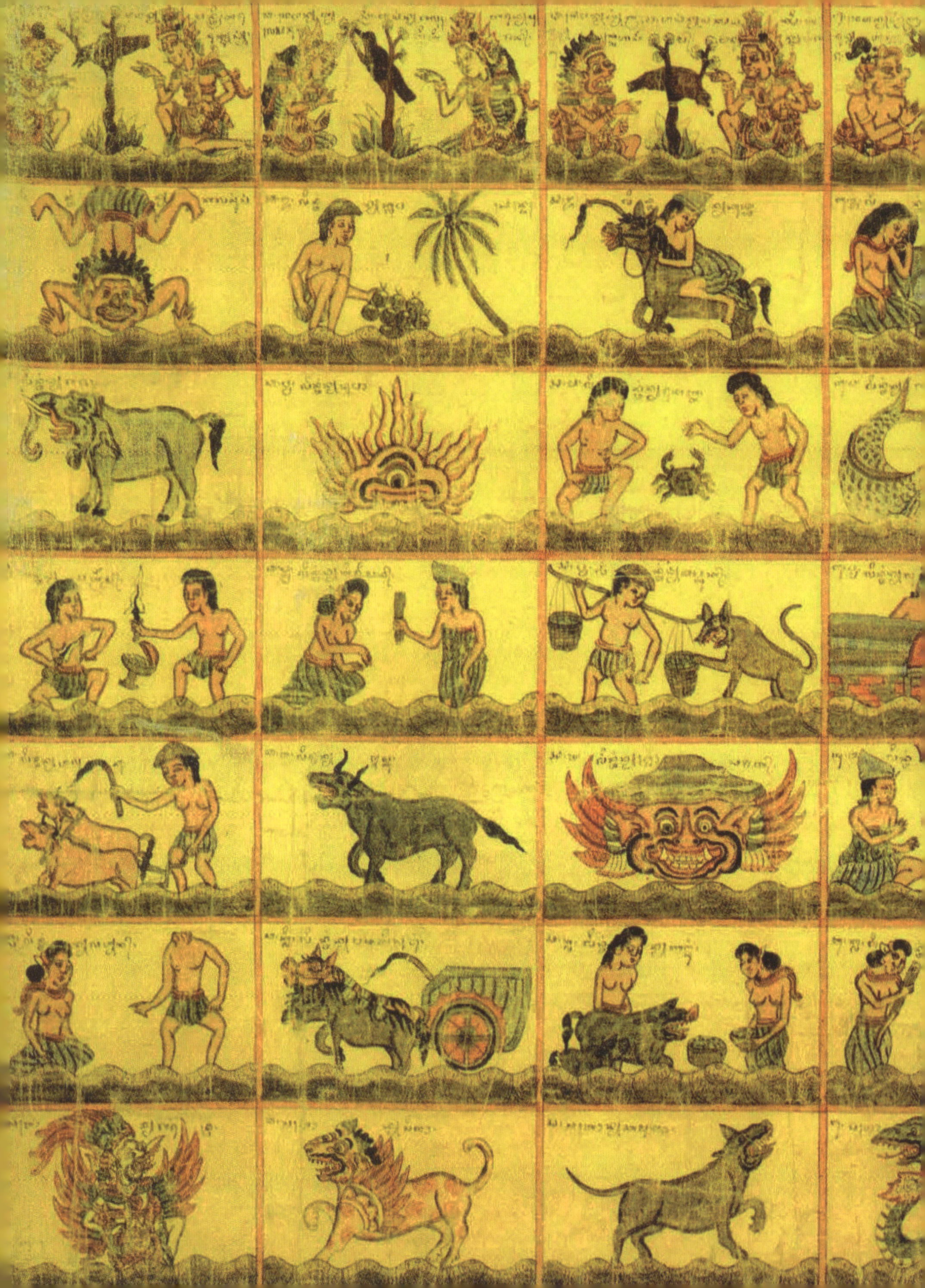